Praise for *Cartographies of Blackness and Black Indigeneities*

"Our education of Blackness and Africanness for political action and social change would be incomplete without attention to the perspectives, frameworks, theorizations, analyses, and visions provided in *Cartographies of Blackness and Black Indigeneities.*"

—*Carl E. James, Jean Augustine Chair in Education, Community & Diaspora, York University*

"Dei, Odozor, and Vasquez Jiminez' edited book *Cartographies of Blackness and Black Indigeneities* brings together a wonderfully wide range of voices on the issue of Blackness and all its complexities. This text therefore is not only relevant to researchers and graduate students but also community workers, policy makers, and individuals in the wider society who need to be aware and ready to act on the challenges facing Black peoples everywhere. Indeed, it is even more important in this political era when to be identified as Black brings with it a host of difficulties. The multiplicity of spaces and perspectives addressed in this volume certainly afford the readers the opportunity to come to "a critical consciousness of our existential and ontological realities as African and Black peoples" that, according the editors, is one of their objectives. *Cartographies of Blackness and Black Indigeneities* provides the evidence for those of us wanting to make the case, in our own voices, for the importance and significance of Blackness, Africanness and Indigeneity and is therefore a must read."

—*Janice B. Fournillier, Georgia State University*

Praise for *Cartographies of Blackness and Black Indigeneities*

"Our exploration of blackness and Africanness for political action and social change would be incomplete without attention to the perspectives, frameworks, theorizations, analyses, and visions provided in *Cartographies of Blackness and Black Indigeneities*."

—Carl E. James, Jean Augustine Chair in Education, Community & Diaspora, York University

"Drs. Ibrahim and Vasquez Jiménez' edited book *Cartographies of Blackness and Black Indigeneities* brings together a wonderfully wide range of voices on the issue of Blackness and all its complexities. This text therefore is not only relevant to researchers and graduate students but also community workers, policy makers, and individuals in the wider society who need to be aware and ready to act on the challenges facing Black peoples everywhere. Indeed, it is even more important in this political era when to be identified as Black brings with it a host of difficulties. The multiplicity of spaces and perspectives addressed in this volume certainly afford the readers the opportunity to come to 'a critical consciousness of our existential and ontological realities as African and Black peoples' that, according the editors, is one of their objectives. *Cartographies of Blackness and Black Indigeneities* provides the evidence for those of us wanting to make the case, in our own voices, for the importance and significance of Blackness, Africanness and Indigeneity and is therefore a must read."

—[illegible], Georgia State University

CARTOGRAPHIES OF BLACKNESS AND BLACK INDIGENEITIES

Cartographies of Blackness and Black Indigeneities

EDITED BY

George J. Sefa Dei, Ezinwanne Odozor

AND

Andrea Vásquez Jiménez

Myers Education Press

GORHAM, MAINE

Myers Education Press

Published by Myers Education Press, LLC
P.O. Box 424
Gorham, ME 04038

Myers Education Press is an academic publisher specializing in books, e-books, and digital content in the field of education. All of our books are subjected to a rigorous peer review process and produced in compliance with the standards of the Council on Library and Information Resources.

LIBRARY OF CONGRESS CATALOGING-IN-PUBLICATION DATA AVAILABLE FROM LIBRARY OF CONGRESS.

13-digit ISBN 978-1-9755-0107-5 (paperback)
13-digit ISBN 978-1-9755-0106-8 (hard cover)
13-digit ISBN 978-1-9755-0108-2 (library networkable e-edition)
13-digit ISBN 978-1-9755-0109-9 (consumer e-edition)

Printed in the United States of America.

All first editions printed on acid-free paper that meets the American National Standards Institute Z39-48 standard.

ooks published by Myers Education Press may be purchased at special quantity discount rates for groups, workshops, training organizations, and classroom usage. Please call our customer service department at 1-800-232-0223 for details.

Cover design by Sophie Appel

Visit us on the web at **www.myersedpress.com** to browse our complete list of titles.

Acknowledgments

Our sincere thanks go to Myers Educational Press for believing in our collective scholarship and publishing this work. We have been moved on this journey by a desire to mobilize our collective thought and politics to promote educational and social change and to further explore the nuances, tensions, contentions and complexities of Blackness and Indigeneity. For all those who have helped us in our intellectual growth we pay homage.

Thank you to the students in my classes for continuing to challenge "the norm" through your works of resistance and to the publishers of this book for your continued support.

— George J. Sefa Dei

To my parents, Ekwutosi & Livinus Odozor, for your example, wisdom, and love. To my siblings—Uzo, Chioma, and Edo—thank you, thank you, thank you.

— Ezinwanne (Ezi) Odozor

Thank you to my parents, Adriana and Jairo Vásquez, for all of your sacrifices, endless love, and support. Thank you to my mentor and amazing professor Nana (Dr. George J. Sefa Dei) for your guidance and for always believing in me. Thank you as well to my friends and community members for keeping me grounded and holding transformative spaces together.

— Andrea Vásquez Jiménez

Contents

Mapping Blackness: An Introduction

George J. Sefa Dei, Ezinwanne Odozor,
Andrea Vásquez Jiménez (Editors)

KNOWING THAT WE have a rich body of scholarly works on Blackness has been transformative for so many of us and in so many ways. We are extremely grateful and humbled to know that this also makes it an arduous task of (co)creating further scholarship on the realities of Blackness and beyond, which truly aims to add new insights, highlight previously left out voices, and offer new conversational spaces. Yet, the difficulty of it is all the more reason why we should engage it and continue to think through our Blackness, our nuances, and its complexities. Responding to that call, this book takes up the multiple cartographies of Blackness and Black Indigeneity. In exploring these cartographies—or mappings—this book queries multiple spaces: geographic, experiential, temporal, and so on. What our discussion hopes to unveil and bring additional perspectives to is the plethora of different and significant ways to theorize the interplay of Blackness, Africanness, Indigeneity, and anti-colonial politics for educational transformation, social change, and Black liberation. What we agree with and believe is the need to think through Blackness and Africanness in ways that connect a broader segment of the global Black/African population dispersed across multiple geographies. We also want to add to the reframing of Blackness for educational and political action from multiple locations. In the Fanonian sense, we believe the power of coming to a critical consciousness of our existential and ontological realities as African and Black peoples is to constantly interrogate the social and academic meanings and understanding that we hold of ourselves and to deploy such knowledge into concrete political action to achieve change. This is all the more reason why today we must seek to articulate a decolonial Blackness as a pedagogic, instructional, and communicative approach to challenge imperial, colonial, Eurocentric, and racist consciousness of what Black, Blackness, Africanness, and Indigeneity have come to signify.

In our articulations of Blackness, we refuse the power of the dominant to codify experiences on our behalf. Refusal is a provocative, productive, and promising stance (Simpson, 2007). In such readings of the "politics of refusal" we see the power of affirming our intellectual agencies and power to name ourselves and our experiences. We see decolonial and anti-colonial "resistance" as reclaiming our collective and self-power, while at the same time refusing the trappings of privilege conferred by the dominant. Black is human and has always been human. Blackness has existed in antiquity. The notion of "Blackness in modernity" is flawed because Blackness has always existed in a context of modernity, where modernity is necessarily recontextualized beyond the Eurocentric frame. Modernity is an ongoing phase characteristic of all peoples, communities, and lands. There have been different conceptions of modernity throughout human history. Euro-modernity possess different questions for our collective existence; however, their questions have been overarticulated and have been centered for quite some time. There is the tendency to claim Euro-modernity as the only modernity worth talking about, a fact that in itself is one of the most dangerous of all delusions, which a people can have or entertain. Not all universalisms are necessarily particularities. Why is it that throughout human history it has always been the dominant with the power to present its particular history as universal history? The dominant has always insisted on having all the space unto itself. Interestingly, when the nondominant bodies offer counter/alternative knowledges and readings to subvert an existing knowledge provincialism masquerading its particularity as universal knowledge, we come face to face with open skepticism, intellectual ridicule, and discursive surveillance and policing.

There is an ethical responsibility for us to listen to each other and, particularly, to accentuate and bring to the fore unheralded voices. Unfortunately, in the current era where the "Friends of Xenophobes" (FOX) have succeeded in being a mouthpiece as a power megaphone, well beyond its local reach, we have a deep responsibility to posit different ways of speaking about our collective human condition. There is a mouthpiece that designs futures for others. This mouthpiece has a definitional power whereby it determines what is worthy of intellectual and political pursuit, establishing what questions must be asked, by whom, when, and why. In a more direct relation to the matters raised in this book, it is a form of legitimation that Blackness is worthy of academic inquiry, intellectual engagement, and contestation.

For sure, there can be no guarantee that our call to reframe Blackness through the different geographies will be heard by the dominant. In fact, they are not our primary audience. We turn our attention to our own. For our part, we are asking to continue the tradition of critical scholarship on Blackness to reach out to the genealogies of thought that have always informed knowledge about Black existence and Black life. An understanding that Blackness is constantly moving and shifting is only significant to the degree that we recognize that the heterogeneity, complexity, saliency of the epidermal, multidimensionality, and simultaneity of Blackness still operate within certain confines and theoretical terrains. We should never pursue our heterogeneity to deny our existential Blackness as a requisite for radical decolonial politics to challenge the entrapments of academia for Black, Indigenous, and racialized learners. Dei's opening piece, for example, responds to the question "Who's missing in education?" by posing new exploratory questions such as "*Why* are they missing?" and "*How* does this absenting occur and reoccur?" His personal, but critical reflections offer an intellectually honest entry point for us to challenge the (white) univocality that surrounds and adjudicates the "legitimacy" of discourses on Blackness and Black theorizing in educational and political spaces.

In this book we conceptualize Blackness as a highlighting and a (re)centering of the totality of Black and African peoples' experiences including our histories, culture, politics, philosophies, and education. We take up Blackness, its synergies, and its convergences with Africanness to highlight Black and African Indigeneity in the context of multiple geographies. Clearly, there must be no totalizing logic about Blackness. Blackness is represented both within and outside selves and communities. Claiming difference as the mark of the "Other" is about the power to acknowledge the multiplicity of knowledge and is also about using our myriad knowledges as counter insurgency and resurgence politics. Within an era of colonialism and ongoing colonializations, the Black struggle for freedom, liberation, and acknowledgment as equally human continues to exact heavy emotional, psychological, spiritual, material, and political tolls on everyone. Part of the work of the book is to anchor at the center, the idea of global Blackness and Black Indigeneities and histories as homing points and legitimate inheritances for Black peoples across geographies.

Working to expand the idea of Black Indigeneity and Indigenous as categories lodged in the space of global Blackness and Africana, this work locates its discussion within lived experience and the multiple encounters of Blackness across space times. Odozor in "Making Peace with Movement" asks us to consider our Blackness and Africanness within new spatial imaginaries, calling on us to theorize diaspora not simply as dislocation or loss, but as lines along which to create new and *new-old* ontologies of Blackness. She articulates this toward the re-existing as Black peoples and narrating possible futures mapped along borderless understandings of Africanness and Blackness. Significantly, our intention in putting this collection together is to contribute to ongoing discussions about the contested meaning of Blackness within the scourge of global anti-Blackness and anti-Black racism. We take up Blackness to extend a discussion of the cultural and racial politics of society to highlight the myriad resistance and agencies of Black and African bodies in different geographies. In seeking to understand the contemporary Black and African human condition we engage Blackness as a sociohistorical existence and human condition as well as an episteme and critical ontology. We ask, for example, how do Black ontologies offer different readings of our worlds? Indeed, an important aspect of this work is the multiplicity of entry points that it highlights. Danvers and Rodney offer discussions of Black womanhood, which make complex our notions of masculinity and femininity, particularly in light of the masculinization of Black womanhood within white supremacist narratives. Hwami and Shiza look at the notion of agency and Black Indigeneity within the Continental context. Their chapter complicates nativism as a decolonial conversation exploring Black ownership—of Land, of body, and of ontology—as fundamental for Black liberations and development. Working at the intersection of Blackness and Ability discourses Thomas takes up the question of "special" education and asks where, when, and how it makes room (or does not) for Blackness. Each of these discussions looks at Blackness across social, political, historical, and/or spatial geographies.

The contributions of Black and African peoples, our global presence and civilizations, and the challenges of our collective responsibilities and accountabilities build strong, viable communities in multiple spaces and are more than mere lessons of history. They are about the study of Black existentialism and the materiality of Black body politics. Our book enthuses that Blackness and Africanness speak to the complexity of a people's lived condition through time and in multiple places. An understanding of Blackness and Africanness evokes complex and contested ontologies and epistemologies of the Black/African social existence. Such understanding also requires a complex theorization of Blackness that engages with different landscapes and geographies, thereby appealing to different bodies and spaces anchored in their Blackness/Africanness and Black Indigeneity.

We acknowledge the saliency of Blackness in contemporary social formations, insisting that how bodies are read is extremely important and that these readings elicit or produce both tangible and intangible social, political, material, spiritual, and emotional effects and consequences on Black and African bodies, globally (see Dei 2017a, 2018). The need to challenge, resist, and subvert a fixed, essential, totalizing, naturalized, criminal, and degenerate Blackness extends beyond a call to affirm the multidimensionality of Black identities and subjectivities. Of course, we must celebrate Blackness in all its complexities (race, ethnicity, class, gender, sexuality, (dis)ability, spiritualties, geographies, etc.). In nuancing the understanding of Blackness, the political project is to insist on Black and African cultural knowings of Blackness outside of Euro-colonial attempts to regulate and define how as Black and African bodies globally we come to understand our own Blackness across different geographies. Blackness is about cultural, social, racial, spiritual, emotional, and psychological productions of knowledge and the pursuit of politics for change and liberation. For the Black and African existence—both on the continent and in diaspora—resistance has been a defining part of heterogeneous Blackness. Such an understanding also implies that Blackness cannot be understood outside a conception of Africanness and the different geographies of Black identities. Blackness has not always been understood as a response to Whiteness, and particularly Euro-Whiteness. That is, Blackness has not always derived its meaning from or in relation to Whiteness. We acknowledge that African ancestral cultural and heritage knowledges about Blackness symbolized holiness, purity, beauty, happiness, fear, anger, and resistance (see Dei 2017a, 2018; Dugassa, 2011; Melba, 1988). This understanding is a far cry from Euro-colonial constructions of Black and Blackness as deviant, criminal, unholy, immoral, sexually deviant, abnormal, and degenerate. In this book Adjei and Akanmori look at the very real implications of reading Blackness, particularly in the youth "justice" system, as deviant and criminal. The authors critically examine the social construction of Blackness in risk assessment of Black youth. This book intersperses discussions of "conceptual Blackness" with "epidermal Blackness," Black racial identity, cultural politics, and the required responsibilities for global Black and African populations to build viable communities, utilizing our differences—knowledges, cultures, politics, identities, histories—as strengths. Such communities can then be used as a platform in the fight for Black social justice and liberation.

A key question the book raises is, "How can we re-envision education to address the many challenges facing global Black populations?" Forde's "search [for] dark stars" explores the crisis of anti-Black racism in Canadian school systems. Her work uses a series of case studies to interrogate hegemonic leadership structures, looking to Afrocentric practices as models for resisting Eurocentric learning monocultures and creating new spaces for liberatory Black-centered learning. Similarly, Kirk locates her reflection on the academy in lived experiences, theorizing the connection between placemaking and her own push for emancipatory practices in educational spaces. Putting forward "Black Graduation(s)" as a case study, she challenges the institutionalized absenting of Black students and the necessary supports, structures, and community spaces, which are fundamental for our thriving. Kirk's exploration of placemaking offers a challenge to White supremacist centrality within the educational space, offering options for new futures.

Thinking through new educational futures is a challenge for our communities. We need new speculative imaginaries informed by Black thought and political action. Our engagement of Blackness links the question of African Indigeneity and education focusing on a proactive Black educational agenda. Emeagwali homes in on futurity, recognizing Indigeneity and Indigenous Knowledge Systems as foundational homing points for theorizing Black continuums, or futures. This agenda is not exclusive for Black and African communities. It simply realizes the severity of the issue for Black communities worldwide. In staking a claim of Black and African Indigeneity, we recognize the different associations and meanings many communities Earth-wide bring to Land, water, seas, and the sky. We also recognize the dispossession from Land as global and as having produced powerful effects and legacies. The fact that many colonized populations worldwide still hang on to particular understandings and relations of the Land and water is enough for us to work with contested definitions of Indigenous. Thus, the book emphasizes that as we seek to understand the nature, contexts, intersections, and role of Indigeneity we must simultaneously engage Black ontologies, philosophies, and epistemologies for transformative political and educational ends.

We must challenge the colonial appellation of the "Indigenous" and think of Indigenous in more broad terms to encapsulate many global communities and peoples. This means to speak of Black Indigeneity. As Dei (2017a) has noted repeatedly, recognizing the contested claims to Black and African Indigeneity is significant. The acknowledgement responds to the tendency for contributions of the local cultural resource knowledge base of Black and African peoples to schooling, education, and global development to be ignored when it comes to thinking through new educational futurities. We need an anti-colonial, anti-racist analysis of how Indigenous cultural knowledges and ideas can subvert colonial relations, processes, and practices to enhance social, political, economic, cultural, and spiritual outcomes for communities in African and global diasporic contexts.

Clearly, we must resist the ways particular identities have been normalized within contemporary social formations for White supremacist, racist, cis-normative, hetero-capitalist, homo-nationalist, and xenophobic ends. In doing so, we must distinguish between the current mobilizations of identity around cultural and ideological constructs of nationalism and xenophobia—including White supremacist formations cloaked under euphemistic terms such as the "extreme Right" or "Alt-Right"—and progressive mobilizations of identity for anticolonial and anti-racist projects (see Dei 2017b, 2017c). The question is not merely that certain identities are denied or devalued. For Black, Indigenous, oppressed, and colonized peoples negating claims to our positive, (solution-oriented) Black and African identities is an affront on our intellectual agencies in the construction of knowledge about ourselves. It is to this end and realization that this book centers some significant questions as well: How do we come to understand Blackness and anti-Blackness in contemporary social formations? How do we know and define ourselves as Black and African peoples in the contexts of our different geographies? How have such articulations of Blackness and Africanness helped us to pursue radical politics of social justice with the ends of liberation? How is reclaiming our social, cultural, political, and spiritual identities a form of resistance to global anti-Blackness and anti-Black racism? How do we begin to locate ourselves as Black and African peoples on the path to decolonization? How do we envision new Black futures? Moreover, what are the challenges and possibilities of Black global futurity?

The study of Blackness has been part of the lived experience of Black and African peoples. Blackness has been part of our everyday realities. The long trajectory of looking to bring complex meanings to Blackness has been fraught with a number of intellectual and political challenges. As we push forward to think critically about Blackness from multiple geographies and intellectual stances, we are guided by a pedagogy of new futures and liberation. We push for new Afro and Black futurism guided by a desire to challenge the Eurocentric authentications of Blackness and the approach to Blackness as merely an exercise in theory or an intellectualized problem. In presenting Blackness as a critical discursive and political prism, we are cautious not to fall into the trap of intellectualizing Blackness. We note in this endeavor that "We note that this endevour is not "antiintellectual, but precisely anti-intellectualist" (Leonardo & Porter, 2010, p. 150).

The phenomenology of Blackness, that is, to be Black in this world, the politics and consequences of epidermalization of racist values and views on Black bodies, as well as the signification of Black body image and schematic representations and subjectivities, have been extremely consequential (Fanon, 1967). We present Blackness as embodied knowing that signifies both the salience of Black body and psyche, as well as the politics required to be in a skin and blood. As many have noted, there is always a visceral Blackness in an anti-Black climate (Sharpe, 2016). We know that historically Blackness has been mapped onto bodies and spaces with ontological and differential material implications and corresponding resistances (see McKittrick, 2006). Thus, our task is not just reading Blackness in multiple spaces and places, but also in speaking to the possibilities, complexities, consequentiality, and precarity of Blackness.

Blackness as episteme, a way of knowing, is steeped in our rich intellectual traditions as Black and African peoples. Such rich radical Black intellectual traditions of our experiences offer us a decolonial prism of reading Blackness not as a counter point of Eurocentric thought nor Whiteness (see Dei, 2017a). Blackness must be viewed as a spiritual ontology that challenges the Anthropocene, Anthropos, and the anthropocentric thinking. We challenge Blackness as viewed in the lens of the Anthropos—that is objectification of Black/Blackness and Africanness—to begin the place of our discussion of Black personhood in the context of critical humanitas—that is Black as living, breathing human subjects. The study of Blackness gestures to our collective memory, heritage, and ancestral visions and values that connect us to shared oppressions and histories. These shared histories do not necessarily mean they are singular experiences. As Castillo explores in "Unlearning Our Blackness," we must unlearn the hegemonic notions of Blackness and (re)conceptualize them as agents and drivers of radical futures.

Black humanhood has always required that Black and African bodies everywhere carry the weight of our Blackness proudly and unapologetically as resistors and creators. We cannot run away from our Blackness and African humanhood. We must be unflinching in affirming our Blackness and not afraid to express our Black rage/anger. To many of us, our scholarship is about embracing our Blackness as a cornerstone to subvert the everydayness of Western academia and its entrapments. Jennifer Mills explores Dei's work as a possible framework for this subversion, while Andrew Allen uses his work to conceptualize decolonial modes of praxis for transforming teacher education. Our decolonial and anticolonial scholarship must affirm our Blackness even as we purport to work for the solidarity of all colonized and oppressed peoples. We need to be proud of our heritage, roots, and ancestry. Paraphrasing what many other Black radical thinkers have alluded to, if we (as Black bodies/scholars) are not for ourselves, who will be, and, who are we to begin with? Clearly, there is nothing wrong in an anticolonial politics speaking to/ for all humanity. Nevertheless, there is great importance and a necessity for partisan scholarly/intellectual politics (see King, Council, Fournillier, Richardson, & Akua, 2019).

References

Dei, J. S. S. (2017a). *Reframing Blackness and Black Solidarities through Anti-Colonial and Decolonial Prisms*. New York, NY: Springer.

Dei, G. J. S. (2017b). "Foreword." In J. Newton & A. Soltani (Eds.), *New Framings on Anti-Racism and Resistance: Resistance and the New Futurity, Volume 2* (pp. vii-x). Rotterdam, Netherlands: Sense Publishers.

Dei, G. J. S. (2017c). "Foreword." In A. Abdulle & A. N. Obeyesekere (Eds.), *New Framings on Anti-Racism and Resistance, Volume 1* (pp. ix–xiv). Rotterdam, Netherlands: Sense Publishers.

Dei, G. J. S. (2018). "Black Like Me: Reframing Blackness and Decolonial Politics." *Educational Studies* 54(2), 117–142.

Dugassa, B. (2011). "Colonialism of Mind: Deterrent of Social Transformation: The Experiences of Oromo People in Ethiopia." *Sociology Mind* 1(2), 55–64.

Fanon, F. (1967). *Black Skin, White Masks*. New York, NY: Grove Press.

King, J., Council, T. M., Fournillier, J. B., Richardson, V., & Akua, C. (2019). "Pedagogy for Partisanship: Research Training for Black Graduate Students in the Black Intellectual Tradition." *International Journal of Qualitative Studies in Education*, 32(2), 188–209. doi:10.1080/09518398.2018.1548040

Leonardo, Z., & Porter, R. K. (2010). "Pedagogy of Fear: Toward a Fanonian theory of 'safety' in race dialogue." *Race, Ethnicity and Education, 13*(2), 139–157.

McKittrick, K. (2006). *Demonic Grounds: Black Women and the Cartographies of Struggle*. Minneapolis, MN: University of Minnesota Press.

Melba, G. (1988). *Oromia: An Introduction*. Khartoum, Sudan: Duke University Press.

Sharpe, C. (2016). *In the Wake: On Blackness and Being*. Durham, NC: Duke University Press.

Simpson, A. (2007). "On Ethnographic Refusal: Indigeneity, 'Voice,' and Colonial Citizenship." *Junctures, 9*, 67–80.

CHAPTER 1

Teaching Race, Anti-Blackness, and (African) Indigeneity: Personal Reflections Of A Black Scholar

George J. Sefa Dei
[Nana Adusei Sefa Tweneboah]

Introduction

BLACKNESS HAS BEEN a cultural, economic, material, political, emotional, spiritual, and racial signification and expression rather than an objective artifact (see Adjei 2016; Dei, 2017; Ibrahim, 2014; King, 2016; McKittrick, 2011; McKittrick & Wood, 2007; Sexton, 2015, 2017; Walcott, to mention a few). Relatedly, anti-Blackness continues to have much global currency because of the "attraction of Blackness" as a commodity, a desirable and yet repulsive embodiment. The duality of the desire and repulsion of Blackness has been consequential not only for the cultural politics of society, but also in the understanding of our colonial engagements and inheritance. The repulsion of Blackness has revealed itself historically in the enactment of everyday anti-Blackness at both individual and institutional levels. There have been many varied interpretations of Blackness, a discussion which itself sometimes reveals codes of anti-Blackness congealed up in the Black body. To "think Black," to come to know as Black subject, to speak of Black theorizing or perspectivism, or to articulate the power of Blacks as "self-knowing subjects" often faces counter arguments and critique of identity politics in the politics of knowledging. I recall being asked by an academic colleague if there is ever something to be called "Black knowledge!" The anti-Blackness that is embedded in the question is masked in the justification of knowledge and scholarly inquiry. To be Black is to know differently, not merely a taking such knowledge as different from other knowledges, but that such knowledge is shaped by the experiences and lived realities of being Black in a White supremacist context. It does not mean all Black bodies/peoples/scholars/learners will necessarily share in such knowledge. However, the legitimacy of such Black knowledge must not continually be held "suspect" nor perpetually questioned.

Without a doubt, anti-Blackness is a dominant expression and practice. However, it is also fair to say Black, African, Indigenous, racialized, and colonized peoples themselves are not innocent of, nor immune from, charges of global anti-Blackness. Internalized racism and colonialism are cases in point. In the academy, anti-Blackness reveals itself in the everyday surveillance of the Black presence, our scholarship and politics. Black bodies have continually been under Eurocentric gaze. There continues to be a Euro-authentication of Blackness, which disciplines us to speak of Blackness in particular ways. What we do not often talk about is the extent to which anti-Blackness reveals itself in knowledge production in academia. For example, the Eurocentric hierarchization and validation of particular knowledges offer the space for even some Black, Indigenous, and racialized "intellectuals" to be complicit in the arrogance of dominant bodies to think they have a corner on what really constitutes anti-Blackness. The assertion of a decolonial Blackness through a re-epidermalization of knowledge has been seen as suspect. Some Black, racialized, and Indigenous scholars have been guilty of being part of the troubling intellectual politics that negate the voices, experiences, and scholarship of fellow Black, Indigenous, and racialized scholars simply because some bodies will not mimic Eurocentric theorizing or knowledge production. Claims of Afrocentric knowledge and anti-racism are ridiculed, dismissed, and often evaluated using a Eurocentric gaze by these intellectuals who live and breathe White theorizing—all of which goes to show the complexity and messiness of Blackness and what is constitutive of anti-Blackness in academia. Anti-Blackness has an institutional and systemic existence throughout human history. Of late, the specificity of anti-Blackness is grudgingly acknowledged. Yet, it was not so long ago when in even speaking of anti-racism, one was quickly branded as creating a simplistic "Black-White binary." I always felt that the charge of binarism was a deliberate ploy, to deflect, obfuscate, and avoid a discussion of anti-Black racism. It was a ploy and a defensive mechanism against White and dominant complicity, and it was used to dismiss the legitimate claims of racism of Black bodies and the everyday oppressive encounters we endure. While White supremacy has re-entered the public lexicon of late, anti-Blackness is quickly mouthed off. I remember very well the reluctance and resistance to admit White racism, let alone to say White supremacy. The whole idea of White privilege was denied and countered with questions about how important it is to complicate this Whiteness and the enactment of such privilege by White bodies. I would like to think times have changed. Unfortunately, no, nothing has changed. My sojourn in academia tells me nothing has really changed. Same old, same old!

Clearly, the complexity of the Black ontological existence calls for a more nuanced understanding of Blackness and anti-Blackness. I see anti-Blackness as reference to sociohistorical and political dimensions of Black existence speaking to the everyday individual and systemic hostilities and violence mapped onto the congeniality of the Black body with profound concrete, material, physical, and spiritual manifestations in Black life. As noted in a forthcoming publication (Dei, 2019) this violence is racialized, classed, gendered, sexualized, and manifested in culture, politics, and a knowledge praxis in multiple geographies. Anti-Blackness is seductive and can entice even Black bodies to create very divisive distinctions among ourselves. Furthermore, it is this complex understanding that extends the meaning of anti-Blackness beyond anti-Black racism. Principally, anti-Blackness speaks to the curious interface of body, skin, culture, race, and politics in the context of a White supremacist racism that foments and cements a breathing culture and climate of anti-Blackness (Dei, 2017; Sharpe, 2016). There is also a global anti-Blackness drawing on the synergies and convergences of Blackness and Africanness in largely negative ways to ensure colonial nation building projects, fueled by the logics of White supremacy. In effect, such institutionalized anti-Blackness is endemic to the normal, everyday functioning of White hetero-patriarchal capitalist society (see also Dumas 2014, 2016; Dumas & ross, 2016).

Before I continue further, let me take a moment to reflect on "Blackcentricity" as a philosophical and political perspective that I am working with in this chapter. Blackcentrcity is centering Black and Blackness in intellectual and political praxis. It is also the idea of unashamed Blackness, a desire to speak with a distinctive Black voice and a discursive politics about upholding the Black spirit and soul in a moment in history when our Blackness is under assault from state-sanctioned violence. This understanding of Blackcentricity owes an intellectual debt to the pioneering ideas of Molefi Asante and his scholarship on Afrocentricity as well. I need not remind anyone about police brutality, the hypervigilance of Black bodies in schools, courts, media, on the streets, and so on. Blackcentricity negates the dominant propensity to design futures for Black and African bodies and communities. Blackcentricity is about a refusal, resistance, resurgence, and commitment to a common cause for humanity. Black must mean "something special," and it behooves Black and African bodies globally to honor our Blackness and Africanness. We cannot only perform Blackness and Africanness to achieve social and educational excellence. We must also embody the true meaning of Blackness as resistance and resilience. Therefore, I reflect on taking the positionality and subjectivity of Blackness as an anti-colonial discursive and political formation. This is accounting for global Blackness (including Diasporic Blackness) that does not simply reclaim the African past, culture, history, and knowledge for social transformation, but also fundamentally sees global Blackness as a place, location, space, and identity from which to theorize the Black/African humanity as spiritual knowing, a collective spiritual ontology encased within Black and African souls. Blackcentricity speaks of African Indigenous ontological existence and claims African Indigeneity as decolonial resistance.

This chapter will focus on the resistances and challenges of engaging race and Black/African Indigeneity in the academy as a Black scholar. Further, it will query what these revelations imply for institutionalized anti-Blackness. From the onset, I reiterate that my intellectual politics do not assume simplistically that (anti-)Blackness is only about race and racial politics. However, I maintain with no apologies that there can be no sound intellectual discussion of (anti-)Blackness that remains silent on race or that does the fancy intellectual dance around race and anti-racism. Blackness is not just about race, and yet it has everything to do with race! Race and racism must be central to a discussion of Blackness and anti-Blackness! I offer this cautionary note to those Black and racialized intellectuals who think anti-Blackness and anti-racism are miles apart and see no point in joining forces. Just as what masquerades as anti-racism may not be anti-racist, what also comes off as anti-Blackness may actually be a nice way of appealing to post-modern preoccupation with complicating everything. There are clearly points of convergence, as well as distinctiveness of racism, anti-racism, and anti-Blackness. For one, anti-Blackness is about recognition of the specificity, preeminence, and prominence of violence meted onto a group and reflected in the everyday embodied experience of Black and African subjects. We say "Black lives matter" precisely because of the perniciousness of systemic racism and state-sanctioned violence on Black bodies in our different geographies and within the context of our heterogeneity. However, irrespective of who we are as scholars/learners in the Western academy, when we fail to openly challenge race/racism and instead simply intellectualize and/or engage with language that talks around race and difference, we merely exhibit how adept we have become with the powerful codes of anti-Blackness. When we posit intersectionality/intersection theory in ways that deny race as a significant and unique entry point in understanding myriad and intersecting oppressions, we reveal our hidden anti-Black fabric. We also demonstrate our anti-Blackness/Africanness with our denial and open questioning of African and Black Diasporic Indigeneities, especially in the settler/colonial context (see also Adefarakan, 2011). As Black/African scholars we need to take up the colonial appellation and apparition of "Indigenous." To deny Black bodies of a history of Indigeneity is to deny a part of our identity and ancestral knowledges. Furthermore, when we misread Black resistance and politics as all about race and nothing more, rather than understand the urgent call to acknowledge race saliency, then our demonstrable intellectual hostility serves only to mask our anti-Blackness. These then are some the different codes of global anti-Blackness that go beyond White dominant and racialized subordinate relations. As we openly resist White anti-Blackness, we must also openly admit to Black anti-Blackness, Black anti-Black racism, Indigenous anti-Blackness, and racialized anti-Blackness. None of these admissions is intended to leave dominant bodies off the hook.

I have been privileged with the opportunity to speak out on the question of teaching race and Indigeneity in the academy as a Black scholar with Indigenous roots in Africa. The intellectual journey, however, has been a perpetual struggle. It has been an emotionally draining journey in an academy where the system of merit badges makes us all complicit in putting our own communities literally "under the bus" in order to gain legitimacy, validation, and acceptance as a "scholar" in White colonial spaces! It pays not to speak race, Black, or Indigenous but to present oneself as a disembodied scholar. It pays when even our racial identification is tempered with a constant questioning of what race, social justice, and Indigeneity mean, especially when such questioning is framed by White theory or White mimicking and ends up delegitimizing these discourses in the eyes of the dominant. We must ask why this constant questioning is well-received by the dominant scholar. We must question, when the dominant puts on us the tag of "scholar/thinker" and draws a distinction of our scholarship from the "angry," "raging," and "romanticizing" Afrocentrists and anti-colonialists, what intellectual politics are being served for consumption.

I will enter into a conversation from an experiential moment. In the fall of 2015, I was invited as a speaker on a public forum titled, "BLACKOUT: Who's Missing in Education?" organized by the Black History Awareness Committee of a local university in Ontario, Canada. All three panelists were asked to address some key questions:

- Why are Black communities underrepresented in education/academic professions?
- What are the difficulties faced when trying to climb the ladder in education/academic focused professions as a Black individual?
- How is systemic racism manifested in education/academic policies, practices, and cultures?
- How are racist and stereotypical attitudes maintained in a classroom setting?
- Why is "critical race theory" and other critical frameworks for analyzing power so marginalized in the discipline of education/academia?
- How does one encourage members of the Black community to view, as legitimate and desirable, a career in education/academia? (Black History Awareness Committee (BHAC), 2015, personal communication).

Without much effort, it became obvious to me that no Black scholar can do justice to these questions without grounding the accounting in the self-experiential knowledge garnered from our lived experiences in the academy. Writing this chapter has taken me back to the questions. Hence, this chapter will be a reflection on the paradox of our (Black/racialized/Indigenous) invisibility and yet hypervisibility in the academy. Both the invisibility and hypervisibility are simultaneously meant as punishment and reward. I locate myself as an African-Canadian heterosexual male, anti-racist pedagogue, teaching and researching race, anti-racism, and Indigeneity in the (Western) academy. I will highlight some of the personal struggles and challenges of this location and the implications for radical politics in academy. I connect the discussion to broader issues of race and educational transformation, for example, what it means for the Black scholar to work with a measured understanding of how we can only achieve educational excellence by addressing race, anti-racism, equity, and social difference in the academy. In ensuring that excellence is accessible to all learners, how have we as educators, researchers, and community workers within institutional settings addressed questions about who is represented, how, what, where, and why? Who is teaching in the academy and to what extent is the school curriculum diversified to ensure that we tell "complete stories?" How are we making the knowledge and education relevant to the communities of our students? Moreover, are we reaching out enough to our communities in ways that make us all define our academic mandates and the corresponding responsibilities? These questions gesture to reframing and replacing the current academy, not simply embarking on the current liberal approach to inclusion.

Before proceeding further let me make some important notations. These questions could also be perceived as limitations of the chapter. The issues raised here are not just concerns for the Black subject in the academy. These issues can be shared as collective experiences of racialized, colonized, and Indigenous bodies, albeit with different narrations and stories. Claiming "shared experiences" does not mean these are singular experiences. As many have also noted, oppressions are shared experiences, which are also experienced differently. These oppressions are varied and include racist, homophobic, sexist, classist, ableist, linguistic, sexual, and colonial violence. Admittedly, there are differences in the narration of our "stories" that cut across lines of ethnicity, class, gender, sexuality, (dis)ability, and the tropes of difference. I have chosen to write on my experiences from a particular vantage position and subject location. In the academy (as in everyday life) I am fully aware how race intersects with ethnicity, gender, class, sexuality, (dis)ability, as well as language and religious differences. The experiences I speak about are therefore demarcated powerfully by the lines and axis of difference. The experiences of a Black heterosexual, able-bodied male on issues of race in academia would be different from a female or even another male colleague (see Maylor, 2009, for example, on the Black academic female researcher and many others). I have put the gaze on my experiences to lead the discussion, fully aware of the complexities and the intersectionality of experiences in the academy that make any particular accounting limited. But I would also emphasize that the "blind spots" do not delegitimize my reflections and nor make my work any "less scholarly." To compound the criticism, I have not found a need to buttress every experience with a written text or citation. I have received knowledge pointing to a scholar's intellectual agency and "agential power" (Daniel & Yearwood, 2002) to reflect on the personal and experiential. To paraphrase Steve Biko (2005), "I write as I like," in a deep reflection, I will speak from my accumulated knowledge grounded in my long experience in the academy learning from and sharing knowledge with others. If I do not reference lines, I still acknowledge many others have shared similar thoughts. This is the story of the Western academy. Our stories look similar for the Black, racialized, Indigenous scholar!

Throughout this discussion I will allude to a collective shared experience that make the Black, Indigenous, and racialized presence in the academy a way to speak about community and the body. Ajamu Baraka (2016) notes that we live in age when "image is dominant and meaning fluid" (p. 1). There is a perpetual need to complexify, and I understand that. The notions we work with (e.g., community, Black, race, gender, sexuality, etc.) are contested, and it is imperative they speak of complexity, contingencies, and ambiguities. For example, I do not think we can and must even expect all Black academics to see themselves as "Black bodies/scholars," let alone as a collective in our pursuit of a radical Black politics. But I want to engage an *epistemic community* (Dei, 1999) that is willing to share ideas in the humility of knowing and to shun intellectual arrogance. I am a Black body in a White colonial space: the academy. The latter has been a community for different reasons and for different people. It has for other reasons not been a community. So not every Black or racialized scholar will share the experiences I recount here. But I am not here to debate notions of Blackness and community. I know for a fact that some of us have found the academy rewarding precisely because we do its bidding (e.g., working with tropes of hierarchies that demarcate "excellence" differently for different bodies). For some of us our scholarship may be validated when we mimic Eurocentric theories that hardly speak about the Black, Indigenous, racialized, or colonized experiences.

Part of the challenge of a decolonized, anti-colonial, and anti-racist education should be to make every member of the academy feel a sense of welcome, a sense of belonging in their educational settings. It is more than a respect for our different scholarship and the ways we speak differently. Racialized and Indigenous scholars must feel empowered to define ourselves in terms of who we are, what we are going to do with our education, and what they see as our broader responsibilities to each other and to our communities. All learners should see themselves in the school curriculum, defined broadly as encompassing textbooks, teaching methods, as well as the culture, environment, and the socio-organizational lives of the academy. This is not the sole responsibility of racialized, Black, or Indigenous faculty. It is our collective responsibility, and we must meet this challenge. We must constantly remind ourselves what we are doing to meet these challenges. We live in a world sanitized to deny frank discussions on race. When race comes into public consciousness it is usually the blatant forms of individual racist acts that make us claim to be shocked. It is frustrating when the public feigns surprise. We conveniently forget that all racisms have structural and systemic components to them.

There is always a subtle interplay of race and other forms of difference. But the saliency of race lies in that it (i.e., the race question) cannot be approached as a subsidiary of any other category (e.g., class). High income is no barrier to being subjected to anti-Black racism. For example, in April of 2014 we witnessed the racist rant of Los Angeles basketball owner Donald Sterling who, while dating a Mexican and African-American female, had such racist misgivings for his female friend's public companionship with Africans. Sterling's performance and the spectacle was itself not surprising in a racist society. It was interesting the way race and capitalism jostled with each other. The so-called philanthropic work of a billionaire and the fact that his businesses employed a number of people was introduced into social condemnations in a way that drew attention away from the severity of his racist rant. This was an issue of morality and there was no room for discussions about capitalism and economics. When it was suggested that we just leave the players to play the game and leave the distraction of Sterling's comments out of sports, I wondered what people are afraid of. I guess I should hold my tongue, play ball, and suffer racist indignities because I am making money! Sometimes people have to forget about the bread-and-butter issues and take clear stances on moral indignation. To ask the question of who in the end suffers if he pulls his monetary power away from the community is a reversal. It could be argued that Donald Sterling made his money on the backs of the very people he hates with impunity. Black basketball players are his bread and butter and not the other way around. Similarly, Black basketball players and, in fact, all professional Black athletes, have to take a stance against racism and not temper their utterances in fear of losing their daily economic survival. To claim that what I am asserting is coming from a position of class privilege is patronizing. It only makes my point about the seductive interplay of race and class. When facts are there we can only argue and debate to a certain point. Is there no room in our society for morality to triumph over wealth?

Experiential And Generative Knowledge

There is one reading that sticks out for me in teaching race and anti-racism in the Western academy over the years: this idea that somehow the focus on race in a scholar's work makes her or him a "single-issue" scholar. This problematic reading usually understands race as simply Black, and it is applied, especially for the Black scholar. She or he is further charged as operating with a simplistic Black-White binary. Or worse, the Black scholar who specializes and/or focuses solely on Black and African experience can be deemed narrow/parochial and yet this charge is not extended to an Indigenous scholar dwelling on Indigenous studies or even a White scholar working on White subjects and/or European studies, which leads me to ponder: Why is it that claims of Blackness are met with a need to recognize its heterogeneity and multidimensionality, something that we do not often hear of when claims of Indigeneity and the Indigenous experiences are made? (See also Dei, 2019.)

As Black scholars we are asked to nuance our analysis and go beyond race. Never mind that scholars take up interstices of difference in their analysis; they are heard as always "speaking race." I have seen a few Black colleagues—claiming to be anti-racists—actually take up interstices of difference in ways that not only dilute a focus on race, but sometimes even push race to the background. Of course, this call to complexify is important because we are not all just about race. To paraphrase Edward Said (1979), no one has ever been one thing. We should at all times complicate race. We should speak of how race intersects with other forms of difference. But as we do so in our work as anti-racists we must maintain the gaze on race. It is always the big elephant in the room, the "taboo subject" (Tatum, 1992), the issue people quickly run away from and conveniently maintain as a blind spot. It is the seduction to complicate, and what such a rhetoric does to the saliency of race makes critical anti-racism hang on to race as a pivotal issue. We must not be apologetic about that. In fact, what is normally lost in the dominant critique of the "race focus" is an important/cardinal tenet of anti-racism: that race is and must be the entry point on which the axis of difference pivots. The politics of anti-racism requires that we foreground race. But in the anti-racist interpretation, this saliency of race is not just about race as Black and Blackness (Dei, 1996). Race is about everything, particularly, White, Whiteness, and the dominant. Whiteness has been the dominant gaze with which everything else is measured (see Kincheloe & Steinberg, 1998).

There is an important conceptual distinction between maintaining a Black-White binary and working with a Black-White paradigm lens. Unfortunately, this distinction is often lost, leading to fault lines in the re-theorization of race. A Black- White binary is a dualism or divide that understands self (White) in relation to the Other (Black) (see also Smith, 2006). It works with the color descriptor of "Black" and "White" as bounded and fixed categories. The Black-White paradigm, on the other hand, is a lens or frame of reference that acknowledges the ways Whiteness becomes the standard bearer. The closer one is to this Whiteness, the greater currency, legitimacy, and validation one is accorded. Society and academy reward a closer proximity to Whiteness. This is why in most contexts those who are closer to Whiteness are given privileges. It happens even in colonized, racialized communities. I know in my own Ghanaian community that those who have lighter skin receive positive attributes and are favorites. This assertion has nothing to do with the politics of the body. I am speaking about degrees of shadism and the "lactification" Fanon (1967) spoke about. The Black-White paradigm gestures to the politics of the body rather than merely the body as a "signifier of difference." The Black-White paradigm allows us to understand the problem of racialized bodies magnetized by Whiteness that Molefi Asante (1999) alludes to in his conception of a "tortured consciousness." Also, the Black-White paradigm allows us to ground the Black experience as cornerstone, or very fundamental to interrogating and understanding social justice struggles and political activism (see also Sexton 2010, 2015; Dei, 2017).

Again, in my years in the academy I have often heard some oft-repeated comments: "This has nothing to do with race" or "We cannot reduce the Black experience simply to race!" Indeed, these are interesting comments. While there may be a point worthy of contention or note, I would ask us to think what we really mean when we make these assertions. Usually, when it is said that "this has nothing to do with race," it is more of a defensive stance. Why do people feel the need to make these claims? And, more importantly, who is able to make these comments? When one seriously looks at what is being denied, indeed it has everything to do with race! This is why the comment is put out there in the first place. It is to deflect. It is also significant to note the body making this assertion and just what is being denied. That body is hiding his or her race privilege. Saying something has everything to do with race is not to deny other interpretations. It merely insists that race is part of the equation. In contemporary society we can and must bring a race angle to our analysis. Of course, this also goes for gender, class, sexuality, (dis)ability, and so on. In my experience it is race that is always in doubt. Race continually has to prove itself! Part of the denial of race in the academy is to throw in a wrench that either dilutes the discussion, implicates everyone, or makes it soothing to the ears of the dominant. It is curious to me why those who equate the anti-racism emphasis on race to Black/Blackness do not question the source of their own (mis)interpretations rather than ask that we interrogate the concept of race itself!

We hardly speak race in the academy, contrary to the assertion that there is too much focus on race. The academy only makes particular kinds of discussions on race possible. It also limits the extent of institutional engagement of race and anti-racism. The academy regulates race knowledge and doesn't deem it scholarly and worthy of pursuit. It seeks to domesticate the anti-racist agenda the same way the nation state does. It is no wonder that some would attribute this liberalizing institutional politics of race and anti-racism as more a problem of what anti-racism stands for, rather than how institutions "regulate" race and anti-racism knowledge. For some, our universities "have too many courses on race!" Let me give an example. In prior years of teaching in the university my department summer courses might include "race studies," "politics of marginalization," and others. I recall in one year there were three courses offered in total, with two courses offered by faculty members from a previously separate faculty that is now joined with my faculty. The other (third) course from my faculty was in French and so was available only to some students. No courses were offered by our critical race scholars, and no courses addressed race substantively. Students who come to the now amalgamated faculty do have access to a well-rounded and critical education, but only during some academic terms, and there is a dilution of the anti-racist, anti-colonial, anti-hegemonic emphasis with the mixing of other courses that use different names to address different levels of some of these aspects.

There are subtle interventions deployed when tensions emerge, such as budget issues, and during these times the perhaps previously sleeping colonial matrix begins to write in departmental discourses and silences at universities. Paying attention to the scope of topics covered in courses in a department or faculty so that a well-rounded, critical education is at least possible for those who choose to pursue it is very important to the spirit of decolonizing the academy and education in general. I have often felt that we need to work to establish critical race studies and equity-based courses as degree requirements with meaningful institutional support. Surely the course content is important because a course named anti-racism, equity, and so on can be limited in its approach to questions of social oppressions. But so is every course taught at a university. There are limits of knowing, and this critique cannot be lodged solely at anti-racism or critical race studies. We do not have this monopoly on this problem I call the "limitation of scholarships." Our critiques must extend to courses in media and culture, feminism and gender studies, Diasporic and transnationalism studies, democratic education, Aboriginal and Indigenous studies, and so on. Courses on anti-racism, critical race studies, however, need to be available with a variety of emphases to support the particular interests and scholarship of students. These courses must fit easily into the academic year and would desirably be available through all terms to respond to the varied need of our students and the multiple roles they engage.

Questions

To be a Black, anti-racist scholar one must be a prepared for the possibility of social and intellectual death given the emotional, psychological, and spiritually draining nature of the academy (see also Baraka, 2016 and Patterson, 1982, in different contexts). Following Patterson, I use "death" in the figurative sense to denote there are subtle ways of silencing the Black, racialized scholars who speak, race and social oppression in the academy. One can go far (albeit within constraints) in the academy when the Black scholar chooses to remain silent and not talk about race, anti-racism, and oppression. The Black scholar always stands the risk of being viewed as confrontational, angry, emotional, and anti-intellectual. For racialized, minoritized, colonized, and Indigenous scholars we need to understand the dynamics of race in the White academy and be political and strategic in order to maintain our own health and sanity. We must engage the academy on its hypocritical levels. We must also be in tune with our communities outside of the academy to secure emotional and spiritual healing and rejuvenation. While the challenges we have to deal with are complex, the genesis of the problem is not that complex. I will reflect on four of the questions that guided my presentation at the university public forum referred to earlier as given impetus to this paper. To use the old adage: "One must know where one is coming from in order to know where one is going." The same can be said of the Black experience in the academy. We cannot solve or address a problem we do not understand or refuse to understand. I bring some truthful frankness and integrity to the discussion. I respect the views of other Black scholars who would disagree with me. I just ask that my reflections are not dismissed as being misinformed.

First, *why are Black communities underrepresented in education/academic professions?* There has been some progress on the question of minority faculty representation in the academy, but by far our academies remain lily-White in terms of the bodies who teach, hold positions of power, and influence and go into these spaces to learn. The problem can be traced to a host of factors. I firmly believe, however, a major reason is the disturbing lack of critical understanding of the strengths and imperatives of diversity and difference. These terms cannot be depoliticized if we want to concretely engage them to bring about social change. These terms cannot be sanitized into comfortable discussions that fail to ruffle feathers. Diversity is conventionally (read liberally) taken as something merely to be celebrated, but not to be concretely dealt with in terms of its implications about representation, identity, and the link with knowledge and the responsibilities of ensuring that school curriculum and classroom pedagogy, reflects this diversity in order to present a more complete account of history, ideas, events, and developments that have influenced and continue to influence human growth and development.

The rhetorical understanding of diversity as mere celebration and simply appreciating difference means while we may take pride in seeing different faces in our academies, we do not feel as a sense of urgency to relate this diversity to the structural transformation of schooling and education. For example, in the face of our diversity we still operate with very narrow and restrictive definitions of "excellence" and "meritocracy" that are understood within the conventional. When issues of diversity and difference arise there is a boundary that cannot be crossed, which is to say not to challenge what has been conventionally accepted as "excellence" and merit. Of course, we all want "excellence" and to be assessed on the basis of merit. But how have these been defined? How inclusive are our understandings? Counter-discourses that are oppositional to the established grain of thought are measured with a Eurocentric yardstick and dismissed. A consequence is that minority scholars are not emboldened to trouble existing definitions and many of us would mimic dominant knowledges, theories, and experiences in order to seek validation and acceptance. Many times when our faculties are hiring they fail to look for scholars who actually trouble hegemonic knowledge and use very Eurocentric measures to assess the candidate's excellence. Similarly, the pervasiveness of color blindness in defense of Whiteness rationalizes the lack of critical diversity in the academy. To interrupt this culture of power we need our academies to teach about excellence in a way that stresses the multiple ways of knowing and what it truly means to concretely address the requirements and expectations of diversity and difference. This can only happen if we bring a more pointed understanding to difference and diversity, placing power and privilege questions at the center. If we cannot do this we will continue to betray what "difference" and "diversity" truly mean.

Second, *what are the difficulties faced when trying to climb the ladder in education/academic focused professions as a Black individual?* For Black bodies who find our way in the academy we confront challenges and expectations that pose huge obstacles to progress through the ranks. There are interrelated academic, health, spiritual, and economic challenges that suggest the academy was not designed for us. To fit in, there are expectations placed on the Black body. Not only must one perform to the criteria of a "scholar" as set out by mainstream definitions and conventional codes of "excellence," but we cannot perform our Blackness to its fullness without posing a threat. The academy makes some forms of Blackness acceptable while others are repulsive, repugnant, and punishable.

We have to perform in terms of engaging academic theories, research scholarship, and educational practice deemed as "knowledge." It is through these conventions that we are validated and accepted. To insist on seeking validation and legitimation under one's own terms is to assume risks and commit "intellectual suicide." Black bodies have designed and ascribed roles in the academy. We are seen as "experts" on race issues and yet our expert knowledge must be validated by the dominant. We can speak race and oppression only to a point. We do not have the same discursive authority and authorial control over race knowledge production that a White/dominant scholar speaking on race does. We are seen as very interested, partisan, and political scholars with no "objective" knowledge.

The challenge and responsibility to confront the racial boundary policing and the fabrication of Whiteness and that Aime Cesaire (1972) wrote about is injurious to our souls and well-being. We always have to be careful how we tread. Certain boundary crossings become transgressions. The spatiality of race also requires that we know our limits and confines in the academy. Black bodies are read differently when we occupy certain spaces within the academy. Blacks in leadership roles have a constant gaze and sometimes it appears as if there is an eye trained to catch the moments we slip. There is also a "thingfication" of our Blackness whereby our subjectivity and agency are always questioned. We continually struggle to insist on our humanity and the objectification of our experiences. When we mimic Eurocentric theories and speak in dominant language we are seen as "smart." When we work within oppositional and counter stances and discourses we become half-baked intellectuals. There is an expectation to maintain our individualities, but this reading is not granted to us when we are being essentialized. Many of us claim "community" and "collective belonging" to politically resist and maintain our sanity. But such reclaiming is dismissed as totalizing and bearing hints of over-romanticism. Notwithstanding counter-claims of our individual and collective agencies, our Blackness is seen as fixed, unchanging, degenerate, deficient, or with deficit. To challenge and resist our continuing sub-humanity our politics is understood as always grumbling. These problems are exacerbated by the fact that there is still a lack of critical mass: not enough Black scholars as role models to learn from. And as if this is not enough, we have dominant discourses that even subvert claims of "role models," insisting the concept itself is problematic. In my experience I see the Black, Indigenous, or racialized scholar who is an academic warrior grounded in community political activism as a role model. It is what I strive to be. Who is to challenge my perception of who a role model is? The coupling of scholarship and political activism is what makes the Black scholar authentic. Authenticity is not about purity nor an uncontaminated ethos. For a scholar, it is about being true to oneself and soul. In the midst of disturbing high school push-out rates, mass incarceration, youth unemployment, community health challenges, children in care, and so on that disproportionately affect Black, Indigenous, and racialized communities to insist that one is simply pursuing scholarship is not enough. Our scholarly pursuit must make sense in helping to address the problems afflicting our communities. Disputing claims of Black scholarly "authenticity" can be hypocritical. Who is the "Other" to tell the "Self" he or she is being authentic/inauthentic? Dominant bodies are *not* the experts to inform us about Black authenticity. It is extreme arrogance for a White billionaire like Rupert Murdoch in reflecting on U.S. election politics to charge that Ben Carson will be the first genuine Black president if elected! It is an insult to Black intelligence, and there is much of that in the academy.

Third, *how is systemic racism manifested in educational/academic policies, practices, and cultures?* Racism in academia is primarily an issue of institutional neglect and the ways systemic exclusions are justified as the normal way of doing things. The open hostility to critical race and anti-racist pursuits and the fact that nothing is being done about the race problem is even more problematic. To speak race and racism is to create a problem, and the least said the better. Racism in the academy is too often conceptualized as the

lack of diversity in faculty and staff and/or as its negation or absence in curriculum, instruction, classroom pedagogies, and representation of bodies. Diversity can be a calling card for our institutions, and the presence of diversity among students, staff, and faculty population is read as an indicator of "no racism." We know academic institutions boast about having policies in place to deal with systemic exclusions and to address race and anti-racist issues. But as Sara Ahmed (2006) notes in her discussion of the "performative speech acts" of our institutions, the policies are often for show and institutional credibility. The policies themselves have become performances of equity (see also Blackmore & Sachs, 2003). The policies often give the appearance that the institution is doing its utmost best to address systemic racist exclusions. The experiences of racialized, colonized, and Indigenous bodies in the academic setting are different. There is a sense we have to continually shout racism; we have to prove ourselves beyond everybody else, and our mistakes are often magnified and attributed to some inherent genetic traits. To be a racialized scholar is to be a naturalized subject. There is a disturbing degree of institutions merely acknowledging difference, but not going beyond to concretely address what the difference signifies in terms of having faculty and staff representation, having more inclusive curriculum, and engaging the multiple knowledges, histories, and experiences that a diverse student body brings into these institutions. Repeatedly, there are enactments and functionality of Whiteness in academic spaces. As noted, what is deemed "excellence," what theory and whose theories count, and the particular understandings of merit(ocracy) are very heavily anchored in individualism, hard work, and achievement skills. There is often not a critical interrogation of the structures of educational delivery that may produce school "failures;" for example a new study that showed that White teachers' expectations for Black boys for academic success are significantly less than Black teachers' predictions for the same students (Papageorge, Gershensona, & Holta, 2016).

Discussions of race are usually interpreted as attempts to establish binaries. As already noted, we have an academic culture that fails to distinguish the important conceptual distinction between a Black-White binary and the significance of using the

Black-White paradigm. Other examples of racism in academia is the appreciation of capitalist/consumptive Blackness, which plays itself out when particular forms of Blackness are very welcome in schools while others are deemed threatening. There is a sense of entitlements restricted to the dominant who insist the academy has to meet their needs. When educational institutions attempt to respond to the expectations and demands of the disadvantaged the dominant's response is, "What about us?" In high schools in particular, it is not uncommon for few White students to complain that at least Black students have African History Month while they do not have any month celebrating their cultures!

The spatiality of race and punishing of what are perceived to be Black transgressions (e.g., showing up Black in unwanted White colonial spaces) is common (see Adjei, 2013). Being perceived as too loud, aggressive, and continuously angry are part of this spatial reading of the Black body. There is a fetishization of theory over community and practice, and Black, racialized, and Indigenous scholars who prioritize politics and activism in their scholarship risk being perceived as anti-intellectual. All this constitutes aspects of liberal democracies and the emphasis on the self, individual, and rights rather than communities and collective responsibility. A clear manifestation of racism in academia is the dismemberment, depersonalization, and wounding of souls, spirits, and bodies.

Fourth, *how are racist and stereotypical attitudes maintained in a classroom setting*? In academic settings there are everyday acts of educational violence—curriculum exclusions, lack of curricular sophistication, speech acts violently directed at racialized bodies, and the dominant's tendency to conscript the idea of fractured communities in order to avoid responsibility and accountability, for example. Denials of people's histories and the pervasiveness of a cultural historical amnesia undergird classroom discussions. While some educators are bold enough to challenge students and faculty colleagues when these racist and stereotypical acts come up, unfortunately not everyone chooses to resist or stand up. The cost of such resistance can be high for different bodies. In classrooms the knowledge and expertise of racialized, Indigenous faculty can be questioned through claims of bias, not presenting "both sides of the story," or a failure to allow contending positions to flourish. Claims of silencing dominant students are usually leveled against Black and minority faculty who teach race simply because they call learners up on their actions. When minority students feel empowered to speak in anti-racist classes they risk being viewed as "dominating class discussions." The faculty who allow such voicing of the subjugated voice are seen as playing favorites and empowering Black and minority students at the expense of disempowering White/dominant students. It is not uncommon to hear charges of "reverse racism" leveled against Black and racialized faculty interestingly by the very people who deny there is any racism in academia. In classroom discussions Black masculinities can often be presented as problematic, deficit, criminal, violent, aggressive, and degenerate. It takes a critical teacher to uncover such racist tropes. It is little wonder that for some minority students and faculty the comfort they may feel in classroom discussions is by amputating a part of themselves (our histories, cultures, and identities).

In my teaching experience I have also seen some subtle and not so subtle ways racism is maintained in academic circles through what I would call the "politics of striking pedagogical favorites in social theorizing." Critical Race Theory (CRT), Critical Anti-Racism Theory (CART), Afrocentric theory, and other critical frameworks for analyzing power can be marginalized in the academy. Because of their critical stances these frameworks can be assessed differently and often their claim to theory can be questioned. In relatively recent years, critical race theory has gotten a following in the academy. But it is more so the case with those of us who push Afrocentric interpretations of social phenomena. No discourse is immune to criticism. Afrocentricity does not lend itself to a postmodern take. And it appears to me that Afrocentricity as a theory of social change and a political ideology is scrutinized with a Eurocentric lens and often dismissed because it seeks to establish a counter hegemony. Never mind the fact that the principles espoused by Afrocentric education, for example, are ideas with which all schools must be engaging. The "anti" posture is always fraught with challenges (e.g., anti-colonial versus post-colonial; anti-racist versus critical race, etc.) The "anti" stance is an "against" stance and it is often very liberatory and action oriented. There is a fascination with the "post" and its articulations of unending ambivalences and contingencies (e.g., postmodernism). I also wonder what is good about racism and colonialisms for anyone to be opposed to the "anti" stance? We can connect these readings to the fear of radical Blackness and radical Black scholarship.

The intellectual hostility to race and anti-racism has two push-pull factors. For some of us this is the more reason we want to study and engage critical race and anti-racist scholarship. In this space we can become the distinctive voice that speaks about our experiences in their complexities. The Black experience is very much about race and more. As acknowledged earlier, there are gender, class, sexual, and (dis)ability dimensions to our experiences as Black, racialized, and Indigenous scholars in the academy. Another push factor is some racialized scholars may not want to speak race because of the consequences and risks which they are unwilling to bear or pay. These scholars, some of whom are progressive colleagues, often hide their fears and anxieties around unfounded intellectual claims of race being very reductionist. If one looks closely at their work, the alternative they offer either makes race a subset of class or takes up the "human" as a (new) universal subject devoid of race, class, gender, sexuality, and (dis)ability identifications. It may also be contended that race has been understood as Black/White binary. Frankly, I do not buy the argument that race scholarship is about a binary of Black/White. This critique becomes a convenient, too-easy escape for not speaking race. By sharing our experiences of the "unspeakability" and "difficulty" of speaking race, we put race on the table for discussion and political practice. Reflecting and acting on our experiences as race and anti-racist educators make us take up the mantle of being change agents wanting to subvert the assumed normalcy of the Western academy. We also begin to unlearn our "miseducation" as our primary responsibility.

Moving Forward With A Self And Collective Implications

In a reflective piece it is empowering to undertake a self and collective examination. What do I see as my/our self and collective complicities as Black, racialized, or Indigenous scholars in the academy? I am (just as we all are) implicated in this discussion. I believe as Black/racialized faculty our presence in the academy make us deeply complicit in the continuing racist, colonialist, and imperialist history of the academy. We have become complacent and too-often accepting. But, it is more than our inaction and the failure to become distinctive Black or racialized voices in the academy that makes us complicit and fosters the deep cynicism that exists in own communities. While I would not go so far as to say that Black academics are simply "taking up space" in our institutions, I believe our mere presence tends to compromise any critiques we may have of the system. There is the *agential power* to reflect on our experiences and ideas to change our own condition, and in this case the institutional settings within which we work.

The continuing alienation and devaluation of Black intellectuality has put us on the defensive. We are often seduced to shy away from speaking for/with our communities for fear of being asked to respond to the questions: "Who speaks for whom? Why speak for a community given that we cannot represent a heterogeneous community?" Many of us do resist, for sure. Despite some resistance, however, there is a troubling assimilation into the Western academic culture and the particular ways this culture approaches intellectuality; for example, in the ways we seek legitimation, validation, and acceptance in White colonial spaces; the unilateral fragmentation around difference—as if our world is all about accentuating our differences—not seeing between the lines when dominant discourse conscripts the idea of a fractured community in order to deny responsibility and accountability; the mimicking of Eurocentric theories that for the most hardly speak to our lived experiences.

We are witnesses to the power of a capitalist modernity and the distribution of rewards in the academy. The politics and intellectuality of Black, racialized, and Indigenous scholars risk being co-opted by the "capitalist bourgeois culture" within a corporate modernity of liberalism (e.g., individualism, competition, greed, hierarchies of knowing, craze for individual excellence and meritocracy). Today many forms and aspects of Black resistance are commodified by the economic, cultural power of neo-liberalism (see also Baraka, 2016). This is part of the political economy of knowledge production in the academy, which has resisted any attempts for cooperation and community building among Black, racialized, and Indigenous scholars. We often compete among ourselves. We put each other down to seek dominant favor. As noted, some may put our communities "under the bus," and we are seduced into thinking that by putting one another down we bolster ourselves and our own scholarship. These oppressive relations constitute spiritual and emotional wounding that hurt of us all. There is also the problem of Black complicities in hegemonic and anti-Black knowledge production. For example, in Canada there still persists the problematic discourse of Blacks as "settlers," which some Black and racialized scholars simply accept without a critical interrogation. Admittedly, some frank and legitimate questions have been raised and continue to be debated (see Lawrence & Amadahy, 2009; Lawrence & Dua, 2005; Sharma & Wright, 2009; Waldron, 2003; Wolfe, 2006). Nonetheless, the politics of inserting the Black experience in White colonial settlerhood has gained traction at the expense of marginalizing the African genocide, which is beyond enslavement: mass incarceration, school "push outs," the very flaky idea of Black citizenship in the colonial nation state (see Dei, 2017).

In reframing the personal and political I want us to insist on our authenticity as Black scholars. We must bring authentic Black, racialized, and Indigenous intellectual resistance through courage and be true to ourselves as academic warriors. One way to achieve this authenticity is to resist the continued commodification of our Blackness as pursued within a capitalist prism. We must begin to appreciate authentic Black transformational politics emerging from within our communities. We must also work on producing our own sociohistorical condition and consciousness through a control of the knowledge production process. We must be the vanguards in cultivating a place of Indigenous/African/local community cultural knowledge (including Indigenous spiritual ontologies) in our scholarship, theorizing, and research.

In conclusion, I note that while a lot has happened, not a lot has changed. As Black/African scholars we must understand what it means to resist an "intellectual nothingness" and to affirm the earthiness of Black radical thought and politics grounded in our rich ancestral histories and cultural heritage. I reiterate that we must reclaim our identities as Black scholars/learners/intellectuals in the academy and be bold to work with possibilities of Black scholarship, to cultivate mutually supportive relations with our diverse communities. This is the way for Black educational futurity and survival in academia. This grounding in community offers us the spiritual strength and rejuvenation needed to survive in the treacherous environments of the academy. There is a need to work to shape our individual and collective consciousness through a control of the anti-colonial knowledge production to inform our lived experiences in a newly imagined community. We may not be able to "replace the academy" but we can seek to transform it. We need an academy that puts in the work. We must learn to play the complex and sometimes conflicting roles of being "in and out" simultaneously. We are "in" working to transform the academy. We step out to work "outside" in the wider community to bring into being a new future in counter-educational spaces. I see this as a form of strategic engagement. It is about working with the possibility of new futures and thinking through new speculative imaginaries for a new future to happen. By bringing a critical and political edge to scholarship we are resurrecting our sense of purpose and honoring our commitments to the historic community and ancestral struggles that made it possible for us to be the "academy we want" in the first place. We have a particular responsibility to search for new and reimagined ways to advance a Black, Indigenous, anti-racist, and anti-colonial agenda and to bring such agendas to the forefront of local, regional, national, and international consciousness.

In speaking race and Indigeneity, pushing anti-racist and anti-colonial activism we are not creating the problem of race, colonial violence, and imperial oppression. We are actually gesturing to the fact that a problem, racism (much like gender, class, sexuality, disability, colonialism, anti-Indigeneity, anti-Blackness, etc.), has not been fully addressed. Race has not been fully addressed, and we cannot go beyond a problem that remains unsolved. It is very cool to center one's Blackness and Africanness in a paper and not be apologetic about it. Some of us may shy away from such intellectual politics because of the colonial gaze and ongoing coloniality of Western knowledge production. Colonialism has either disturbed or dismantled many aspects of our lives: our histories, cultures, and spirituality. Fortunately, through creative intellectual and political resistance, we are beginning to put all this back together (with no help from the colonizer, of course). We are drawing on our imaginative imaginaries and potentials to build and restore relations and community. In this process our African ancestors have been called back into action and to help in restoring our lost relationships. Throughout this power, I have articulated the conjunction of Blackness and Indigeneity to seek and offer new Black and Indigenous futurities in the academy. In this futuristic journey we must be looking to the epistemologies and pedagogies of Blackness and Indigeneity that help to restore our humanity in academia. Through speaking out on racism and anti-Blackness we are restoring our sense of collective wellness and living well together.

Acknowledgements

I would like to thank Anila Zainub of the Department of Leadership, Higher, and Adult Education and Ezinwanne Odozor and Andrea Vásquez Jiménez Vasquez of the Department of Social Justice Education, Ontario Institute for Studies in Education of the University of Toronto (OISE/UT), Canada, for reading through and editing initial drafts of the chapter. I also thank the audience at the public forum, "BLACKOUT: Who's Missing in Education?" organized by the Black History Awareness Committee of Ryerson University in Ontario, Canada, in November 2015 for comments during my presentation, which have filtered through my thoughts for the paper.

References

Adefarakan, T. (2011). (Re)Conceptualizing "Indigenous" from Anti-Colonial and Black Feminist Theoretical Perspectives: Living and Imagining Indigeneity Differently. In G. J. S. Dei (Ed.), *Indigenous Philosophies and Critical Education: A Reader* (pp. 34–52). New York, NY: Peter Lang.

Adjei, P. B. (2013). When Blackness Shows Up Uninvited: Examining the Murder of Trayvon Martin through Fanonian Racial Interpellation. In. G. J. S. Dei & M. Lordan (Eds.), *Contemporary Issues in the Sociology of Race and Ethnicity: A Critical Reader* (pp. 25-41). New York, NY: Peter Lang.

Adjei, P.B. (2016). The (Em)Bodiment of Blackness in a Visceral Anti-Black Racism and Ableism Context. *Race and Ethnicity in Education, 21*(3), 1–13.

Ahmed, S. (2006). The Non-Performativity of Anti-Racism. *New Spaces in the Humanities* 5(3), 1–10.

Asante, M. K. (1999). *The Painful Demise of Eurocentrism: An Afrocentric Response to Critics.* Trenton NJAfrica World Press.

Baraka, A. (2016, February). Beyonce and the Politics of Cultural Dominance. *Black Agenda Report.* Retrieved from http://blackagendareport.com/beyonce_politics_social_dominance

Biko, S. (2005). *I Write What I Like.* A. Stubbs C. R. (Ed.). Johannesburg, Africa: Picardo Africa.

Blackmore, J. & Sachs, J. (2003). Managing Equity Work in the Performative University. *Australian Feminist Studies, 18*(41), 141–162.

Cesaire, A. (1972). *Discourse on Colonialism.* New York, NY: Monthly Review Press.

Daniel, B. & Yearwood, M. (2002). African-Canadian Women's Bodies as Sites of Knowing and No-ing. In S. Abbey (Ed.), *Ways of Knowing in and through the Body* (pp. 25-45). Welland, ON: SOLEIL.

Dei, G. J. S. (1996). *Anti-Racism Education in Theory and Practice.* Halifax, Nova Scotia: Fernwood Publishing.

Dei, G. J. S. (1999). Knowledge and Politics of Social Change: The Implication of Anti-Racism. *British Journal of Sociology of Education, 20*(3), 395–409.

Dei, J. S. S. (2017). *Reframing Blackness and Black Solidarities through Anti-Colonial and Decolonial Prisms.* New York, NY: Springer.

Dei, G. J. S. (2019: Forthcoming). Black Theorising: Indigeneity and Resistance in Academia. In S. Styres, & A. Kempf (Eds.). *Troubling the Trickster.* Edmonton: University of Alberta Press.

Dumas, M. J. (2014). "Losing an Arm": Schooling as a Site of Black Suffering. *Race, Ethnicity and Education, 17*(1), 1–29

Dumas, M. J. (2016). Against the Dark: Antiblackness in Education Policy and Discourse. *Theory into Practice, 55*, 11–19.

Dumas, M. J., & ross, k. m. (2016). "Be Real Black for Me": Imagining BlackCrit in Education. *Urban Education, 51*(4), 415–442.

Fanon, F. (1967). *Black Skin, White Masks.* New York, NY: Grove Press.

Ibrahim, A. (2014). *The Rhizome of Blackness: A Critical Ethnography of Hip-Hop Culture, Language, Identity, and the Politics of Becoming.* New York, NY: Peter Lang.

Kincheloe, J. & Steinberg, S. R. (1998). Addressing the Crisis of Whiteness: Reconfiguring White Identity in a Pedagogy of Whiteness. In J. L. Kincheloe, S. R. Steinberg, N. M

Rodriguez, & R. E. Chennault (Eds.), *White Reign: Deploying Whiteness in America* (pp. 1–29). New York, NY: St Martin's.

King, J. E. (2016). Anti-Blackness in the Academy and in Community Activism [Keynote Address]. Decolonizing Conference on Race, Anti-racism and Indigeneity: Anti-Colonial Resurgence and Anti-Colonial Resistance. Ontario Institute for Studies in Education, University of Toronto. Toronto, Canada.

Lawrence, B. & Amadahy, Z. (2009). Indigenous Peoples and Black People in Canada: Settlers or Allies? In A. Kempf (Ed.), *Breaching the Colonial Contract* (pp. 105–136). Netherlands: Springer.

Lawrence, B., & Dua, E. (2005). Decolonizing Antiracism. *Social Justice*, *32*(4), 120–143.

Maylor, U. (2009). Is It because I'm Black? A Black Female Research Experience. *Race, Ethnicity and Education*, *12*(1), 53–64.

McKittrick, K. (2011). On Plantations, Prisons, and a Black Sense of Place. *Social & Cultural Geography*, *12*(8), 947–963.

McKittrick, K., & Woods, C. (Eds.). (2007). *Black geographies and the politics of place*. Toronto, Canada: Between the Lines.

Papageorgec, N. W., Gershensona, S., & Holta, S. B. (2016). Who Believes in Me? The Effect of Student-Teacher Demographic Match on Teacher Expectations. *Economics of Education Review*, *52*, 209–224.

Patterson, L. (1982). *Slavery and Social Death: A Comparative Study*. Cambridge, MA: Harvard University Press.

Said, E. (1979). *Orientalism*. New York, NY: Vintage.

Sexton, J. (2010). People-of-Color-Blindness: Notes on the Afterlife of Slavery. *Social Text*, *28*(2), 31–56.

Sexton, J. (2015). Unbearable Blackness. *Cultural Critique*, *90*(1), 159–178.

Sexton, J. (2017). On Black Negativity, or the Affirmation of Nothing. Interview with D. Colucciello Barber. *Society & Space*. Retrieved from http://societyandspace.org/2017/09/18/on-black-negativity-or-the-affirmation-of-nothing/

Sharma, N., & Wright, C. (2009). Decolonizing Resistance, Challenging Colonial States. *Social Justice*, *35*(3), 120–138.

Sharpe, C. (2016). *In the Wake: On Blackness and Being*. Durham, NC: Duke University Press.

Tatum, B. D. (1992). Talking about Race, Learning about Racism: The Application of Racial Identity Development Theory in the Classroom. *Harvard Educational Review*, *621*, 1–24.

Walcott, R. (2003). *Black Like Who? Writing Black Canada* (2nd ed.). Toronto, Canada: Insomniac Press.

Waldron, J. (2003). Indigeneity? First Peoples and Last Occupancy. *New Zealand Journal of Public and International Law*, 1, 55–82.

Wolfe, P. (2006). Settler Colonialism and the Elimination of the Native. *Journal of Genocide Research*, *8*(4), 387–409. </ref>

CHAPTER 2

Black Indigenization As Politics of Transformation: Implications of the Zimbabwe Experiment

Munyaradzi Hwami and Edward Shizha

Introduction

ZIMBABWE, UNDER THEN President Robert Mugabe, will be recorded in history as one of the very few developing countries in the world that attempted to transfer the means of production from minority White people of European descent and multinational corporations to Indigenous Black Zimbabweans, and in the process made political independence from European powers realistic and meaningful to ordinary people (Moyo & Yeros, 2011; Sadomba, 2011), further proclaiming the Black race as owners of national resources, a feat rarely seen throughout the world, including in the rest of Africa. That the implementation of the Indigenization program was an affront toward international capital and White racism (a system that has benefitted from Black skins more than from any other race) could not escape many critical eyes, and its representation of Black empowerment and progress, Black/African emancipation, anti-racism, and anti-anti-Blackness were evident.

In this chapter, we examine and locate African/Black struggles for development in the context of the much-publicized Indigenization program that was deployed in Zimbabwe. We argue that Black Indigenization is a philosophy for African/Black emancipation and genuine independence, marked by ownership of economic resources after political control (independence). This de-colonial perspective is analyzed through an examination of Zimbabwe's Indigenous Black Empowerment law and policy. The (in) ability to control a nation's means of production is at the center of Black subjugation and the many hegemonies that Blacks' struggle against, including neoliberalism, anti-Black racism, and anti-Blackness, among many others. The chapter exposes Black African Indigenization of the economy as a genuine attempt to reverse centuries of Euro-America domination of Black Indigenous peoples. An attack on international capital by ensuring that the means of production were transferred into the hands of Indigenous peoples, long perceived as hewers of wood and drawers of water, answered the call for Black emancipation and equal rights. It also sparked a Western hostile reaction, further demonstrating the association between capitalism and racism.

Claiming to represent the majority of Black African people in the country, the Zimbabwe African National Union-Patriotic Front (ZANU PF) party embarked on a program that aimed at transferring national resources, for example, land, into Indigenous Black hands and control (Government of Zimbabwe, 2007; Moyo & Yeros, 2007), and this is considered here from an anti-hegemonic and pan Black African analytical standpoint to

- expose the meaning of Indigenous and locate it in broader conceptions of being Black African;
- examine the Indigenization policy and program as liberatory, a philosophy for the liberation of Black peoples, and ownership of means of production (Indigenization as anti-colonial and a de-colonial perspective), targeting the twin authors of Black suffering, racism and capitalism; and
- consider the epistemological implications of Black Indigenous empowerment (Indigenization as an educational philosophy informing education for sustainable development/empowerment, liberation, and anti-colonial and global/diasporic citizenship).

The analysis in this chapter is informed by theoretical explanations and critiques regarding decolonization and neo/anti-colonialism in post-independent African states (Fanon, 1963; Nkrumah, 1965) and in the global south/developing countries in general (Escobar, 2004; Mignolo, 2000, Quijano, 2007), aimed at achieving Black African emancipation through economic empowerment and reversal of colonial and neo-colonial economic arrangements that were against Blacks and openly in favor of Whites of European descent. The Indigenization nationalist policy of the government of Zimbabwe is informed by the idea of nativism (Ndlovu-Gatsheni, 2006, 2009a; Mbembe, 2006), "a socio-political position taken by those who consider themselves as native-born and followed by a policy favoring native-born citizens over immigrants" (Ekeh, 1975, p. 623). Nativism is also seen as a belief in the importance of asserting an authentic ethnic identity, perpetuating native cultures in opposition to acculturation and multiculturalism (Appiah, 1992). Post-2000 Zimbabwe's nationalist paradigm "contains strong and fertile seeds of nativism in the sense that it entailed rolling back colonialism and giving back the power to govern and control the economy to Black sons and daughters of the soil" (Ndlovu-Gatsheni, 2006, p. 11). Nativism amplifies local and global struggles for justice, emancipation, and development in the formerly colonized countries. Ashcroft, Griffiths, and Tiffin (2000) define nativism as "a term for the desire to return to Indigenous practices and cultural forms as they existed in pre-colonial society" (p. 36). However, the Zimbabwe Indigenization process envisioned a modern Zimbabwe with the means of production in the hands of Black autochthons.

Furthermore, this "nativist revolution" (Ndlovu-Gatsheni, 2006, p. 5) in Zimbabwe is also a descriptive analysis of Robert Mugabe's socioeconomic and political policy framework put into practice since 2000 that was significantly different to the reconciliation policy enunciated in 1980 when the country obtained independence from Britain. ZANU PF called it the "Third Chimurenga" (Chimurenga means struggle for liberation) (Gandhi & Jambaya, 2002; Ndlovu-Gatsheni, 2009a; Tendi, 2010) and involved the promotion of Afro-radicalism and the valorization of African culture and patriotic history. This nativist perspective, as expressed by public intellectuals (faculty members/academics who speak to a wider/public audience or one that extends beyond their professional academic colleagues as political analysts and commentators), mostly from the University of Zimbabwe, allied with ZANU PF (Tendi, 2010), and the media considers Zimbabwe as a Black African country, and all of its challenges were given a colonial explanation that blamed Britain and its Western allies. Analyzing the rise of nativism in Zimbabwe, Ndlovu-Gatsheni (2006) wrote:

> The Afro-radical ideology relies on a troika of rhetorical rituals that involve refutation of Western definitions of Africa; denunciation of what the West had done and continues to do in Africa; and frantic efforts to provide ostensible proofs disqualifying the West's fictional representations of Africa and refuting its claim to have a monopoly on the expression of the human in general and in that way opening up a space in which Africans can finally narrate their own fables without imitation of the West. . . . Therefore, nativist struggles for autonomy must not only involve economic emancipation but consistent and systematic refutations of Western definitions of Africa predicated on anti-neo-liberalism, anti-globalization, and anti-cosmopolitanism. (pp. 10–11)

The nativist strategy was located within a particular historical discourse around national sovereignty, liberation, and redemption, which also sought to capture a broader

Pan-Africanist and anti-imperialist audience (Raftopoulos, 2004). Through the use of national institutions, specifically the media and education, the ruling party ZANU PF was able to suffocate the public sphere with its ideology and, importantly, to monopolize the flow of information to the majority of the people. Through this control of national institutions, the idea of the nation being conveyed was one that was racialist. A report on the ways in which Zimbabwe Broadcasting Corporation (ZBC) delivered views on the nation in 2002, concluded that:

> ZBC's conceptualization of "nation" was simplistic. It was based on race: The White and Black race. Based on those terms, the world was reduced to two nations—the White nation and the Black nation and these stood as mortal rivals. The Black nation was called Africa. Whites were presented as Europeans who could only belong to Europe just as Africa was for Africans and Zimbabwe for Zimbabweans. (Gandhi & Jambaya, 2002, p. 4)

As Raftopoulos (2004) noted, ZBC's definition of a nation is captured in the same report as showing that:

> Blackness or Africanness was given as the cardinal element to the definition. The exclusion of other races deliberately or otherwise from the "African" nation was an attempt to present Africans as having a separate and completely exclusive humanity to any other race. (Gandhi & Jambaya, 2002, p. 5)

One of the public intellectuals from the University of Zimbabwe proclaimed:

> Since the value system of the Europeans, of the White man, of the Rhodesian in Zimbabwe, is exclusive, it is racist, it does not have any place for us. . . we should come up with this kind of ethos: Zimbabwe for Zimbabweans, Africa for Africans, and Europe for Europeans. This is the starting point because that's what they do. (p. 8)

Citizenship became redefined in nativist terms that excluded White races as President Mugabe proclaimed the Zimbabwe for Zimbabweans ideology. In an interview with Christine Amanpour (2009), on CNN, Robert Mugabe reiterated his government's seemingly racialist policy:

> Zimbabwe belongs to the Zimbabweans, pure and simple . . . white Zimbabweans, even those born in the country with legal ownership of their land, have a debt to pay. They are British settlers, citizens by colonization.

The view was later cemented by the passing of Indigenization and Empowerment Act that defined an Indigenous Zimbabwean as Black and African (Government of Zimbabwe, 2007). It implies that no White person can claim to be Zimbabwean. Articulating the philosophy behind nativist and Afro-radical discourses, Mbembe (2002b) said:

> Nativist and Afro-radical discourses of the self are both projects of self-regeneration, self-knowledge, and self-rule. Self-knowledge and self-rule are justified in the name of autochthony. According to the argument of autochthony, each spatio-racial formation has its own culture, its own historicity, its own way of being, and its own relationship with the future and with the past. Each has, as it were, its own certificate of origin and its own telos. In all cases, the idea is that the encounter between Africa and the West resulted in a deep wound: a wound that cannot heal until the ex-colonized rediscover their own being and their own past. (p. 635)

Others see leaders like President Robert Mugabe as having deployed Afro-radicalism and nativism as part of taking the "decolonization struggle to the further level of economic liberation from the snares of neocolonialism" (Osaghae, 2005, p. 1). The Indigenization program was explained and justified by President Mugabe in the following words:

> We are now talking about the conquest of conquest, the prevailing sovereignty of the people of Zimbabwe over settler minority rule and all it stood for including the possession of our land. . . . Power to the people must now be followed by land to the people. (*The Herald*, 6 December 2005)

Mbembe (2006) noted that nativism "historically has always been about racial supremacy and the defense of immoral privilege while Black nativism is a by-product of dispossession" (p. 3). Mbembe further noted that:

> [n]ativism is a discourse of rehabilitation. It is a defense of the humanity of Africans that is almost always accompanied by the claim that their race, traditions, and customs confer to them a peculiar self-irreducible to that of any other human group. (p. 44)

To Ndlovu-Gatsheni (2006) this type of thinking informs some African leaders and intellectuals' quest to rebuild their nations, recreate African confidence destroyed by colonialism, and recreate African creativity as opposed to dependency. This view is corroborated by the way some provided prolific and sharper formulations of nativism in support of the government of Zimbabwe.

The Indigenization Policy in Zimbabwe

The law that established the Indigenization policy in Zimbabwe quoted widespread controversy with some describing it as there to institutionalize anti-white racial discrimination in perpetuity (Ranger, 2004). Another school of thought saw it as a form of affirmative racism meant to redress decades of immiserating European colonial rule and a genuine attempt at empowering Black Zimbabweans. Indigenization is thus understood as both a redress and reconstruction strategy for former colonies, enabling the post-colonial government to correct past imbalances of racially biased social and economic policies (Wilson, 1990). The local ownership of resources includes the transfer of shares from foreign-owned companies to Indigenous people or ring-fencing certain social and economic activities for the local people (Kobrin, 1985). Indigenization principles are premised on the need to eliminate poverty and promote economic development (Mawowa, 2007). Without ignoring the violent manner that marked its implementation, this brave project in Zimbabwe witnessed the interplay of Blackness, Africanness, Indigeneity, and anti-colonial transformational politics and economic programs rarely witnessed by Black people throughout the world and aimed at making Black Africans owners of the country's resources. According to the Indigenization and Economic Empowerment Act Government of Zimbabwe, 2007, (Chapter 14:33), an Indigenous Zimbabwean is defined as:

> [a]ny person who, before April 18th, 1980 was disadvantaged by unfair discrimination on the grounds of his or her race, and any descendant of such person, and includes any company, association, syndicate or partnership of which Indigenous Zimbabweans form the majority of members or hold the controlling interest.

This definition excluded almost every White person and included every non-White person. In other words, the intention of the Act and accompanying regulations was that all "foreign-owned businesses and all businesses owned by white Zimbabweans or permanent residents valued at a prescribed amount cede a controlling 51% share to Black Zimbabweans" (Government of Zimbabwe, 2007). And where in today's neoliberal world do you find Blacks controlling such a share in businesses, even in Africa? The definition of Indigenous foregrounds the status of being underprivileged and the racial discrimination that occurred during the colonial era. The Act also defined Indigenization as a purposeful attempt to involve the Indigenous people in the economic arena of the country, to which previously they were denied access, so as to guarantee the equitable ownership of the country's resources (Murombo, 2010).

In line with this policy, the land was seized from white farmers after 2000 and the rationale was that the policy simply restored land, misappropriated from autochthonic Zimbabweans without compensation, to the rightful owners (Moyo & Yeros, 2007;

Raftopoulos, 2004). Similarly, an ideological argument was developed that Zimbabwe's mineral resources belonged to Zimbabweans as a whole rather than multi-national companies that leave Zimbabweans with but a large hole in the ground when the resource is depleted. The concomitant of this argument is that it is Zimbabweans as a whole that should benefit from the exploitation of mineral resources within Zimbabwe. This, in turn, suggests full or partial nationalization of mining companies. The government claimed that Indigenization is a way of empowering the Indigenous population for a "truly independent Zimbabwe, whose resources and the economy will be controlled by the Zimbabweans" (Ministry of Youth, Indigenisation, and Empowerment, 2012). The aim of this policy was to reduce the aid-dependency syndrome currently in the country. The policy allowed local people to contribute to the economy, not just as employees but also as shareholders is. Ultimately, Indigenization aimed at reclaiming people's patriotic commitment and national pride (Murombo, 2010). When all these are attained, the result, according to the Ministry of Economic Empowerment, will be sustained long-term growth and economic development, which would eradicate poverty and other socioeconomic challenges (Magure, 2012).

That this policy was for the advancement of Blacks could not be denied. The Indigenization agenda promoted an autochthonic paradigm that proclaims that Zimbabwe is for Zimbabweans (Hwami, 2013; Ndlovu-Gatsheni, 2009a). It came under intense scrutiny from all those interested in post-colonial developments in Africa and the formerly colonized world as a whole. The Indigenous law was accompanied by what Terence Ranger termed *patriotic history* (Ranger, 2004). Beside commemoration, concrete steps were taken to forcibly inculcate liberation struggle history on the nation in general and the youth in particular in an endeavor to create what was termed a "patriotic citizenry."

Beyond Nativism: Black Indigenization as Liberatory

The story of the Black African peoples is one of oppression under white Europeans, and this unpalatable narrative stretches back hundreds of years when slave ships dominated international trade. All across the contemporary world, the injustices meted against those in Black skins continue unabated. In Israel, Africans are being chased away (Essa, 2018), in the United States the advent of the Black Lives Matter movement (Taylor, 2016) together with Donald Trump's "taking back our country" nativist policy (Anderson, 2016; Mishra, 2017), and the United Kingdom's Brexit, among many other policies in the West, are cause for concern for people of African descent. These anti-Black international sentiments are surging at the time when in the former colonies where nationhood after independence is still to stabilize, and memories and consequences of racial discrimination and apartheid are still fresh, any expressions aimed at restoring Black dignity and agency through economic empowerment is considered not only favorably, but as genuine emancipation.

Many have realized that political independence was a hollow gesture, where once again Blacks lost as the economy remained in the hands of the "former" colonizers, now represented by multinational corporations (Madeley, 2008). It is difficult for Black African peoples to separate capitalism, racism, and Europeans. African underdevelopment was written by European development (Rodney, 1972), and continued poverty can largely be traced to the same Euro-America dominated economic system. The Indigenization thrust as laid out in Zimbabwe was an attack against Black domination, against anti-Blackness as expressed by continued control of Zimbabwe by international capital or multinational corporations. The Black Indigenization process in Zimbabwe was revolutionary and excited the anti-colonial base. It was given political and philosophical underpinnings, hence the acronym Mugabeism in consideration of then President Robert Mugabe's leadership and rabid anti-colonial ideas (Hwami, 2013; Ndlovu-Gatsheni, 2009b) and represented nationalism, pan-Africanism, and pan-Indigeneity (Ranger, 2004).

Black Indigenization became a rallying point for many Black Africans who were beginning to question political independence and their leaders, who they began to perceive as stooges and puppets of the West and international capital. Black Indigenization or Mugabeism became a discourse designed to unite and free the oppressed Black peoples of the world. "Mugabe-ism," concluded Manheru, was "an imposing outward fact in Southern African politics." On April 18, writing in *The Sunday Mail*, Sabelo Sibanda was cited (Ranger, 2004) to have proclaimed that "Zimbabwe sets example for Africa." He argued that most of Africa, in theory, had yet to really enjoy independence. Only Zimbabwe had taken radical steps toward the total emancipation of African people and their motherland. According to him, Zimbabweans enjoyed the right to take occupation of their land, which a lot of their other African brothers and sisters had yet to enjoy. Zimbabwe was setting a new African agenda for the global African family (Ranger, 2004). Then, Sibanda made reference to the history of Zimbabwe and Africa:

> As we Zimbabweans weigh our role in as far as our significance to Africa is concerned, we do not only do so by looking at our present and future contribution but also to the past. Historically, Great Zimbabwe is the last of the Great African civilizations to fall and, unlike the likes of Egypt, Zimbabwe remains truly African.... What better place for us to pick up the pieces again than in Zimbabwe, where we still have a traceable history of the greatness of our ancestors in a land still truly Black? Being the last to fall, it is most fitting that it be the first to arise out of the mud and in turn pull the rest of the continent, and its people globally, upward. Great Zimbabwe is not a ruin as the colonizers had us believe but "a sacred spiritual place." Hence, to connect from it spiritually and move on up is a most significant spiritual starting point for all Africans. (p. 9)

Black Indigenization, in Zimbabwe, can also be read from the perspective of African modes of self-writing as defined by Achille Mbembe (Ndlovu-Gatsheni, 2009b). Mbembe argued that Marxism and nationalism as ideologies gave birth to two narratives on African identity, namely nativism and Afro-radicalism (Mbembe, 2002b).

Nativism was defined as a discourse of rehabilitation and a form of defense of the humanity of Africans predicated on the "claim that their race, traditions, and customs confer to them a peculiar self—irreducible to that of any human group" (Mbembe, 2006, p. 8). Nativism is conceptualized as one of the culturalist responses Africans have given to the fact of denial of their humanity. While nativists accepted that Africans were human beings like any other person, they "nevertheless emphasized the difference and uniqueness of their traditions or what they call culture" (Ndlovu-Gatsheni, 2009b, p. 1146). Mbembe argued that Afro radicalism and nativist thought were founded on three historical events, namely slavery, colonization, and apartheid. At the first level, the historical processes of slavery, colonialism, and apartheid are said to have resulted in a loss of African familiarity with the self to the extent that the African subject became estranged from him- or herself. The net effect of all this was that the African self became not only unrecognizable to the "Other", but "the self no longer recognizes itself" (Mbembe, 2002a, p. 241). Black Indigenization in the form of Mugabeism constantly articulated this politics of estrangement and victimhood. At the second level of property relations, slavery, colonialism, and apartheid were blamed for having led to dispossession, "a process in which juridical and economic procedures have led to material expropriation" (Ndlovu-Gatsheni, 2009a, pp. 266). This process is said to have unfolded alongside the broader agenda of "falsification" of Africa's history, culminating in estrangement. It is within this context that Black Indigenization/Mugabeism located the controversial fast-track land reform within the broader agenda of African resistance to colonialism. Nativist Black Indigenization was galvanized around:

> the idea of historical degradation in which slavery, colonization, and apartheid plunged the African subject not only into humiliation, debasement, and nameless suffering but also into the zone of nonbeing and social death characterized by denial of dignity, heavy psychic damage, and the torment of exile. (Mbembe, 2002a, pp. 239–240)

The sum of all this thinking is the desire by Africans to know themselves, to recapture their destiny (sovereignty), and to belong to themselves in the world (autonomy). Added to this is the idea of an African destiny that is not proceeding from free and autonomous choices, but from a terrible legacy of a history imposed on Africans by the West.

Black Indigenization was also observed as a politics of self-regeneration, self-knowledge, and self-rule, all increasingly justified in the name of autochthony (Ndlovu-Gatsheni, 2009b). Autochthony is defined as a claim that its articulator was an original inhabitant of the land, a "son of the soil" (Dunn, 2009, p. 115). It revolves around questions of citizenship and the concept of a citizen as the bearer of rights. To Mbembe (2006) the idea of autochthony proceeded through a belief that "each spatio-racial formation has its own culture, its own historicity, its own way of being, and its own certificate of origin and its own telos" (p. 635). In all cases, the idea is that the encounter between Africa and the West resulted in a deep wound: a wound that cannot heal until the ex-colonized rediscover their own being and their own past (Mbembe, 2002b).

Epistemological Implications

That the conditions of Blacks in Africa and in the Diaspora are a topical question is beyond debate. In a world witnessing the rise of the far right and nationalist politics as witnessed by the triumph of leaders like Turkey's Recep Tayyip Erdogan, India's Narendra Modi, France's Marine Le Pen, and America's Donald Trump (Mishra, 2017), the Black Africans in the Diaspora and in Africa have reasons to be apprehensive as Blacks, of all colored people, are always the first point of anti-immigration policies. Black Indigenization policies and programs become necessary. President Robert Mugabe, as the face of Black Indigenization, was viewed by some Africans as a representation of pan-African memory, a reclaimer of African space, and the African power of remembering the African legacy and African heritage which slavery, apartheid, and imperialism thought they had dismembered for good (Ranger, 2004). Others saw Mugabeism as the base of a new way of thinking, one aimed at freeing the wretched of this earth (Ndlovu-Gatsheni, 2009b). Mugabeism is an ideology that believes in not only the transference of political power, but also an unwavering commitment to shift the means of production—land, minerals, and corporations—from the privileged white minority to the Zimbabwean majority. Mugabeism is a pan-African revolutionary philosophy, the final onslaught on imperialism on the continent, and for Africans to use the war against the imperialists (Chengu, 2014).

Political developments in the global North clearly indicate to the Black Africans that they are not welcome and that colonial relations have been reinvented in a benign format. Black Indigenization in Zimbabwe was deployed as part of taking the "decolonization struggle to the further level of economic liberation from the snares of neo-colonialism" (Osaghae, 2005, p. 1). For this struggle to succeed, there is a need for epistemological support. African thinkers like Fanon sought to deal with the perennial issue of how to release possibilities of human existence and history that have been imprisoned by "the colonization of experience and the racialization of consciousness" (Sekyi-Otu, 1996, p. 17). Any agenda with a scope encompassing the realization of the restrictions and impediments of imperialism and colonialism would be expected to resonate with all formerly colonized peoples. While many African revolutionaries and progressive organizations sympathized and identified with Marxism and other socialist-oriented theories to expose, and struggle against, the inhuman nature of colonialism and its associated racist and capitalist principles, many have unmasked Marxism as Euro-centric and racist cultural realism (Hobson, 2012), a European line of thinking that could not identify and speak on behalf of the colonized peoples, particularly Blacks, whose racialist suffering is unmatched by any other race on Earth.

Black Indigenization as laid out in Zimbabwe is a thesis concerned with the realization of Black people's potential as human beings equal to other races, especially the Whites. That colonialism was a European and, in particular a white race, project (Mignolo, 2000; Quijano, 2000, 2007) is well established. It is arguably the root cause of the suffering Black people all over the world. Some scholars and analysts argue that colonialism is still present in modern times but in benign forms. In order for colonized Blacks to regain their humanity, Fanon justified revolutionary violence or what Nayar (2013) calls "reconstructive-recuperative violence by the colonized whose end goal is the rediscovery and reconstruction of the colonized" (p. 3). Fanon (1963) wrote that "the colonized man liberates himself in and through violence" (p. 44). According to Haddour (2006), Fanon wages war against colonialism and against capitalism in the post-independent era, and as a result, some have dismissed Fanon as an "apostle of violence, a preacher of hate" (p. xviii), and similar charges have been posted against Black Indigenization in Zimbabwe. This violence is "an attempt on the part of the desperate, frustrated, and alienated colonized subject to retrieve a certain dignity and sense of the self that colonial violence had destroyed. It takes the form of anti-colonial struggles" (Nayar, 2013, p. 70).

As was observed by Fanon, Black Indigenization should be seen as both an assertion of the agency, as well as a means to recover it after years of colonial subjugation and humiliation. Violence, in the form of forced eviction of international capital, represented by White commercial farmers, for example, was therefore seen here "as praxis, an act of acting out, or a performance in which the Self is rediscovered" (Nayar, 2013, p. 88). Fanon (1963) further writes, "The colonized subject discovers reality and transforms it through his praxis, his deployment of violence and his agenda for liberation" (p. 21). Thus, liberatory violence inherent in the Black Indigenization program is not only justified by Fanon but it is encouraged, and the struggles for independence and dignity in many Black African countries were successful after nationalists resorted to violence. The issue though is with the violence prevalent in post-independent Zimbabwe that is widely acknowledged by all political parties in the country (Bond & Manyanya, 2003). Is it targeted at modern forms of colonialism? Or is it as asked by "absolute violence that exceeds the goal of merely evicting the colonizer and seeks a purging of the ideas, myths, and notions planted in the colonized by the colonizer—a process we can think of as the decolonization of the mind?" (Nayar, 2013, p. 87). The Black African Indigenization program in Zimbabwe aimed at economically and politically empowering Black people and hence can be viewed as a moral theory identifying with struggling groups in society such as rural peasants and the urban poor. Because of their role in the liberation struggle, the peasantry in Zimbabwe is seen as revolutionary and not the workers as established by Marxism. The land occupation movement in Zimbabwe, the hallmark of the Indigenization program, was largely shaped by the participation of rural peasants (Moyo & Yeros, 2011; Sadomba, 2011).

Race and racism is another important idea running through the Indigenization program. Even decades into independence, the living conditions of Black people, compared to that of the Whites in Africa, is a reminder of the colonial past. Corroborating this idea, Nayar (2013) noted that post-independence conditions of living, notably social services and class structures, remind the generality of the population more of the ills brought about by colonialism than with the joy of independence. When Fanon (1956/2008) pronounced his project as "nothing short of the liberation of man of color from himself" (p. 2), he was speaking of a movement beyond racial identities. This means "a movement beyond colonial constructions of identities of Blackness but [that] also transcends the essentialisms of negritude" (Nayar, 2013, p. 114). In doing this, it should be noted that a necessary part of colonialism was the process whereby the colonizers problematized the culture and the very being of the colonized, where the latter come to accept the "supremacy of the white man's values" (Fanon, 1967, p. 43). This facilitated the development of an inferiority complex among Black people. Fanon's (1956/2008) response to this is emphatic and empowering to Black people, and he said, "Since the white man chose not to recognize the Black, there remained only one solution open to the Black: to make himself known as a Black man" (p. 87).

There is no doubt that President Mugabe's Indigenization program in Zimbabwe made Black Zimbabweans known, and caused shock in the Western capitals, resulting in targeted sanctions placed against Zimbabwe's leaders, and the United States went further to identify Zimbabwe as part of an axis of evil and passed legislation, the Zimbabwe Democracy and Economic Recovery Act (ZIDERA), to impose same sanctions on Zimbabwe. That these policies were aimed at enforcing democracy in Zimbabwe has been the official position, but there are far worse despotic nations in Africa and throughout the world, and these have not attracted the U.S. Senate and Congress to pass legislation. The Euro-America block was simply protecting white capital. The processes of national development after the attainment of independence are centered on the phenomenon of decolonization. Fanon (1967) considered decolonization as "truly the creation of new men" (p. 3). Fanon further warned against mimicking Europeans (Bhabha, 2007) and he wrote, "Let us decide not to imitate Europe, let us combine our muscles and our brains in a new direction" (Fanon, 1967, p. 236). Black Indigenization implies the reversal of colonial conditions and includes restoring pride among Black Africans after decades of being racialized and dehumanized. Black Indigenization is a form of decolonization. Decolonization is the only way out of the absolute dehumanization in which the (former) colonized lived (Haddour, 2006, p. xii). Decolonization should therefore not only refer to the transfer of political power to the Black colonized, but economic and cultural aspects of life should be addressed as well. Fanon (1967) concluded that "national culture or cultural nationalism involves generating continuity with a community's past, it alerts the colonized to colonialism's agenda of ensnaring them to Western culture" (p. 148) and it helps "retrieve those cultural practices that the colonial regime had thought to erase or reject" (Nayar, 2013, p. 99). This means:

> We need to make a clear distinction between liberation and decolonization. When liberation moves into the zone of transforming the sociopolitical, economic and discursive mindset of the oppressed/colonized and that of the colonizer/oppressor, then it becomes decolonization. (Dei, 2010, p. xvii)

This resonates with President Mugabe's view of his Indigenization program when he argued that Zimbabwe's Indigenization was about the conquest of conquest, sovereignty of the people of Zimbabwe over settler minority rule, and the possession of Indigenous land.

The epistemological relevance and implications to Black studies and progress were captured by Gandhi and Jambaya (2002) when they argued that Mugabeism was a pan-African revolutionary philosophy and an African revolution against imperialism in Zimbabwe, in the form of Third Chimurenga, another name for pan-African nationalism. Revolutionaries see and equate President Mugabe's stance as an anti-capitalist creed. True Indigenization liberates. Fanon (1963) argues that there can be no authentic liberation without decolonization, while Dei and Simmons (2010) suggest that "decolonization must be complete and must overcome exploitation, alienation and oppression, and dehumanization" (p. xvii). Indigenization of education must go beyond ownership and wealth accumulation if authentic liberation from global and local capital is to be attained. Educational transformation should consider *unhu* as the framework for restoration of education in Zimbabwe and Africa in general. As Dei (2010) observes:

> Decolonizing education brings to the fore questions of power relations among actors and different players in the school system while at the same time upholding the agency, resistance and local cultural resource knowledge of all learners. . . . [It] is about change, it is about a particular way of knowing that emerged through bodies of difference, it is about embodied knowledge, it is a particular process that encounters the foreign and the local of imposition. It is about resistance and the fight for social justice. (p. 6)

The Indigenization program advocated the end of the inhuman doctrine of European colonialism in its various historical and modern forms and the social injustices committed on fellow human (Black) beings.

The Indigenization program is informing a new African humanism, one where Black Africans are not just hewers of wood and drawers of water for the white people. The new humanism called for by Fanon cannot borrow and learn from Europe because of her imperial and racist activities in Africa. Black Indigenization is the antithesis of European hegemony and racism. The idea that Africans cannot learn from Europe is in line with the government of Zimbabwe's policies and other radical nationalists from the global

South who argue that the West failed to respect the human rights of African Indigenous peoples during colonial times, and hence contemporary calls for respect of human rights and democracy are dismissed as hypocrisy. President Mugabe has many times reminded his British critics that they did not and never attempted to introduce democracy during their close-to-a-century rule of Rhodesia (Zimbabwe). Nativist education that seeks to create a new and free Zimbabwe has been introduced throughout the school system with the objective of glorifying Black African heroics. History texts used in Zimbabwean schools can best be described as the literature of negritude because of their radical and revolutionary nature (Ranger, 2004; Tendi, 2010). They spring from a need to reverse an intolerable situation, a negative principle. They challenge Western expansion and an imposed Western ideology that led to the subjugation and humiliation of Africans.

For Black Indigenization to succeed there is a need for the reorientation of the mind, and, consequently, nativist education in Zimbabwe can be seen as "decolonization, a struggle for an anticolonial space, entailing educators and learners working together to address questions of power, history, knowledge identity, and representation" (Dei, 2010, p. 8). It is through this approach that African Indigenization should be an exercise in epistemological provocation and a model to put an end to a long imitative tradition and dependency of Africa over European philosophy. Black Indigenization as a form of decolonization should involve self-discovery of African philosophy (Mudimbe, 1998), and the thrust on African culture in Zimbabwe's education can be understood from this standpoint. This is meant to fulfill Fanon's observation and would enable the dispelling of the idea that "all the elements of a solution to the great problems of humanity have, at different times, existed in European thought" (Fanon, 1963, p. 237). The formerly colonized Blacks have had to fight inferiority complexes, and the continued high levels of poverty have not helped to look at the West with admiration. European imperialism reduced that idea of humanity to the figure of the settler-colonial White man (Quijano, 2000). The educated in decolonizing Zimbabwe were mainly schooled along the British education system, further exposing them as European copycats unfit to lead any ideological decolonization as currently required in the country. Fanon (1963) charged that "the intellectual is overwhelmed by the colonizer's culture, is rootless and uncertain" (p. 84). It is crucial for Zimbabwean scholars, though Western educated, to recognize that the totality of Western epistemology is no longer valid for Africans (Mignolo, 2003). Zimbabwean "intellectuals should be the ones to question patriotic nationalism, corporate thinking, and sense of class, racial or gender privilege" (Said, 1994, p. xiii). Creating a decolonizing learning space is a process of affirming multiple knowledges and having learners come to claim a sense of ownership and responsibility for their own knowledges. It is about bringing to the fore subjugated knowledges, histories, and experiences (Dei, 2010). Nativist education for Black Indigenization must go beyond Black against white, Europe against Africa, or Britain against Zimbabwe, but must interrogate all forms of hegemonic tendencies.

Conclusion

The Zimbabwe Indigenization program is a radical attempt at reclaiming Black African Indigenous agency in the face of continued assault from international capital and racist Euro-America that could not afford to see the success of this project. The Black Indigenization program informed anti-colonial politics and education and, despite the crisis it created in the country, it still remains as one gigantic attempt at empowering and transforming the ownership structure of a country's means of production. It is a fact that today in Zimbabwe resources are in the hands of Black Indigenous Africans and there are few countries that can claim the same feat (Moyo & Yeros, 2011). This shows that Indigenization went beyond rhetoric and cultural refrains such as "Black is Beautiful" that characterized nativist thought. Indigenization became an examination of the extent to which liberal capitalist order is ever capable of accommodating the demands of Black emancipatory movements. The response from the developed countries in the Western world was clearly informed by anti-Blackness and anti-Black racism as the European Union, the United States and the white commonwealth imposed sanctions on Zimbabwe (Raftopoulos, 2004) to stop the government from taking away land from white commercial farmers. The Indigenization program in Zimbabwe was an affirmative action meant to uplift the condition of Black Zimbabweans. It represents a rare experiment of Black African bodies' resistance against neocolonial neoliberalism represented by multinational companies that dominated the ownership of land and minerals among many other national resources. It was an affront to racial capitalism.

The dominant narrative on the Black Indigenization program has been informed by anti-Black perspectives and anti-Black racist scholars (Hughes, 2010; Meredith, 2007; Scarnecchia, 2006). This means a study of the Black Indigenization program is more than a study of Black peoples and Black body politics. It is a creation of cultural, political, and economic knowing of Black African agency outside of Euro-America-colonial attempts to regulate and define Black and African narratives of development. Furthermore, it is about the continued presence of anti-Black racism as perpetrated by and in Western capitals. The significance of knowing and understanding racism is a powerful and empowering tool for all Black peoples, including those in the Diaspora. It is a politics for change and freedom that has the potential to inform theory and practice in the Black people's quest for equality and dignity all over the world.

References

Amanpour, C. (2009). Mugabe denies blame for Zimbabwe woes. CNN. Retrieved from http://www.cnn.com/2009/WORLD/africa/09/24/zimbabwe.mugabe.amanpour/index.html

Anderson, C. (2016). *White rage: The unspoken truth of our racial divide.* New York, NY: Bloomsbury.

Appiah, K. A. (1992). *In my father's house: Africa in the philosophy of culture.* Oxford, UK: Oxford University Press.

Ashcroft, B., Griffiths, G., & Tiffin, H. (2000). *Post-colonial studies: The key concepts.* London, UK: Routledge.

Bhabha, H. K. (2007). *The location of culture.* New York, NY: Routledge.

Bond, P., & Manyanya, M. (2003). *Zimbabwe's plunge.* Harare, Zimbabwe: Weavers Press.

Chengu, G. (2014). Mugabeism: A model for African liberation. Retrieved from https://www.herald.co.zw/mugabeism-a-model-for-african-liberation/

Dei, G. J. S. (2010). Rereading Fanon for his pedagogy and implications for schooling and education. In G. J. S. Dei & M. Simmons (Eds.), *Fanon and education* (pp. 1–27). New York, NY: Peter Lang

The Pedagogy of Fanon: An Introduction Author(s): GEORGE J. SEFA DEI and MARLON SIMMONS Source: Counterpoints, Vol. 368, Fanon & Education: Thinking Through Pedagogical Possibilities (2010), pp. XIII-XXV Published by: Peter Lang AG Stable URL: https://www.jstor.org/stable/42980663.

Dunn, K. C. (2009). "Sons of the soil" and contemporary state making: Autochthony, uncertainty and political violence in Africa. *Third World Quarterly, 30*(1), 113-127

Ekeh, P. P. (1975). Colonialism and the two publics in Africa: A theoretical statement. *Comparative Studies in Society and History, 17*(1), 91–112.

Escobar, A. (2004). Beyond the third world: Imperial globality, global coloniality, and anti-globalization social movements. *Third World Quarterly, 25*(1), 207–230.

Essa, A. (2018). Israel: no country for Black people. *IOL.* Retrieved from https://www.iol.co.za/news/opinion/israel-no-country-for-Black-people-12900274

Fanon, F. (1956/2008). *Black skin, white masks.* C. L. Markmann (Trans.). London, UK: Pluto.

Fanon, F. (1963). *The wretched of the earth.* R. Philcox (Trans.). New York, NY: Grove Press.

Fanon, F. (1967). *Toward the African revolution.* H. Chevalier (Trans.). New York, NY: Grove Press.

Gandhi, D., & Jambaya, L. (2002). *Towards a national agenda on Zimbabwe Broadcasting Corporation: Vision 30 revisited.* Harare, Zimbabwe: Media Monitoring Project of Zimbabwe.

Government of Zimbabwe. (2007). *Indigenization and Economic Empowerment Act, Act 14.* Harare, Zimbabwe: Government Printers.

Haddour, A. (2006). Foreword: Postcolonial Fanonism. In A. Haddour (Ed.), *The Fanon reader* (pp. vii–xxvi). London, UK: Pluto.

The Herald. (2005, December 6). President Mugabe on the third chimurenga. Retrieved from https://www.herald.co.zw/third-chimurenga-is-the-great-teacher/

Hobson, J. M. (2012). *The Eurocentric conception of world politics: Western international theory 1760–2010.* New York, NY: Cambridge University Press.

Hughes, D. M. (2010). *Whiteness in Zimbabwe.* New York, NY: Palgrave.

Hwami, M. (2013). Neoliberal and Indigenous capitalist intrusions in higher education: An anti-colonial analysis. In E. Shizha (Ed.), *Restoring the educational dream: Rethinking educational transformation in Zimbabwe* (pp. 152–164). Pretoria, South Africa: Africa Institute of South Africa.

Kobrin, S. (1985). Diffusion as an explanation of oil nationalization. *Journal of Conflict Resolution, 29*(1), 3–32.

Madeley, J. (2008). *Big business, poor people.* London, UK: Zed Books.

Magure, B. (2012). Foreign investment, Black economic empowerment and militarized patronage politics in Zimbabwe. *Journal of Contemporary African Studies, 30*(1), 67–82.

Mawowa, S. (2007). *Crisis, state, and accumulation in Zimbabwe* (Doctoral dissertation). University of KwaZulu Natal, Durban.

Mbembe, A. (2002a). African modes of self-writing. *Public Culture, 14*(1), 239- 273.

Mbembe, A. (2002b). On the power of the false. *Public Culture, 14*(3), 629–630.

Mbembe, A. (2006). *The cultural politics of South Africa's foreign policy: Between Black (inter)nationalism and Afropolitanism.* Paper presented at Wits Institute of Economic and Social Research (WISER), University of Witwatersrand. Johannesburg, South Africa.

Meredith, M. (2007). *Mugabe: Power, plunder and the struggle for Zimbabwe.* New York, NY: Public Affairs.

Mignolo, W. D. (2000). The many faces of Cosmopolis: Border thinking and critical cosmopolitanism. *Public Culture, 12*(3), 721–748.

Mignolo, W. D. (2003). Globalization and the geopolitics of knowledge: The role of humanities in the corporate university. *Nepantla: Views from the South*, 4(1), 97–119.

Ministry of Youth Development Indigenization and Empowerment. (2012). *Community share ownership schemes: Operational framework for community share ownership schemes or trusts (CSO) in terms of the Indigenization and Economic Empowerment Act* (Chapter 14:33). Harare, Zimbabwe: National University of Sciences and Technology.

Mishra, P. (2017). *Age of anger: A history of the present.* New York, NY: Farrar, Straus, and Giroux.

Moyo, S., & Yeros, P. (2007). The radicalized state: Zimbabwe's interrupted revolution. *Review of African Political Economy, 34*(111), 103–121.

Moyo, S., & Yeros, P. (2011). After Zimbabwe: State, nation and region in Africa. In S. Moyo & P. Yeros (Eds.). *Reclaiming the nation: The return of the national question in Africa, Asia and Latin America* (pp. 78–104). New York, NY: Pluto Press.

Mudimbe, V. Y. (1998). *The invention of Africa: Gnosis, philosophy, and the order of knowledge.* London, UK: James Currey.

Murombo, T. (2010). Law and the Indigenization of mineral resources in Zimbabwe: Any equity for local communities? Sabinet, 25(2), 568-589. Retrieved from: https://journals.co.za/content/sapr1/25/2/EJC153229

Nayar, P. K. (2013). *Frantz Fanon.* London, UK: Routledge.

Ndlovu-Gatsheni, S. J. (2006). The nativist revolution and development conundrums in Zimbabwe. *ACCORD Occasional Paper Series, 1*(4), 1–40.

Ndlovu-Gatsheni, S. J. (2009a). Africa for Africans or Africa for natives only? New nationalism and nativism in Zimbabwe and South Africa. *Africa Spectrum, 1*, 61–78.

Ndlovu-Gatsheni, S. J. (2009b). Making sense of Mugabeism in local and global politics: "So Blair, keep your England and let me keep my Zimbabwe." Third World Quarterly, 30(6), 1139–1158. http://doi:10.1080/01436590903037424

Nkrumah, K. (1965). *Neo-colonialism: The last stage of imperialism.* New York, NY: International Publishers.

Osaghae, E. E. (2005). The state of Africa's second liberation. *Interventions, 7*(1), 1–20.

Quijano, A. (2000). Coloniality of power and Eurocentrism in Latin America. *International Sociology, 15*, 215–232.

Quijano, A. (2007). Coloniality and modernity/rationality. *Cultural Studies, 21*, 168–178.

Raftopoulos, B. (2004). Nation, race, and history in Zimbabwean politics. In B. Raftopoulos & T. Savage (Eds.), *Zimbabwe: Injustice and political reconciliation* (pp. 160–175). Cape Town, South Africa: Institute for Justice and Reconciliation.

Raftopoulos, B. (2006). The Zimbabwean crisis and the challenges for the left. *Journal of Southern African Studies, 32*(2), 203–219.

Ranger, T. O. (2004). Nationalist historiography, patriotic history and the history of the nation: The struggle over the past in Zimbabwe. *Journal of Southern African Studies, 30*(2), 215–234.

Rodney, W. (1972). *How Europe underdeveloped Africa.* Cape Town, South Africa: Pambazuka.

Sadomba, Z. W. (2011). *War veterans in Zimbabwe's revolution: Challenging neo-colonialism and settler and international capital.* Harare, Zimbabwe: Weaver Press.

Said, E. W. (1994). *Culture and imperialism*. New York, NY: Vintage Books.

Scarnecchia, T. (2006). The fascist cycle in Zimbabwe, 2000–2005. *Journal of Southern African Studies, 32*(2), 221–237.

Sekyi-Otu, A. (1996). *Fanon's dialectic of experience*. Cambridge, MA: Harvard University Press.

Taylor, K. Y. (2016). *From Black lives matter to Black liberation*. Chicago, IL: Haymarket.

Tendi, B. M. (2010). *Making history in Mugabe's Zimbabwe: Politics, intellectuals, and the media.* London, UK: Peter Lang.

Wilson, J. (1990). Strategies of state control of the economy: Nationalization and Indigenization in Africa. *Journal of Comparative Politics, 22*(4), 401–419.

CHAPTER 3

Making Peace with Movement: Dislocation and the Black Diaspora

Ezinwanne Toochukwu Odozor

To be Black, and to be African, is to be tethered to movement and to the enduring question of belonging and self-determination. We move and have been moved through enslavements, colonialisms, and White supremacy, but also through our own articulations and explorations. We, even in our homelands, even without ever setting foot elsewhere, are connected to shift, to the "massive gravity of the middle passage," and to the mutability of Blackness (Lubrin, 2019). Blackness is not homogenous. There is no one way to be Black, but to be Black is to be indomitably connected with the Continent (Africa and Africa before Africa), and it is fundamentally tied to Black skin and thus about race and racism, which is used as a marker and made real. But, to be Black or to engage Blackness is also to be bound to resistance, resurgence, and re-existence (see Asante, 2005, Dei, 2017; Fanon, 1963; hooks, 1997). Black peoples have endured many dislocations—spatial, temporal, cultural, and so on—and in search of a repair, this chapter turns to the idea of belonging. In doing so it asks, "How does belonging function in the face of dislocation? How can rearticulating community, particularly community in Africaness and Blackness, across geographies—temporal, spatial, and experiential—heal dislocations toward engendering radically free and Black-centering futures?" In exploring these questions, I will interrogate the notions of "identity" as well as those of "Blackness and Africaness" and how these shape belonging. I will then come to reflections on the multiplicity of Blackness and how it is mapped—spatially, temporally, and experientially. This chapter further seeks to propose an understanding of Africa as being a diverse unity beyond the continent and questions the displacement of non-Continental diasporic personhoods or cultures as non-African. I will turn to cultural studies, anti-colonial, anti-racist, and Black feminist discourse and scholarship for theoretical guidance and grounding. The aim of this chapter is not to resolve all questions of dislocation, but rather to look at how we conceptualize our connections in hopes of more expansive conversations and conversational spaces that will allow us to work across our divergences, while holding fast to a radical, Black, unifying root.

But what is Blackness? Derived as a juxtaposition, it thrives as a marker of difference, but has also been transformed as a political, racial center from which to articulate resistances and re-existences, which center bodies raced, along the spectrum, under that category and history. While Blackness is connected along a spectrum to Whiteness, it is fundamental to understand that the fluidity of this spectrum is not itself a privilege. That while a proximity to Whiteness engenders greater acceptance by the dominant, it does not engender humanity or Privilege (capital P) itself. It simply complicates and reminds us of the various intersections encountered. Similarly, while Whiteness is tethered to the idea of Blackness, people raced as Black do not, and should not, derive their determination, history, existence, and identity from Whiteness, but all the while must be in opposition to its dominance. Black people—in all geographies—existed long before the Euro encounter and long before Europe itself. Blackness, under white supremacy, is constructed and read by the dominant as a dis-invitation to belonging. It is not meant to be unifying or generative. The Black subject is not meant to be master of anything—of Land, of body, or of self. To be Black under this logic is be of the pejorative. Within the psyche of the self, tormented by these logics, there comes, then, a desire to seek separation from Blackness. To live in such desire is to sit in dislocation, at odds with one's self and one's experience, and it is to suffer (Fanon, 1963). Yet, we must resist the tethering of Blackness to absence, to non-productivity, to the ahistoric, to the negative. Whether in Diaspora beyond or on the continent, Black bodies are simultaneously read as being from nowhere and as being of elsewhere. Africa is seen, by the dominant ideology, as nowhere, in the sense that its significance as a space of productivity, history, or culture (i.e., civilization) is denied. It is also read as elsewhere as a mechanism to refuse space, citizenship, and validity to Black bodies in non-African (continental) geographies. The African Diasporic body in Canada, for example, is always of elsewhere; its presence within the contrived Canadian landscape is shaped as being recent, atypical, and otherwise shocking (McKittrick, 2006). The question, "Where are you really from?" is one that the Blackness must answer, but never seems to have the right to ask. The continental African in Kenya, on the other hand, is a no one from nowhere. Their validity as a creator or host of knowledge, civility, and value writ large is not given the benefit of the doubt. Africa is thus seen as a *country* of non-persons: nowhere. We cannot—and surely I do not—rely on White Supremacy's reading of Blackness. It becomes important then to turn to the question of unities, histories, identities, and centers: ones that can thrive in the face of our movements and shifts; ones that will repair the dislocations of time, space, and ideologies; and ones that create generative solidarities across the bountiful cartographies of Blackness. The nowhere-elsewhere narrative is part of the mechanism of colonialism. Whether through enslavement, colonial dominations, or persistent anti-Blackness, our attachment to physical Land is constantly denied and our sense of landedness, or belonging, as a metaphysical attachment to space and place, is deliberately set in question. As Dei (2017) reminds us, the construction of Africa is not simply about racist ideologies at the individual level, but about the systemic disruption of African/Black being or personhood.

The colonial construction of Africa, as a set of regions, closed in around groups of people, collectively called Africans, separately marked as variable, supposedly identifiable as ethnicities, projected further within a Black race, needs to be problematized. Specifically, it needs to be troubled with respect to how we as Black people read and define our identities. When I told a friend and colleague of mine that one does not need to return to Africa to connect with one's "Africaness" her reply—understandably—was, "That's easy for you to say. It is easier for those of you from the continent to feel connected." The sentiment that my colleague expressed was and is not unfounded. As an African—specifically, as someone who can locate myself within the narrative of the continent having been born there and having a family and cultural group for whom tradition and an understanding of tradition is significant—I have a groundedness. That said, I too am Diasporic, and I too struggle with the idea of rootedness, both in the sense of a connection to the continent as well as to Blackness as a location always in transit. The need to feel situated is something that has been deliberately excised from the Black experience. This is what I refer to as dislocation. To become rooted then is the goal. To be rooted is to be centered. To be centered is to be located in a place from which one can actively resist and determine possible futures.

On the Question of Identity

Canada is not my birthplace and English is not my first language. I was born in Nigeria in the 90s and came to Canada as a very young child who spoke no English at all, but rather who conversed fluently in my native Igbo. As far as citizenship, I hold a Nigerian and a Canadian passport. If identity is to be so simply ascribed, one would say that I am a Black, Igbo, Nigerian-Canadian woman: race, ethnicity, nation, place, and gender. The apparent simplicity of identities is also what hides the complexities of belonging and the illusion of agency in determining the totality of who it is that we are. What those ascriptions—Canadian, Nigerian, woman, and so on—elide is the interplay between history, narrative, and power. Identity in a sociopolitical landscape is about more than simply locating the "I" in relation to the Other, or identifying the self through binary oppositions. It is about the meaning that those relationships create or are given and, in Eurocentrism, it is about the particular hierarchical-dominant value that those relations reveal.

The *Oxford English Dictionary* tells us that *identity* is "[t]he sameness of a person or thing at all times or in all circumstances; the condition of being a single individual; the fact that a person or thing is itself and not something else; individuality, personality." However, the experiential tells us that identities are often shared and relative, constituted in relation to circumstances, and mutable depending on those circumstances, not to mention across time. This is not to say that identities are so fluid or entirely subject to a particular space-time such that the next logical step is for us to do away with identity altogether, but rather that identity can be located differently under different conditions and mobilized for particular uses in particular time-spaces. Identity then, in a useful configuration, is about subjectivity—not the essentialist Enlightenment subject that lies at the center of all things, but the subject that is part of the constitution of the whole, and that reflects the strategic, non-essentialist position of the self in a particular location. So to say that I am a Black, Igbo, Nigerian-Canadian woman is not to state who I am in this fixed moment or where I came from, but as Stuart Hall (1996) writes, it is a dialogue of "what [I] might become, how [I] have been represented and how that bears on how [I] might represent [myself]" (p. 4). In truth, it is less about Me (I) individually and more about the We, which the original quotation maintains.

The political utility of *identity* and of *belonging* cannot be overstated. By belonging, I mean a sense of rootedness, which is important for orienting one's self as subject, rather than as object to be read, defined, controlled, and used. As Hall again writes,

> Precisely because identities are constructed within, not outside discourse, we need to understand them as produced in specific historical and institutional sites within specific discursive formations and practices by specific enunciative strategies. Moreover, they emerge within the play of specific modalities of power, and thus are more the product of the marking of difference and exclusion, than they are the sign of an identical naturally constituted unity—an "identity" in its traditional meaning (that is, an all-inclusive sameness, seamless, without internal differentiation). Above all, and directly contrary to the form in which they are constantly invoked, identities are constructed through, not outside difference. This entails the radically disturbing recognition that it is only through the relation to the Other, the relation to what it is not, to precisely what it lacks, to what has been called its *constitutive outside* that the "positive" meaning of any term—and thus its "identity"—can be constructed. (p. 4)

A connection to Black identity, or *becoming Black* as Dei (2017) writes, is "a politicized process and identity that involves connecting with one's roots and history" (p. 48). A reconstruction of belonging toward a subject orientation requires understanding those histories that give rise to our present, cultural identities, including those events that sought, and continue to disembody and dislocate us, through a vilification of Blackness and an impoverishing of Africaness.

The Colonial

To say "the colonial" is not simply to evoke the historical Euro-Indigenous encounter, with Indigenous being read multiply. Rather, it is to enter into a discussion about systems of oppressions and their various logics; thus, it is about colonialisms in the plural. As Dei and Asgharzadeh (2001) note, colonial "is conceptualized not simply as foreign or alien, but rather as imposed and dominating... colonial in this case functions as a set of relations, and imperial as political/institutional structures that sustain the relations of domination" (pp. 300–301). As a response, the anti-colonial must challenge those relations at their multiple sites: in "ideas, cultures, histories of knowledge production" and in this case in the conception of nation, boundaries, communities, and belonging" (p. 300).

Blackness and Africaness

Whiteness and its desire for its supremacy does not necessarily create the Black subject, but rather creates a code through which to read that subject and makes every attempt to have that code be received as it is designed. The colonial here derives and inscribes a particular narrative of Blackness, and at the center of that narrative is racism, which uses race. The narrative of race as biological was, and despite its discrediting, continues to be "the centerpiece of a hierarchical system that produces differences. These are differences, moreover, of which W.E.B. Du Bois once said in 1897, that 'subtle, delicate, and elusive though they may be... have silently but definitely separated men [people] into groups'" (Hall, 2017, p. 33). These groups have taken up ranked, antagonist meanings, rather than constitutive positions within the social dialectic. More simply put, Blackness does not have an inherent meaning; rather, it has been made to mean a set of things, and those things have largely been negative. While racism is multiple, this discussion centers skin-color racism, namely anti-Black racism. Thus, by association, those bodies, which have been read as Black racially (e.g., the African, the Caribbean, the Indigenous of Oceania, and Black/Afro-Latinx) as well as Black politically (e.g., the South Asians in the UK), have also adopted those negative connotations in the White imagination. It is from this location that the Black American decides that to be African is to be backward, or the African decides that the Black Caribbean is uncultured, or the Dominican comes to believe that Blackness is something to be denied.

The danger of the White imagination is not only that it produces and institutionalizes a harmful, fictitious narrative of the Other, but that it common-senses the narrative of Whiteness such that it is not a story at all, but rather an invisible reference point for all things (hooks, 1997). It seats itself at the center and so does not look on itself as others must, but looks outward from its place as "innocent, normal, natural and objective" (Dei, 2013, p. 2). The seduction of this position sometimes causes the Other to engage certain behaviors and orientations as a means to shift themselves along the Black-White paradigm toward a closer proximity to Whiteness, thus the "race to whiteness" (p. 2). However, running away from Blackness is no solution. Beyond the fact that Whiteness preserves its position through a distancing from the Other, Blackness is not simply about an essential character, but rather the ascription of multiple, mutable characteristics, in negative. For the same reasons, under the logics of white supremacy, as Andrea Smith (2010) calls them, African, African American, Caribbean, Black/Afro Latinx, Oceanic Blacks, and all Black affiliated signifiers are also encoded within the same system of negatives.

A rejection of Blackness in favor of an unquestioning, ethicized affiliation must also respond to the risk of an essentializing narrative, which replaces race with ethnicity or nation, two concepts that are also socially constructed and that like race have material implications. As Gupta and Ferguson (1992) write,

> The distinctiveness of societies, nations, and cultures is based upon a seemingly unproblematic division of space, on the fact that they occupy "naturally" discontinuous spaces. The premise of discontinuity forms the starting point from which to theorize contact, conflict, and contradiction between cultures and societies. For example, the representation of the world as a collection of "countries," as in most world maps, sees it as an inherently fragmented space, divided by different colors into diverse national societies, each "rooted" in its proper place. It is so taken for granted that each country embodies its own distinctive culture and society that the terms "society" and "culture" are routinely simply appended to the names of nation-states. (p. 6, internal citations omitted)

There is no essentialist quality of Africaness or Blackness that finds its proof in the body or in the borderlines of a map. Rather, the Black body who results from the shared history of continental dislocations, a long history of dehumanization (i.e., slavery and colonialisms), and rich histories of resistance and ingenuity does find its route (rather than root) in the political identification of Africaness and thus begins to write a new story of origin and establishes new trajectories for the future. As Kobena Mercer (2017) writes, "[R]econceptualising diaspora not as a tragic loss of organic *roots* but as a polycentric network of cross-cultural *routes* that give Black culture is transnational dynamism" (p. 8). This African is equally situated whether continental, American, Caribbean, Oceanic, Latinx, or otherwise.

Toward New Cartographies and Communities

The Black Diaspora does not arrive as reflex to the colonial encounter. That Eurocentric temporality reads the story of the Black body as having begun with the European and claims a false, static history on behalf of the African ancestor. The ancestry of the Black subject extends in all directions geographically and temporally. What is truly ancestrally African is the art of meaning making in wondering and through wandering. As the Igbo saying goes, *onye njenje ka onye ishi awo uzo ahu*: Wise is the old man, but wiser still is the traveler. Part of the ancestral knowledge of my people is founded in exploration and the extension of communities. If we turn to history, more "objectively" Africans have been recognized as travelers, creators of knowledge, and founders of societies since, at least, Biblical/Koranic times. The use of movement to build and exchange knowledges and communities is a well-documented aspect of precolonial African life. Mansa Musa's wanderings are only one example of this. Thus, the colonial displaces not simply communities, but ways of understanding histories, community, and culture. I have no wish to center a White understanding of Blackness, but rather to acknowledge the circumstances under which Blackness in the Black imagination must struggle to reconstitute itself. It must make its own meaning despite colonial codes.

Meaning is not simply made by the encoder, but also by the receiver. Meaning making is a dialectic process in which the messages are sent, but enter into conflict with the receiver to either successfully implant the original message or become contravened toward a new understanding. There is, as Mercer (2017) notes, "always 'the possibility of struggle over meanings.' It is precisely the possibility of breaking with oppressive regimes of racial meaning that is at stake in the polysemic agency of difference, which makes discourse the medium in which historically subordinated subjects can transform the dominant code and activate resistance" (p. 18).

To say that decolonization happened is to misread the events of the past and the present. Decolonization is a process that is underway. At the center of a decolonial or, rather, anti-colonial, response is the necessity to uproot Whiteness as the dominant code. As part of this, we must also trouble Eurocentric cartographies—cultural and terrestrial—as being natural reference points for mapping our worlds, including our cultural geographies and histories. An anti-colonial response troubles the Eurocentric construction of *the global* and thus of boundaries to, and of, belonging. The world as it has been drawn up in nation-states cuts across connectivities to suit imperial needs. If we are to have an anti-colonial, decolonizing response, we must challenge the interruption of our transnational communities by not taking as natural or as right the construction of nation states. We must interrogate how these constructions have served to dislocate us as African peoples—globally—from a sense of belonging to the lands of our origin, but also a sense of landedness where we are now.

Andrea Smith's (2010) work "Indigeneity, Settler Colonialism, and White Supremacy" protests against "the givenness of the white-supremacist, settler state" (p. 10). Her work articulates the importance of foregrounding the interconnectedness of the oppressive logics of white supremacy as part of constructing an anti-colonial response. Smith (2010) asserts that white supremacy is not singular in expression, but rather that it "is constituted by separate and distinct, but still interrelated logics" which "in the U.S. context include: (1) slaveability/anti-Black racism, which anchors capitalism; (2) genocide, which anchors colonialism; and (3) orientalism, which anchors war" (p. 1). Smith notes that these logics vary, but that they serve to articulate how groups of people have been narrated and conscripted toward serving particular purposes under white supremacy. Dislocations of Africaness can be read as parts of these logics. In fact, the logic of slavery takes a different form continentally than it does in the Americas, but ultimately it works with the same understanding: Black people and spaces are property to be exploited to forward the goals of capitalism. This logic requires the separation between the Black body and the land—physical and metaphysical—in the sense of claim to land, but also in the sense of place of origin, and by extension to those places of resulting (forced) migration, through a denial of space and place. So in reimaging the cartographies of Blackness, it becomes necessary to understand these logics so as to uproot and dismantle White supremacy.

A contestation of Eurocentric readings of space and place brings new possibilities. Diasporic communities now become sites for articulating the ever-growing—forward and backward—African community, where articulations of Africaness emerge, even in relocation. It also gives room for the kind of solidarities to which Smith's article calls attention. If by reimagining the African global community as an extension, or multi-center, of the continental ancestry we begin to see new realities, then we can also ask—and indeed have the responsibility to ask—what realities have been disturbed or displaced by colonial interruptions? This brings us to necessary solidarities with the Indigene of the world and with those communities who share experiences of subjugation, displacement, and dislocation. As Smith (2010) writes, we can then "organise around the differential impacts of white-supremacist logics" (p. 3).

If education, particularly anti-racist and anti-colonial education, is to be part of the anti-colonial, Black liberatory quest, then it must center the histories of the displaced and dislocated. We must learn about ourselves and about how our lives have intersected and how those intersections have been interrupted to disrupt the potential of Black peoples and Black emancipatory movements. We should be concerned by those shared histories, which give rise to our present conditions, and we should create political communities that respond to and challenge the normalcy of these conditions. It is not even that we will all have the same goals. In fact, we must be able to relate in difference, but if we can create communities that understand histories of domination and disturb the normalcy of domination as a logic by introducing other ways of being, this will move us forward in a radically different and necessary direction.

A reimagining of diaspora and of cartographies offers the Black subject a way to articulate a new ethnos. An African identity that recognizes that Africans have always been in movement—that globalization as movement and exchange is not the brainchild of the West, but the way of the world since the beginning of time—recognizes that movement has contributed to the shaping of the world, and that precolonial Africans, and thus Africans through descendancy, have long since been at the center of that shaping. As Mercer (2017) writes, "[N]ew ethnicities do not seek to eternalize identity in myths of purity and origin that rely on exclusionary closure against difference, but instead accept that all collective identification are subject to fluctuating historical conditions" (p. 5).

What, in a very practical sense, would it mean if Africa began to redraw its own boundaries toward collecting and organizing across points of solidarity, both within the continent and beyond it, including other, global Black Diasporic subjects within its community, even in an extension of citizenship in a reconceptualization of Black sovereignties? As Dei (2017) notes,

> The search for Black solidarities is about building communities that are not necessarily reliant on the nation state. We do create communities, and these are "communities of differences." Our communities are about differences and sameness because shared experiences are never singular. The nation state often homogenizes "communities." But the community is also a site and place of learning and healing. Colonial violence and on-going colonial injustice have wreaked havoc on colonized populations. We must all come together and recognize that although our histories are different, they are intertwined. It serves no purposes other than those of the dominant to continue a unilateral fragmentation around difference. We witness how the dominant often conscripts the idea of a fractured community in order to deny responsibility and accountability. (p. 145)

New cartographies of Blackness allow Africa to be reimagined as not a singular locale, but as an extensive network of ancestries, which continue the heritage and give life and voice to it in a variety of ways, at multiple locations. Tradition is a living thing, which forms ways of doing and of being in response to needs, a new cartography—a new mapping—as a new tradition responds to the very real need of Black solidarities and revolutions. This doing away with sameness and essentialist notions of community is anti-colonial. African-centered ways of knowing recognize the centrality and continuity of the spirit and the spiritual ancestry. A reconceptualization of Black geographies makes room for this African-centered way of knowing by asserting a tripartite connectivity of mind, body, and spirit (Dei, 2017), thus opening new spaces of belonging and new frames for reading and articulating liberated Black lives, making space for peace and repair, in the context and reality of movement.

References

Asante, M. K. (2005). Blackness as an Ethical Trope: Toward a Post-Western Assertion. In G. Yancy (Ed.), *White on White/Black on Black* (pp. 203–216). Oxford, UK: Rowman and Littlefield.

Dei, G. J. (2013). Reframing Critical Anti-Racist Theory (CART) for Contemporary Times. In G. J. Dei, & M. Lourdan (Eds.), *Contemporary Issues in the Sociology of Race and Ethnicity: A Critical Reader* (pp. 1–14). New York, NY: Peter Lang.

Dei, G. J. (2017). *Reframing Blackness. Anti-Blackness and Black Solidarities through Anti-Colonial and Decolonial Prisms.* New York, NY: Springer.

Dei, G. J., & Asgharzadeh, A. (2001). The Power of Social Theory: Towards an Anti-Colonial Discursive Framework. *Journal of Educational Thought, 35*(3), 297–323.

Fanon, F. (1963). *The Wretched of the Earth.* New York, NY: Grove Press.

Gupta, A., & Ferguson, J. (1992). Beyond "Culture": Space, Identity, and the Politics of Difference. *Cultural Anthropology, 7*(1), 6–23.

Hall, S. (1996). Introduction: Who Needs Identity? In S. Hall, & P. du Gay (Eds.), *Questions of Cultural Identity* (pp. 1–17). Thousand Oaks, CA: SAGE.

Hall, S. (2017). *The Fateful Triangle: Race, Ethnicity, Nation.* Cambridge, MA: Harvard University Press.

hooks, b. (1997). Representing Whiteness in the Black Imagination. In R. Frankenberg (Ed.), *Displacing Whiteness* (pp. 165–179). Durham, NC: Duke University Press.

Lubrin, C. (2019). Perhaps You Have Not Heard This Story: In Conversation with Canisia Lubrin (E. Odozor, Interviewer). *Room Magazine, 42*(2).

McKittrick, K. (2006). Nothing's Shocking: Black Canada. In M. Katherine, *Demonic Grounds: Black Women and the Cartographies of Struggle* (pp. 91–119). Minneapolis, MN: University of Minnesota Press.

Mercer, K. (2017). Introduction. In S. Hall & K. Mercer (Ed.), *The Fateful Triangle: Race, Ethinicity, Nation* (pp. 1–30). Cambridge, MA: Harvard University Press.

Smith, A. (2010). Indigeneity, Settler Colonialism, White Supremacy. *Global Dialogue (Online)*, 1–13.

CHAPTER 4

Black Life: Theoretical Underpinnings

Marlon Simmons

Introduction

THOUGH BLACK COMMUNITIES have been in Canada for centuries, their experiences as citizens have been slowly becoming better. From being underpaid to unemployment, to credential devaluation, to perennial housing discrimination, Black communities continue to face substantial challenges integrating into the civic and economic life of Canada. What is needed are different ways of interpreting Canadian citizenry, which could inform their human rights, build transformative practices for educational policies, and critically inform leadership practices for Black youth as well as the broader context of Canadian communities. One of the foci here is to theoretically trace the untold social formations of Black life to understand how these different cultures engage intergenerational knowledge and cultural memory of the past and present to deal with the challenges of a globalized world in the context of Canada. I address the complex dynamics of how diverse Black communities come to situate their place of belonging within respective Canadian societies. The aim is with providing an alternative means of understanding how Black life experiences different forms of belonging through particular cultural understandings embedded within the African Diaspora. I conceptualize Black life through particular encoded discursive fields with historical specificities to colonization and plantation life that locate the socio-material on African peoples. In this discussion, I tend to the socio-materiality of Blackness by thinking through variant histories of Black life. Though these histories speak to the relational experiences of Black life, of movement—wittingly or unwittingly—the concern here is with how Black life becomes positioned within the nation-state and what sorts of becoming are made possible. These experiences cannot be denied historically. As such, the intention is with extricating Black ontologies as embodied within the land and Black life, to situate Black histories as unfolding within the nation-state and the ensuing text, rather than always already tangential.

Let me say a bit about how I am working to conceptualize these everyday moments experienced in Black life. I am interested in the variant modes and procedures of Black social formations in which Black peoples come to know and govern the self through particular identifications and popularized social media desires, which materialize in everyday performatives or ritualized practices. I am curious about how particular Black social formations come to accept these identifications as being performed through a constellation of histories as a continuity. My interest is with knowing how race and culture concomitantly produce performative desires that form the conditions of existence for Black life. I am thinking of Black life through innumerable material embodiments of time and space and socio-historic-cultural processes as interwoven by way of difference immanent to Black cultures as shaped through the uncertainty of Diasporic movement. I am writing to ease the tension of a historical, homogenous, singular, immutable read on Black life. Yet, as method, writing through the Diaspora presents complexities. With its shifting terrains, contoured historically through different sociocultural enactments, the Diaspora, as configured through the local and the global, materializes through uncertainty in ways in which Black life and its ensuing relationship with its social world speak to the infinitude of possibilities of what it means to be human (Mignolo, 2015; Walcott, 2003; Wynter, 2003). I am intrigued more so by the way in which Black life has become autonomous through the continuous absorption and withdrawal of local stories, traditional narratives, which inevitably come to propel the ordering of thought, the sociality, the peopling as imbued through the transferring of ideas as embodied within Diasporic relations.

Black Life

With Blackness, my foci involve understanding the ways in which meanings of Black life have been discursively and materially constituted and how such meanings are made anew in their contemporaneity. In so doing, and as a method of social inquiry, I draw from raw materials such as Blackness, race, relationships with the land, Indigeneity, nation-state governmentality as conditioned through colonial modernity, and immigration policies constitutive of the nation-building initiative in Canada. Black life gives us a place to think of historic specificities of expropriation of Indigenous lands, racism, Diaspora, White supremacy, African enslavement, and the project of settler nation-state.

Through its anachronistic temporality as conditioned by way of colonial forays, Black life became organized, regulated, and recognized through the governing socio-material techniques of colonial power. Black life provides the social and material practices necessary for creating imaginative directions that can help with refashioning the historical work of writing difference and belonging. Such writing congeals through epistemological Diasporas, as embodied through African enslavement and made wholesome by quotidian events that are actually linked through time and place to current issues and a particular past.

We know Black life is deeply embedded within colonial enslavement of African peoples, that it concerns a way of thinking that orients itself through resistance, struggle, and social justice (Fanon, 1963). With Black life, I am thinking about the sociopolitical thought experienced among African peoples concerning the human condition of post-plantation life. In a sense, I am taking up Black life as an approach to understand how Diasporic African peoples worked through the imperial contours of the contested terrain of sovereignty. I am thinking of Black life as temporal, as an anachronistic interruption to colonial governance, which situates through space and time, liminal Diasporic sensibilities that integrate Black life by way of contrapuntal pedagogies. I am suggesting that writing and reading Black life involve Diasporic enactments, which holistically speak to the historical, cultural, and spirituality of African peoples. I would imagine then that Diaspora invites inclusivity amidst historical classifications of Euro-colonial modernity and Black life.

Of particular interest to Black life is the economic and social movement of peoples to Canada. Often enough this movement has been one dimensional, from archipelagos historically steeped in colonial manacles to harvesting territories that reap the materials of enslavement. This movement has also been enacted in ways that promulgated unbelonging for Blackness, as outside of what it means to be a citizen and engaging in civic participation as governed within the prescripts of a self-identifying democratic nation-state. Nested within this movement are troubles immanent to colonial-settler governance that saw educational systems, finance economies, and jobs being difficult terrains to navigate for Black peoples. Public sphere conversations concerning Black life have come under discursive surveillance (Browne, 2015), in which Black life comes to be articulated and socio-materially represented in ways that place their positionality as secondary within the history of the colonial nation-state. Indeed, the constitutive makeup of the nation-state is deeply entrenched within colonial violence; consequently, as the nation-state renews itself through imperial space and time, belonging for Black life continues to be positioned and marked through colonial inscriptions. With this in mind, I am seeking to write Black life beyond the parochial conduits that repeatedly shape Blackness through devalued forms of citizenry. In so doing, I want to have a conversation that speaks to the experience of Diasporic African peoples, in the context of being transnationally located. I want to trouble the ways in which these transhistorical experiences have been framed through particular theoretical frameworks. I am asking, "How might we begin to understand questions of what it means to belong for Black life when historically belonging becomes ontologically contrapuntal and co-terminously situated to the archetype human"; an understanding that dialectically speaks to the experience of belonging, through historical acts of movements. As a starting point, I want to consider how Black life, as located within the Americas emerging from Africa through Civil Rights encounters, comes into personhood through the unfreedoms of emancipation. In a sense, I am thinking about how Blackness comes to understand the variant terms and conditions of belonging through different articulations of the African Diaspora.

If, and as Hall (2007) reminds us, immanent to the self are histories of the past, then much of Black life involves working through the materiality of these narratives to get a sense of how synergies of the past and present come into discursive and material enactments in particular public spheres such as schools, job settings, community building, friendships, family relations, and just civic participation. Circumscribing these synergies of Black life are contingencies of globalization that mitigate Diasporic life. Understanding Black life in the context of self, difference, and sociocultural environments involves some mind work with specific questions cognizant of histories in the global context of coloniality and the attendant modernity. The study of Black life involves a host of methods and techniques, which have congealed into a discipline. Black life has become a place where scholars, students, activists, community, and family members can draw from to make sense of, or extend upon, the literature. With this approach Black life is less interested in being reduced to one fixed thing, but more so Black life is made durable through the different embodied practices and relational experiences.

You might ask, "What constitutes Black life in its distinctive forms? What are the ways in which the study of Black life becomes a field of knowledge, institutionalized and at the same time forming epistemological modes of inclusion and exclusion within academe?" After all, the study of Black life concerns understanding human practices, understanding human relations within the broader ecological sphere. What then are the ways in which the study of Black life diverges and converges from other schools of thought? And how do these diverging and converging pathways relate to the broader political relations of the world? These epistemic moments need not be neatly bound into some even compartmentalized moment as if human relations were evenly fashioned. Black life, like other socialites, has its own ontologies with specific characteristics and sensibilities as imbued through certain historical conditions. If one of our aims is with understanding how the relational experiences of Black life come to be consolidated through particular engagements with their broader, or let us say Diasporic, world, one could imagine, then, these narratives concern moments of resistance, survival, and self-determination as contingent to plantation struggles and embodied within Black life (McKittrick, 2006). I am suggesting Black life is contextually bound to the conditions in which it emerged. With the foci being material change, one of the aims is to make sense of how Black life comes into the means of this materiality when the starting point in a sense becomes the self.

For Black life to have to attend to the colonial, political, and economic organizing practices of employment involves deciphering public sphere institutional alignments, as well as designing particular ways of knowing that correlate to the past through public memory, which mitigates the present in its immediacy. I am asking, then, how does Black life, as interwoven with coloniality and Diasporic histories, come to share ways of living with heir own as well as with other communities (Simmons & Dei, 2012)? What are the ways in which Black life learns about the conditions in which it acquires its reality? If the concern, then, is about how Black life makes meaning of the conditions of its reality, then part of this project is with tracing what counts as knowledge when making intelligible the crystallization processes immanent to their ensuing sociocultural register.

Perhaps we should discuss some of the underlying assumptions regarding how we are thinking of Black life. What I am working through is the domain of transmissions that enable Black life with distinctive sensibilities as situated within particular sociocultural networks, institutions, organizations, and community establishments, conveying bearings, generative of synergies in the quest of solidarity through social memory. As Black life traverses through the different pathways of globalization, the ongoing route, in due course, sifts through historical modes of thought when socializing in its everyday life. At times, depending on how Black life is situated, it then becomes experienced through discontinuous histories or temporalities proving to be delayed or have latent growth, not yet materializing into actualizing the self.

Mbembe's Critique of Black Reason

Achille Mbembe's (2017) compelling account in *Critique of Black Reason,* situates a re-reading of Black life through the historical contours of colonization, race, capitalism, and modernity. His underlying concern is with understanding what it means to be human through historical codifications of Black life. Weaving entwined narratives of Black experience as anchored within complex contact zones of Africa, apartheid, the Caribbean, America, and Europe, Mbembe provides signifiers and notes from the African Diaspora to signal the importance of linking plantation sensibilities in making sense of the enslavement of African peoples, the ensuing commodification of Blackness and simultaneous socioeconomic material production of Europe. With this discursive material making of Europe, Mbembe points to the stitching of colonial boundaries, which places Black peoples outside, as external to Europe. He amplifies how the colonial boundaries of modernity work to govern the institutional process of the unplaceability of Black peoples, of unbelonging; in a sense it speaks to the reification of Blackness into nonhuman entities. Attendant to this unplaceability, Mbembe points to the colonial affect imbued through the psychosocial insertions of colonization. His writing is less interested with some linear narrative of history, which provides cohesion to the coloniality of African peoples. Instead, he writes to uncover the entangled geographies of Black life as encumbered through indeterminate histories of racial classifications, cultural aesthetic practices, religion, language, and literature.

Mbembe is also thoughtful about the means of knowledge production and how these modes of relations allow for a re-identification of Black life within colonial logics. He leaves us thinking of how these terms and conditions of coloniality are made recognizable in ways that endow Black life with sociocultural practices as being contained within colonial conduits, yet at the same time moving beyond the boundaries of colonial logic. Through these historical trajectories, Mbembe presents particular sensibilities for Black reason—sensibilities allowing for different embodiments, constellation of voices, Enlightenment discourses, intergenerational knowledge, and shared consciousness of Blackness, sensibilities that make anew enactments immanent to everyday negotiations necessary for the self-determination of Black peoples as experienced within the globalized forays of modernity. Given the ethical proximity of essentializing Blackness, Mbembe invokes Blackness to historically dialogue with Europe's duplicitous conception of man and Blackness as nonhuman. He leaves us thinking about the set of epistemic-material practices wherein which Blackness is made fungible in ways that promulgate colonial logics. Blackness becomes desired and made abject through interchangeable performatives, making permissible belonging and unbelonging of the human. In tacit ways Mbembe notes how fungibility as concomitant to market interests becomes surreptitiously steeped within practices of militarization, privatization, and digital technologies.

Across these layered textual readings of Blackness, Mbembe's work is rife with language of the Black man. One is left wondering about the myriad ways in which Blackness becomes constituted through gender and Euro-modernity. How might such a gendered reasoning of Blackness and modernity make intelligible Black reason? And how might such reason help with offering different possibilities for Black life? What we are left to work through is the elision of the Black subject as configured through the said Western consciousness. At the same time we are pushed to think that counterhegemonic to this elision of Blackness resides anti-colonial critique. As such, this anti-colonial way of being provides *reservoirs of life* necessary for understanding what it means to be human in the global context of eco-planeterization. African enslavement, colonization, and apartheid are three events Mbembe recalls as bringing foreclosure to Black discourses. For Black subjects the resultant effects are social death and alienation of the self. Governing these historical events are the auspices of memory and religion, concomitantly infused through the politics of representation as constituted through ahistorical synchronic readings of Black life. With *Critique of Black Reason,* Achille Mbembe offers futures for humanism through carefully retrieving genealogies of unmapped archives of Black life. Linking the material of Blackness through racism and histories of capitalism, Mbembe journeys through the historical consciousness of Black life to unearth what he calls the *reservoirs of life.* In marking these reservoirs as embodied by Black reason, Mbembe does well to identify possibilities for Black reason as such possibilities co-identify with racial classifications and stern organizing principles of life that suggest different ways of thinking about the social and the political.

History, Place, and Black Life

What it means to be human is constantly being reconfigured through different forms of belonging. How might Black life help one with understanding these shifting modes of sociality? Let us think of Black life and the history of movement as archived through Black memory. Thinking of Black life as emerging through anti-Black racism, survival, resistance, and modes of self-determination calls for remembering through histories of textual and public erasure. Movement of African peoples globally gave rise to social, material, economic, and political implications regarding historical questions of belonging and sovereignty, as these moments were embodied and constituted through the land. Black peoples are filled with difference and possess a unique history. Sometimes these distinctive histories provide possibilities; sometimes they prove to be a limiting factor as these linguistic, religious, spiritual, cultural, gendered, ethnic, and national constructs bind with or against themselves to form cohesions or tensions that act in ways to form global markers. Understanding how Black peoples traverse these socio-material places in ways that strategically distance themselves, de-race, or make anew social networks through Diasporic epistemologies, affords sensibilities to fecund an understanding of Black life as situated through the psychic terrain of coloniality (Wynter, 2003).

One method of writing Black life as a diachronic approach is to note that particular experiences of Black life result from traversing within and across historical archives of nation-state citizenship. Here, I am thinking about historical archives that have become enacted through museums, oceans, flags, text, and national artifacts (Sharpe, 2016), at the same time shaping the socio-material terms and conditions that immutably evoke the memory of Black life. Memory then becomes assembled at one level through public documentation that invariably encodes meaning and experiences of Blackness. At another moment we have memory of Black life being lived and archived through oral histories, ancestral knowledge, and cultural enactments. Embodied within this memory are Diasporas, with their specific epistemes, as constituted through histories of place and time—histories that are resilient to the hegemonic documentation of Black life and have surreptitiously worked to form modes of displacement within particular governing public spheres. This is to also note that concomitant to these histories are socio-material practices that come into relations of resistance with the governing coloniality of power, at the same time productive of particular terms and conditions as a way of becoming human for Black life. What I am troubling here when working with the idea of writing history as a social method of inquiry is to acknowledge history is written from different experiences, epistemological assumptions, and philosophical paradigms as culturally shaped through an embodiment of time and place. It is also to say such an inquiry becomes circumscribed with practices imbued though colonial documentation of Black life. Critical writing of Black life ought to vigorously conceptualize these embedded contestations residing within history to tend to the diverging and converging contours that embody Black oral histories, as these subjugated histories are colonially interwoven.

Three distinct moments emerge here, one of which confronts history as a signifier of Blackness resulting materially in disenfranchisement, debasement, and devalued forms of representation of Black life. The second speaks to the disjunctures governing the innumerable historical beliefs, customs, values, and culture of Black life as these moments congeal through shared histories of the Middle Passage (Wright, 2015). And third is the epistemological interest that continuously negates knowledge residing from Black geographies. To write Black life cognizant of such trajectories is, to some extent, to disrupt colonial histories of knowledge by way of opening possibilities for Black life through a language that unremittingly probes what was said, what was unsaid, and what needs to be said about Black life. One can imagine trying to ascertain such practices of Black life is to unearth congruent experiences of coloniality with predispositions to essentialism and absolute debasing conceptions of identity. By contradistinction, Black life can be typified through Middle Passage memory to cogitate about situatedness, place, and future economic pathways as organized by current arrays of social settings within said public spheres of the nation-state. Such writings of Black life make anew ethical promulgations that could respectfully account to the racial disjuncture embedded within history and work toward embracing alterity that avows the future through an immediate present. In this way, attending to Black life can fecund meaning-making sensibilities that differ from archived essentialist texts.

Given the periodization of history in the context of African enslavement, the emphasis is on the past and present alike. In that, understanding the relationship with coloniality and Blackness entails making sense of the formation of Black history with respect to time and place, one that vehemently tends to sociocultural and economic growth, institutional and structural barriers, and quality of life (Dei, 2017). This involves working with an arrangement of alterity that becomes traversed by way of compound Diasporic temporalities, acting intermittingly through diverging and converging paths, resulting not necessarily with some totalizing negation of history, but one that works to create ecological continuities with particular linkages to the land, humanism, social values, and cultural traditions. The pedagogical necessity here is with writing Black life through an intelligible comprehension of Diasporic sensibilities as entrenched in the present. It involves engaging in reading and writing Black life as constituted through the transatlantic movement to understand historical interpellations of citizenship, the integration of Black life as localized within imperial Americas, and the particular Diasporic conditions on Black life within the Americas.

Working through this Diasporic epistemic formation affords a method of determining how to broach the many tensions amidst theory and practice, to instead allow for the pursuit of a mode of thinking that can attend to histories of Black life as these histories materially become coalesced to some essentialist present. We ought to be cognizant with the layering of problems encoded in such a pursuit, for writing Black life involves a hermeneutic sense as is imbued through experience and is contextualized diachronically to the phenomenon under inquiry. If we are thinking of Black life through oppression, disenfranchisement, housing, unemployment, and social health, then these instances ought to be thought of from a close reading of particular moments, such as colonization, African enslavement, nation-state, and modernity. To situate Black life within the politics of social economies involves concomitantly addressing the conditions of the Middle Passage and attending plantation politics that continue to provide material readings of experiences onto Black peoples. In one instance, futurity of Black life concerns writing against contingent racial codifications, whereupon writing Black life as a social method of inquiry has to be absconded from the circuitous colonial grip that continues to offer formations, contours, and pathways regarding how Black life comes to makes sense of the past and how Black life can be realized and accomplished in the present and future. This brings us to some of the ethical concerns regarding the politics of writing Black life. To say this, then, I am less interested in some utopian totality, a writing of Black life that makes permanent a suggestion of avowal, which discursively works to invest within historical linear narratives of progress to distinguish elements of economic growth for Black peoples. In terms of ethical considerations, one ought to be aware of the proximity of being seduced to political representations of being modern that serves the undoing of Black life.

As a method of social inquiry, relocating the politics of Black life allows one to interpret the local and the global situatedness of Blackness. Relocation also allows one to interpret the ensuing nation-state itself as being transhistorical and political, providing for the self-determination of Black life beyond the parochial confines of the sovereign nation-state and engendering of sociocultural economic growth within existing post-plantation territories. I can think of two moments arising here, that for Black life to think of home, to think of Africa, was to think of the present, the here and now, and at the same time, home materialized through a dialectical reading of Africa, the Caribbean, and the Americas. If we are thinking of what is at stake politically and intellectually with Black life, then situating transatlantic histories becomes a necessary site of intervention to understand the syncretized experiences of Black life as transnational, cosmopolitan, and constituted through discontinuous histories. Through these discontinuous histories, one of the tasks with writing Black life is seeking to relocate Black life in ways that allow for a cultural undoing of the hegemonic contours of modernity, which inherently de-linked systems of thought that called for ontological linearity to primordial origins (Simmons, 2010, 2011).

Making sense of the coloniality immanent within Black life becomes arduous, involving diligent work about speaking to the points of identification and points of dis-identification, points of histories, points of culture, and points of sociality, which come to constitute Black social formations. These quotidian points are well augured through memory and oral histories and are embedded with socio-material forms of the present, not fixed points that speak to us from the past, as outside of history, waiting to return to through some final, absolute mode of what it means to be human. What does it mean, then, to be grounded to the past through a particular historical continuity? What does it mean to speak to the present through the intervention of history, through discontinuous histories as entrenched within colonialism, Euro-modernity, enslavement, plantation life, Indentureship, and Euro-Enlightenment narratives? And how do we come to understand Black life through these spatiotemporal moments produced through the intervention of history in which Black life is always already produced in and through its continuity? We also need to be cognizant of the cultural inscriptions within the disquiet of Black life, for Black life cannot simply be encapsulated through some binary. Instead, Black life ought to be read through a constitutive historical complexity that through a continuum of ways brings life to a particular place, a particular time that identifies, in combination with, the cultural codifications of the African Diaspora. Writing Black life can invite or facilitate an understanding of belonging that moves beyond the narrow confines of a boxed belonging to nation, which speaks to very contained, rigid performances and desires of knowing the self.

In Closing

Historical terms of citizenship and the concomitant ethics have well been spatiotemporally archived as modes of thought and made intelligible through particular socio-material practices. Yet Black life and the relationship with the land is asking us to rethink these said modes of thought as accepted "truth" systems (Foucault, 1994). Black resistance provides for a counter-hegemonic culture that in a sense turns liberal sensibilities of individualism into ethical questions concerning hope, community, and belief in the self as constitutive of different forms of citizenry. For Black life to conceptualize and simultaneously perform a particular type of citizenry as overdetermined against archived ritual practices of late modernity, it has, in a sense, produced a precarious relationship to the historical classificatory system of belonging. The precariousness of Black life remains constantly in question and surreptitiously marked as fugitive within the nation-state. Belonging for Black life invites us to think of how prevailing governmental conditions of the nation-state have interwoven, in a profound way, encumbered moments and possibilities of the freedoms of citizenry. Shaping a future for Black life might involve asking what types of citizenship are made possible and through what political philosophies are these futures of citizenry being materially constructed. Indeed, within our present epoch, imagining a social contract that refashions the fugitiveness of Black life into the humanness of citizenry invites addressing the liminal spaces of the entrapments of Black life through such questions of surveillance, risk, security interests, and modes of violence.

References

Browne, S. (2015). *Dark matters: On the surveillance of Blackness.* Durham, NC: Duke University Press.

Dei, G. J. S. (2017). *Reframing Blackness and Black solidarities through anti-colonial and decolonial prisms.* Gewerbestrasse, Switzerland: Springer.

Fanon, F. (1963). *The wretched of the earth.* New York, NY: Grove Press.

Foucault, M. (1994). Subjectivity and truth. In J. Faubion (Ed.), *Michel Foucault: Ethics, subjectivity and truth,* Vol. I. New York, NY: New Press.

Hall, S. (2007). Fundamentalism, diaspora and hybridity. In S. Hall, D. Held, D. Hubert, & K. Thompson (Eds.), *Modernity: An introduction to modern societies* (pp. 629–632). Oxford, UK: Blackwell.

Mbembe, A. (2017). *Critique of black reason.* Durham: Duke University Press.

McKittrick, K. (2006). *Demonic grounds: Black women and the cartographies of struggle.* Minneapolis, MN: University of Minnesota Press.

Mignolo, W. D. (2015). Sylvia Wynter: What does it mean to be human? In K. McKittrick (Ed.), *Sylvia Wynter: On being human as praxis* (pp. 106–123). Durham, NC: Duke University Press.

Sharpe, C. (2016). *In the wake: On Blackness and being.* Durham, NC: Duke University Press.

Simmons, M. (2010). Concerning modernity, the Caribbean Diaspora and embodied alienation: Dialoguing with Fanon to approach an anti-colonial politic. In G. J. S. Dei & M. Simmons (Eds.), *Fanon and education: Thinking through pedagogical possibilities* (pp. 171–189). New York, NY: Peter Lang.

Simmons, M. (2011). The race to modernity: Understanding culture through the Diasporic-self. In N. Wane, A., Kempf, & M. Simmons (Eds.), *The politics of cultural knowledge* (pp. 37–50). Rotterdam, The Netherlands: Sense.

Simmons, M., & Dei, G. J. S. (2012). Reframing anticolonial theory for the diasporic context. *Postcolonial directions in education, 1*(1), 67–99.

Walcott, R. (2003). *Black like who? Writing black Canada.* Toronto, Canada: Insomniac Press.

Wright, M. (2015). *Physics of Blackness: Beyond the Middle Passage epistemology.* Minneapolis, MN: University of Minnesota Press.

Wynter, S. (2003). Unsettling the coloniality of being/power/truth/freedom: Towards the human, after man, its overrepresentation—an argument. *New Centennial Review, 3*(3), 257–337.

CHAPTER 5

Navigating Being a Tall Black Female in Hostile Environments

Carla Rodney

As a tall Black female, I have had to look for my sheroes in the mirror, in my family, or the community because girls like me were not represented anywhere else, not in the popular culture at the time, then, or now. Then, I came across this—an ode in recognition and honor of our many Black sheroes—and I felt compelled to share it. I acknowledge and dedicate this to all my Black sisters past, present, and future, especially my tall queens who I will direct to stand straight, and stand tall, because you stand on the shoulders of giants and should not feel compelled to shrink or alter your proportions for anyone or thing.

Introduction

Black women have historically been endangered at the hands of White male oppressors, dating back to slavery. Black women, as with Black men, were considered slavable, labor providers, both in the sense of work and also in the sense of creating new chattel through birthing. The commidifcation and distorition of Black women's bodies would become an identification that would shadow Black bodies through the advent of Sarah Baartman, who was born in 1789 and displayed to Europeans as the "Hottentot Venus." Baartman, a South African Indigenous woman, was paraded as a freak show attraction under the name Hottentot Venus because of the differences her body signified in comparison to White women. She was paraded and abused and even after her death; her remains were kept until 2002 when she was finally returned and buried in the Eastern Cape on South Africa's National Women's Day. She suffered years of indignity, as many Black women have, being multiply determined and excluded by constructions of variances. She was seen as subhuman based on imperial definitions of race, sexuality, class, and gender. Black female bodies were, and contintiue to be, seen as a phenomenon, thus drawing in the imperial gaze that created zoos and other exhibitionist sites, used to examine us from head to toe.

The imperial gaze continues to take note of our skin, size, and assumed sexualities, with our physical differences signifying to them a need for deeper scrutiny that has resulted in torture, rape, and other dehumanizing efforts that we Black people continue to experience today. Yet, in our contemporary times, focus seems to remain fixated on the plight of our Black men, who we acknowledge as being targeted for incarceration, whilst our missing and dead female bodies fail to grab media and other forms of attention. As a professor, American civil rights advocate, and leading scholar, Kimberlé Crenshaw said in response to a report she authored on the discriminatory treatment of Black girls, "[W]e must challenge the assumption that the lives of girls and women who are often left out of the national conversation are not at risk" (Columbia Law School, 2015) indicating that we must advocate for Black women instead of assuming that they are not also being targeted.

My work argues that the exclusion of Black women from research and dialogue is detrimental to their health and well-being, especially when we consider our complex intersections. Thus, by focusing on the endangerment of the Black population beyond men, this work submits that tall Black women are not afforded the same privildges as men, and that they are endangered too. This is even though "[c]onsiderable research demonstrates that Black men are specifically threatening and imposing. [And for] this reason, height may impact judgments of threat more strongly for Black men than for White men" (Hester & Gray, 2018, p. 2711) meaning that when a Black woman is tall, she too can be considered imposing and/or threatening, especially considering that the imperial observation has never ceased to surveille and misjudge us. Yet the research does not exist connotating that Black women and children are rendered indiscernible with only our labor and physical bodies seeming to be of interest while our minds remain unappreciated, a situation no different within many Black families who also, in the habit of our colonizers, reduce Black women and children into "something," whose only value is limited to fetishization and the fulfilling preconstructed roles that include but are not limited to caretaking, sexing (willing or unwilling), and/or other positions of servitude to male wants and whims, leaving them to encounter dangerous situations alone, especially given that when your frame is tall it can be interpreted as threatening, confrontational, and/or as a signifier of the "angry Black female" who must/can take care of herself. Being myself, a tall Black woman, I have personally experienced that neglect and observed the implications of height when also intersected by race and gender. These experiences lead me to believe that further research is necessary if intervention and decolonialization is to happen. Researching Black bodies in our multiplicities, particularly from this intersection, could help elucidate more on the relationship between height, gender, and colonial violence that needs our attention and mediation. Bear in mind that "for people who already perceive Black men as threatening, height confers extra threat" (Hester & Gray, 2018, p. 4) and that threat is also bestowed onto the body of the Black woman who is many times masculinized and yet "no work to date has investigated the effects of height for perceptions of Black women" (Hester & Gray, 2018, p. 4), which is a perspective that places them in positions of potential violence, bearing in mind Kimberlé Crenshaw's (1991) caution that:

> [t]he failure of feminism to interrogate race means that the resistance strategies of feminism will often replicate and reinforce the subordination of people of colour, and the failure of antiracism to interrogate patriarchy means that antiracism will frequently reproduce the subordination of women. These mutual elisions present a particularly difficult political dilemma for women of colour. (p. 1253)

Given these gaps in our popular and academic discourses, this research addresses what it means to be a tall Black female in Canada. While some hold on to the belief that height offers privileges of preferential treatment and possibilities to succeed over being shorter, this work questions the essentialism of that reading, considering that what might be true for males, especially if they are White, may not hold true for tall females, especially racialized bodies. As one of the few researchers who do look at height in women states, "[F]rom a feminist perspective, pathologizing tall height in women reflects both a current societal trend toward medicalization to 'treat' any number of normal physical variations deemed socially undesirable, as well as a reaction to tall women's violation of traditional gender role expectations" (Farman, 2010, p. 58), meaning that when females are judged to be abnormally tall, then they are diagnosed to be in need of some form of treatment—a perspective that fails to address the multiplicities of people's lives. By analyzing the interlocking systems of oppression that plague Black females, especially for those who are tall, this work hopes to shed some light into the question posed by researcher Tanya Farman:"Should tall women fear being too tall?"

Research Question and Approach

The research question guiding this study is part of an ongoing project that will not only ask if tall Black women should fear being tall, but will also examine what feeds the fear and how Black women are impacted by the racialized violence that is perpetrated by the White subjectivity of imperialism instituted in North America.

This question will be examined through a qualitative study using social media and blogs on tall Black women, newspaper reports, and my personal experiences. My examination of the literature and various media addressing the intersections of race, gender, and height will be engaged with an autoethnographic approach and will be interwoven with personal narrative and observations. This data is analyzed through content analysis that reveals themes or categories that arise through the media, undertaken by listening to the experiences of Black women as well as employing an anti-racist praxis to "[amplify] the social construction of race, [by] disrupting the hegemonized discourses of the inevitability of racism through biologizing narratives of race" (Dei & McDermott, 2014, p. 4). In an intellectual pursuit toward advocacy for social change and justice, delving further into the plight of Black females allows for us to gain an understanding of how heightism factors into the violence against Black women, in their homes, schools, and larger society.

Situating Myself

My earliest childhood experiences in the colonial school system was in England, attending St. Jude's Catholic institution. It was part of the system that would privilege and enrich its own children with stories of conquering and planting flags, while Black children were told at home that they either "work twice as hard" to access what privileged children inherit or risk leaving school early to seek work. Many people of color were struggling within what was, and still is, an oppressive system. As a child of the 60s, I would not have articulated my experience this way because violence has been normalized in school since caning as a form of corporal punishment existed. What that dominant ideology taught to me was that "children should be seen and not heard," and that if I failed and strayed from the place in which society had designated me to fit, the colonial system could and would show their disapproval by exacting punishment onto me at their own discretion. This included, but was not limited to, spiritual and physical violence.

At school, I would sometimes ask the teachers about the differences in our bodies and about how and why people interacted with our bodies differently. When asking how to account for those differences, I found that I was shut down since discussions of race were not permitted, or at least not encouraged. The teachers responded to my questions as though they were taboo or irrelevant to the lessons that they preferred we learn. Nevertheless, I kept asking, failing to understand that I was to keep my mouth shut and just blend into the room. Only I failed, being perhaps an anomaly or a misfit who did not know her place. This was even more pronounced by my physical presence as I am also a tall female who was encompassed in a society that subscribed to the belief that height is preferable for males. This confirmed to me that a tall woman is an abnormality, which made my standing out inevitable. In addition, being Black in school was not what might have been the ideal to fit into imagined mainstream society when I am already not the definition of normal. Hence, for me there was no shrinking or disappearing into the scenery, and it probably did not help that I was a curious child who responded to others by asking "Why?" frequently, though my teachers did not hear inquiries, but instead took my questions to be forms of interrogation and read me not as a child, but as a confrontational upstart. These experiences informed my development as a child, and student, where I learned that inequality and oppression not only existed in the classroom and in every fabric of existence dominated by colonial culture, but that they were also dangers to my well-being.

My time in the school system included going to a school that specialized in maladjusted children, only at this school, they seemed to be more unreasonable toward us since the demographic of students had changed from my previous one of mainly White children to children of color. Many of them, like me, had been diagnosed as suffering from mental and or behavioral challenges, though, like my previous school, there were no safe spaces to go for help for students of color who faced different forms of subjugation. Therefore, we improvised, creating our own therapeutic group that convened at night, and I recall many of us whispering as we talked about how we would escape what I now see us being in a jail that was dressed up as a teaching facility for "special" children.

Upon returning from England to Canada, where I had no memories of the country where I was born, or knowledge of the culture I was to reencounter, I began school looking forward to starting over, making new friends, and putting the past behind me. I had no idea that this was not going to be the case. In many ways, the school system in Canada was like what I had experienced in England because it failed to incorporate any relevant pedagogies to address the experiences that children of color experienced in the colonial school systems. An example of this is the school I would attend following my experiences in England.

Zion Heights Junior High school was an attractive-looking school that allowed me to make some friends who lived in the same housing complex as me. This school also gave me access to children in the neighborhood just outside the complex that we lived. Their parents enjoyed a higher socioeconomic status in comparison to the complex in which I lived, which was a space designated for families who were new to the country and/or living below the poverty line, though as children we did not care. I started my time at Zion in grade 8, so my time in this school was short since most children in my grade were moving on to high school. It would not have mattered much to me because most of the pedagogy centered on Eurocentric, patriarchal instructions similar to England—benefitting boys while continuing to marginalize girls and gender non-conforming peoples. This inevitably meant that the diversity of the students attending was not acknowledged, as teachers presumed that students of color were intellectually inferior to Caucasian students or otherwise culturally deficient. It was not surprising to me that many of the students of color appeared to be disengaged.

However, I escaped that designation due to my English accent that held a certain cultural currency since English is and continues to be associated with Whiteness, and as the primary language, becomes superior. This social currency benefited me when graduation came, and I was informed that I would be moving on to AY Jackson Secondary School while the majority of the children of color from the complex where I lived would not. This caused many of my friends (and a few bullies) to refer to me as a "brainer" while making fun of my British accent. That difference gave as much as it took away, as it hindered me from fitting in with children from either side. I was uninterested in "acting White" and being further alienated, just as Gloria Ladson-Billings (1995) writes, the "fear [of] being ostracized by peers for demonstrating interest in and succeeding in academic and other school related tasks" was a real and present concern (p. 161). This influenced my lack of drive to interact or to make new friends. However, a few children of color befriended me, which I assumed was due to their own alienation from the majority of the student body for their own differences.

Yet, not all the Caucasian students were the same, as there were a few who got to know us (the children of color), but the rest stayed clear, treating us as if we were of an alien category. Oftentimes, I struggled with this categorization, sometimes responding violently, eventually regressing and becoming a loner and leaving AY Jackson to attend George Vanier Secondary School, which was reputed as the school for "the less-smart children," though for me it was where the majority of Black children and other racialized children attended. And for me it was there where a sense of camaraderie existed. What was unfortunate was that the pedagogies they presented remained the same so that the psychological conditioning deliberately done during the educational development of Black students maintained its social dominance over us. I spoke to teachers in it, citing that the instructions we were receiving seemed to be dumbed down, but they seemed uninterested in anything I had to say so that even the brightest of students were being suppressed in class with little hope of extracting themselves from their assigned low positions in life.

In my case, this may have contributed to my skipping school with other disengaged students, becoming pregnant at 15, and living life as prophesized by the inequitable and oppressive behaviors of colonialists, who saw me and people of color in deficit terms, not keeping in mind that in order to engage students of color in classrooms, we should be mindful of what colonialism is and is not. And what it is not is a system created to empower anyone else's children but its own, which is why culturally relevant pedagogies would not be included, because in order to maintain itself, a colonial education system has to empower its children with myths and maintain its victims through those same myths.

Becoming pregnant at 15 and giving birth to my son at 16 put me in an even lower position in life because the society I had inherited was not as liberal minded 34 years ago as it has become today. Instead, because of my condition, I was discouraged from continuing high school, so I pursued employment. Regrettably, not many work positions were available to me since I lacked specific skills other than light clerical and babysitting experience, leaving me ill-prepared for many available well-paid positions, but with persistence I continued searching for employment and answered an advertisement in the back of a local newspaper that advertised that it was seeking women to "exotically dance." Initially, I had no clue what being an exotic dancer meant, but I soon found out and acquiesced since hunger and a needy baby can motivate you to do many things, and I began my adventures in burlesque entertainment. I came to find out that many women engage in the sex industry for a variety of reasons including finishing school, enjoying the job, self-empowerment, as well as paying bills. My reason was the latter.

It was in this context that I encountered many of the more privileged citizens in Canada, who included, predominantly, White businessmen, White professionals, White "family" men, and ordinary working White men looking to be entertained. Interestingly, the stage provided its own education and I learned a great deal from the White men who entered the various establishments I entertained in. Over time and communication, I came to understand that many of these men knew little about themselves and how to live "happily" up to the traditional gender expectations passed on to them. I also learned more about how these privileged people see themselves in relation to Black people, especially Black and queer folk, similar to myself. Tall and small, I learned from their interactions with me and the other entertainers, about the culture they grew up in, as we conversed and they shared. At times, we compared the conditions of our lives, and they discovered fewer differences between us than they had initially been taught, thus allowing me to become a more "normal" female, in contrast to the earlier teachings they had received that delineated women as less than men: less intelligent, less assertive, and less able. Patriarchy was still afoot, but our conversations disarmed them enough to allow me to socialize with them as I entertained them, posing no threat while opening opportunities to learn.

The first bar where I answered the advertisement was owned by Italian brothers, who employed eight to ten women per shift. Those women were a variety of Caucasian women, varying in age and background. I was the only Black female. Many nights, new to this setting, I sat in observance of the "action" that brought in the various businessmen, who started their relaxation process with the untying of ties and the loosening of collars and engaged in the heteronormative opportunity to hang with the boys and drink and frolic with the women, who were only too happy to oblige, and maintain their illusions of being "captains of industry." Each of us performed our own skit on stage to which the "boys" responded with loud chants and applause in appreciation. And on the odd occasion, they tipped.

In those early days, we were not allowed to get completely undressed since we risked being charged by people conducting surveillance who anonymously entered the club to catch girls in the act. Many girls pushed the boundaries when they felt like it, getting as close as they could without "crossing the line" because to do so stimulated profit.

During this time, I sat in corners listening carefully to comprehend what it was that the White men responded most favorably to and feminize myself accordingly. This recasting mirrors the ways in which many of us Black people *code-switch*, or go to various lengths in order to fit in, in certain spaces. The gender norms in these spaces paralleled and enhanced those already existing in many of the White institutions and communities today. Clubs controlled female bodies, which were chosen to entertain because "contrary to the notion that male customer taste is objective, it is carefully socially constructed through club marketing techniques, as well as the media at large, which overproduces images of White and mixed-race people as sexually desirable" (Brooks, 2010).

So, being a dark Black, tall woman I did my best to pay attention to the subliminal and overt codes of behavior and messaging, which included keeping up to date with varying mass media and sports to aid in conversations with them in order to penetrate their constructed illusions of intelligence and their definitions of beauty. It was empowering, and as I became more familiar with the environment, I learned how to keep an eye out for the clients who came alone and were lonely, since they were more likely to pay for companionship once their reservations and defenses against their constructed fears of differences abated. This was not an easy task. No matter where you work in clubs in North America the imperial teachings that aid in the construction of fear, racism, and gender inequality have been so well ingrained in so many of them that changing their minds provided challenges. On some occasions when you tried to breach those defenses, as many women of color attempted do, your attempts could result in rejections, ignorance, and violence. As entertainers in one San Francisco club discovered, "the degree of symbolic anti-Black racism at the Lusty Lady often was overwhelming, but not discussed among the White, Black, and non-Black dancers of colour" (Brooks, 2010). This is no different to Canada, where it is not unusual for ambiguity to occur in situations of violence. So, as the younger females became the older females, women began to organize to change their conditions by choosing to guide the dialogues around acceptable behaviors and women's safety so that issues previously buried could come to light. Sex workers became more politically oriented in trying to unionize to create safer conditions to work in, as in the case of the Lusty Lady Theater in San Francisco. The Lusty Lady made history on August 30, 1997, by unionizing with Service Employees International Union (SEIU). This was a move that many women throughout North America supported in various ways, feeling like this was imperative to their survival, particularly since under the influence of alcohol some of the men liked to show off their bravado as well as act entitled, a regular pastime that White men seemed more inclined to do in groups with little to no consequences. Many times, they would engage in degrading antics aimed at whichever female was unfortunate enough to be called over, because the gender norms seemed to support their viewpoint that (boys will be boys) women in the sex industry, especially those who are Black, deserve nothing better. These gendered ideas and the social stigma attached to our form of entertainment are more than likely why "the Lusty

Lady became the only strip club in the United States to successfully unionize" (Brooks, 2010), though many of us women never stopped trying.

While at work, we often became more like therapists rather than dancers, as we sat listening as the men spoke, laughing at their jokes, attending to their life views, hopes, accomplishments, and disappointments on any day, month, or year. The more seasoned women knew how to respond, displaying more than feigned interest. Yet on occasion, these "boys" could get upset, especially when alcohol or emotions took them over, believing that our entertainment extended beyond entertainer, to prostitute. In many cases they read entertainer and prostitute as being the same thing; we would have to know how to deescalate the situation. As such, we would tread lightly to assuage their ego, since making money and then making it home safely to my children each night were my foremost desires. I did not want to end up in some (entitled) man-child's bed. So, following the example of the more seasoned entertainers, I learned how to tread carefully when establishing boundaries that would assist me and the other women in keeping emotions within the space of the change rooms we shared with each other. However, no matter the level of caution, it did not prevent women from being assaulted, raped, and killed. In fact, it is estimated that more than 60,000 Black women are missing, which to my mind meant that if, or when, something did happen to us, not much, if any response or investigation was going to take place. Therefore, we soon learned how to create our own communities to look out for and protect one another. In our formed alliances, we walked each other to our cars or gave each other rides. We paid attention to those customers with tendencies toward abuse and informed one another, slowly becoming organized and educated by the circumstances by which we earned our living. Over time I began to notice that it was rare that Black men or men of color came into the bar and I became nosy, thinking to myself that surely they might enjoy these clubs too, so where were they? I then discovered that they were discouraged from coming in since the negative and racist stereotypes of many of the owners and some dancers had described them as being unable to afford or behave in these settings. Puzzled with the suggestion of them not being able to afford it, I spoke to managers and owners over the years who suggested that their presence would bring discomfort to the privileged class, who we were meant to entertain. In fact, when Black men did come in, we were discouraged from speaking to them, as it was thought they could be dangerous. But from my own knowledge and experience, the only violent men I met in my years as an entertainer were White. Truth be told, from my own perspective, I think they were scared to see us in large numbers.

I remember one particular evening when I first began entertaining and violence broke out. I was still naïve and did not understand the hostility my body brought with it. It had not occurred to me that the men employed as security at the establishment to protect the business and women would focus their attention on me in any way negatively and attack me. I was gaining in popularity and, on this occasion, that status infuriated some of the girls to the point that they planned to teach me a lesson. This night was the first time I had been happy since I had started dancing, since many of the men, especially those in groups, seemed reluctant in the beginning to call me over. It seemed to me like they were embarrassed for anyone to notice their attraction to and interest in a tall Black female, so that night's attention gave me a false sense of security that allowed me to let my guard down. I was preoccupied with thoughts of returning home with money, which could take care of some of my family's needs. All night I was delightedly praying that my popularity would never end. However, it did when one of the security guards asked to speak to me at the end of the night. I thought nothing of it since I thought the night had gone well, so I was eager to return home and distractedly followed the security guard's instructions to our prearranged meeting place by the office. As I opened the door to enter, I realized I was in a stairwell and looked up to the security guard jumping off one of the higher stairs straight onto my face. I lost consciousness; the last thing I recall was his shoe making contact with my head.

When I regained consciousness, I was in an ambulance on my way to the hospital, only to find out later that no investigation would take place and no charges would be laid against the guard, the bar, or the dancers who set everything up. Instead, I received chastisement for being in such an establishment as an underage entertainer. Their attitude is explained by Katie McDonough (2014), who notes in an article that "perceptions of the essential nature of children can be affected by race, and for Black children this can mean they lose the protection afforded by assumed childhood innocence well before they become adults." Coupling this attitude with sex work, I found out I was of no interest to the establishment insofar as my being deserving of protection. I was also now unemployed, given that the owner "did not want trouble" and the money I earned was gone from my person. All I had left to show for that evening were bruises. Once healed, I searched for other bars and learned to become more cautious of men, and some Caucasian women too, as I found out later that the security guard's girlfriend, who also worked at the bar, was the person who instigated the attack on me. She was jealous of my popularity. Apparently, she and her boyfriend laughed with others, sharing how my presence had always irritated her and how they planned to take me down to put me back in my place. With that and other experiences I came to realize this incidence as a symptom of larger societal problems that include elements of racism, sexism, and other isms based on stereotypes and biases, imposed by an imperialistic system on Black tall women such as myself. These systems utilize various oppressions, violence, and the "rape of Black women by white males to obtain absolute allegiance and obedience to the white imperialistic order" (hooks, 1981, p. 27). And the violence I experienced was meant to humble me. With my height and demeanor designating me with dominatrix-type categorizations, when you removed the sexual component all that was left was a threat that contributed to the intimidation some men felt, especially when I donned my stilettos, and on special occasion the props of a whip, which some imagined as an implied threat. When I was on stage, I embodied that character not fully comprehending that I was designated as the originator of sexual sin. Black women were naturally seen as the embodiment of female evil lust, which at times gave me a false sense of empowerment as I played along, performing their fears whilst donning my dominatrix attire. I allowed my queer/nonconforming self out and felt proud as I transgressed the gender expectations they had been taught to live up to, even though my choices brought danger with it. I began to see that the need of Caucasian men to consider my height and gender performances as sources of constant danger and sexiness, which was seducing. It was a delicate balance where at times I feared for my own safety and learned to become more conscious of my surroundings and very being. I consistently endeavoured to try to disarm them off stage, to put them at ease, so that they would know that I came in peace. I wanted to profit and continued reassuring them that I was no different from the other females who entertained them, just differently sized and colored. My time on stage was just an act for the purposes of entertainment. And when the make-up was off I was, to me, a regular person with an irregular job who only wanted to accomplish what so many parents desired, which was then, and is now, to take care of my family regardless of my gender, race, or height, and to do so safely.

One strategy of resistance I employed was getting an agent; my hope was that I would become safer in my environment. Furthermore, because my agent handled bookings with the various clubs and he managed so many girls throughout Ontario, coupled with his being a Black man who had some experience in dealing with the resistance clubs gave me due to my race, I hoped this would improve my prospects. This was not always an easy thing to accomplish since, as mentioned before, many bars across Ontario were not favorable to hiring Black women. This meant that we were policed in ways that Caucasian females were not. Moreover, one could arrive at a bar that would let you work for the week only to refuse payment, knowing that it would be a waste of time for us to call the police in the hopes of justice. We learned that in the eyes of the system fairness was not available to Black females, queers, or any other person who is different from male Whites who measure themselves as "normal," preferring instead to situate our differences to them as the problem. As the years wore on, so did my age, health challenges, and financial opportunities. Contrary to popular belief, not all women in North America who entertain make the same money. Caucasians make more and have the opportunity to make more, a point elucidated on by Alice, a Black Canadian entertainer who interviewed with author Siobhan Brooks (2010):

> You have to try harder to talk to the customers and ease them into buying a lap dance from you, smile at them, engage them more, because many White men are scared of Black women and sometimes Black men don't want to see a Black woman either, whereas the White women have an easier time talking to the customers [since] the erotic value of Black bodies remains decidedly unequal to those of White ones.

So, I hung up the G-string and decided to look beyond burlesque entertaining and focus my life in a way that I had not been able to do when I was younger due to the biases existing in the educational system. Knowing that the adult entertainment business offered no long-term security, insurances, or assurances, I looked to try again at completing the education that had been interrupted when I was a teenager. Feeling confident that I had now accumulated sufficient knowledge and courage from life experience to pair with what I was to hopefully glean from traditional methods of learning, I aspired to increase the probability of giving voice to a section of the Black community that is rendered invisible or that gets very little if any attention.

In writing about heightism, it is impossible to ignore the intersectionality of "isms" that Crenshaw draws our attention to that impacts the lives of Black women. Crenshaw (1991) in writing on intersectionality, states succinctly that "the experiences that Black women face are not subsumed within the traditional boundaries of race or gender discrimination as these boundaries are currently understood, and that the intersection of racism and sexism factors into Black women's lives in ways that cannot be captured wholly by looking at the race or gender dimensions of those experiences separately" (p. 1244). These are points with which I can agree and attest to while still asking society to ask itself, "What is it that makes tall Black women targets for satire, violence, misrepresentation, and other acts of denigration?"

What Informs Heightism?

Heightism is based on a measure of "normal" height expectations constructed by a the differencing between *normal* and *abnormal* reinforced by gender expectations for girls and boys. There is very little research available that explores the results of heightism from a gendered and raced perspective, meaning, stereotypes associated with stature have not been investigated as thoroughly as certain other components of physique, such as weight or attractiveness.

Heightism for this research is defined as discriminatory practices against individuals based on height and not limited to shortness. This is counter to popular literature on heightism that tends to ignore the discrimination tall women experience in favor of focusing on shortness. As a bias, "heightism" impacts racialized female bodies differently than those of paler skin who have not traditionally been labeled as inferior and subject to social media that present tall females as counter to racist ideologies of "normal," especially, I would suggest, because "the definition of 'normal' height was constructed by a combination of medical and social forces" (Cohen & Cosgrove, 2009, p. 298), who have traditionally (mis)labeled Black female bodies as inferior, unnatural, and suitable only to and for servitude. As Dei (2013) writes:

> In a racialized society, skin colour drives and maintains a degree of saliency and persistence primarily because as a phenotypical characteristic, skin colour is a biological marker conventionally viewed as absolute, fixed and

> determinate of race. The currency of skin colour is that is either "a harbinger of inferiority" or a mark of valued "property." (p. 27).

Much like skin color, size has effects that I did not fully comprehend until I witnessed it occurring to my daughter from the moment she began school and began to experience hostility toward her person. I suppose I, like many Black people, wanted to believe that racism was starting to let up. I wanted to believe that change was happening. I was unaware that an understanding of heightism and females dated as far back as the 1930s when science began its pursuits on how to reduce female height. As I began to explore it, I was unable to find much research to show how, or if, tall Black women figured into what was available. What we do know is that doctors prescribed the treatment of what was considered a "new 'wonder' drug—the synthetic estrogen diethylstilbestrol (DES), which when administered during early puberty would keep their adult height within socially accepted norms" (Munro Prescott, 2010, p. 298). The research presented at the time was used to convince Caucasian women that medical intervention would prevent their daughters' heights from escalating and by so doing improve their life chances. To my knowledge, this "wonder drug" was not offered to Black people. So, while White female bodies were being pathologized in pursuit for "success," Black women's bodies were excluded of this practice. This is relevant in a society that currently displays as much hostility toward Black bodies as it does because it gives context to the neglect of our well-being. In further research Farman (2010) notes that prejudice and discrimination based on height exists in our society, and furthermore that this bias shows that not only was height an issue with respect to the norms that took the body of healthy girls and disabled them, but that they also marginalized the bodies of tall Black women, leaving them out of research and treatments that were offered at the times, as Black women were not regarded as worthy or human enough to be included in su,ch investments. So, although the medicalization of tall women has since been stopped for Caucasian women for the improvement of their health, for Black women of certain height the surveillance of their body continues with no considerations given for the enhancement of their lot. This is not to say that we would welcome such "considerations"; rather, the point is that under the category of female, girl, or woman, Black women were not considered as fitting into that designation, standard, or associated care.

Height and the Education of the Black Female

Returning to education as a mature student I began my academic journey through the Transitional Year Program (TYP) at the University of Toronto (UofT). The program began with the basic viewpoint of "providing opportunities for participation to students from groups and communities who were traditionally under-represented in postsecondary education" (Braithwaite, 2003, p. 11). It was certainly a change from what

I had experienced as a teenager since for the first time I had Black teachers and was surrounded by mature students who like me had previously experienced the streaming, rejection, and marginalization that was common to many people of color. TYP "was developed from two summer programs the first of which was organized by Black students, Black educators, and associates, and housed in the Home Service Association building on Bathurst Street in the Black community in Toronto in 1969" (p. 13), though by the time I was enrolled it was closer to the university on St. George Street, and the space provided a supported learning environment that allowed for me to gain access, through the completion of its program, to UofT as a full-time student.

While embarking on my academic adventure an incident occurred that resonated strongly with me. A 28-year-old Black woman named Sandra Bland was found hanging in a prison cell in Waller County, Texas. Ms. Bland's incarceration was already being discussed via social media. Looking at her in videos and pictures I realized how easily Bland could have been my daughter, as she stood 6 feet tall too. I immediately heard familiar alarm bells, like the kind I hear each time I shop and security immediately begins their surveillance of me as I enter, or like what I have and had experienced when I enter certain spaces in school and am ignored or not treated as a student due to my appearance. Ms. Bland, being tall and Black like me, had been pulled over for a broken taillight and was met by a hostile officer who proceeded to arrest and detain her, leaving her to ask the rhetorical question "How did switching lanes with no signal turn into all of this?" This is relevant to the question, "Should tall women fear being too tall?" These are questions that inspired me to consider her encounter from the perspective of being a tall Black female and to wonder how heightism may have participated in her death that fateful day, since knowing that, as tall Black women, we are forced to confront typecasts of being viewed as less than female, no matter our accomplishments. Our bodies' "failure" to assimilate leaves Black women to "experience gendered and classed forms of racism that are rooted in societal stereotypes and controlling images; images that exist to marginalize and objectify Black women based on racist and sexist perceptions of womanhood" (Lewis, 2016, p. 761).

It also raised for me the question why when we consider racism, sexism, and other isms, Black women are still stereotyped as confrontational, argumentative, and scary, especially when they are tall. I was livid in response to her death, remembering back to my previous educational experiences and encounters within society that left me victimized, not only for being Black, but also for not fitting into the gender expectations of size. Sandra's death, in my mind, could have been prevented had her body not intimidated the officer who pulled her over. Rather than ticket her, he chose to exhibit hostilities to her questions and incarcerate her, which in Bland's case I believe contributed to the escalation of the situation that left her having to face fear, solitude, and ultimately death. While "race has no scientific meaning, it has a 'pragmatic, [and political] meaning that depends on what is valued in concrete situations in which ideas of race are invented or applied'" (Dei, 2013, p. 25). In her case, White superiority was in effect, and she had no power to stop it.

For me, as a tall Black woman, these passive aggressive and violent behaviors have accompanied me since I began school. They have been the indirect and direct, relentless, noxious behaviors one must live with daily, only to be compounded by "the subtle and everyday slights and insults . . . [including] assumptions about criminality, cultural values, and citizenship, as well as the minimization or denial of the racialized experiences of people of colour" (Lewis, Mendenhall, Harwood, & Huntt, 2016).

Microaggressions

> The Canadian Association of University Teachers (CAUT), provides the following as a definition of **microaggressions:** [T]he subtle, stunning, repetitive event that many whites initiate and control in their dealings with Blacks can be termed a racial microaggression. Any single microaggression from an offender to a defender (or victimizer to victim) in itself is minor and inconsequential. However, the relentless omnipresence of these noxious stimuli is the fabric of Black-white relations in America.

Though microaggressions are not limited by geography, these issues of violence can be understood in context of microaggressions that are launched against tall Black female bodies, questioning their femininity and also excluding them from the benefits of protection that are usually reserved for White women.

These encounters of ongoing microaggressions come partly from the sense of White people seeing being Black (i.e., race) people as abnormal. Then when you add in height and standardization to what is considered standard, or "normal," especially since tallness is understood as the legitimate way of being in the world and the only version of the "good life" (Titchkosky, 2009), you appreciate that this "good life" of normality does not pertain to tall Black women. Instead, many times, in our case, you are left with "deviant" bodies asking the question of why tall Black women are impacted by racialized violence, perpetrated by the imperial system instituted in North America, without much mention.

Race, Space, and Confronting Heightism

Given the paucity of research on the experiences of tall Black women from the research literature, I found media—websites for tall women and blogs—were the areas to discover how some of these women think about navigating the existing hostility in their daily lives. Thematically, the conversations can be categorized into three areas: ostracism, confronting stereotypes, and humor. In terms of ostracism, many women described experiences of exclusion from those around them. On one site called Black Women are Tall, members share experiences ranging from daily encounters of racism to experiences with dating. One blogger links her experience of exclusion to not only racism, but also sexism in having to deal with Black males, who because of their bruised egos cannot handle her stature and skin shade and resort to then insulting and demeaning her. This points to the fact that it is not just White people who mistreat Black women, but reveals that it happens within the Black community too.

It is interesting to note that Black Women Are Tall is a website asserting itself as "a space for women who self-defined as tall, Black . . . who are 6 foot +, and for the men who love tall Black women" (Black women are tall, n.d.). Though some do still hold on to that belief because it is ingrained and approved of by science, which is held within the highest regard. As Oliver (1990) suggests, almost everyone accepts the cognitive authority of medicine; however, this does not dissuade tall women from continuing to educate themselves and society by promoting information to the contrary.

Confronting Stereotypes

In confronting stereotypes about tall Black women, the website titled Tall Society is geared to women with height; though not race specific, it is run by Bree, a tall Black woman, who creates social events, bringing tall women together. Her YouTube contributions are used to empower tall women who, without these groups, might remain excluded and try to shrink to fit into a society that has not made room for their existence. This is a sentiment confirmed and displayed in most retail shops when tall women attempt to purchase clothes only to find that these stores have shirts with sleeves too short or pants that never reach their ankles, as well as shoes that rarely fit their feet. Bree, with other allies, also created the High Heel Freedom Movement (n.d.) that states as a guiding principle:

> You already stand tall. Get ready to stand taller with the High Heel Freedom movement. Are you a female identified person who stands 5'9" and taller in your bare feet? Have you ever felt embarrassed to wear high heels or been told that you shouldn't on account on [sic] your height? Or have you always been confident in the highest of heels? No matter your story, during High Heel Freedom events tall women and girls from all over stand tall together.

This is important because many tall women tend to slouch, or fear wearing heels, as it brings unwanted attention and opens uninvited conversations that center around them having to justify their desire to wear high heel shoes as so many women and some men do.

Humor Addressing Microaggressions

On many of the websites I visited, women discussed their everyday encounters of stereotypes about being tall and Black and the various strategies they take to face and cope with passive aggressive behaviors and microaggressions. Some tall women choose to engage with humor, as exemplified in YouTube videos called Tall Girl Problems. On these two sites, tall women, using the monikers Drea KnowsBest (2016) and Just Call me Wah (2016), discuss their heights and the advancement of stereotypical assumptions they encounter, and the lack of knowledge in existence. Both use humor as a tool for education, working to neutralize conceptions previously believed. Both women's approaches are effective; furthermore, their following is in the thousands, with women laughing and sharing their own stories, including one woman who states,"I'm 5'9" and people freaking act like I'm 7ft' I'm like…ok" (DreaKnowsBest, 2016). She suggests that many times we disguise so as not to disturb and worsen opinions that already have us confused and confined to social typecasts. Essentially, this means that tall women, who do not want to attract any trouble, oftentimes ignore those microaggressions. Instead, some choose to laugh to deflate what could turn into violent confrontations. In so doing, they prove that humor is an excellent way of disarming hostility.

Humor then, for tall Black women, is a source of empowerment that Black people have practiced historically when dealing with issues of race and space. This is interesting when discussing microaggressions, given that little or no focus is allocated to how tall Black women cope with being violated. Thus, YouTube can be viewed as a forum of empowerment and healing that many Black females use as a safe space in which to share. This use of technology not only engages heightism with humor, but it also exposes and informs people of the violence tall Black women encounter, while creating everlasting friendships.

Summary/Conclusion

I believe that there are many occasions when tall Black women suffer in plain sight without acknowledgment of the discrimination being heaped on us resulting from our size. Taller women are read as more aggressive, as older, as less vulnerable. This connected me to my earlier ventures of burlesque and made clear to me why at the age of 16 I was allowed to work in establishments that sold alcohol. Like many before me, I was a novelty or property for the amusement of White men by participating in something that could be identified as a contemporary freak show. My personhood did not exist. Thanks to the ejection of my person from school I became the "Hottentot Venus," a statistic that is not counted since my humanity, like so many other Black women, is and was not acknowledged.

What comes through to me from this project is that there are so many methods used in society to construct height as an omnipresent privilege reserved for men, starting in church where we as children are on our knees looking up when receiving sacrament from the priest, and we must look up to pay homage to his authority. Similarly, in legal institutions judges are elevated to survey us while we look up to their authority. And in movies, which inform our popular culture, the male protagonist is portrayed as being tall, strong, and authoritative while the little woman, who is meant to represent women, looks up to him in admiration. Thus, when a woman is taller, perhaps she is read to be to authoritative and therefore she has exceeded her place, and by doing so, shifts the "natural" order of things as prescribed by the White male population. Adding to their outrage are tall Black females whose height not only breaks with social conventions, but also intersects with many of their existing fears of her race and gender, and she becomes the demarcation of the "deviant girl" who is then studied and under surveillance under the alias of "science" who then looks for treatments for her, which can include that she might (and most likely will) be abused, incarcerated, or killed. Thus, since Black women do not stay in their allotted place by White society's standards, they must be forced back through the various measures, including microaggressions, that are used to protect normative spaces invented for them through policies of self-preservation enacted on by their self-serving colonial agenda. Being tall and Black does not confer to me the benefits that tallness confers for those who are White, particularly those who are White and male.

My experiences as a Black woman, in reflection, have taught me that there is, and was, nothing wrong with me that a lot less racism couldn't cure, though from my perspective this is not possible in Eurocentric educational systems that assess Black children as anything other than a problem because of where we as Black people come from in their ideologies that equate us with savagery, inferiority, and/or being inhuman. As a child questioning my experiences, which was perceived as aggressive, was in fact a healthy curiosity toward a world that misidentified me. Blacks to this day were and are prevented, dissuaded, and discouraged from participating in Eurocentric societies that adhere to capitalistic ideals. In entertainment we were and are demarcated for roles in servitude, sex, and or incarceration, while in schools many of us as are treated as "absent" presences to be negatively addressed every time we stepped out of line, which could mean for those whose differences stand out more than others that we are being marked for abuse each time we raise/d our hands.

So, to answer Tanya Farman's (2010) question as to whether tall women should fear being tall, I would answer yes, especially if you are Black, because it could mean the difference between life and death.

References

Black women are tall (@blackwomenareta). https://twitter.com/blackwomenareta?lang=en

Braithwaite, K. S. (2003). Access and Equity in the University: An Introduction. In K. S. Braithwaite, *Access & Equity in the University* (pp. 11–31). Toronto, Canada: Canadian Scholars' Press Inc.

Brooks, S. (2010, December 12). Black Exotic Dancers: Undervalued and Underpaid. *The Scavenger.* Retrieved from http://www.thescavenger.net/feminism-a-pop-culture-sp-9560/feminism-a-pop-culture/537-Black-exotic-dancers-undervalued-and-underpaid-69223.html

Cohen, S., & Cosgrove, C. (2009). *Normal at Any Cost: Tall Girls, Short Boys, and the Medical Industry's Quest to Manipulate Height.* New York, NY: Penguin.

Columbia Law School (2015). *New Report from Columbia Law School's Center for Intersectionality and Social Policy Studies Recommends Including Girls of Color in Policies to End School-to-Prison Pipeline,* Retrived from https://www.law.columbia.edu/media_inquiries/news_events/2015/february2015/black-girls-matter

Crenshaw, K. (1991). Mapping the Margins: Intersectionality, Identity Politics, and Violence Against Women of Colour. *Standford Law Review, 43*(6), 1241–1299.

Davis, L. (1995). Constructing Normalcy. *Enforcing Normalcy: Disablity, Deafness and the Body,* 22-49.

Dei, G. J. (1994). The Challenges of Anti-racist Education Research in the African Context. In G. J. Dei, *Africa Development / Afrique et Développement , Vol. 19, No. 3* (pp. 5–25). CODESRIA Stable URL: https://www.jstor.org/stable/43657955

Dei, G. J. (2013). Reframing Critical Anti-Racist Theory (CART) for Contemporary Times. In G. J. Dei, & M. Lourdan (Eds.), *Contemporary Issues in the Sociology of Race and Ethnicity: A Critical Reader* (pp. 1–14). New York, NY: Peter Lang.

Dei, G. J., & Mcdermott, M. (Eds.). (2014). *Politics of Anti-Racism Education: In Search of Strategies for Transformative Learning.* Toronto, Canada: Springer.

Derald, W. S. (2010). *Microaggressions in Everyday Life: Race, Gender, and Sexual Orientation.* Hoboken, NJ: Wiley.

Dixson, A. D., & Rousseau, C. K. (2005). And We Are Still Not Saved: Critical Race Theory in Education Ten Years Later. *Race Ethnicity and Education Volume 8*(1), 7–27.

DreaKnowsBest, D. (2016, December 26). Tall girl problems! [Video file] Retrieved from https://www.youtube.com/watch?v=jMMPU43nQDM&t=156s

Farman, T. C. (2010). *Should Women Fear Being Too Tall? A Study Examining the Experiences of Very Tall Women.* (Doctoral Disseration) Texas Woman's University. Denton. Texas.

Hester, N & Gray, K. (2018). For Black men, being tall increases threat stereotyping and police stops. *Psychological and Cognitve Sciences. 115*(11), 2711-2715.

High Heel Freedom Movement [The Tall Society] (2015, May 21). #HighHeelFreedom. Retrieved from https://www.youtube.com/watch?v=I-SULx1wpTo

hooks, b . (1981). Ain't I a woman? Black women and feminism. Boston, MA: South End Press.

Jackson, L. A., & Ervin, K. S. (2001). Height Sterotypes of Women and Men: The Liabilities of Shortness for Both Sexes. *Journal of Social Psychology, 132*(4), 433–445.

Jones, A. (2016, May 16). Alex Jones: Is Michelle Obama Transgender? It would explain a lot. *Info Wars.* Retrieved from https://www.infowars.com/is-michelle-obama-transgender-2/

Just Call Me Wah. (2016, August 6). Tall Girl Problems [Video file]. Retrieved from https://www.youtube.com/watch?v=UbcGoK-AZyE

Ladson-Billings, G. (1995). But That's Just Good Teaching! The Case for Culturally Relevant Pedagogy. *Theory into Practice*, 34(3), 159–165.

Lebron, C. (2016, January 15). The Invisibility of Black Women. *Boston Review*. Retrieved from http://bostonreview.net/blog/christopher-lebron-invisibility-Black-women

Lewis, J. A., Mendenhall, R., Harwood, S. A., & Huntt, M. B. (2016). "Ain't I a Woman?": Perceived Gendered Racial Microaggressions Experienced by Black Women. *The Counseling Psychologist* 44(5), 758–780.

Louhiala, P. (2009). On the Ethics of Estrogen Treatment for Tall Girls: An Update. *Journal of Medical Ethics*, 35(11), 713–714.

McDonough, K. (2014, March 11). Study: Police See Black children as Less Innocent and Less Young than White Children. *Salon*. Retrieved from http://chathamavalonparkcommunitycouncil.blogspot.com/2014/12/police-see-black-children-as-older-and.html

McGinnis, S. (2017, February 2). The Fact That People Still Seriously Call Wendy Williams a Man Is Really Sad. *Sheknows*. Retrieved from https://www.sheknows.com/entertainment/articles/1043529/wendy-williams-a-man-the-talk-show-host-comes-clean/

Munroe-Prescott, H. (2010). Normal at Any Cost: Tall Girls, Short Boys, and the Medical Industry's Quest to Manipulate Height (Review). *Journal of the History of Childhood and Youth*, 3(2), 298–300.

Oliver, M. (1990). The politics of disablement: A sociological approach . New York: St. Martin's Press.

Tall N Curly. (2013, August 24). *A Tall Girl's Life "Short Menaces."* Retrieved from http://tallncurly.com/2013/08/24/a-tall-girls-life-short-menaces-meeting-short-n-curly/

Titchkosky, T. (2009). Introduction. In T. Titchkosky & R. Michalko (Eds.), *Rethinking Normalcy*, Vol. 1 (pp. 1-10) Toronto, Canada: Canadian Scholar's Press.

Titchkosky, T. A. (2009). Coming Face-to-Face with Suffering. In T. Titchkosky & R. Michalko (Eds.), *Rethinking Normalcy*, Vol. 1 (pp. 91-114), Canada: Canadian Scholar's Press.

Wendell, S. (1989). Towards a feminist disability studies. *Hypatia* 4 (2). 104-124. Retrived from http://ieas-szeged.hu/downtherabbithole/wp-content/uploads/2018/02/Wendell_Towards-a-Feminist-theory-of-Disability.pdf

Chapter 6

In Search Of Dark Stars: Addressing Anti-Blackness in Schools through Critical Racial Embodiment in Educational Leadership

Michelle Forde

In North America, there is an ongoing crisis in the education system concerning the growing opportunity gap for Black students. A significant amount of scholarly research has been directed toward the careful study of this situation. The systemic inequity of educational outcomes for Black students persists, despite volumes of existing literature analyzing the phenomenon. In the absence of an immediate solution for this complex social condition, a rising chorus of voices has pathologized the Black community as the source of this problem. The dominant narrative has erroneously embraced a number of narrow constructions as the cause of this crisis, such as family breakdown, socio-economic status, or, worse yet, cultural and attitudinal factors. These surface analyses misdiagnose the symptoms of the opportunity gap for a far deeper social disease.

Educational equity will not be attainable for Black students until the problem of anti-Black racism in school systems is eradicated. The opportunity gap for Black students is a crisis caused by an absence of representative racial embodiment in educational leadership; the learning outcomes for Black students will not change until we critically examine and address these absences at the leadership table. It is imperative to underscore that while the lived experience of racial embodiment is essential for the effectiveness of educational administrators, it must be coupled with a carefully studied critical awareness (and application) of an anti-oppression educational framework; an in-depth awareness of the concepts and principles connected to critical race theory, for example, is one such framework that would serve these ends. With this understanding in place, there are three ways that this crisis of leadership can be effectively addressed: We must ensure that multiple ways of knowing and being are represented within the school culture, curriculum, and staffing models. An effective example of these multiplicities of knowing can be found within the principles of Africentric education; a meaningful and balanced application of these practices within our learning spaces would serve to effectively redress the inequities in our current Eurocentric system. It would be dangerous to assume that best practice in education prescribes the replacement of one way of knowing (Africentrism) with another (Eurocentrism). Rather, the understanding is that the learning monoculture within current school systems is ill-suited to address the complexity of needs reflected in the classrooms of our 21st-century globally connected learners. These homogenous practices of knowledge construction in schools must be interrogated. The resultant rising tide will not only uplift the collective minds and spirits of Black learners, it will also bring positive learning outcomes for all students. Critical race theory (CRT) provides the necessary discursive framework for this analysis; it offers a number of useful tools with which to identify and dismantle the hegemonic structures embedded within North American educational systems. As an analytical lens, CRT also provides possibilities for emancipatory futurities for Black learners; it compels educational leaders to move beyond the existing pathologized structures.

Locating the Self: Race, Place, and Identity

I come to this analysis as a Black female activist-educator with over 17 years of experience teaching in the Toronto District School Board (TDSB). It might be assumed that my span of time in the system has afforded me a certainty of knowledge regarding its machinations. Instead, I find the institutional landscape perpetually shifts beneath my feet; there is growing uncertainty with every additional year I work in the system. My formative years in the North American educational system also failed to afford me any lasting foundation of understanding regarding its operations. If anything, my childhood experiences served only to compound my confusion surrounding the loudly championed egalitarian ideals of this system versus the dramatically differing learning outcomes predicated on racial factors.

I completed my primary and secondary education in London, Ontario, in predominantly White school and community settings. I was typically the only Black student in my class, in an environment where there were very few racialized students in general. I never saw my Caribbean (Bajan) heritage reflected in the Eurocentric curriculum, although I do recall one instance when one of my Canadian history teachers personally apologized to me for failing to cover material on Africville in our unit on Nova Scotia. As I recall, he claimed to have "run out of time" and awkwardly offered this unsolicited and defensive rationale to me in front of the entire class. Thinking back, I've come to realize that my early learning experiences were filled with thinly veiled hostility directed at me in a multitude of ways: through strained interactions with teachers, absences and erasures in the curriculum, and constant reminders of my existence as a Black body "out of place."

In high school, I was extremely fortunate to have one Black teacher, Carol Talbot, who took personal responsibility to ensure that my heart, mind, and soul remained intact while I struggled through those turbulent years. She introduced me to stream-of-consciousness journaling, spoken-word poetry, and critical readings by insightful Black women like bell hooks, Gloria Naylor, Alice Walker, and Toni Morrison. It is critical to note that Ms. Talbot was the only Black staff member in the entire school; there were few racialized teachers of any background in the board itself, which underscored the magnitude of the systemic barriers to advancement, at the time. Given the benefits of my years of education (both formal *and* informal) in Black scholarship, I now recognize that Carol Talbot's careful investment of time and energy in my early adolescence was a conscious act of resistance. By exposing me to a body of creative work written within the Black Diaspora, nurturing my developing Black consciousness, and connecting me to a community of supportive elders through our local chapter of the Black Women's Congress, Carol Talbot affirmed my humanity as well as her own. Carol Talbot's critical and caring mentorship would become the catalyst for my future career as an activist-educator, though at the time, I did not grasp the gravity of this relationship. For centuries, it is these selfless acts of sisterhood that have served to sustain us, by ensuring that our collective wealth of embodied knowledge is vested within successive generations.

My older sister was much less fortunate in terms of her timetable and was made to bear countless classroom indignities, which I will not chronicle here. Walcott (2003) reflects on this uneasy experience in his assertion that "Blackness in Canada is situated on a continuum that runs from the invisible to the hyper-visible" (p. 44). In time, my sister also experienced this cruel shift toward invisibility.

Her creative spirit, unapologetic Blackness, and clever tongue formed a dangerous combination; she exited the system in grade eleven. Paradoxically, my sister was more intellectually curious than I ever was, yet she was pushed out of the system. While I went on to pursue post-secondary and graduate studies, it was her dreams that were deferred. She eventually returned to the system as an adult learner and completed her remaining credits, but something inside her had permanently shifted. There were no Black teachers in the building during the span of my sister's high school years. She was forced to fight for her education, while others were entitled to receive theirs. For every affirmation I experienced in Carol Talbot's classes, my sister endured endless negations. Walcott (2003) elaborates on this negative peace in his assertion that "to be Black and at home in Canada is to both belong and not belong" (p. 50). If my educational timeline shifted by a mere three years, I would likely not be writing this chapter.

My sister's story is one chapter within the countless volumes of inequities in the North American system. There is a psychic cost for all Black students when Blackness is pathologized in the classroom. The resultant push-out reflects a broader social cost in terms of the lost human potential. I left London as quickly as possible, at 17, to continue my learning in an environment that offered new possibilities. I entered the teaching profession with the goal of becoming an advocate for students (like my sister) who are pushed to the margins. Now that I am situated on the other side of the classroom desk, I've come to appreciate the many ways in which the promise of advocacy is constrained by the politics of my positionality as a Black female teacher in the TDSB.

On Language: Positionality, Politics, and Power

Before venturing further into this analysis regarding the crisis in educational leadership and its effects on the learning outcomes for Black students, it is necessary to address the issue of language and the intentional ways it will be applied in this work. When referencing identity, the following terms will be utilized: Black, Blackness, Black Canadian, and Black American. Rinaldo Walcott (2003) shares a meaningful rationale to support this choice in his book *Black Like Who*:

> When I use the term blackness, I mean to signal blackness as a sign, one that carries with it particular histories of resistance and domination. Questions of blackness far exceed the categories of the biological and ethnic. I employ blackness as a discourse, but that discourse is embedded in a . . . set of histories which are messy and contested. (pp. 27–28)

In centering the capitalized term "Black" within this analysis, a common history and struggle "living in the wake of slavery . . . [in] the afterlife of property" is signaled, which reflects shared identity politics (Sharpe, 2016, p. 15). These "particular histories" combine to form the beautifully intricate fabric that is Blackness.

At the outset of this analysis it is also necessary to address the common criticism that investigating the experiences of "Black learners" reinforces monolithic constructions. The charge is often posed that this language will legitimize stereotypes and obscure individual experiences. An additional charge is that this language encourages essentialism, given the scholarly discussions of race as a social construct. Dei (1997) challenges the notion that race is irrelevant to discussions of identity:

> Race is a useful analytical category. Its saliency rests on the fact that race has powerful currency in Euro-American society. Race language is used to

> differentiate people. The meaning of race pervades social life, affectingindividual and collective identities, as well as social structures. The commatisation of race is nothing short of academic gymnastics. It is always very tempting to deny the site from which we oppress, subordinate, or gain privilege. The academic explanation that race does not have scientific validity or that it is not a useful analytical tool can be worn out to the victim of racism. (pp. 26–27)

In his body of research on race, Dei has shared ample evidence to exemplify the "salience of race" as it shapes the lived experiences of people of color. According to Dei, (1999) youth engage in the performativity of their Blackness in school communities as a conscious method of resistance for three reasons: "to create [their own] spaces; to interrogate, critique and engage conventional academic knowledge; and to define and acquire the requisite social skills" (p. 26). For racialized students, the threads of positionality, knowledge construction, and survivance (within increasingly violent learning spaces) are inextricably interwoven. Any meaningful analysis of the schooling experiences of Black youth must foreground the "salience" of race.

Critical Race Theory: A Discursive Framework

The North American educational system operates as a social hierarchy; it is by design that Black youth are held subordinate within this system. Critical race theory (CRT) provides the necessary lens by which to study and subvert social hierarchies. According to Ladson-Billings (1998), CRT is a theoretical framework that originated within the academic field of critical legal studies. Ladson-Billings asserts there is "no canonical set of doctrines or methodologies" that all CRT scholars follow; however, there is a common commitment to understanding the ways in which systems of White supremacy are created and maintained for the purpose of restricting the fundamental freedoms of racialized peoples (p. 12). The initial legal contexts for CRT were expanded and applied to other fields requiring nuanced analyses, such as education. López (2003) clearly articulated the goals of CRT studies in educational settings:

> We have a duty to challenge oppression in all forms and an obligation to interrogate how schools and administrators oftentimes silence students who are culturally different. We have a duty to transform schools from being sorting mechanisms. However, we cannot adequately prepare future leaders to achieve these goals if we avoid exposing them to issues of race, racism, and racial politics and demonstrate to them how these issues still permeate the educational landscape. (p. 71)

Perceptively, López has identified the main barrier to equitable learning conditions in school systems as a problem of leadership.

López also asserts that leaders must develop an understanding of how racism "intersects with other areas of difference," which is challenging as they often fail to "comprehend the ways in which they . . . perpetuat[e] white racism in their schools" (p. 71). In Canada many educational leaders believe the language of diversity, color-blind ideals of multiculturalism, the patchwork approaches of inclusion, are sufficient tools to ensure equitable learning outcomes for all students. Board-level and school-level practices underscored by these toothless policies serve only to maintain the status quo, as James (1995) explains: "Multiculturalism as practiced in Canada, has not made schools [into] fair, objective, and unbiased institutions. Canadians have a false perception of equality of opportunity and outcome" (p. 43). Multicultural practices entrenched within school-based policies work to falsely inflate administrators' impressions of themselves as progressive leaders. It is necessary to move beyond the empty promises of multiculturalism in order to understand how race is weaponized within school systems.

Four core elements of CRT as extracted from scholarly research will be reviewed. As outlined by López (2003), one CRT principle holds that racism should be understood as an intentional construction that is part of "everyday reality" as it is entrenched within "our institutions, relationships, and ways of thinking" (p. 84). Racism is functional as it serves to reinforce the "natural" social order. Another CRT principle holds that "whites will tolerate and advance the interests of people of colour (POC) only when they [align with] the self-interest of whites" (p. 84). López builds on this idea in his assertion that this "ensures social progress advances at the pace that white people determine is reasonable" (p. 84). A third CRT principle holds that racism functions as a "privileging of white stories," which are centered as the "dominant reality," which serves to obscure the "racial reality" of the lived experiences of POC. According to López (2003), CRT recenters "the counter-stories" of POC in order to "demystify the notion of a racially neutral society and tell another story where social institutions serve the interest of white individuals" (p. 85).

A final tenet of CRT sourced through Gooden (2012) details that "white supremacy is utilitarian and serves psychic and material purposes for the dominant culture" (p. 70). According to López, CRT reveals the truth that "beliefs in neutrality, democracy, objectivity, and equality are not just unattainable ideals, they are harmful fictions that obscure the normative supremacy of whiteness in society" (p. 85). Applications of the CRT framework as outlined by López, provide possibilities for educators to "recognize the reproductive functions of schooling and have the courage to envision different [ends] . . . for the most marginalized youth, [by utilizing] a new set of tools, mindsets, and dispositions than what is commonly taught in leadership preparation programs" (p. 71).

The four understandings of CRT, as detailed, will be applied throughout this chapter. As the leadership crisis in North American educational systems is investigated, the ways in which it functions to directly reinforce the inequitable outcomes for Black students (through anti-Black racism) will be analyzed. Particular emphasis will be placed on the need for critical racial embodiment in school leadership at all levels—and the attendant harms linked to its absence. A CRT framework will be applied in a careful analysis of the following areas: school culture, school curriculum, and school staffing models.

Exposing the Leadership Crisis: Anti-Black Racism in the School Culture

Directly and indirectly, anti-Black racism is reinforced in educational systems through pedagogical practices, novel and textbook selections, and the construction of school-wide cultural "norms." Rampant anti-Black racism is the reason why a significant proportion of racialized students are caught in the opportunity gap. Collective failures in educational leadership have led our students, and our system, to this point of crisis. At the classroom level, teachers have the ability to wield their power and politics over a captive "audience," should they be so inclined. Oftentimes, however, anti-Black racism in learning spaces manifests itself in far more mundane ways, as an outgrowth of ignorance and general ineptitude.

I've witnessed a team of predominately White female educational leaders (one of whom was the vice principal) attempt to organize a school spirit food and music festival in the middle of Ramadan. The population of the school in question was comprised of a sizeable number of Black Somali students. An observant Black Muslim staff member raised the concern that the event would be exclusionary because a significant proportion of students would be fasting during the school day. The team of White women resolved to proceed with the event as planned, and to provide observant students with "take-out containers" in order to avoid "punishing" the rest of the (nonobservant) students by postponing or canceling the event. The resolution was deemed to be favorable as all students would have an "equal" opportunity to participate! Curry (2010) would describe this disregard for the needs of Black Somali students as a *microaggression*: "[These] are brief, commonplace, and subtle indignities (whether verbal, behavioural, or environmental). [Microaggressions] have been shown to produce feelings of racial rage, guilt, doubt, sadness, frustration, low self esteem and depression" (p. 406).

What message is sent to Black Muslim students when their faith is regarded as an inconvenience? What statement is made about who belongs when school-wide activities (and school leaders) fail to acknowledge major events on the multi-faith calendar, beyond those associated with Judeo-Christianity? Dei (2007) provides a fitting response to these seemingly rhetorical questions on identity formation: "We need to question all discriminatory educational practices that negatively impact upon the minority students' sense of connectedness and identification with the school, and their development of positive self-esteem" (p. 47). Dei also suggests an action plan to address these problems of systemic exclusion: "Canadian educational policies maintain an existing hegemony that continually excludes most people of colour and women from positions of power. We must pursue a political agenda to remove those systemic barriers to educational equity" (p. 47). Accordingly, Dei's analysis links the twin problems of Black student alienation and push-out to the root cause of poor educational leadership.

A CRT framework can be applied to analyze the school spirit festival case study. The predominately White school leadership team did not show any concern that a major school-wide event had been scheduled during Ramadan, even after an observant Muslim teacher explained the implications. The exclusion of observant Black Somali Muslim students from a marquee celebration reflects the mundane *everyday reality* of racism that is entrenched within our public institutions. A solitary member of the leadership team spoke in support of deferring or canceling the event, in order to be sensitive to the Black Muslim students. It is important to note that this White female staff member experienced resistance from school administrators regarding her previous attempts to organize queer-identity awareness workshops and events for students and staff. It is likely that the CRT concept of *interest conversion* played a role in this staff member's decision to speak up; it is reasonable to expect she may seek her colleague's support in the future, when she is faced with issues of queer identity–based intolerance in the workplace. The organizing group's blunt dismissal of the Muslim staff member's concerns serves the *psychic and material purposes* of *centering White supremacy* as the *dominant culture*.

The school spirit festival case study is one of many examples of problematic leadership linked to the learning community in question. In the absence of critical racial embodiment and a formal commitment to the careful study and application of an anti-oppression educational framework, our schools are governed by the slippery politics of misinformed White administrators. The same vice principal, for example, opted to "decorate" a bulletin board for International Women's Day (2018) with an oversized portrait of Aung San Suu Kyi. This embattled Burmese politician was recently stripped of a number of previously earned human rights honors—including the U.S. Holocaust Memorial Museum's Elie Wiesel award—due to her complicity in the targeted massacre and mass displacement of Rohingya civilians who fled Rakhine State. A significant portion of students at the school in this case study are newcomers to Canada, from racialized communities, who identify as Muslim. A fair number of these students have come to Canada as refugees; many are in the process of navigating a complex landscape of trauma linked to their collective experience of religious and political persecution. When a racialized female teacher questioned this vice principal as to how she selected the women featured in the bulletin, the reply was that she merely "Googled it" and chose the "most popular" internationally decorated figures. She then proceeded to voice the callous assumption that Aung San Suu Kyi must certainly have "fought on the good side" since she had been previously awarded a Nobel Peace prize. This casual disregard for the lives of racialized peoples can be likened, in some ways, to McKittrick's (2014) discussion of the "mathematics of black life" as it relates to the transatlantic slave trade: It is an assumption that the "killability" and "throwing overboard" of Black bodies from the ships is a mere "sacrifice of parts of a cargo for the benefit of the whole" (p. 17). If it were not for the critical intervention of this politically aware staff member, and the repeated pleas to remove the display, this visual assault would have been mounted for all to see. This singular example underscores the need for much broader representation in school leadership teams.

The White female vice principal's alarming ignorance of current global geopolitical issues and faith-based persecution of the Rohingya community, coupled with her lack of facility with anti-oppression education, allowed for this alarming transgression to occur. In turn, some of the most marginalized students in the school (newcomer refugees) were confronted with the *everyday reality* of racism, as detailed in CRT theory; the focus of the bulletin board reinforced their position at the bottom of the *natural social order* in the school. The planned public celebration of Aung San Suu Kyi served to negate the *racial reality* of these students, while simultaneously reinforcing the *dominant reality* that their experiences and concerns are peripheral to special event programming.

When White educational leaders (particularly vice principals) in racially diverse, multi-faith schools have no understanding of who their students are, there can be no meaningful progress in terms of school improvement. The practice of White supremacy in schools is not exclusive to White administrators; the same limiting principles apply to other racialized educational leaders who perpetuate anti-Black biases. This transgression of leveraging one's proximity to Whiteness is also a problem for teachers of color who lack (critical) racial embodiment and, thereby, the necessary lens for interrogating and subverting dominant colonial mythologies. In choosing to refrain from speaking truth to power, these racialized staff members fail to grasp the reality that their silence will not spare them.

Exposing the Leadership Crisis: Anti-Black Racism in the School Curriculum

Anti-Black racism in schools is also manifested in formal, direct ways, through the classroom curriculum. Teachers have the latitude to weaponize their institutional power and personal politics. Recently, a colleague ("Patricia") in the Durham District School Board sought my advice regarding a curriculum-related conflict she was attempting to resolve, connected to her son's ("William") ninth-grade English class. William's teacher announced his plans to teach Harper Lee's *To Kill a Mockingbird* as the core text for the mandatory novel study unit. William attends a predominantly White high school; he is the only Black student in his class, and his teacher is White. There were no previous classroom discussions critically addressing race issues in any context, historical or contemporary. This novel would mark the problematic beginning and end of the conversation on race in William's class.

Patricia contacted the teacher and shared multiple concerns regarding this unit: the dangers of "White savior" narratives studied without a critical race lens; the dramatic racial divide in the classroom; abundant racial slurs in the text and their attendant psychic harms; the disconnect between the Jim Crow setting of the novel versus the contemporary experience of Blackness in Canada. In response, the teacher became defensive and refused to consider alternatives. He accused Patricia's of censoring the classics and subsequently sought the support of his union, who backed his position. By contrast, Patricia sought informal support from within her network of Black female educators. I do not know Patricia personally, but a mutual friend introduced her to me. I offered support by sharing my own similar stories as a way of validating her lived experiences and her racial reality. At the time, I happened to be enrolled in a graduate course with Professor Dei, so I also connected her with him. My goal was to ensure that she too had formal, professional support from a critically recognized leader within the Black community to back *her position*. Apugo's (2017) research on graduate millennial Black women's (GMBW) experiences in predominately White professional settings also speaks to this importance of critical racial embodiment: "GMBW indicated that the peer relationships they held . . . acted as a means for psychological and emotional sustainability against perceived racial micro-aggressions by white colleagues, and lack of perceived institutional support" (p. 353).

After notifying the offending teacher that she was now consulting with Professor Dei of Ontario Institute for Studies in Education, he suddenly became much more receptive to working in partnership with her. Even a cursory review of Dei's work (2007) would reveal the teacher's positioning on the wrong side of social justice education: "Why is it that the defence of free speech and individual freedom is often carried out at the expense of minorities? Examining classroom texts to see whether they contain [hateful] materials and how they offend people is not creating an atmosphere of censorship. It is living up to the responsibilities of academic freedom" (p. 40).

Patricia's concern was not with the novel exclusively, so much as it was with the way the White male educator sought to "teach" it in the class. Regardless, it is a fair question to ask why the teacher selected this particular text. What "lessons" would the sole Black student in the class extract from this unit "developed" by a White male teacher? What are the psychological harms posed by this text for Black students? Tatum (1997) asserts, for example, that "racial grouping is a developmental process in response to an environmental stressor—racism. Joining one's peers for support in the face of stress is a positive coping strategy" (p. 60). As the only Black student in his class, William would not have access to this protective strategy.

Every time a Black student encounters racial slurs in an educational setting they are encountering acts of violence; the n-word appears over 50 times in *To Kill a Mockingbird*. The psychological harm is compounded by the fact that these reading exercises are governed by a White male teacher! bell hooks (1995) has written extensively on the mental wounds of racism: "Failure to address the psychic wounds inflicted by racist aggression is the breeding ground for a psychology of victimhood wherein learned helplessness, uncontrollable rage, and feelings of . . . despair abound in the psyches of Black folks yet are not attended to in ways that . . . promote [healing]" (p. 137).

As a beginning English teacher, I found myself in the awkward position of being asked to teach *To Kill a Mockingbird* to a junior class that was almost exclusively White in a privileged Toronto-area neighborhood. I would have been the only Black person in the room! I chose not to expend my mental energy on such a questionable endeavor; a lifetime of experiences in hostile learning environments afforded me the knowledge that I would need to conserve my energy for future challenges. As the only racialized teacher in the English department, I understood it would be unwise to enter into a battle of words and wills with my White colleagues. Instead, I borrowed a set of alternate books from a friend at another school. My lived experience of racial embodiment reinforced by my critical awareness of an anti-oppression education framework and provided the necessary tools for me to effectively address the situation. Fifteen years have passed since this incident. I have changed school sites, completed a graduate degree, and earned the title of English department head. Disturbingly, however, I am now the only Black teacher in my entire school. I am currently mentoring a Black female English teacher who is new to the profession and working in a school on the opposite end of the city from mine. She, too, is the only Black staff member in her entire school; she is grappling with the same issues I faced nearly two decades ago. With time, I've found that the levels of anti-Black racism in schools have increased, in direct proportion to the decreased numbers of Black staff members.

With time, I've also found that these battles to topple White savior literature from its lofty perch have not subsided. In winter 2019, I attended a board-wide professional development planning session on enhanced pathways. Beginning in fall 2019, this program will require all ninth-grade students be placed in academic level courses in English and mathematics. On the surface, through this program, it may appear as though the board has taken bold steps to address the opportunity gap for Black and Indigenous students. In practice, however, I've found that the levels of teacher resistance and open hostility toward progressive educational programming have not subsided. During a workshop on critical literacy, when the facilitator asked a room full of educators to justify why they are still teaching *Mockingbird*, a White male teacher called out: "White men can't jump, but they CAN write!" Disturbingly, his words were met with laughter from the majority of the group. He was not directly challenged by any of the professionals in the room, even after I voiced my concerns to the facilitator. Recognizing the need to conserve my energy, I exited the session.

A CRT framework can be applied in order to analyze in the *Mockingbird* case study. The teacher's initial selection of this "White savior" text underscored the *utilitarian aims of White supremacy*, as the voices and experiences centered in the novel are those of the White characters. The teacher's investment in this novel as a progressive exploration of race issues served to reinforce *harmful fictions* linked to *beliefs in neutrality and democracy,* while also fulfilling the *psychic purpose* of re-centering the *dominant culture.* Patricia took pains to present a list of carefully considered reasons why the novel was a poor choice for her son, and for that specific class. The teacher disregarded her concerns and refused to consider alternatives until she wielded the institutional power of Professor Dei. The principle of *interest conversion* can be applied, as the teacher prioritized his professional *self-interest* (avoiding exposure) over his initial urge to wield power over Patricia.

My own early experiences as a beginning English teacher seeking to creatively avoid this core novel serve as a powerful example of the *privileging of White stories* as the *dominant reality.* I had never been rescued from racism by benevolent White people. As a Black female teacher, my anecdote functions as a *counter-narrative* to the illuminate the *everyday reality of racism* embedded within our school communities. Yet the novel perpetuates the false *notion of a racially neutral society,* while simultaneously obscuring my *racial reality.* The novel also *serves the interests of White individuals* by entrenching their one-dimensional *narratives* within our *social institutions.*

Exclusionary cultural practices serve to strengthen underlying currents of anti-Black racism in schools. The crisis of weak educational leadership is the host that enables these parasitic conditions to flourish. In both the school spirit festival and *Mockingbird* case studies, the lack of diverse racial embodiment at the leadership table and the subsequent erasure of multiple ways of knowing and being resulted in the further marginalization of Black students.

Exposing the Leadership Crisis: Anti-Black Racism in Staffing Models

Given the pervasive nature of anti-Black racism in North American society, particularly within educational institutions, it is critical that racialized students see themselves reflected in the teaching staff. When there is racial representation on staff, the positive ripple effects to students' self-esteem and motivation are unparalleled. Unfortunately, the inverse is also true, especially in terms of the school administration team. Gooden (2012) highlights the critical influence of administrators on school communities in his assertion that "principals are second only to teachers in effecting school change. Principals who make . . . decisions without regard to the racial realities [of students], particularly the counternarratives of these students, will unconsciously work to promote negative outcomes" (p. 74).

When attempting to put forth an argument for increased Black racial representation in teaching staff, a criticism is often leveled that embodiment alone is not a sufficient guarantee for pedagogical competence. We must be cautious against a total dismissal of the benefits of critical embodiment, as Ryan, Pollock, and Antonelli (2009) explain:

> Teachers of colour are particularly well positioned to establish relationships with Students of colour, deliver relevant pedagogy, and prepare students

> of colour for a world that marginalizes them. White teachers—no matter how dedicated and skilled—can take their talents only so far. They cannot stand as symbols as teachers of colour can. Nor will most be in a position to understand, communicate, or identify with students of colour the way educators of colour are able to do. (p. 595)

My own lived experience as a Black female high school student in a predominately White school, neighborhood, and city is reflective of this particular truth shared by Ryan, Pollock, and Antonelli. I only had access to one Black teacher in my high school, yet her effect on my developing mind, body, and spirit was transformative. I can confidently state that were it not for Carol Talbot's firm guidance and loving care, there is little doubt that I would not have pursued an education beyond the secondary level.

As discussed earlier, my older sister did not have the benefit of working with a Black teacher in her formative years; she was then pushed out of the system in grade 11. At the time, her levels of creative skill and critical self-awareness were more developed than mine, and her unconventional nature, in retrospect, was likely part of the problem. Despite her innate talents, the fundamental difference between our future paths was one Black teacher—and it made all the difference. Dei (1997) provides further evidence to support my statement: "For many students, negative experiences of school [are] related to differential and unjust treatment. This treatment was most strongly and most frequently related to issues of race" (p. 78). I feign no modesty in the following assertion: There is nothing particularly special about me; my level of academic capability is solidly average.

Carol Talbot's high expectations pushed me far beyond the limits of my own middling standards, as Beady and Hansell (1981) further explain: "Black teachers expected more of their students to enter and complete college than white teachers" (p. 191). The deciding factor in my high school success was my good fortune; Carol Talbot's classes were an escape from the low expectations and daily racial hostilities I faced in the school community and beyond. To this day, I remain the only member of my immediate family to complete my education at the undergraduate and graduate levels. A CRT framework can be applied to my early learning experiences with Carol Talbot: By introducing me to the writings of self-possessed Black feminists, she validated my *racial reality* through these *counter-stories*; by affirming my intelligence and character, she subverted the *everyday reality of racism* and its attendant ills; by repeatedly asserting that she expected I would become an educated professional, she directly challenged the *normative supremacy of Whiteness* in Canadian society.

Balanced racial representation on staff is as important for teachers as it is for students. The Black students' learning environment is also the Black teacher's working environment, as Dei (1997) elaborates: "The narratives of Black students have shown that racism exists unchecked within schools, and even when incidents are brought to the attention of school authorities, just and decisive measures to address the problem are lacking. This is particularly true when [staff] are the perpetrators" (p. 79). If school boards cannot retain

Black students due to high levels of racial harassment and push-out, similar factors will serve to undermine the well-being of racialized teachers. While I have not been directly targeted with racial epithets, over the years I've been confronted with a significant number of unsavoury "jokes" and passive-aggressive commentary.

Current data indicates that the number of racialized teachers in the GTA is declining, while the racial and cultural diversity of our students is rapidly increasing, as Ryan, Pollock, and Antonelli (2009) assert, "[T]he proportion of visible minority teachers in the overall teacher workforce is *consistently* less than the proportion of visible minority citizens. The proportion of visible minority teachers in the workforce declined between 2001 and 2006" (p. 597). The trio of researchers refer to this disturbing trend as a "filtered pipeline" where systemic factors such as hostile workplaces and discriminatory hiring practices serve to "systematically prevent some elements from passing, while allowing other substances to move through" (Ryan et al., 2009, p. 607).

Recently, a gradual shift is occurring whereby scholarly research on school push-out is beginning to influence social policy. At the provincial level, for example, the liberal government established an anti-racism directorate with Members of Provincial Parliament (MPP) Michael Couteau positioned in a newly created role as minister of anti-racism. Of course, impressive job titles and expansive office spaces are insufficient tools to combat racism. The funding of this department, however, is a promising first step toward a better future for all Canadians. On Thursday April 19, 2018, the Durham District School Board (DDSB) held its first ever recruitment night for Black teachers. The event came into being as a response to increasing reports of systemic racism in the DDSB, along with the extensive data documenting the declining educational outcomes experienced by Black students in the board. The large turn out was widely covered by mainstream media outlets; it is likely that other boards in the Toronto area will follow Durham's lead in terms of progressive hiring strategies.

The Way Forward

A lack of diverse racial representation in educational leadership is the root cause of many ills within the North American educational system. The weight of this erasure has been hefted upon the shoulders of our Black students. The attendant harms of this skewed racial representation in school leadership are intensified by a corresponding lack of awareness and application of the core principles of an anti-oppression educational framework in schools. The antidote for this condition is threefold: We must ensure that multiple ways of knowing and being are represented within the school curriculum, culture, and staffing models. Our community of young Black students are in crisis; we must immediately begin the process of transforming their learning conditions. We cannot effectively progress as a society if a significant portion of our youth are being left behind. Corresponding measures must also be taken to ensure there is formal accountability and oversight for maintaining these new standards within school systems; transformational institutional change cannot occur based on good intentions alone. The language of progressive policy must be reinforced by material consequences for school leaders who reject these practices and weaponize their privilege by choosing not to engage. Diverse racial representation in our educational leadership is an essential part of this revolution; however, there are additional steps that must be taken.

The scourge of anti-Black racism has negatively affected our communities socially, mentally, and spiritually. Our healing must begin by re-centering our diverse cultures and histories within the process of knowledge construction. Embedding the principles of Africentric education into our learning spaces is one powerful way to dismantle the inequitable structures in our current school system and thus allow for new possibilities of engagement for all students. As it stands, Eurocentric world views and practices form the core of our existing educational systems; these narrow frameworks must be reconstructed to reflect the racial realities of multiple learning communities. There can be no universal template that will meet the complex needs of every school; it will be necessary for educational leaders to work in partnership alongside parents, students, and elders in order to determine the best way forward within a given community. With this particular caveat emphasized, a number of general points of entry can be shared as potential seeds that may germinate, if the environment is suitable.

Co-create the school curriculum: Teachers and administrators cannot effectively engage the community if the school doors remain closed. Educational leaders must recognize (and utilize) the rich cultural knowledge of parents and elders by inviting them into classrooms and engaging them in the process of program development. Living histories projects are an excellent example of this practice.

Situate the spiritual: Allow for explorations of personal growth, values, and beliefs in connection to core subject material. Foreground mindfulness and connectedness to nature within the learning environment. Reflective journal writing activities and practices that incorporate meditation and creative movement in the natural environments are accessible ways for students to form spiritual connections.

Integrate indigeneity: Traditional teachings and practices must be centered within learning activities. Storytelling and visual arts are powerful ways of celebrating cultural heritage; creating space for the meaningful expression of first languages is an important part of the process. It is imperative for school leaders to draw from a multiplicity of cultural texts (oral, visual, spatial) in order to ensure that learning is culturally relevant and responsive for all learners.

Embrace collaborative leadership: In effective school communities every member is a leader and a learner. This practice holds true for students, teachers, and administrators. Reflect on the decision-making protocols in your learning community and find creative ways to ensure many voices have input. The integration of restorative circle practices and restorative justice are powerful ways to ensure every member of the learning community plays a role. As a critical element of these restorative practices, it is necessary to recognize the ongoing legacy of racial trauma experienced by Black and Indigenous teachers working in institutionalized settings. As such, it is imperative that measures are taken to ensure additional resources are made available to racialized teachers. These tools may include additional release time for educators to form collaborative mentoring networks across a variety of sites within a family of schools or additional funding for professional learning opportunities sourced within racialized communities.

Nurture professional networks: Many researchers, including Apugo (2017), have found that Black activist professionals working in predominately White school settings undergo "definite trauma" as a result of their experiences with racial microaggressions. These harms are compounded by a lack of formal institutional supports to address the toxic circumstances. A supportive learning environment for Black youth cannot be possible when dangerously unhealthy working environments for Black teachers are allowed to persist. Apugo's research encourages Black professionals to draw support from their own professional networks through peer-mentor relationships: "Graduate millennial black women actively sought out peer relationships in their respective programs . . . because they knew how vital they were to their psychological, social, and emotional well-being. Participants did not express any expectation for the university in regards to providing support" (p. 363). Strength-based problem-solving approaches empower us to look within the Black community to identify existing strategies for resistance and resilience. Ideally, these informal methodologies could be used in concert with additional resources made available through the school boards. In the absence of formal supports to challenge systemic anti-Black racism embedded in schools, however, it is essential to remember that the most powerful forms of resistance and resilience are born within racialized communities, at the grassroots level.

Politicize pedagogy: Encourage students to approach learning as a problem-solving project. Privilege discussions of personal politics, social issues, and community concerns. Educational leaders must work in partnership alongside students, in a co-learning community. There must be a collective critical exploration (and interrogation) of the ways in which knowledge construction is a political exercise; this process can be leveraged to power or disempower particular communities, depending on the pedagogical approaches that are applied. With this awareness, classroom projects can be conceived as social learning labs where meaningful change in the school community can be realized.

As Black activist-educators, we must remember our power rests within the collective. We must continue to situate ourselves within our cultural identity and draw on the strength of our traditions, across the Black Diaspora, in order to move our community forward. In this way, our cartographies of Blackness will inform our practice and offer us an instrumental framework for sustaining Black creativity and consciousness.

References

Apugo, D. L. (2017). "We All We Got": Considering Peer Relationships as Multi-Purpose Sustainability Outlets among Millennial Black Women Graduate Students Attending Majority White Urban Universities. *Urban Review, 49*(2), 347–367. doi:10.1007/s11256-017-0404-2

Beady, C., & Hansell, S. (1981). Teacher Race and Expectations for Student Achievement. *American Educational Research Journal, 18*(2), 191-206. Retrieved from http://www.jstor.org.myaccess.library.utoronto.ca/stable/1162381

Curry, J. (2010). Addressing the Spiritual Needs of African American Students: Implications for School Counselors. *Journal of Negro Education, 79*(3), 405–415.

Dei, G. J. (1997). *Reconstructing "Drop-out."* Toronto, Canada: University of Toronto Press.

Gooden, M. A. (2012). What Does Racism Have to Do with Leadership? Countering the Idea of Color-Blind Leadership: A Reflection on Race and the Growing Pressures of the Urban Principalship. *Educational Foundations, 26*(1–2), 67–84.

hooks, b. (1995). *Killing rage: Ending racism.* New York: Henry Holt and Company, LLC.

James, C. (1995). Multicultural and Anti-Racism Education in Canada. *Race, Gender & Class,* 2(3), 31–48.

Ladson-Billings, G. (1998). Just What Is Critical Race Theory and What's It Doing in a Nice Field Like Education? *International Journal of Qualitative Studies in Education, 11*(1), 7–24. doi:10.1080/095183998236863

López, G. (2003). The (Racially Neutral) Politics of Education: A Critical Race Theory Perspective. *Educational Administration Quarterly, 39*(1), 68–94. doi:10.1177/0013161X02239761

Masko, A. L. (2005). "I Think about It All the Time": A 12-Year-Old Girl's Internal Crisis with Racism and the Effects on Her Mental Health. *Urban Review, 37*(4), 329–350. doi:/10.1007/s11256-005-0014-2

McKittrick, K. (2014). Mathematics of Black Life. *Black Scholar, 44*(2), 16–28.

Ryan, J., Pollock, K., & Antonelli, F. (2009). Teacher Diversity in Canada: Leaky Pipelines, Bottlenecks, and Glass Ceilings. *Canadian Journal of Education, 32*(3), 591–617.

Sharpe, C. E. (2016). *In the Wake: On Blackness and Being.* Durham, NC: Duke University Press.

Tatum, Beverly Daniel. (1997). *"Why are all the Black kids sitting together in the cafeteria?:"* New York :Basic Books,

Tatum, Beverly Daniel. (2003). *"Why are all the Black kids sitting together in the cafeteria?:" and other conversations about race.* New York :Basic Books,

Walcott, R. (2003). *Black Like Who?* Toronto, Canada: Insomniac Press.

CHAPTER 7

Unlearning our Blackness

John P Castillo

Introduction

THIS CHAPTER EXAMINES implications of adopting a discursive *unlearning* framework within the context of contemporary education. Throughout Western society a civilizing narrative propagates learning through dominant hegemonic knowledges, colonial narratives, oppressive teaching, learning, and schooling practices. A Western educational paradigm seeks to maintain a citizenry that recognizes and rewards the efforts of constituents who contribute to subverting anti-colonial agendas that interrogate hegemonic narratives. Ilmi (2011), Ladson-Billings (1998), Schick (2010), and Wane (2003) discuss the importance of rethinking learning, teaching, and schooling paradigms within the framework of anti-racist education, consequently offering an anti-colonial lens as a form for progressive and anti-oppressive pedagogy wherein the lived experiences of contemporary—particularly students of African ancestry—are authentically represented in the classroom. In addition, I consider the significance of recognizing that the permanence of skin color should not be utilized as a marker to dispense microaggressions on students with African ancestry. These microaggressions emerge from implicit biases that are constructed, supported, and sustained through hegemonic political agendas to maintain the power structures that privilege the dominant Eurocentric body while marginalizing and punishing Black/racialized bodies.

The construction of implicit biases leads Ilmi (2011) to discuss the phenomena that "there is a complex colonial ideology that is used to create racial hierarchies within society with the sole purpose of rewarding dominant bodies, while simultaneously racializing Black/minority bodies" (p. 220). Continuing with the notion of implicit bias is recognizing that "[i]mplicit biases position us to choose and not choose what to look for, hear, and see alternative possibilities in racialized bodies more specifically black bodies. Assigning or not assigning value on individuals depending the information received" (Sharpe Silverthorne, 2018). Implicit biases make the possible impossible in that Black bodies are viewed through a deficit assumption whereby Black bodies are deviant because they present a threat to the safety and well-being of dominant bodies. Implicit bias often constructs a single narrative sustained by the multiple media platforms, which inflict traumatic harm and emotional pain originating from violent forms of oppression by dominant bodies protecting a sacred worldview regarding racial differences. For Dei (2017), unlearning our Blackness must "[c]onsciously challenge and subvert the construction of Black/African identity within Euro-American hegemony" (p. 72).

In her June 11, 2018 piece written for the *Chicago Tribune*, Michelle Sharpe Silverthorne (diversity and education director for the Illinois Supreme Court Commission on Professionalism) chronicles her experience with implicit biases when she writes:

> I often walk around my neighborhood with my two biracial kids. My kids could pass for white. And because I am black, I am often assumed, by some well-meaning parents, to be my children's nanny. I am asked how much I am paid, do I have any friends looking for work, or am I looking for work... it's not just what's said. It's what unsaid. When they treat you like someone who just doesn't belong. Now they would never claim they were doing it on purpose, or that they were acting biased at all, until you ask them, "Why do you think I am the nanny?" See, this is implicit bias. It's because (in part) they think one thing should only be this way, because they have only ever seen it this way, and cannot adjust their mind to seeing it any way else.

Before moving on with my discussion about unlearning, I want to investigate the validation of learning as the central paradigm through which individuals, more specifically Black and racialized bodies, are measured, identified, and valued in the world cultivated from an invented schema in which the Black body is problematized and vilified within Eurocentric understanding of education, teaching, and learning. In moving through places and spaces of learning, racialized bodies by default are positioned within the White imaginary as inadequate or rather impaired to engage in learning endeavors. For Adjei (2013), "[W]ithin the white world, there is an active political assertion that certain bodies, especially black bodies, represent a homogenous social group in which degeneracy, criminality, destitution, illiteracy, immorality, and violence are part of their normative history, culture, and identity" (p. 28). Drawing on Adjei's articulation enables me to highlight and reflect on the notion that to learn is to be human, to learn is to think, to learn is to reason, to learn is to question, to learn is to understand, to learn is to imagine, to learn is to remove restrains, to learn is to enlighten. The paradox presented in the structures of learning is this notion of unlearning, which will be discussed in further detail. Not to negate the importance of learning and the benefits of moving from ignorance to knowledge, it is essential to highlight the many forms of learning within different racialized groups as transmitting indigenous knowledge(s). For Ilmi (2011), "Indigenous knowledge[s] are generated and passed down intergenerational through storytelling, observations, and traditional ceremonies. Moreover, once embodied knowledge depends on the age of the person and the role they play in society" (p. 226) These indigenous stories require intentional listening and learning on the part of the receiver(s) to preserve indigenous knowledge(s). Through the lingering effect of colonial structures, our stories are often convoluted, misrepresented, misremembered, and underrepresented, leaving us (Black/racialized bodies) to sift through shattered pieces of our fragmented history in efforts to connect our violent past with an oppressive present while looking toward an imagined future of endless possibilities. It is through the complexity of learning how to unlearn our Blackness that Blackness is primarily remembered and reclaimed.

My reference to remembering and reclaiming Blackness positions me to consider my childhood on the small Caribbean island of Trinidad and Tobago where my father instilled in me the lifelong lesson of living my life as a human who is being in the world. I vividly remember comparing myself to my three older brothers and unconsciously constructing and learning my Blackness using their changing pubescent masculine bodies and deepening voices as a reference point. Remembering the experience as an adult allows me to recall my father's authoritative yet calm voice reassuring me of the dignity and power of my Blackness when he said, "Son, no one before your time, during your time, and after your time will have your fingerprint. Chances are, you will die a Black man; however, live your life as a human who is being in the world." I remember hearing these words before my 10th birthday and engraving them on the tablets of my heart. My father's voice not only became the catalyst to my understanding of Blackness, his words were etiological in constructing my Blackness. Consequently, as an adult I often return to the sacred altar my dad constructed on my heart to remember my Blackness as being a human in the world apart from defining myself within the limits of hegemonic narratives.

Fanon's (1967) seminal work *Black Skin White Mask* spoke to my Blackness through the corridors of time when he states, "I came into the world imbued with the will to find a meaning in things, my spirit filled with the desire to attain to the source of the world, and then I found that I was an object in the midst of other objects" (p. 109). For hooks (1992), remembering is searching through "the debris of history . . . wiping the dust from past conversations, to remember some of what was shared in the old days" (p. 338). hook's reference to "the debris of history" positions me to examine the process of reclaiming Blackness.

Turning toward reclaiming Blackness, I consider examining recovering my Blackness. The implications of Blackness reclaimed moves my discussion to explore intersectionalities within the African-Caribbean Canadian Diaspora. In reclaiming Blackness, I engage in deliberate action to dismantle singular narratives wherein Blackness is "understood to be the material expression of black culture which is defined as a cycle in which the negative effects of black matriarchy and family pathology wrought destructive changes on the inner city by internally breeding deviancy out of deprivation and discrimination (Gilroy, P, 1987). Contrary to hegemonic racial constructs to erase our Blackness by reducing our African ancestral and Indigenous knowledge(s), Blackness is more than an entry point for legitimizing oppressive colonial agendas. Envisioning Blackness beyond a single lens in favor of a prismatic outcome with multiple entry points allows us to critically analyze anti-racism education and interrogate sustained anti-Black racism practices consequently unlearning our Blackness.

Theoretical Framework

I will use an anti-colonial and anti-racism discursive framework to carry out a comprehensive discussion of unlearning our Blackness as a transformative process of engagement within an educational context. The anti-colonial framework and reference to an education context highlight the pivotal role education played in navigating intersectionalities of my African-Caribbean Canadian Blackness. My understanding of Blackness was limited to my childhood and early adolescent years on the island of Trinidad that was part of the British colonial empire until it gained its independence on August 31, 1968. Framed entirely within a colonial paradigm, my educational experience did not provide me with any knowledge of my African ancestry. With my Blackness eliminated from my textbooks, my learning centered on a Eurocentric canon that celebrated the discovery of Trinidad and Tobago by Christopher Columbus in 1498. Ilmi (2011) explains that an anti-colonial theory "will enable [us] to proceed forward with a comprehensive understanding of the complex colonial ideology that is used to create racial hierarchies within society with the sole purpose of rewarding dominant bodies, while simultaneously racializing Black/minority bodies" (p. 220) .

Using an anti-racist framework allows me to optimize my discussion in considering the lingering effects of the violent colonial project to subjugate Black bodies through dehumanizing physical oppression and invasive mental instruction that Blackness is synonymous to being inferior and uncivilized. To buttress my discussion, I will also employ an anti-racism framework highlighting that by "placing race squarely in front of us, 'we can challenge the state, the institutions of civil society, and ourselves as individuals to combat the legacy of inequality and injustice inherited from the past' and continually reproduced in the present" (Omi &Winant, 2003, p. 159). Adopting an anti-racism framework allows me to place race at the center of my discussion. According to Schick (2010):

> [U]nless racism is understood as a systemic and political problem of unequal relations, solutions will not be forthcoming. An anti-racist education takes place in and through direct acknowledgement of power relations found in everyday systems and practices. Critical pedagogy, of which anti-racist education is one formation, recognizes that people are marginalized through hierarchies of socially constructed identifications. Racism is not simply a pre-existing condition or an inevitable fact of life that would render the social world helpless to change it, but something with a history that is learned across time and geographic location." (pp. 47–49)

For Ilmi (2011), "Anti-racism provides the space for one to speak about their lived experiences in their own voice" (p. 221). Considering this, I see myself having survived my colonial education in Trinidad to now embracing and journeying toward becoming through a triangulated intersectional lens of my Blackness as an African-Caribbean Canadian.

A Historicity of Blackness

In concert with Dei (2017), "Blackness is about knowledge production, representation, and politics centered on race, Indigeneity, culture, and history" (p. 15). Writing about a history of Blackness is engaged by many scholars who "all make the distinction between being Black, which is a socially, historically, and culturally constructed, and becoming Black, which is a political act of constructing, negotiating, and shaping identities that encompass resistance" (Ilmi, 2011, p. 218). Blackness in the White imaginary is collectively perceived as a homogeneity wherein Black bodies are fixed in a constant space of disrepair, as the Other (see Adjei, 2013; Ilmi, 2011; hooks, 1992; Ladson-Billings, 1998; and Wane, 2003). For Fanon (1967), the history of Blackness is akin to color being a marker by which a standard of competence, goodness, perfection, purity, and reasoning is synonymous to Whiteness:

> It [color prejudice] is nothing more than the unreasoning hatred of one race for another, the contempt of the stronger and richer peoples for those whom they consider inferior to themselves and the bitter resentment of those who are kept in subjugation and are so frequently insulted. As colour is the most obvious outward manifestation of race it has been made the criterion by which men are judged, irrespective of their social or educational attainments. The light-skinned races have come to despise all those of a darker colour, and the dark-skinned peoples will no longer accept without protest the inferior position to which they have been relegated. (p. 89)

It was in a Canadian high school when my African-Caribbean Canadian Blackness came to the forefront of many conversations with my peers and interactions with my teachers wherein dominant bodies marveled at my ability to speak proper English without the need for intensive remedial ESL classes. After numerous attempts to curtail the veracious appetite of my peers to investigate the source of my civility and their insatiable curiosity and desire to reconcile their cognitive dissonance to my strong command of their language, I concluded that my peers were unaware of my forced colonial education in Trinidad where I was taught the queen's English. The cruel duality of me mastering English eliminated any history of my African ancestry and Indigenous language, to which I have no memory of or reference to. In addition, my command and mastery of spoken English became a point of contestation in the imagination of my predominantly White teachers. Being raised in a two-parent family where both mom and dad attended parent-teacher interviews (much to my chagrin), added to the daily discomfort my teachers experienced when I entered their classrooms. My Blackness in the classroom was not an opportunity to engage in critical pedagogy that subverts hegemonic biases and narratives, consequently engendering opportunities for transformative anti-racism pedagogy, but rather, my Blackness became a Herculean task to resolve the cognitive dissonance that plagued the White imaginary. In support of my discussion, I reference Dei (2017) when he states, "The truth about Blackness is that it is consequential, complex, contested, and yet affirming" (p.3).

I vividly remember being one of two or perhaps three Black bodies in most, if not all, my classes during the first two years of my secondary school. As a response, "I was responsible at the same time for my body, for my race, for my ancestors. I subjected myself to an objective examination, I discovered my Blackness, my ethnic characteristics; and I was battered down by tom-toms, cannibalism, intellectual deficiency, fetichism, racial defects, slave ships, and above all else, above all 'Sho good eatin'" (Fanon, 1967, p. 112). Living in the permanence of my Blackness during secondary school was a courageous undertaking requiring me to continually disprove the rigidly fixed implicit racial biases and stereotypes in the imagination of my White teachers. I performed Whiteness by adopting a Canadian accent to suppress the melodious sonority of my Trinidadian accent hoping to diminish the harmonious inflections, rhythms, and syntax entrusted to me by my ancestors as forms of resistance to encode the language that was imposed on my ancestors and me by our colonial oppressors. In the classroom I was considered an imposter, where I was not welcomed because of the rich mocha color of my skin; my Blackness was always under surveillance in the classroom. Building on Dei's (2017) work, "To be Black is to be aware of such embodiment and what it means to embody the practice of Black identity/Blackness in positive (solution-oriented) ways as opposed to oppressive and dominating trends. Affirming a strong Black identity to challenge anti-Blackness is about a personal racialized embodiment" (p. 77). In concert with Ilmi's reference to Solomon, Ilim (2011) states "Blackness was synonymous with being a dysfunctional learner, and to being predisposed to criminality, social, and moral disorderliness within the school system" (p. 222).

My resolve to not only challenge but unapologetically resist violent epistemologies inflicted on my darkened skin positioned me to traverse the dominant landscape filled with racialized landmines that, if triggered, would inflict unrelenting trauma on Black bodies because "[c]olonialism and colonial relations have an uncanny ability to self-preserve. Colonialism has continually reinvented itself to ensure dominance. This reinvention is not a postcolonial experience but an ongoing colonial experience—one that is a daily struggle for peoples at the receiving end of colonialism" (Dei, 2017, p. 11). The visual trauma inflicted on Black bodies is constant, a feeling of always being under scrutiny and surveillance within the White gaze. Trauma and unlearning Blackness are intrinsically linked to dismantling socially constructed and racially charged biases targeting Black bodies. These microaggressions are "subtle and stunning assaults people of color encounter based on their race, assaults that have a cumulative effect over the course of an individual's life" (Garcia, 2018) and that produce single narratives and racial stereotypes constructed and sustained by dominant Eurocentric bodies reveling in power and privilege. By comparison, "[N]arrative is one of the most powerful tools available to paint a multidimensional portrait of a community's experience" (Ilmi, 2011, p. 225).

In concert with Ilmi, Toronto journalist, broadcaster, and co-host of CTV's *The Social*, Marci Ien's 2018 piece in *The Globe and Mail* gives her readers an introspective first-person glimpse at the trauma she encountered for a third time after being stopped by Toronto Police. For Ien, "Who you are doesn't matter; it's what you are. If you are black in Canada, you are subject to a different standard and, often, seemingly, different laws." The enduring racial trauma became the catalyst for Ien, an award-winning journalist. Her Blackness validated the police officer's interrogation protocol; Ien's Blackness positioned her as a villain within a dominant colonial narrative, consequently paralyzing her with racial trauma. In concert with Ien, Adjei acknowledges, "In the white world, blackness is quintessential evil that needs to be policed and quarantined before it causes any harm to whiteness. Thus, when blackness appears where it is not supposed to appear, in particular, at a space reserved for whiteness, serious questions need to be asked and urgent actions need to be taken" (Adjei, 2013, p. 27). Returning to Ien (2018), when she poignantly concludes her article, leaving her readers to corroborate and substantiate their lived experiences with her trauma she writes, "I lingered behind the wheel for a long while, too shaken to go inside." How long shall we have to linger in the shadows of our beautifully darkened skin?

In describing his Blackness, Toronto activist Desmond Cole's 2015 *Toronto Life* article recoils at his internal and external conflict: "My skin is the deep brown of a well-worn penny. My eyes are the same shade as my complexion, but they light up amber in the sun, like a glass of whiskey. On a good day, I like the way I look. At other times, particularly when people point out how dark I am, I want to slip through a crack in the ground and disappear." This relentless and unending trauma inflicted on Black bodies delivers a ubiquitous blow on the psyche. For Cole, his Black skin is a site of trauma violently imposed on him by White police:

> After years of being stopped by police, I've started to internalize their scrutiny. I've doubted myself, wondered if I've actually done something to provoke them. Once you're accused enough times, you begin to assume your own guilt, to stand in for your oppressor. It's exhausting to have to justify your freedoms in a supposedly free society. I don't talk about race for attention or personal gain. I would much rather write about sports or theatre or music than carding and incarceration. But I talk about race to survive. If I diminish the role my skin colour plays in my life, and in the lives of all racialized people, I can't change anything . . . too many black men are "known" through a foggy lens of suspicion we've done nothing to earn.

In her piece "The Ubiquitous Trauma of Blackness" when writing about defensive end for the Seattle Seahawks Michael Bennett's experience with police, Serene Hitchcock (2017) articulates, "The trauma sustained when someone is racially profiled, abused, threatened or beaten because of their race permeates and affects them deeply. Sometimes for their entire lives. The post-traumatic stress incurred by the victims, the shock and horror that bystanders and witnesses endure is unending and often insurmountable." I propose exploring the possibility of rethinking the term Black within Western thought to describe individuals of African ancestry. For Adjei (2013), "The implication is that black bodies must be viewed and read as imminent threats whenever they trespass through spaces reserved for whiteness. In a sense, blacks are already pathologized, criminalized, and degenerated even before they enter the white world," and by default Black bodies are seen "through a violent colonial imaginary story that scripts black bodies like me as the quintessence of evil, less educated, lazy, dishonest, and inferior" (p. 28). In rethinking the term "Black" when describing and referring to individuals of African ancestry, permit me to interrogate and decolonize the term as a form of resistance to violent Western epistemologies of Blackness. The innate negative undertones associated with the term Black when conceptualizing Black bodies in Western societies violently erases our history and replaces our Indigenous knowledge(s) with Eurocentric ideologies and understanding of ourselves.

Minimizing our humanity to a shade of color displaces our connection to the African continent by simplifying our complex and intersecting narratives. In the Western imagination and the context of education and schooling, "blackness was synonymous with being a dysfunctional learner, and to being predisposed to criminality, social, and moral disorderliness within the school system" (Ilmi, 2011 pp. 222). Adjei (2013) goes on to say, "[T]he body of a black male comes to be constituted as a criminal in the Euro-American/Canadian society" (p. 37). Historically Blackness is linked to negative overtones that negate our deep and rich culture, our ways of knowing, our stories of enduring the brutality of slavery, our ability to continue to survive and thrive as a people displaced from our land. Unlearning our Blackness is being "aware of such embodiment and what it means to embody the practice of Black identity/Blackness in positive (solution-oriented) ways as opposed to oppressive and dominating trends. Affirming a strong Black identity to challenge anti-Blackness is about a personal racialized embodiment (Dei, 2017, p. 77).

Unlearning Blackness

The fundamental understanding of learning is acquiring knowledge by instruction, experience, and observation. My reference to instruction expresses the primary objective of traditional colonial mechanisms to deny indigenous bodies' access to knowledge. For Dei (2017), it is "[t]hrough colonial and Eurocentric knowledge [that] Black bodies have been rendered homogenous. Coloniality highlights the lived realities of Black bodies being racialized based on assumptive inferiority and how this plays out into everyday interactions resulting in global power. We see this othering in Black bodies in all realms of life. From birth to death, the Black body is categorized, questioned, and disposed through time and across space. Our humanity has always been questioned" (p. 12). In addition, the evolution of colonial education and subjugation of colonized bodies became "embedded in a social structure designed to erode traditional knowledges and values. Colonial education succeeded in planting seeds for the expansion, growth, and sustainability of imperialism" (Wane, 2008, p. 185). By comparison, unlearning speaks of emptying the self of imposed epistemologies more specifically, dominant colonial narratives wherein Black and racialized bodies are dehumanized and vilified. Unlearning is "the anti-colonial struggle about body, mind, soul, and spirit . . . [f]or the Black body that is continually, consistently, and constantly shamed; to reclaim Blackness and Black identity the challenge is equally about pride," self-determination, and self-preservation (Dei, 2017, p. 1).

Unlearning speaks of changing the context of Blackness and shifting the widely accepted notion that Blackness and knowledges of Blackness originating from ancestral African thought must be eliminated, if not eradicated, from main educational discourses. Unlearning Blackness presents a binary in which Black bodies must antagonize the status quo that articulates a single narrative of Blackness as non-intellectual; unlearning requires dispelling the myths and dominant stereotypes of Black males as hypersexual and violent men.

Through reclaiming our African identity akin to our fragmented Indigenous knowledges, we unlearn Blackness as constructed and defined by colonial knowledge and dominant ideologies of race. In speaking of race, I am considering Dei (2017) when he states, "[T]he race concept was used to categorize people because of perceived differences of intelligence and physical prowess. An important justification for the enslavement of African peoples was that we were a sub-human species, like cattle. We supposedly did not have the same capacities for language, communication, and culture as our European oppressors" (p. 70). Unlearning Blackness is a resistive stance to piece together that which has been lost and violently fragmented by dominant European conquests to subvert and dehumanize Black bodies through cruel and harsh punishments with the barbaric institution of slave ownership. Unlearning our Blackness is the transitory process of transcending beyond the White imagination of the "socially constructed dominant understanding of Blackness as violent, criminal, deviant, and evil" (p. 71) and moving toward emancipatory practices of becoming with considerations to endless possibilities of new futures.

Unlearning Blackness requires the deliberate and ongoing action to empty the self of pre-existing colonial paradigms; unlearning Blackness is changing the content and context of conversations filled with anti-Black racism rhetoric and moving toward new knowledge(s) and practices, toward considering new realities. Unlearning Blackness is a freedom from preexisting Eurocentric ideologies of Blackness, dispelling myths of what it means to be Black in the Western world. Unlearning Blackness is moving in the direction of relearning because "[w]ithin the white world, there is an active political assertion that certain bodies, especially Black bodies, represent a homogenous social group in which degeneracy, criminality, destitution, illiteracy, immorality, and violence are part of their normative history, culture, and identity"; in addition, the Black body is "a fearsome and evil monster, a source of danger, a threat to white bodies, and therefore needed to be stopped and prevented from causing any havoc to white population" (Adjei, 2013, p. 35).

Unlearning Blackness in an educational context is the corporal refusal of Black students to accept the pre-scripted roles assigned to Black bodies in the classroom by the "rhetoric of white supremacy" to supply the "fantasy of Whiteness" (hooks, 1992, p. 340). Unlearning Blackness speaks of "[r]upturing the myths that [are] utilized to pathologize Black communities, when it comes to issues of education of our children" (Ilmi, 2011, p. 221). For hooks (1992), unlearning Blackness is deconstructing stereotypes that propagate the notion that Blackness speaks to "the Other who is subjugated, who is subhuman, lacks the ability to comprehend, to understand, to see the working of the powerful" (p. 340). This inability to comprehend and understand often plays out in the White imagination, subsequently maintaining colonial structures. Unfortunately, Black students (predominantly males) subconsciously accept the assigned roles assumed in the White imagination and often accept these socially constructed roles. For Dei (2017), "The truth about Blackness is that it is consequential, complex, contested, and yet affirming. A critical scholarship on Blackness is, and must be, about anti-racist practice, and particularly resistance to anti-Black racism, as well as, the pursuit of decolonial and anti-colonial praxis. There are implications for the study of Blackness as 'living knowledge' about ourselves, our histories, cultures, and identities" (p. 3).

In unlearning Blackness, I speak of knowledge decolonization and refusal to accept the roles assigned to Black bodies from dominant narratives. My daily interactions with Black students in the classroom and the halls grant me access to their lived experiences.

My teaching career in the secondary panel gives me a firsthand account of Black students (more specifically males) buying into and accepting the notion that their Blackness equals laziness, unintelligence, inability to learn and therefore must maintain what I refer to as hallway culture. In the paradigm of hallway culture, many Black students maintain a nomadic existence, wandering through the halls rather than going to their designated classes. In my travels through the halls, it is quite easy for dominant bodies to dismiss Black students' nomadic tendencies of hallway culture. Rather than circumvent hallway culture, implicit biases dictate the disengagement of White teachers to propagate Black students feeding on regurgitated Eurocentric ideologies to sustain the need for the class clown, the underachiever, the one who is always late for class, the one who skips, the one who takes physical education classes and not academic-based courses. Black students are coerced to implicitly learn:

> [b]y perceiving Blacks as not Whites[;] Blackness is 'justifiably' equated with darkness, laziness, dirt, and criminality while Whiteness is about light, purity, innocence, and cleanliness. Blackness becomes repulsive, unwelcoming and hostile, while Whiteness is attractive, welcoming and friendly. Such binary notions are not innocent practices. It allows for a discursive space and positioning of Black [ness] as terror in the White imagination. (Dei, 2017, p. 72)

The convergence and divergence of my Blackness within the White imagination mobilizes me to acknowledge the necessity of (re)connecting and (re)animating African memories.

My reference to memory focuses on the "recollection of someone or something; awareness, consciousness" (Online Etymology Dictionary, n.d.). For Beatrice Culleton Mosionier (2008), "memories are" elusive, fleeting, like a butterfly that touches down and is free until it is caught. Others haunting: you'd rather forget them, but they won't be forgotten. And some are always there. No matter where you are, they are there too. I always felt most memories were better avoided, but now I think it's best to go back in my life before I go forward" (p. 1). In articulating the lived experiences of Black students, I propose reconnecting the misremembered and the fragmented images of an authentic present. There is an ongoing dialogue with the present as an antecedent to conceptualizing an anticipated future. In our re-collective experience, we manipulate and negotiate our cultural and ethnic identity, our sense memories accessed through hearing Indigenous stories to reconstruct autobiographical narratives void of the dominant paradigm. Our memories position us within a polarized space where we encounter a going to and coming from; our current experiences in and of themselves confide in the past; subsequently, our imagined self alters within the current space of becoming. In seeking to acquire cohesion within our polarized memory-space, we construct a schema of memory that encapsulates events that tie our lived experiences together.

Our life story and memories interconnect narratives that are selectively strung together within our Blackness. For Conway (2005), memory is "a major component of the self . . . memories may be altered, distorted, even fabricated, to support current aspects of the self" (p. 595). These "altered, distorted, even fabricated" memories become the catalyst for disremembering wherein failure to remember our Blackness originating from African Indigenous knowledges renders members of the African Diaspora virtually catatonic. Misremembering is the opposite in that Blackness is imperfectly remembered. For Conway:

> coherence is a strong force in human memory that acts at encoding, post-encoding, and re-encoding, to shape both the accessibility of memories and the accessibility of their content. This is done in such a way as to make memory consistent with an individual's current goals, self-images, and self-beliefs. Thus, memory and central aspects of the self form a coherent system in which the healthy individual, beliefs about, and knowledge of, the self are confirmed and supported by memories of specific experiences. (p. 595)

In hindsight, we are perpetually accessing, creating, and recreating memories simultaneously with the past, present, and imagined future to circumvent the internal and external dilemma of unlearning our Blackness. In addition, memory should be considered "not as an ability to revive accurately impressions once obtained, but as the integration into the whole personality and their revival according to the needs of the whole personality" (p. 595). Turning toward defining memory within the framework of African-Caribbean bodies Stuart Hall (1990) states that memory is:

> the retention of old customs, the retention of cultural traits from Africa; customs and traditions which were retained in and through slavery, in plantation, in religion, partly in language, in folk customs, in music, in dance, in all those forms of expressive culture which allowed men and women to survive the trauma of slavery. Nevertheless, in everyday life, in so far as it was possible, maintaining subterranean link with what was often called "the other Caribbean," the Caribbean that was not recognized, that could not speak, that had no official records, no official account of its own transportation, no official histories, but nevertheless that oral life which maintained an umbilical connection with the Africa homeland and culture. (p. 7)

Memory for African-Caribbean Canadian Diaspora is an ongoing process of deconstructing imposed Eurocentric ideologies to (re)construct representations of an imagined self within a larger education and social context. The African-Caribbeans engage with their past, present, and future and consider "the representations of the conceptual self" that are "socially constructed schema and categories that define the self, other people, and typical interactions with others and the surrounding world. These schema and categories are drawn largely from the influences of familial and peer socialization, schooling, and religion, as well as the stories, fairytales, myths, and media influences that are constitutive of an individual's particular culture" (p. 597). The goal of unlearning Blackness is to reconsider the images represented in our memory as the building blocks to reconstruct an identity akin or rather affixed to African Indigenous knowledges. These "self-images are mental models of the self in relation to past, current, and future goals and form part of the conceptual self" (p. 600). Memories situate us within specific cultural, ethnic, and social narratives; "each individual has a set of 'self-defining' memories which contain critical knowledge of progress on the attainment of long-term goals" (p. 600). It is plausible to affirm that memories are analogous to knowledge of our Blackness.

Knowledge connotes a global awareness of the self within educational and social contexts; it constructs internal and external self-awareness, produces familiarities with people, places, and objects through direct and indirect experience(s). Our etiology of knowledge is interconnected to different learning possibilities demarcated by hegemonic narratives and dominant power structures. Knowledge in itself underscores the innate functions of our senses, giving us a glimpse into the sense images akin to personal narratives constructed and reconstructed by memory; it is therefore plausible to consider the implications of knowledge as specified concepts affecting unlearning our Blackness. In unlearning our Blackness, "[w]e resist continually, and we become subjects and agents of our own history. But we must recognize the power of the colonial dominant" (Dei, 2017, p. 4). In unlearning our Blackness, we move from an abstract and intangible understanding of the *self* to tangible representations of fragmented and interconnected images. Furthermore, knowledge as an acquisition propositions a return to these fragmented and interconnected mental images to recover and reconstruct these sense images into representations of the self. The recreation and reformation of the mental images positions us to consider an etiology of our knowledge wherein Hall (1990) states:

> Africa was in fact present everywhere: in the everyday life and customs of the slave quarters, in the languages and patois of the plantations, in the names and words, often disconnected from their taxonomies, in the secret syntactical structures through which other languages were spoken, in the stories and tales told to children, in religious practices and beliefs, post-emancipation society. Africa, the signified which could not be represented directly in slavery, remained and remains the unspoken, unspeakable 'presence' in Caribbean culture. It is 'hiding' behind every verbal inflection, every narrative twist of Caribbean cultural life. It is the secret code with which every Western text was 're-read.' It is the ground-bass of every rhythm

> and bodily movement. This was-is-the 'Africa' that 'is alive and well in the diaspora. (p. 230)

Furthermore, Hall (1990) understands Caribbean knowledge when he states:

> I don't want to speak about the nature of this rupture, with much of the population wrenched from their own cultures and inserted into the cultures of the colonizing plantation relations of slavery. I don't want to talk about the trauma of transportation, of the breaking up of linguistic and tribal and familial groups. I don't want to talk about the brutal aftermath of Indian indenture. I simply want to say that in the histories of the migration, forced or free, of peoples who now compose the populations of these societies, whose cultural traces are everywhere intermingled with one other, there is always the stamp of historical violence and rupture. (p. 6)

For Fanon (1967) his knowledge of himself is:

> [a] slow composition of myself as a body in the middle of a spatial and temporal world—such seems to be the schema. It does not impose itself on me; it is, rather, a definitive structuring of the self and of the world—definitive because it creates a real dialectic between my body and the world. All I wanted was to be a man among other men. I wanted to come lithe and young into the world that was ours and to help to build it together. I wanted to be a man, nothing but a man. Some identified me with ancestors of mine who had been enslaved or lynched: I decided to accept this. It was on the universal level of the intellect that I understood this inner kinship—I was the grandson of slaves. (pp. 112–113)

In addition, it is essential to consider the possible implications of the African-Caribbean Canadian's colonial/post-colonial knowledge in relation to unlearning Blackness. The unrelenting plight of the African-Caribbean Canadian constitutes an ongoing tension of coming and going within converging and diverging colonial narratives. These narratives interlocking and intersecting subsequently garner implicit knowledge (knowledge implied and often hidden); according to Roberts (2008):

> [W]hen Europeans began to write about the New World, they already had an exotic vision of people, places, things and events elsewhere that had been formed by Greek mythology and beliefs about 'the Indies.' Colonial societies in the Caribbean were artificial, in the sense that they were imposed on the land and controlled from outside. In addition, the islands themselves seemed to have encouraged movement, nomadic and migratory, even before

> the advent of Columbus. Thereafter, though rigid systems remained in place, the rate of population replacement was consistently high, especially where sugar and slavery thrived. (pp. 2–3).

In comparison, Hall (1990) argues that explicit knowledge (knowledge easily transmitted to others by observation or verbalization) positions the African-Caribbean Canadian to "belong to the marginal, the underdeveloped, the periphery, the 'Other.' We are at the outer edge, the 'rim,' of the metropolitan world—always 'South' to someone else's El Norte. The common history—transportation, slavery, colonization—has been profoundly formative. For all these societies, unifying us across our differences. But it does not constitute a common origin, since it was, metaphorically as well as literally, a translation" (p. 228). In other words, African-Caribbean Canadian's encounters are framed within an ongoing process of deciphering implicit and explicit knowledge of their colonial/post-colonial past in conjunction with unlearning our blackness through deconstructing hegemonic narratives imposed on members of the African Diaspora.

Conclusion

From the foregoing discussion, it becomes plausible that by nature humanity is inherently complex with intersecting metanarratives of Blackness. Subsequently, unlearning our Blackness will "encourage creative, Indigenous ways of knowing, teaching and learning to flourish via curriculum and language adapted for each indigenous community created and sustained by its members" (Wane, 2008, p. 195). As such, this discussion seeks to generate further interrogative pedagogical practices toward unlearning our Blackness within anti-colonial education in the 21st-century classroom, creating spaces for African-Caribbean Canadian students to unapologetically articulate their voice(s). Considering this, "I believe that it is imperative we as a society not only ask critical questions about why society assigns racial hierarchies and that we also collectively demand our rights, armed with the power of ideas and hope for humanity from an anti-colonial/ anti-racist angle" (Ilmi, 2011, p. 219). Therefore, it is imperative that we consider a paradigm shift in an education system that dismantles anti-Black racism practices, legitimizing multiple entry points of knowledge production, by acknowledging the lived experiences of Black and racialized bodies in the classroom. Seeing Blackness through indigenous prisms of knowing circumvents colonial legacies, consequently refracting the single dominant narrative of Black and racialized bodies and giving space for multiple centers of knowing. When considering a pedagogy of possibilities, I propose the following: What are the implications, antecedents, and intersectionalities associated with the politics, process, and practice of unlearning our Blackness within the framework of circumventing anti-Black racism in education? I trust that this discussion offered insight to and created space for discussing, conceptualizing, and unlearning our Blackness within the framework of anti-colonial and anti-racist education. I believe Black resistance against violent epistemologies (taking a BRAVE stance) will trouble the whole notion that Blackness is to be pushed aside for a widely propagated and accepted hegemonic narrative that bestows social benefits on the dominant while simultaneously oppressing Black bodies. Unlearning Blackness is essentially unlearning Eurocentric ways of knowing in favor of constructing and celebrating Blackness.

References

Adjei, P. B. (2013). When Blackness Shows up Uninvited: Examining the Murder of Trayvon Martin through Fanonian Racial Interpellation." In. G. J. S. Dei & M. Lordan (Eds.), *Contemporary Issues in the Sociology of Race and Ethnicity: A Critical Reader.* New York, NY: Peter Lang.

Cole, D. (2015, April 21). The Skin I'm In: I've Been Interrogated by Police More Than 50 times—All because I'm Black. *Toronto Life.* Retrieved from https://torontolife.com/city/life/skin-im-ive-interrogated-police-50-times-im-black/

Conway, M. A. (2005). Memory and the Self. *Journal of Memory and Language, 53*(4), 594–628.

Dei, George J. Sefa. (2017). Reframing Blackness and Black Solidarities through Anti-colonial and Decolonial Prisms. 10.1007/978-3-319-53079-6.

Fanon, F. (1967). *Black Skin, White Masks.* New York, NY: Grove Press.

Garcia, N. M. (2018). You Don't Look Like a Professor. *Diverse.* Retrieved from http://diverseeducation.com/article/113239/

Hall, S. (1990). Cultural Identity and Diaspora. In J. Rutherford (Ed.), *Identity: Community, Culture, Difference* (pp. 222–237). London, UK: Lawrence & Wishart.

Hitchcock, S. (2017). The Ubiquitous Trauma of Blackness. *Black Excellence.* Retrieved from https://blackexcellence.com/the-ubiquitous-trauma-of-blackness/

hooks, b. (1992). Representing Whiteness in the Black Imagination. In L. Grossberg, C. Nelson, and P.A. Treichler (Eds.), *Cultural Studies* (pp. 338–346). New York, NY: Routledge.

Ien, M. (2018, February 26). The Double Standard of Driving While Black—in Canada. *The Globe and Mail.* Retrieved from https://www.theglobeandmail.com/opinion/driving-while-black-in-canada/article38107157/

Ilmi, A. (2011). The White Gaze vs. the Black Soul. *Race, Gender & Class, 18*(3/4), 217–229.

Ladson-Billings, G. (1998). Just What is Critical Race Theory and What's It Doing in a "Nice" Field Like Education?. *International Journal of Qualitative Studies in Education 11*(1), 7–24.

Mosionier, B. (2008). *In search of April Raintree.* Winnipeg, Canada: Portage & Main.

Omi, M., & Winant, H. (1993). On the Theoretical Concept of Race. In C. McCarthy, W. Crichlow, G. Dimitriadis, and N. Dolby (Eds.), *Race Identity and Representation in Education* (pp. 3–10). New York, NY: Routledge.

Online Etymology Dictionary. (n.d.). *Memory.* Retrieved from https://www.etymonline.com/word/memory

Roberts, P.A. (2011). *Roots of Caribbean Identity.* Cambridge University Press.

Schick, C. (2010). Whatever Happened to Anti-Racist Education? In C. Smith (Ed.), *Anti-Racism in Education: Missing in Action* (pp. 47–58). Alberta, Canada: Canadian Centre for Policy Alternatives.

Sharpe Silverthorne, M. (2018, June 11). "Implicit Bias": The Problem and How to Interrupt It. Plus, the Beads Test. *Chicago Tribune*. Retrieved from http://www.chicagotribune.com/news/opinion/commentary/ct-perspec-black-white-families-implicit-bias-0611-story.html

Wane, N. (2003). Anti-Racism in Teacher Education. *Orbit* [Special issue], *33*(3), 6–9.

Wane, N. N. (2008). Mapping the Field of Indigenous Knowledges in Anti-Colonial Discourse: A Transformative Journey in Education. *Journal of Race Ethnicity and Education, 11*(2), 183–197.

CHAPTER 8

The Black Woman Who Has Learned to Fear Herself: An Inquiry of the Myth of the Angry Black Woman

KE'SHANA DANVERS

"African women in general need to know that it's OK for them to be the way they are— to see the way they are as a strength, and to be liberated from fear and from silence."

—WANGARI MAATHAI

A MYTH IS a false, but commonly held ideology or belief. When the homogenizing narrative of the angry Black woman is taken up, or theorized, it is often contested as a myth; as simply untrue. However, I argue that this needs greater exploration. The label of the angry Black woman contains ugly falsehoods, but that Black women are angry, or that they can be, or have the right to be, does have merit.

The widespread discourse of the Black woman as inherently angry has long acted as a trope that has synthesized Black womanhood into the unpolitical and the unwomanly. The narrative of the *angry Black woman,* as coopted by White supremacist projects, is one that is rife with perversions and distortions. The attitude bred by colonialism, in which desirability resides in homogeneous Whiteness, strengthened through the privileging of synthetic social likenesses, has required the peripherizing of Black women. Without consent, the Black woman's body is used for the purpose of fulfilling the message of White purity and centricity. More wicked, still, is the internalization of these falsehoods by

Black women who have become a conduit of its ubiquitous discourse. This Black woman has learned to fear even the mere relationship with the anger itself, and with the idea of anger and Blackness. The label makes attempts at the removal of Black women's subjectivity toward essentialism, which facilitates the denial of human status for Black women and also removes available agency. As such, I ask how the angry Black woman—who is and has been implicated in the realization of various Black politics—can effectively be depoliticized? In considering the implication of Black women in these processes, narratives attempting to dispel the "myth" of the angry Black woman serve as another means by which Black women have been made responsible for educating others out of their ignorance. We must perform the physical, psychological, and emotional labor of meeting White supremacy where it is and subsequently engage it in discourses and actions that draw it away from itself. In this performance, which ends in the Black woman disassociating herself from herself, there has been a lessening of the naturalness of who we are to gain greater access to, and acceptance from, what and who we are not. Would our time not be better spent healing what has been internalized, to then liberate us from the colonial and from the tropism of *angry Black womanhood*?

Colonial logic has made rational Black women blame themselves for valid emotional responses and for crimes perpetrated against our bodies. That said, there is collective action that we as Black women, who cannot, and do not, stay victim bound, must take. Though the *angry Black woman* is a trope that has disseminated the ghettoizing of the Black woman to reduce political action and to support the denial of her womanhood, a critical engagement of the implication of the Black woman in these progressions is also required. In this chapter, I conceptualize the *angry Black woman* as a trope that attempts to depoliticize, invalidate, and defeminize the Black woman. The argument here is not that Black women are not angry, but that Black women are angry and that that anger is not unfounded, irrational, or misplaced; further, that there is a political and productive basis for that rage and that it is engaged practically, and that finally, it is not the sum or crux of Black womanhood, but an essential response to coloniality and pervasive White supremacist violence. Simply put: The Black woman is angry; more than that, she *should* be.

This work extends my scholarship concerning Black masculine representations of Black womanhood. In writing this, it is imperative that I speak of my entry point into this conversation. A comprehensive mindfulness of one's positionality is critical in hopes of preserving the honesty of this work. I am an Afro-Jamaican woman, born and raised in the colonial state of Canada. To challenge Canada's misleading civil rights narratives, it is critical that I acknowledge the land. The long-standing view of Canada as an ahistorical state has made acceptable the continued denial of Indigeneity for its Indigenous peoples. This denial also maintains White normalcy and dominance (Montgomery, 2005). I do not align myself with the colonial settler project and negotiate my position in this settler state, both as a physical and psychological status. Peoples of African descent were forcibly brought as enslaved subjects to provide slave labor for peoples living in Canada

(Donovan, 2014; Rouillard, 2007). My presence on this land can be viewed as physical occupation; however, I do not willingly operate within the colonial framework. While I do not contextualize myself as a settler, given the complexities of Black life within colonial realities, it does not mean that I do not have responsibilities to the Indigenous peoples of this land. As *Canadians,* we should all consider how we are wrapped up in the impacts of colonialism, particularly in the context of Turtle Island. As Dua (2008) explains, we cannot claim we are doing anti-racist work without engaging a precedence of what is anti-colonial, especially as we do this work on stolen land. Thus, racialized people have responsibilities to resist coloniality and colonialism in this space. As such, my coalition politics must prioritize African and Turtle Island Indigenous solidarities and relations due to our shared and interrelated histories. Thus, it is with an anti-colonial, anti-Black racist, and Black feminist discursive framework that I undertake this topic. Black bodies within Canada have occupied positions of absence within the colonial state (McKittrick, 2006; Walcott, 2001). This erasure of Black presence is indicative of the purposefulness of the colonial project to whiteout Black peoples from Canadian histories and imaginaries, thus making us rootless and furthermore binding our visibility to the position of immigrant (Walcott, 2003). Black civil rights movements are often placed exclusively within the United States, a misconception that is uncontended by the White Canadian hegemony. It maintains a falsified harmony, which has been crafted through our *celebration of multiculturalism*. Wane (2002) speaks to the importance of using our critical works to challenge the distorted histories and the realities of our peoples. Black women living in Canadian society live with the imposition of White patriarchal racism, historically and contemporarily. Within Canada, Black women struggle against silencing and invisibility due to the constant centering of Whiteness within the Black woman's representations (Wane, 2018). The assignment of Black women to the extremes of the spectrum is how White supremacy continues to decenter the Black woman in her own narratives and steals her ability to self-identify. Our *good* Canadian society has profited from the suffering of Black women, both historically and presently. While both can be examined, I will engage the historical as a means of further situating racism as part of the foundation of Canadian society, which then leads to the demand to undo what has become fundamentally systemic and institutional. It is my hope that I can contribute to theorization that offers a counter narrative, that pushes back against the nationally upheld misconception of Canada as a racially harmonious state that has not been, and is not, an anti-Black state. As such, in advancing what has been excluded, I will be exploring the idea of the *angry Black woman,* relying on the theorization of Black Canadian intellectuals, Black feminist/womanist thinkers, and anti-racist scholars.

The representation of the Black woman has undergone and undergoes a mythologizing that has left her in a position where her multiple, possible, and true presentations are ever compromised. The Black woman, in contemporary society, is read from the gaze of Whiteness—fundamentally through that of White supremacy—but also through the lens of patriarchy. While I speak of the *angry Black woman* and the White supremacist processes that seek to depoliticize and masculinize her (in the negative) so as to alienate her from the *human*, it is important to also reflect on the implication of Black manhood. Black men are implicated through patriarchy, sometimes referenced as *misogynoir*, as it is not necessarily a White invention. However, Black women in society being read as the doom of Black men, through masculinization, is a White supremacist construction in the metanarrative of Black familial dysfunction. In "Complicit Victims," Roulliard (2007) speaks to this proclivity that has dominated research:

> bell hooks cautions us, however, against being like some "contemporary feminists [who] tend to act as though black male sexism is more heinous than white male sexism." The goal in this comparison is not to suggest that one expression of racism or sexism is worse than the other. Rather, it is to illustrate that just as racism plays out its fantasy of white superiority on the backs of black women, sexism also uses black women's bodies to demonstrate male (black and white) superiority. (p. 1102, internal citations omitted)

Within research, we too must avoid distraction. The question of patriarchy does not avoid them, and certainly the masculinization of the Black woman would result in her becoming more akin to Black "malehood." Thus, we must interrogate the question of masculinity and gendered relations. That said, an exploration of the masculinizing of the Black woman does not equate to working within a dichotomy whereby there exists absolute maleness and absolute femaleness. Such juxtaposition is a Western propensity. The Western framework has made it so that nothing can exist outside of a binary composition. Even within the periphery, it has become normal to name what is from what it is not and then take up these differences as deficit. The so-called maleness of Black women has also been held up as the reason (or cause) for which Black men have become emasculated. Furthermore, this maleness has also been cited as the root of disruption within the Black family. It is from the evil nature of colonial agendas that a façade has been crafted, wherein Blacks are illustrated as being largely responsible for the divergences in their gender-conforming (and nonconforming) relationships. On the flipside, certain arguments have concretized the dichotomy and the disjunction by then placing responsibility on Black men, asserting that it is they who have followed the schema of White patriarchal racism, which has assigned the woman to subordinate positions (Wallace, 1979). This is irresponsible. Access to power and legitimated ways of knowing are gendered and racialized based on a priori privilege, which constructs systems of power that serve to determine who has the privilege to access spaces such as research (Simpson, 2007). The privileges created from colonialism have given particular persons the ability to control what can and should be said and about who, both in academic circles and beyond. As such, research has reproduced pathologized communities by only allowing the Black woman to speak her narrative in a particular way (hooks, 1990b; Tuck & Yang, 2014a, 2014b). If we continue to refuse the way in which our stories are researched and published, there is space to disrupt the reproduction of the "metanarrative of damaged communities and White progress" (Tuck & Yang, 2014b, p. 231). Therefore, I refuse to make this an issue of *this* or *that*. This is on its own. The Black woman is the Black woman, the Black man is the Black man, and White supremacy is and always is White supremacy. Here, there is no inherent opposite that subsists and no colonial gaze to commodify the pain and stories of the subaltern (Tuck & Yang, 2014b).

In speaking to the Black woman, and at times alluding to the Black man, and in recognizing the gaps that exist within this work, it is important that I acknowledge that these two groupings speak to what is included, but more saliently it speaks to what has been excluded. The use of the pronouns *he* and *she*, rather than the gender-neutral *they*, is not meant to erase the identity relevance of gender diverse persons from this dialogue that concerns the masculinizing of Black women (Thorpe, 2015). As a piece of work related to gender-conforming roles, it is my responsibility as the writer to bring matters of inclusivity to the forefront to maintain the integrity of the work. This is not an omission that is meant to cause harm or discursive violence, rather an investigation of the Western propensity to control the image of the femme-presenting Black woman in order to reestablish dominance within social hierarchy (Kiesling, 2017). What is understood as gender and the colonial binary that has been constructed from it requires much undoing, as does the socialized characteristics that we are bonded to and allow ourselves to be bonded to for group acceptance purposes. The White supremacist project has long used gender as a means of securing a perceived dominant. The notion of being a masculine woman is simply false as masculine is a determinant of manufactured social ideologies and images that are in fact not real. However, these falsehoods have been the operational standard by which we have functioned and thus must indeed be taken up as very real.

In this chapter, I question how processes of White supremacy and patriarchy inform the way that the Black woman's body has come to be identified. White supremacy has spoken to the Black woman's ability to act within the political, while White patriarchy has excluded the Black woman from womanhood. I will argue how the trope of the *angry Black woman* has been used as a tool to convince the Black woman to supress her anger in order to depoliticize her and rob her of her humanity. As such, I assign the *angry Black woman* to the White supremacist trope, while the angry Black woman (without italics) calls on the truth. Exploring the mythologizing of the Black woman and speaking to the benefit of embracing the angry Black woman, I begin by grounding the angry Black woman in Canada through an engagement of Marie Josèphe Angelique's life. I will then explore how Black women have been standardized within womanhood, as well as look at how the label and the image of the angry Black woman have worked to blame the Black woman for her circumstances. I will speak about the instructional and pedagogical implications for the angry Black woman in and out of educational spaces and conclude with an engagement of the respectability politics, which have made Black women do the White supremacist work. In all of this, my key objective is to explore how the ability to self-identify contributes to *the angry Black woman* and to understand how this process can be used to liberate the Black woman toward a Black womanhood where anger is considered a legitimate response to coloniality and its associated violence.

Counternarratives of Black women, such as Marie-Josèphe Angélique, confirm the enduring subjugation of the Black woman's body within Canada. White Canadian history narrates that Angélique, who had a record as a runaway, set fire and burnt down most of what is known as Old Montreal in 1734 (Cooper, 2006; McKittrick, 2006). It is alleged that she did this as a means of covering her tracks during an attempt for freedom. One wonders why a woman who is trying to escape enslavement would conceal her path by something as conspicuous as fire. It cannot be ignored the possibility of cooptation, which supports the false legacy of Canada as a refuge. Angélique's existence in that space was used to grow a particular narrative of Blackness and that of the Black woman. There is a meticulous and natural centeredness of Whiteness, which focalizes White passions, synonymous with goodness and viewpoints. There is a blatant overlooking of the fact that Angélique was enslaved, rather a pervasive centeredness on her "crime," which is abusive to White goodness. How dare this Black woman cause harm to her White dominants who wanted nothing but to see her delivered from herself. The probability of her purposeful politicization is quickly stripped and renounced, and she is reduced to a reckless arsonist. The story is told in such a way that justifies her torture, conviction, and subsequent hanging. What if we considered that her actions were a manifestation of her anger? What if Angélique was an angry Black woman? She was an enslaved woman. Need more be said to warrant her anger? In *The Uses of Anger*, Lorde (1981) speaks to the validity of anger:

> Women responding to [injustice] means women responding to anger; the anger of exclusion, of unquestioned privilege, of racial distortions, of silence, ill-use, stereotyping, defensiveness, misnaming, betrayal and co-optation. (p. 278)

I must note that though Canada has sought boundlessly to deny its deep participation in the institution of slavery and its practice within Canada, here Canada is willing to admit its involvement to avoid having Angelique's actions be associated with personal political actionizing. What if her arson was the product of her politics? Angélique had a history of fleeing for freedom, so how is it that her incendiarism as resistance has been made implausible by White Canadian historical accounts? Angélique's account follows the societal practice that controls the labeling and imagery of the Black woman's actions. There is an unashamed indifference toward the multitude of injustices that the Black woman is subjected to; the crimes of White supremacy are whitened. Angélique's "crime" is as a result deemed an unjustifiable act of disorder, while the root is unsourced. Further, if anyone dare align her actions with the political, conveniently a White man named Claude is present for purposes of accompliceship (Cooper, 2006). Angélique's story is one of many that speaks to the way White Canada has made attempts at the removal of the Black woman from the realm of the political (Collins, 2009). As with the *angry Black woman*, certain knowledges about the Black woman have been normalized. Who can be charged for the normalization of these knowledges and who are the beneficiaries of these same propagated knowledges?

The *angry Black woman* is not an issue of feelings. White supremacy does not operate from such a place. The *angry Black woman* is a whitewashing of the lack of humanity that White supremacy has and continues to inflict on the Black woman's body. The Black woman's anger is often elicited by feelings of powerlessness, fearfulness, oppression, and injustice. So, if she has been taught to repudiate that anger—those feelings—and the Black woman who in reality embodies and experiences these very feelings, then it can be propagated that they are not being felt, but irrationally imagined, giving us the nature of the trope. This teaching convinces the Black woman to suppress or deny her anger because ultimately her reaction will allow her to be labeled as an *angry Black woman* whose actions are always deemed unprovoked and unrooted. Coloniality, which is completely responsible for the creation and recreation of the *angry Black woman*, therefore cannot be held accountable for the triggering of the angry Black woman because these Black women have learned not to react. This fragmented means of taking up the angry Black woman has made Black women appear unreasonable and continued the narrative of the ill-tempered. Anger does not act singularly; rather, it functions in response to, and has been denied as such in relation to the Black woman. The homogenizing narrative refuses to take up the oppressions of Black women's anger as valid, which facilitates the removal of accountability from the White subject. We cannot continue to pick up at random points and decide that this shall be the site from which we begin to dissect an issue; by this notion the liable are continually acquitted. There must be a deliberate movement from the reactions toward the causes. This begins with uncovering White supremacy, which finds itself at the base of our oppressive society—and "finds" because it has always gone where it was not invited. When the angry Black woman begins to operate outside of systems of oppressions, she is pictured as unjustified and her continued rejection is made justifiable within social spaces. However, the spirit, and not the social, is a separate condition that ultimately must be answered to. There has been a very strategic attempt to rob the Black woman of her femininity, which serves as an insidious justification for the omission of her experiences.

Anger suggests expression, which is not afforded to the Black woman. The hierarchical ranking of the White woman, who is regarded as the epitome of womanhood, has defined the cultural construct of what it means to be a real woman, as standardized by White patriarchal passions. Fanon (1967) speaks of "the Negro, [who] is full of rage because he feels small, he suffers from an inadequacy in all human communication, and all these factors chain him with an unbearable insularity" (p. 35). Due to our socialization, we stray from the title of angry Black woman because it has been made into the direct opposite image of the gentle White woman, which has become the prevailing right woman since colonialism. The value systems in womanhood, which include the value of certain emotions as expressed by certain women, have rendered the Black woman without access or representation in this feminine space. We are exiled to the margins, fighting the whole way to be accepted into a realm that was not made for us. The application of Western standards to non-Western women has been a means in which systems of Whiteness have reified the ideology that the Black woman is somehow less fitting for womanly features (Spalek, 2005). Black women have been measured within hierarchies that have structurally ensured our lack of competition every time. I am, as a Black woman, to internalize a desire to conform and mirror that of the White woman, while always knowing my place as never being able to achieve it and also dare not believe that I ever could—and so my unbelongingness is reified. What does this mean for the Black woman's emotional and psychological state? The emotional labor that this creates for the Black woman is a ubiquitous performity to be accepted into a framework that has never and will never picture her (Neville, 2001). There is sometimes an instinctive response by Black women to perform in a way that dissipates how they believe and know their bodies are being read. Wane (2002) speaks of the "need to take an inventory of the traces of colonialism that remain within us" (p. 192), as Black women, in order to circumvent the use of our bodies as a reproduction of coloniality. We take this inventory by engaging processes that allow us constantly to question the body and self (Fanon, 1967). If this is not done, the angry Black woman is lost and the Black woman who is seeking to fit into the margins of society steps back into her proverbial place, not understanding that her place is in the margins and she must learn to operate from there.

Particular women have been selected and allotted the internal and external spaces to act and react to their circumstances, the White woman taking up the majority of this plot. Hierarchically, it has been made more legitimate for certain bodies of women to cry louder than others in their attempts toward justice. This legitimization has created a fear within the Black woman, which convinces her that her anger and subsequent action is a threat to herself. And so, she flees from the notion. She is correct in her sensibility; her anger can lead to cooptation, criminalization, and marginalization—but have all these things not been committed to us regardless of being angry? So why not resist? Did Viola Desmond not act in her feelings of powerlessness and injustice to create political and social reformation? Lorde (1981) so eloquently captures this ideal when she writes:

> For it is not the anger of Black women which is dripping down over the globe like a diseased liquid. . . . It is not the anger of Black women which corrodes into blind, dehumanizing power, bent upon the annihilation of us all unless we meet it with what we have, our power to examine and to redefine the terms upon which we will live and work; our power to envision and to reconstruct. (p. 285)

Black women, we cannot fear ourselves, for we are not the real source of terror. The *angry Black woman* has been wielded as a tool to provoke fear within society, but also within us. It is difficult to engage with Black women who do not see the power and legitimacy of being an angry Black woman. Validly, who would run toward the idea of embracing that which is reviled? But when has the angry Black woman not moved us forward? Lorde speaks to a power that anger engages, which realizes political and social reformation, highlighting the collective "Black women" as the carriers of this power. There is a responsibility that extends beyond the individual to attain the collectivity necessary to reclaim the individual and collective Black woman identity.

It is critical that language politics, and the social power dynamics therein that legitimize Whiteness in such a way that privileges it the ability to create truths of whatever it names, be considered. Language has been used as a tool of control over the Black woman's body and, as such, many have theorized on the controlling labels and images of Black women (Collins, 2009; Norwood, 2013; Spalek, 2005). In *More Myth than History: American Culture and Representations of the Black Female's Athletic Ability,* Vertinsky and Captain (1998) speak to history's seduction to control the image of the Black woman into a space which only produces what is negative:

> Historical interpretations or distortions of the [Black] female's past have thus functioned to perpetuate a set of cultural images which together have shaped a composite picture of black women as both damaging and unwomanly. (p. 542)

When studying the Black woman as the *angry Black woman,* there is often a deliberate separation of the label and image from its context. Why is the Black woman unremittingly labelled angry without consideration of what or who is making her angry? The answer would reveal the intentions of the White hegemonic project that publicizes controlling labels and images that remove Black women from womanhood, to make of us a monolith that holds no definition outside of what White supremacy has given it. It cannot be neglected how the label, which is the language, makes the image, the Black woman, have salience. Whiteness provides an uncontested truth to whatever it names. It is only when the adjective is associated with particular social classifications that it is deemed unacceptable. The terror of Whiteness that has reigned over Black women has meant our ghettoization for the means of political control and further quelling to serve the interests of the elite White male (Collins, 2000; hooks, 1997). It is through tropes such as the *angry Black woman* that this has been achieved. Black women have been subjected to the generational rebirth of a subwoman status, made unfit for the normalcy of feeling, for fear that it lessens White power. In this power struggle, there is an introduction of a dichotomy between anger and power. Anger is not measured as a valid emotion, especially for those who are being oppressed (Fanon, Bhabha, Philcox, & Sartre, 2004). This dichotomy is crafted to make bad whatever is done in response to that which holds and uses the power, the power always being made synonymous with good. And so, White supremacy can safely go on acting bad while presenting good, always being accredited with acting with the Whitest and purest of intentions, while Blackness, which attempts to simply be and live, presents as threatening with the most deviant of plans. Anger is regarded as unacceptable and having no place within polite society and therefore needs to be controlled. Anger brings exposure to the dynamic that one group is affecting power over another, revealing that the given society operates according to social constructs, which in an essentialist society such as Canada's cannot be exposed. Because society operates in constant consideration of the elite White man's interests, it must be queried how the *angry Black woman* serves the interest of the White male elite. In order to best serve the interests of this group, it has been made impermissible for Black women to be practicing citizens who are lawfully allowable to practice political agency. At all levels, Black women are called to operate within a space they have no business working within or with. The colonial paradigm has built a wall that has pushed Black women to the margins. This wall has been strengthened in part by the misrepresenting of the female Black body. It is recognized that gender, in the way we know it now, is a socially constructed binary that was birthed out of colonialism, and therefore we can acknowledge that all that is gendered requires problematizing and is inherently illusory. The Black woman has been treated in such a way that does not even allow her to exist according to the standards of imposed colonialism, and so how does that speak to her social value? More, there has been an unfortunate adoption of the *angry Black woman* by people who are non-Black women, which furthers the valuelessness of the Black woman and the inevitable irrationality chained to her anger.

The trope of the *angry Black woman* shows itself as well in the education space by "the educated Black bitch" (Collins, 2005). I speak of the educational space because it is an incredible site of violence for the angry Black woman. Educational spaces have always served as a generational rebirth of status quos. In *Black Women Having It All*, Erigha (2018) speaks of the educated Black bitch's experience:

> [The] educated Black bitches cannot find partners because they work too much, have unappealing traits, or do not support men effectively. . . . As domineering matriarchs, educated Black bitches emasculate their often unemployed male partners by wielding their money, power, and sexuality as weapons of control and treating their relationships as sexual conquests. (p. 11)

Education and the level of education that a Black woman acquires play a part in her defeminizing. The characteristic of being educated is given inherent association to malehood and, further, Whiteness. As such, yet another affirmative characteristic, when paired with the Black woman, is made harmful. In the academy—which I must iterate is not the only site of intellectualism—a diverse many are seen; however, a diverse many are never heard. As Dei and Simmons (2010) assert, "[A]nti-racism is structurally different from anti-oppression" (p. 110). And so, I strongly believe that the anti-oppression approach, which is preferred in educational spaces, has facilitated violence. We need to avoid color-blind approaches, which take ease in essentializing and doing away with issues of difference in an avoidance of discomfort. We must name the thing. There is nothing humanly natural about racism and operating in the role of oppressor and oppressed; however, it has been historically reinvented to thrive in modern society. There is a deliberate need to restore humanity and morality back into educational spaces and sites. The entire moral fabric of education has been compromised for the immoral gain of a few, and so applying goodness and ethics back into education must be the principle priority of practice. How does the mythologizing of Black women and girl representations impact the way in which education is delivered to this group? By exploring this, can we begin to fill the gaps that have been widened and deepened by anti-Black educational procedures, policies, and practices that have violated Black women? In order to avoid the weaponizing of education when it is held by the Black woman, an anti-racist approach to education needs to be prioritized.

In a four-part series entitled *Fix My Life, House of Healing: The Myth of the Angry Black Woman*, Iyanla Vanzant challenges eight Black women who were labelled *angry Black women*. The series, which was announced as "her toughest challenge yet," makes claims at an attempt to "debunk" the myth of the angry Black woman. Episode one featured a clip of Vanzant refusing to "participate in [her] own dishonour" as a Black woman, which she identified as being caused by the angry Black woman. Throughout, Vanzant holds that the angry Black woman serves as a "stereotype" that has allowed Black women to display "inappropriate behaviour that then becomes [their] identity." There were several ideas in this nationally broadcasted show that were problematic; of these I believe the politics of respectability are the greatest. The respectability politics of the angry Black woman has seen Black women police other Black women on the appropriateness of their responses to anger. This "appropriateness," which is standardized by White "civility," demonstrates misguided blame, which makes Black women answerable to White normalcy and systems, instead of to Black resistance and expression. The "myth" of the angry Black woman pushes for the conformity to Whiteness, with the result of never being considered as normal or acceptable to White systems. Some Black women, from within, have begun to do the work of White supremacy, knowingly and unknowingly, by relegating their sisters and their self to a standard that should not want to be achieved, resulting in tireless work that serves only the interest of the oppressor. If the Black woman is not engaging in some kind of resistance, then she has depoliticized herself and thus cannot want for anything that implicates the betterment of her social statuses. The Black woman must understand that her anger is political and it in many ways reflects her individual and collective politics; this is the politics of the body. Rejecting the label of the angry Black woman is a strategy used by Black women for conditional increased mobility, sometimes with a complete disregard for communal futurity. In this way, we need to grapple with the ways Black women have performed, which has reproduced a status quo, stagnating all Black women. We must be uncomfortable with this truth and hold ourselves accountable.

Black womanhood expresses itself through a multiplicity of identities. Black women have been made nonexistent within Canada, largely by the ability of others to determine how our bodies are read (St. Amand, 2010). Resistance occurs through self-definition and therefore dominant groups continue to control the labels attached to Black women. Black women desperately need to grow the ability to be self-determining, such that even in the face of being labelled, we are unaffected psychologically and emotionally. hooks (2003) speaks to the ability Blacks have to exercise agency in order to regain self-esteem: "We know that while race and racism may overdetermine many aspects of our lives, we are still free to be self-determining" (p. 19). Our capacity to be self-defining allows us to carve out space within the margins and operate from there on our own terms (hooks, 2003). We must do away with the deceptive discourse that engages us to believe that it is better for Black women to be anywhere but the margins. Wane (2018) speaks to the ability that other people have to define Black women, however she states that if "you know who you are, if you know yourself, then you don't feel the need to articulate credentials and legitimize yourself in a space—this is what it means to be grounded." Why as Black women do we expend so much effort diverting the labels put on us? Would this be necessary if the Black woman knew and loved who she is? Who earns from the emotional labor of the angry Black woman who is angry, but spends her time performing as if she is not? The internalizing of the *angry Black woman* trope rather than the angry Black woman reality, by Black women, has allowed us to be pathologized. The label has profitably operated as a tool of the silencing, but only because the Black woman has tolerated being silenced by it. The Black woman has known trauma her entire life, so she must be angry—you are angry. It is through the expression of this anger, through a catharsis, that change of social circumstances has been realized. Healing is required. There are those who, after being passed through this kind of psychological blender, have managed to overcome. They have pieced together the fragments, bonded themselves through processes of learning and unlearning, and are OK—more than OK. It can be done. As Black women we must, as well, come face to face with our reflection, our greatest discomfort, and sit in it to produce change and facilitate growth, individually and collectively.

Why am I not allowed to be an angry Black woman? Am I not angry? Am I not a Black woman? For too long, the *angry Black woman* has been used for the conservancy of coloniality. She has been used to dissuade the Black woman from venting her anger, which has kept her angry. Anger has been treated as an unacceptable emotion for Black women to express or use. The *angry Black woman* label is meant to silence our experiences by creating shame in us for being angry. There is a history within the Black woman, whether acknowledged or unacknowledged, which is always angry and will remain that way until justice is realized. The discourse among Black women should surround the normalizing of the angry Black woman for the purpose of making her treatment abnormal. As Black women, we are allowed to be angry Black women in any way we embrace—you can no longer tell me I cannot be angry. She is a Black body who has been in forced relation with Whiteness, and on that basis alone she is justifiable in her anger. She is Black, she is a woman, and most importantly, she is a Black woman. We need to continue to center the narrative of the *angry Black woman* with an agenda of our own that contains radical plans and action that work to the repossession of our bodies and subsequent resistance. It is invaluable that we as Black women take responsibility for the reclamation of our histories and struggle for our self-definition—we must rewrite our stories. Lorde (1981) vents the use of her anger as a Black woman, presenting a value for anger that counters how White supremacy has defined it:

> Women respond to racism. My response to racism is anger. I have lived with that anger, ignoring it, feeding upon it, learning to use it before it laid my visions to waste, for most of my life. Once I did it in silence, afraid of the weight. My fear of anger taught me nothing. Your fear of that anger will teach you nothing, also. (p. 278)

Beyond what Lorde names as anger, she speaks to the utility of engaging anger. As a Black woman, I will be an angry Black woman until society becomes as angry as I am and as angry as they should be at my continued oppression. The angry Black woman has used action as a means of improving her positionality. We have been distracted by labels in order to hide our eyes from the work being accomplished by the Black woman. Because of this, I hold tight to my angry Black woman because it is she who has given me the hope and strength I need to keep speaking back to and resisting what I know as morally wrong. Black women, let us be liberated by knowing that it is not what we are called, but what we answer to that defines who we are; let us start doing the correct work.

References

Christian, B. (1987). The Race for Theory. *Cultural Critique, 6*(1), 51–63.

Collins, P. H. (2005). *Black Sexual Politics: African Americans, Gender, and the New Racism.* New York, NY: Routledge.

Collins, P. H. (2009). *Black Feminist Thought: Knowledge, Consciousness, and the Politics of Empowerment.* New York, NY: Routledge.

Cooper, A. (2006). *The Hanging of Angeliqué: The Untold Story of Canadian Slavery and the Burning of Old Montréal.* Toronto, Canada: Harper Perennial.

Dei, G. & Simmons, M. (2010). Educating about Anti-Racism: The Perils and Desires. *Our Schools, Our Selves, 19*(3), 107–120.

Donovan, K. (2014). Slavery and Freedom in Atlantic Canada's African Diaspora: Introduction. *Acadiensis: Journal of the History of the Atlantic Region, 43*(1), 109–115.

Dua, E. (2008). Thinking through Anti-Racism and Indigeneity in Canada. *The Ardent: Anti-Racism & Decolonization Review, 1*(1), 31–35.

Erigha, M. (2018). Black Women Having It All. *The Black Scholar, 48*(1), 20–30.

Fanon, F. (1967). *Black skin, white masks.* New York, NY: Grove Press.

Fanon, F., Bhabha, H. K., Philcox, R., & Sartre, J. P. (2004). *The Wretched of the Earth.* New York, NY: Grove Press.

hooks, b. (1990b). *Yearning: Race, Gender, and Cultural Politics.* Boston, MA: South End.

hooks, b. (1997). Representing Whiteness in the Black Imagination. In R. Frankenberg (Ed.) *Displacing Whiteness: Essays in Social and Cultural Criticism* (pp. 341–346). Durham and London: Duke University Press.

hooks, b. (2003). *Rock my Soul: Black People and Self-Esteem.* New York, NY: Atria.

Kiesling, E. (2017). The Missing Colors of the Rainbow: Black Queer Resistance. *European Journal of American Studies, 11*(3), 1–21.

Lorde, A. (1981). The Uses of Anger. *Women's Studies Quarterly, 25*(1/2), 278–285.

Lorde, A. (2007). *Sister Outsider: Essays and Speeches.* New York, NY: Ten Speed.

McKittrick, K. (2006). Nothing's Shocking: Black Canada. In *Demonic Grounds: Black Women and the Cartographies of Struggle* (pp. 91–119). Minneapolis, MN: University of Minnesota Press.

Montgomery, K. (2005). Imagining the Anti-Racist State: Representations of Racism in Canadian History Textbooks. *Discourse Studies in the Cultural Politics of Education, 26*(4), 427–442.

Neville, H. A., & Hamer, J. (2001). We Make Freedom. *Journal of Black Studies, 31*(4), 437–461.

Norwood, C. (2013). Perspective in Africana Feminism: Exploring Expressions of Black Feminism/Womanism in the African Diaspora. *Sociology Compass, 7*(3), 225–236.

Rouillard, L. M. (2007). Complicit Victims in «Les Anciens Canadiens» and «Le Mulâtre." *The French Review, 80*(5), 1095–1107.

Simpson, A. (2007). On Ethnographic Refusal: Indigeneity, "Voice" and Colonial Citizenship, Junctures. *Journal for Thematic Dialogue, 9,* 67–80.

Spalek, B. (2005). A Critical Reflection on Researching Black Muslim Women's Lives Post September 11th. *International Journal of Social Research Methodology,* 8(5), 405–418.

St. Amand, A. (2010). "We, the Invisible": Women of the Civil Rights Movement in Canada. *Journal of Undergraduate Studies at Trent* 3(1), 28–37.

Thorpe, A. (2015). Towards the Inclusion of Trans* Identities: The Language of Gender Identity in Postsecondary Student Documentation. *Antistasis,* 5(2), 81–89.

Tuck, E. & Yang, K. W. (2014a). R-Words: Refusing Research. In D. Paris & M.T. Winn (Eds.) *#Humanizing Research: Decolonizing Qualitative Inquiry with Youth and Communities,* (pp. 223–248), Thousand Oaks, CA: Sage Publications

Tuck, E. & Yang, K. W. (2014b). Unbecoming Claims: Pedagogies of Refusal in Qualitative Research. *Qualitative Inquiry, 20*(6), 811–818.

Vanzant, Iyanla. *Fix My Life, House of Healing: The Myth of the Angry Black Woman.* http://www.oprah.com/own-iyanla-fix-my-life/house-of-healing-fix-a-blak-mans-heart-part-1

Vertinsky, P. & Captain, G. (1998). More Myth than History: American Culture and Representations of the Black Female's Athletic Ability. *Journal of Sport History, 25*(3), 532–561.

Walcott, R. (2001). Caribbean Pop Culture in Canada: Or, the impossibility of Belonging to the Nation. *Small Axe, 5*(1), 123–139.

Walcott, R. (2003). *Black Like Who? Writing Black Canada.* Toronto: Insomniac Press.

Wallace, M. (1979). *Black Macho and the Myth of the Superwoman.* New York, NY: Dial.

Wane, N. N. (2002). Carving Out Critical Space: African-Canadian Women and the Academy. In N. N. Wane, K. Deliovsky, & Lawson, E. (Eds.), *Back to the Drawing Board: African-Canadian Feminisms* (pp. 175–196). Toronto, Canada: Sumach Press.

Wane, N. N. (2018). Black Feminist Thought. University of Toronto, Ontario Institution of Studies in Education. Toronto, Canada. Class Discussions

CHAPTER 9

Special Education: When and Where Does Blackness Fit in?

Shaniqwa Thomas

Locating Myself

I COME TO this topic first as an able-bodied Black woman. Talking about Blackness and having to define it is a bit unsettling to me. Blackness is who I am, and it is unsettling for two main reasons. First, as I am abled bodied and do not have a visible or nonvisible disability; because of ableism I have the privilege of moving in and out of spaces without having to spend much time thinking about if the structural design is made for my body. Have I been envisioned in the planning as the "person" to physically use the space? Do I need to think about what it means to publicly commute to work today? How will I get to the second floor in a building? Due to ableism in society and my body instinctively fitting the normal view of ability, I have avoided this self-dialogue, but it has also caused my race to be the forefront of how my body is initially read. Composed of many experiences and parts, these all come second to my physical appearance of a Black woman. As a Black woman, my body is constantly covered in a veil that cannot escape the gaze from outsiders who presume my race, culture, history, and heritage. Nor can my body escape my own gaze that is refracted by societal norms. My Blackness is understood through my double consciousness, which gives me the strength to wear my afro puff proudly, while simultaneously I can spend the day facing my own biases and societal pressures that attempt to define parts of me as valuable and accepted. This unsettling discomfort inside me in trying to answer and define Blackness—a socially constructed identity—helps give context for the preceding conversation. I believe the social construction of the identity of Blackness is defined according to who is answering and defining the term. There is power and strength in defining my Blackness; for me, it simply comes down to what my body and my Blackness symbolizes for me. As I see it, White settlers and their lasting systems of oppression have continuously seen me and my body as a threat and something not of value. So, to be here and to define my Blackness and all its beauty is delicate, rebellious, and fills me with pride, to acknowledge that I am here and that they did not win. Consequently, in reading this chapter as a Black body you may agree with my argument and my use of the words *Blackness* and *Black bodies* or you may not. This is because my understanding of Blackness is relational to me and my experiences growing up in Canada and more particularly Dartmouth, Nova Scotia, and spending the last 14 years living between Barrie and downtown Toronto, Ontario. Thus, depending on what you as a reader perceive as important to you in your personal definition of Blackness, we maybe differ. Second, the unsettling feeling of defining my Blackness and how I understand my Blackness stems from Black people being forced to define who they are to appease and seek validation from the White gaze, which contributes to the control of Black bodies. In this manner, defining Blackness in reference to bodies and identities becomes a tool for capitalization.

As someone who does not identify as Black and disabled, I do not have to actively think about leaving my bed and navigating through these social structures and the intersections. Thus, I must be clear that my intentions in writing this chapter cannot and will not speak for all Black disabled people in the public school system. However, as a proud older cousin to two younger males in my family, who are of different ages and social class and who will have different experiences in life and the school system, I believe part of my job as a big cousin is to help make a better future for them and to do so is to help echo their voice or use my platform to give them space to be heard. The combination of firsthand knowledge of the experiences of individuals living in the margins, gained in my years as a disability support worker along with the stories that are out there in the world that I have heard and gathered over time, has aided in guiding my thinking on this topic. Thus, I feel a bit of an obligation and some responsibility given my current academic and class privilege to start and carry on the discussions that are happening inside and outside the walls of the Ontario Institution for Studies in Education. I come to this discussion with the belief that the intersections of race and disability have not been sufficiently discussed or fully examined in our curriculum, nor within our educational structure. The lack of intersectional conversations among individuals, including myself, in numerous academic fields and backgrounds has led me to question why is there a lack of normative discourse about this visible intersection. Why are racialized bodies within the academic field of disability studies or the individuals who identify as disabled not visible in critical race theory? When attempting to find literature around my questions and supporting research, this was a struggle and frustration because there are huge gaps in the literature that is currently accessible.

There are numerous writings about intersectionality, disability education, and Blackness within our schools, yet there is not a clear dialogue fully exploring the overlaps within academia around these spaces. I am not saying these conversations are not happening, as they are happening within small clusters outside of the academic realm. They are taking place in parent support groups in person and online, and students are in the margins voicing their experience through various forms such as social media, blogs, school papers, friends, and so forth. They are also happening in group homes and by special education teachers; however, when these conversations are not being passed on and highlighted enough to governing officials and authority members to make change, then the content has become lost. Failure to pass on this information hinders the reach of such information to our school boards effectively and with little to no pressure to help create institutional change through disruption. Unfortunately, when school administrators, whose current practice is to make decisions heavily guided by academic research mainly in the form of statistical data, it perpetuates gaps in academic literature. As I see it, there is clearly a need for conversations in this area not just because the current practices, dialogue, and literature is lacking, but because there are lives that are existing within the overlap and their voices and experiences have been silenced.

Introduction

This chapter is intended to trouble the notions of disability education within public schools, influenced by anti-racism theory, and my experience within disability studies at both an undergraduate and graduate level has helped me to ground this chapter in dis/crit theory, coined by Subini A. Annamma, David Connor, and Beth Ferri. Dis/crit theory is the combination of dis/ability studies and critical race theory and

> acknowledges how these normalizing processes of racism and ableism position unwanted bodies outside of the category of normal in order to justify their exclusion, segregation, and even termination. Dis/Crit explores how perceptions of race and ability are built upon each other, socially constructed in tandem, and how those labels impact the embodiment and positioning of those who are constructed as less than. (Annamma et al., 2017, p. 153).

I want to be careful in saying disability education; I am not looking primarily at the field of study known as disability studies. I am looking at special education within schools (primary to high school) and how these classes are intended for those who are seen strictly through a lens of their disability, though in saying that I acknowledge how these two areas overlap. The troubling notions of being Black and disabled leads me to question and examine how Blackness, as an identity, fits into, and how and when it does not fit into, the current Eurocentric school framework, as our current school system (in the Western context) is heavily embedded with notions of White supremacy and ablest ideology. I use the word *Blackness*, noting that there are various meanings and use for the word in the Black community; however, for my purpose I use the term to engage with bodies who are Black and are read racially as Black in Canada. Additionally, being seen and read as Black by others (frequently by the White gaze) often means that one's skin is viewed through a fixed lens that reflects the body being connected to Africa and the association of one as African. It is important to note and continuously be thinking about the entangled relationship between Blackness and Africanness and the lived reality and experience of and within the two. Furthermore, being seen and read as Black often equates to being seen first as a negative due to non-affirming and pessimistic norms that have been associated with the Black body due to colonialism. Thus, Blackness and Black bodies wither in the classroom or are consistently having to defend their worth and beauty; this has tremendous implications on their experience within our school system.

Around the world schools are seen and valued as a part of our societal institutional regulation and division of humans. In their function, they can directly be implicated in producing raced, classed, and gendered subjectivities. This is the result of schools upholding and reinforcing the dominant beliefs of society with little to no resistance, which stems from schools mirroring the same social hierarchies and inequality of the world around them. Additionally, looking at the practices of many school boards within Ontario, Canada, and noting the racialized history of schools within Canada. It is not hard to find many examples of Blackness and the experience of Black students not fitting into the school system, yet schools continue to position themselves as being inclusive and equitable. In order to have a conversation about Blackness and special education and the relationship between the two, I will begin by looking at the operationalization of Blackness, disability, and intersectionality before moving on to examine how there is a sub-school category within our schools. The practices within these spaces push these students aside and reduce them down to their singular identity, an identity of their diagnosed disability that often views individuals through their ability and how they are differently abled. This view of differently abled suggests that there is only one normal model of being and that it is the only correct way to be abled in society.

Understanding the notion of a single identity calls us to reflect on the consciousness of categorization and its relation to the human body, the result being the human naturalization that we need to know and understand everything around us. Additionally, categorizing of bodies is heavily influenced by colonial power. Members of society often categorize things in relation to Whiteness being in the center, which results in all things made to be in correlation and in comparison to Whiteness. From this understanding, I will shift our conversation to discuss how this correlates to streaming Blackness in and out of the classroom, and how in special education classrooms only Whiteness stands to benefit from being reduced down to a single disability-first identity. Identity formation of the body and being seen as a singular identity of disability first does the work in Black bodies of suppressing and pushing aside their Blackness as if its natural, rendering the Black body in these spaces to be seen either in place or out of place. Additionally, a singular identity disregards students' lived experiences that are present when they leave the classroom as well as when they enter the classroom. For Black students, this suppression of themselves contributes to them being reduced to their physical appearance, which is contradicting to say the least. Consequently, for those living in these two spheres, one of their identities is consistently being read as invisible. If racial disabled bodies are read as invisible in either sphere, this leads me to question what practices are being used to reinforce racial bodies to be overrepresented and streamed at higher rates into special education classrooms. In talking to the parent(s) and grandparent(s) of my cousins(s) who are Black, autistic, and nonverbal who currently can become aggressive when misunderstood, they reveal a fear for their child(ren) going to school in the public system and risking misinterpretation by others.On both sides of my family (though they had not spoken to the other side) they have made the claim that they are scared to send my cousin(s) to public schools simply because of the well-known poor treatment and stereotypes Black boys face daily in these spaces. For them, the thought of going to school brought excitement, but that excitement quickly turned to concern over how to keep these bodies safe before they even step foot into the school, the hallway, or the classroom.

This leads our conversation to look at the possibilities through Afrocentric schooling, as I have come to understand the theory and concept through the work of George J. Sefa Dei. Afrocentric schooling is argued on the basis that Afrocentric schooling puts an emphasis on the importance of centering students in their own culture, experience, and history. The consequence of this system of schooling is that students in these spaces are better equipped to understand and interact with other cultures more empathetically (Dei & Kempf, 2013). In examining these two phenomena through an intersectional lens, I come to terms that using the foundational principles of Afrocentric schooling is imperative and allows for the use of race as an entry point, highlighting the overlaps. It finds gaps in theory and practices that relate to individuals and groups of people that often arise out of complex relationships between different attributes. Similarly, disability has been used as an entry point to highlight societies' oppressive history toward human bodies, shedding light onto societies' cultures of ableism. Yet, in both these categories neither race nor disability is discussed enough, even though the two have become overarching concepts that are separated from one another. Finally, I believe calling for the use of intersectional disability education in our classrooms and education spaces, opens and reshape the space so that the bodies and voices of those living in the margins of disability and being Black can coexist and be heard. Intersectional disability education from this perspective raises many questions about the link between special education and anti-racist educational praxis, as well as what it means to practically and pragmatically work with this intersectionality in classrooms and the school systems.

Operationalization of Blackness, Disability, and Intersectionality

In this discussion, I believe it is important to first to engage with the operationalizing of Blackness, disability, and intersectionality in their own spheres, which will allow for a more comprehensive understanding of how all three are independent but work together.

Blackness

In understanding the structured organization of society and how Blackness came to be understood, with a critical lens we can trouble the notion of Blackness further, analyzing the complexity of Black performativity and Black political identification. For me, the operationalizing of Blackness shifts between Black performativity and Black political identification. Rinaldo Walcott (1997) explains this notion in his book *Black Like Who? Writing Black Canada* through a series of essays that examine in depth the complex limits and the possibilities of Black lives, cultures, and events in Canada. Walcott draws attention to the seesaw relationship between reproducing and challenging Whiteness and colonial ideology that underlies Black performativity and Black political identification, which sit on opposite sides of the seesaw. This is the result of the normalization by outsiders and insiders of the Black community to label and create definable characteristics of the Black body and of Blackness.

These presumed measurable characteristics of Blackness and the Black body have been reworked into our social dynamics to help tell Black bodies who they are, as well as tell White and other bodies what Blackness is and how bodies are to be identified as Black. Jennifer Kelly (1998) in her book *Under the Gaze: Learning to be Black in White Society,* demonstrates this notion in her work with Black high school students in Canada. Her research is produced through interactions with students where their voices give light to the challenges they encountered that affect their identity formations. Various sources and meanings aided both positively and negatively for these students in "coming to understand and know themselves as Black students through societal processes that happen inside and outside the walls of the school and classroom" (p. 136). These identity interactions can look like statements from their peers, assuming the only sport males play is basketball or that Black females know how to braid hair. In these situations, and many others where Blackness is put into questioning, Black bodies have to actively decide how to respond consciously, reaffirming the balancing act between Black performative and Black political identifiers.

Disability

When hearing the word *disability* our societal norms have conditioned us to understand this term and use of it to be captured through the medical or social model of disability, with either model focusing on what identifies as the source that causes an impairment of an individual and group or the social limitation. In the words of Tanya Titchkosky (2003) in her book *Disability, Self, and Society,* the working "common sense" understanding of disability is a

> social model of disability [that] is understood by some as to represent a paradigmatic shift in that it is taken as a rejection of the World Health Organization's medicalized conception of impairment/disability/handicap. The Social Model claims that while there is a problem of bodily impairment . . . the focus of disability research should be on how societies disable their members. (p. 248)

The medical model of disability has come to be the norm and the hegemonic control of society. The medical model of disability is based on the foundation of scientific empiricism of medicine that links a disability diagnosis to an individual's physical body (Titchkosky, 2003). The belief and perception is that having body limitations, whether they be physical and/or mental, may reduce the individual's quality of life, which all goes back to one's societal production. Therefore, in our current society the aim is that, with medical intervention, the individual's disability will be diminished and/or corrected. The medical model in combination with the education system, is "used to justify a wide range of educational strategies in special education, and it has a major influence on special education methods and strategies" (Massoumeh and Leila, 2012, p. 1). As Leila and Massoumeh write, the result of using the medical model and its presumptions

> is that a disease or organic dysfunctions are critically important in the etiology of learning problems and deviant behavior. This complex interwoven relationship between the medical model and the education system is also shown by the regular consultation between medical and educational personnel on appropriate ways of educating and caring for persons with special needs that teachers and parents both engage with willingly or not. (p. 2)

Yet in the same breath, it is the same doctor note/verification or testing result that is a major component in moving students out of special education classrooms and off independent education plans (IEP).

Intersectionality

In looking at Blackness, special education classrooms and the intersections of the two, informs us where and how to engage with these two separate but connecting topics. My understanding of Kimberlé Crenshaw's use of the word and concept of intersectionality is the definition I rely on. Crenshaw argues that intersectionality employs us to see what work is being done and to imagine other kinds of work to open the space. In this sense, intersectionality is a practice and theory that is always a work in progress (Carbado, Crenshaw, Mays, & Tomlinson, 2013). Intersectionality "invites us to look for places where it is doing work and not to stop there but to keep asking questions as if it is a starting point to see where it is not doing work and where it has not gone" (p. 312). The use of intersectionality and its fluidity keeps us from being stuck and pigeon toeing to one category, allowing us to look at special education classrooms, policy, and the school system at large. We can look at these areas and the overlap and ask, "What's going on here?" Examining how intersectionality may be used in our school system and by educators will determine if it is being use partially or with "full integration." Intersectionality may be shown and taught to look like A, B, C and not X, Y, Z, which is a static view. However, this static understanding is limited in that it does not go on to look at the other possibilities that exist between C and X, as well as the possibilities that exist within A, B, C. In the case of special education classrooms and Blackness fitting into and out of it, intersectionality may have been shown to educators to look like a diverse set of bodies in the classroom. Yet, intersectionality when fully integrated into the school system looks like us continuing our thinking around who is in the classroom. What does it mean to have these bodies here collectively? Furthermore, what does it mean to have Blackness in this space? Questioning and dealing with the complexities that arise will create friction as it is the consequence of our questioning clashing with and rubbing up against current structures of power that exist out of Eurocentric thinking. (Carbado et al., 2013)

A School within a School

On the surface, there is a well-crafted image of what public schools should look like and how they should perform. Within Canada, no matter what level of education the school caters to, they all, as Sium (2014) writes

> share a public perception of schools being a community resource which serves all children and youth equally. The results being they create equalizing opportunities later in life, for all students. Ideally, schools then transcend race, class, gender, ethnic and other differences and enable its graduates to achieve desired economic and social mobility, irrespective of their background. (p. 105)

A simple Google search of racialized bodies in public schools will show that the ideas of the schools being a space that is all equalizing for all is not the case. Within the school system, there are subcultures that exist because of the systems of power at play that create schools within schools. One of the ways the schools are separated within is with special education classrooms. I define special education classes as they pertain to students in congregated classes that fall under the category of mild intellectual disability that includes behavioral, autism, and learning disabilities and developmental disabilities. These classrooms are projected to parents, guardians, and the community as a space for students "who have behavioral, communication, intellectual, physical, or multiple exceptionalities who may require special education programs and/or services to benefit fully from their school experience" (Ontario Ministry of Education, 2018). Special education programs and services are structured in the classroom to give students "instruction and assessments that are different from those provided to the general student population. These may take the form of accommodations such as specific teaching strategies, preferential seating, and assistive technology and/or an educational program that is modified from the age-appropriate grade level expectations in a particular course or subject" (Ontario Ministry of Education, 2018). What is underlining the narrative of special education spaces is the medical model of disability in which students using these spaces will continue to learn the same material, but through their accommodations. The idea is held that these accommodations will enable students to overcome their disability. From my experience, what this narrative does in practice is swallow up the many layers that contribute to student identities, leaving their disability as the only identifier to which they are visible. Thus, students and teachers interact solely through their relationship to the disability. This view is also harmful on a larger systematic scale in that it opens the conversation and interaction to be solely on how these individuals are "differently abled." This further minimizes who they are by suggesting that the term *disability* is uncomfortable and should be avoided, with preference being to associate individuals as differently abled. To that I ask, "Are we all not differently abled from one another? Does using the term differently abled create a hierarchy, as it implies that only those deemed disabled are able to be classified by this term?" This avoidance yet complexity to highlight a disability due to ablest thinking goes back to my early point of one identity. This has a silencing effect on who the individual is as a whole, and for those racialized bodies it has the effect of silencing that individual's race. I saw this limited interaction play out when I was working in a special education classroom as an education support worker, where the only Black bodies in the room were myself and another, a little Black girl. This little girl was a joy to be around, and as soon as I met her, she asked me if I was Jamaican just like she was. In responding that I partially was, she was ecstatic; for the rest of the day anytime she interacted with the teacher, her peers, or anyone else she came in contact with, she voiced our connection as Black bodies. She would take the time to let them know that her and I were similar because we were both Jamaican.

This young girl voiced her Blackness and our connection for several months. After she voiced our connection I noticed it was followed by her big smile and a little dance. Her excitement after the initial few days was quickly met with disapproval by her teachers. When she shared about her Blackness, she was repeatedly told by her teachers to talk about it during recess and to focus on her current task. This young girl's experience was in a space where she was overly consumed with Whiteness. Anytime she could connect with another aspect of who she was, she was dismissed. I attribute this consistent highlight of our connection to be the result of the classroom being structured and normalized so she did not see all aspects of herself reflected. Thus, in the moments where she did, she claimed it! I brought up this issue to the teachers and school, citing that this may be an indicator she was longing for more cultural experiences and learning. It was no surprise that I was met with the dialogue of, "Those conversations need to happen outside the classroom unless they pertain to the curriculum at hand." It was recommended that because I also worked in the group home after school with this young girl, that the group home was a more appropriate place for these conversations to take place. The school, focus was getting her through the class material as her learning was only seen in comprehending and completing their predetermined material and the only accepted learning material came from the teacher and the predetermined literature.

My experience with the education system and the little girl's experience in her school comes as no surprise. The school curriculum has been scrutinized for years for not being inclusive. The school system is Eurocentric in its teachings, and in such it routinely denies minority students' personal experiences and knowledge and pushes their voices to the margins. Special education classes, like its counterparts, mirror the image of the space being predominantly teacher centered and around getting students to graduate by understanding the curriculum, which reduces them to their disability. This reduction of individuals solely to their disability is very much like the medical model of disability, a model in which individuals get swallowed up by the stereotypes of their disability and are only seen through their disability. For schools, the individual's limitation shifts the schools' focus on students becoming active and productive citizens in society by overcoming their limitations. If these students are perceived as not able to overcome and re-intergrate, then they are simply provided with the skills to get them through life. This reduction, as I perceive it, is preventing students inside and outside the classroom from fully engaging with themselves and the material being taught. The intersections of sex, race, class, gender, disability, and how they are in relationship with each other are not being fully taught or talked about in the classroom but outside of it. In one study, Community Living Ontario (2018) found that students with a disability still experience inordinate barriers to accessing meaningful academic and social engagement in their classrooms. This begs the question, again, "How does Blackness fit in and when does it not fit into special education?" In short, students with multi-complex identities and embodied experiences are entering their classrooms and are simply being told to leave their Blackness at the classroom door and pick it back up on the way out, which is unacceptable.

If classrooms are to be perceived as spaces where there is great emphasis on knowledge, beliefs, individual skills, and experience, where students are able to learn in a constructive, uninterrupted space, then classrooms must actively acknowledge Blackness and racialized bodies in these spaces. Students begin to create, shape, and see their identity in these spaces; thus, it is not an adequate learning environment for students to be seen and taught in spaces where people do not see the color of skin. Under the belief of doing so the curriculum is the focus, and consequently, every student is given equal opportunity. This use of color evasion through the rhetoric of color-blind language and policies within our schools comes as no surprise to minority groups (Annamma, Jackson, & Morrison, 2017). When it is said that color evasion is a tool of colonization "built upon a commitment of white supremacy . . . it uses that power to attack racial remediation and simultaneously defend structural racism" (p. 158). Acknowledging the intersections within the classrooms and using the principles of Afrocentric schooling would effectively establish intersectional disability education. Students in such educational environments would not be reduced to their disability and viewed as a subculture within the school and their classroom placement. In doing so, we would create the space for special education to be more intersectional where disability is not the only sense-making tool. Rather, it would be the entry point to view the world around the classroom and within the classroom, thus allowing for the voices in the intersections to be heard, and in this case, Black bodies would not have to operate solely by their disability in the classroom. We start asking questions about being Black and disabled: Who speaks for me? What does it look like to be Black and be in a special education classroom? I'm Black, but in class my race is seen as invisible. In starting to reject the current system we can start to sit with these questions and in sitting in the messiness of these questions we can start to examine the vast overrepresentation of Black students in special education classes.

Streaming Blackness in and out of the Classroom

In this next section, I want to look at how streaming within Ontario schools has become a product that further suppresses Black bodies due to the disenfranchisement of their academic choices that places them into special education classrooms and limits post-secondary school opportunities. Educational streaming, a "policy in which students are grouped based on ability, was supposed to have ended in 1999 but the Toronto District School Board data shows that Black students continue to be directed toward essential and applied programs of study and away from academic courses, more so than white and other racialized students" (Gordon, 2017). The "dynamic interplay between racism and ableism," the intertwined relationship within schools without a full intersectional engagement with the two (Connor & Ferri, 2005, p. 463) has resulted in consistent biased practices and the growth of them that maintain the segregation of bodies in classrooms. The result has been overrepresentation of students of color in special education classes. When students IQs are not used as the determining factor in school classroom placement, underlying bias is and that enables discrimination based on a student's perceived ability.

As previously discussed, the history of schools in Canada and Ontario have shown that Whiteness has functioned as a form to signal authority and authorize property over, to own property through the objectification of Blackness "through the reification and subsequent hegemony of white people. Whiteness was then transformed into 'common sense' and the law" and what society deems to be the law, and these laws have steeped themselves into the schooling system and consequently into school practices (Leonardo & Bounderick, 2011, p. 2210). Robert L. Haymen, cited in Leonard and Bounderick's article "Smartness as Property: A Critical Exploration of Intersections Between Whiteness and Disability Studies," made the argument that "intelligence has been inextricably intertwined with the construction of race … [and] race, in turn, has been defined in part through intelligence and intellectual inferiority and superiority" (p. 2216). Noting the histories of race, disability, and the school system, it is no surprise then that "racialized conceptions of ability have allowed some parents and educators to use special education categories as a tool for continued racial segregation" (Connor & Ferri, 2005, p. 454). For some parents, at one-point in time, "special education classrooms were a way to allow their child to get more attention and prevent them from having to mingle with Black children" while on the other hand "special education classrooms have been and continue to be used to remove Black children from classrooms so that teachers d[o] not have to deal with them" (pp. 454–456). Given this information and the history of the schooling system, it is not overly alarming for the Black community to hear that race still has an immense impact on students' streaming process.

A recent race-based data collection taken between the years of 2006 and 2011 found that "Black students in Toronto, Ontario schools continue to face an achievement and opportunity gap" (Gordon, 2017). The report cited that "Black students have been strongly encouraged by teachers and guidance counselors to take applied level courses instead of academic courses; despite, their aptitudes or life goals." Despite the effort of school educators, policymakers, and community activists, schools are still adopting and producing ideology and practices that cater to the notions of a hierarchy between races. In this pattern of encouragement, if a teacher is the one doing the pushing, then the likelihood of that teacher attempting to help catch students up as they are falling behind is relevantly low. Students are then pushed on to the next teacher and the next grade, while they continue to fall behind and with no intervention. They are placed into special education classes or given accommodations through an individual education plan (IEP). Robert S. Brown and Gillian Parekh found in their 2010 research into special education programs within the Toronto District School Board that "in looking at students who identified as Gifted, white students were significantly overrepresented (52%) as were East Asian (27%) and mixed students were approximately (6%). In contrast, all other self-identified racial groups were significantly under-represented in overall students identified as Gifted" (p. 43). Without looking too far into the data produced from this study, it is clear that racialized notions of valued ability are still being upheld within our schools. As such, they have reaffirmed stereotype norms of racial segregation and exclusion of bodies.

Special education "It actually reads:

"despite being designed to meet the needs of diverse groups of learners, has nonetheless been used to both create and perpetuate the marginalization of individuals" (Connor & Ferri, 2005, p. 461). By this same notion, when passing students onto the next teacher, students become unprepared for the challenges that they need to overcome academically. Thus, they are left to feel like they have no academic strengths and are unsure how or where to look for supports. This challenge may play itself out in a few ways; one way could be that students may do just enough to pass or students may come to see that their behavior may allow them to elude the challenge (Moore & Lewis, 2012). If this behavior is deemed disruptive to the Eurocentric model of students following the teacher's instructions, students may be deemed as having a behavior problem, resulting in their placement into special education classrooms or an IEP. Another factor to consider in the streaming process of students into special education classrooms is students' behavior and the root cause of their behavior. For minority students, their behavior could be impacted by the racism they face in their day-to-day activities in school. These interactions may appear small like overhearing a racialized "joke" between peers to something bigger, like a teacher making negative remarks about their appearance in the classroom. Navigating these interactions every day can have a negative effect and in some cases may lead to students disassociating with the school, which contributes to them leaving or acting out. These students are then labelled as having behavior problems, with the recommended solution for Black bodies to be placed into special education classes, reinforcing normalized cultural stereotypes of Black bodies to have behavioral issues (Moore & Lewis, 2012).

This aptitude to quickly label behavior as a disability is concerning when we contrast this knowledge to what is known about our school systems failing our young Black children, especially Black boys who evidentially play into the benefit of the school-to-prison pipeline complex. The combination of an internal battle of hate mixed with bullying, hate rhetoric, and racism is an easy gateway for racialized minority students to exclude and isolate themselves from their peers and school community (Daaisma, 2017). The negative feeling associated with the school's rules, regulations, and authority figures can be reflected and displayed through behavioral problems and chronic absences for the student. Being labeled as a student with behavioral problems, with the solution often being suspension, further places the student at a disadvantage due to having missed school. Absenteeism then leads students to be held back or recommended for testing to see if they are intellectually delayed or have a learning disability. Statistics on Black students over the past decade consistently show that "Black students are at least twice as likely to be suspended than their white counterparts who engage in the same misbehavior" (Daaisma, 2017). If students are suspended enough, the skills they would have gathered from being in class are lost if they are unable to be taught outside the classroom.

I believe that this racial bias of streaming in and out of classrooms engages us to ask the question "How do we resist this?" Intersectional disability education enables us to see how Black bodies in special education classrooms are seen either in place or out of place. When our bodies are read by others as visible, it is often because we are out of place and simultaneously in place. While bodies are performing in spaces and they adhere to the norms of behavior, they are read as invisible or in place. However, in the same breath, if bodies are performing in that same environment, but their behavior is not the norm these bodies are read as a visible and often seen as not belonging to that space. Applying this same thinking of "to be seen" to special education classrooms and to approaches to the Black body is imperative, particularly given that the statistics from the last decade show that White bodies are being streamed at higher rates onto paths that have more opportunity for success than Black bodies. Failure to question these practices is seen as normal, and this process, heavily inflicted with racial biases, continues to go unseen. The same can be said when we look at the high rates of Black bodies being suspended with no intervention technique(s) put into place, while on the other hand, when Black bodies do not perform to the acceptable norms of behavior in the class, these bodies are seen because they stand out against the norm. Black bodies stand out in a Western society because they are compared to Whiteness and Whiteness still operates in the center to which all things are compared, for it is seen as perfection. They also stand out when they do not conform and align to our ideals and boundaries of how a Black body should perform. Thus, Blackness fits into special education classrooms and the school system when it performs within the ideal stereotypes of who should be in special education. Consequently, when Black bodies perform and affirm these biased notions they are not seen or treated as valued members of society. Special education classrooms are viewed, then, as a place for Black bodies to operate within. Furthermore, these bodies in these spaces go unquestioned because these spaces are already viewed as "Othered" by the current school system and political environment. In the same breath, this explains why Blackness does not fit into special education because Blackness and Black bodies cannot be reduced down to a singular identity; thus, under Eurocentric schooling they are always in conflict with the system.

Possibilities through Afrocentric Thinking

Blackness does not fit into Eurocentric school system, yet at the same time, Blackness does fit into the systems of power that Eurocentric thinking is founded on. This means that the school system was created on to better white children, with Black and racialized children only being considered on the margins. These excluded groups are simply "permitted" to enter the space, without the space making any accommodations for their particular needs. Minority children needed to mirror the behavior, appearance, and mannerism of White settlers. Yet, Blackness has been and will continue to be defined as the opposite and other to Whiteness, so if our schools are built on and around the White body, Black bodies will never fit into the equation. We see this complexity play out in the case of Indigenous people in Canada where minority bodies did not fit into the school system, yet they did fit into school system because the school is a tool of settler colonialism, where the school became a tool to commit genocide of Indigenous people, culture, and their ways of knowing. Through assimilation tactics into White Eurocentric ways of being, Indigenous bodies were seen as belonging in school. This complexity of fitting in yet standing out alone is enough to argue for the use of Afrocentric thinking in our schools. African-centered thinking in our school systems creates the space for intersectional disability education due to the culturally and politically salient , or specific, content, design, and delivery (Dei &Kempf, 2013). In order for the necessary changes to occur, I firmly believe our schools and spaces need to adopt the principles of Afrocentric schooling where the needs, perspectives, and interests of all student bodies in the classroom are central to the learning environment. I am cautious and want to note that simply adopting Afrocentric principles into our classrooms is not enough as it remains in a Eurocentric structure, which is how terms and ideologies get warped back into and become agents of the continuation of Eurocentric thinking. I am purposely calling for the use of intersectional disability education to begin disrupting and interrupting settler colonial thinking rather than investing in the futurity of settler thinking. Afrocentric thinking in school systems allows the opportunity for Black bodies to center themselves in the school system and teaching material and has the possibility to transform due to systematic disruption from within.

Keeping the discussion of the intersections at the forefront rather than in the margins will allow for all students in the classroom, either inside special education classrooms or not, to be visible. Dei and Kempf (2013) state that where students are able to identify with the teaching material and express their thoughts without fear, such environments "reaffirm multiple identities through centering difference in order to foster educational excellence—broadly defined" (p. 141). I believe this would eliminate the reduction of students within special education classes to a single identity and prevent them from being pushed aside. An intersectional disability education approach, I believe would wholeheartedly empower students, as they no longer would have to decipher and navigate how to identify in class versus at home. Intersectional disability education challenges the normalized Eurocentric thinking by pausing and engaging with the numerous complexities that arise in and out of the intersections. Engaging with these complexities compels us to respond and demand change. At the same time, this educational structure is able to look at streaming in the school system, directly counteracting and responding to the question, "What happens when a student's IQ becomes irrelevant in the streaming process?" Using the foundation created through Afrocentric schooling, gives way to dis/crit theory to enter our classrooms, enabling us to expand our knowledge and challenge and reject the current Eurocentric framework. The reward is that our education system and in particular our special education classes are able to better to engage with the two spheres and the students may operate the intersections, pulling them out of the margins they are currently being forced within and enabling them to no longer have to silence who they are by picking only one sphere to stand in.

Putting It All Together

Examining special education and how Blackness fits into it presents the need for intersectional disability education, raising questions around what it means to practically and pragmatically work with this intersectionality in schools and the school systems. When it comes to applying sense-making mechanisms through our identification markers, we need to understand the implications of those indicators and identifiers. Identification markers are not limited to, nor are they locked into, the parameters of how we identify these things. For me, understanding the fluidity and consistent movement of intersectionality is the staple that is needed in our school system. This foundation is only fully able to happen when we open the space by means of dismantling our Eurocentric/traditional school systems, thus proving the importance of Afrocentric schools as well as embracing Afrocentric thinking in our current schools. It is the practicality of intersectional disability education that aligns with and reinforces Afrocentric schooling in that those same principles of empowering students for who they are (all encompassing) are able to be seen. Intersectionality in combination with African-centered education thinking allows us to go further in our practice and not get stuck nor content with just highlighting the intersections. The current "inclusive education policies" in schools, from my perspective, are practices that have become stuck and are no longer transformative and liberating. Additionally, current educators who may or may not have had extensive experience working and engaging with intersectionality are taught that intersectionality look like "this" and "this"; however, in these spaces and practices they do not always mirror those structural examples. Thus, when educators are doing this, they may believe that and deem their actions are creating a safe, acceptable, and comfortable environment and no longer need to be critical to the space.

Furthermore, intersectional disability education needs to operate in a space that is Afrocentric to be used in its full potential to conflict with the current Eurocentric school system. The reason for this conflict is that our current schooling system does not allow Blackness and Black bodies to grow and flourish wholesomely. Eurocentric classrooms are designed to be fixed and for all bodies to fit into what is deemed the appropriate norms of behavior and identity. However, Blackness is never fixed, nor can it fit into one model because our bodies are not fixed. Special education through a full intersectional lens and anti-racist education forces us to ask questions about the complexities involved and to deal with these complexities as they engage with power structures. In doing so, we are able to see how power reproduces itself so as to uphold its power and notice that where there is power there are also power imbalances. Intersectional disability education, like anti-racist education, allows for us to respond to power imbalances by questioning our relationship to one another. When we look to our one-to-one relationships, it creates the space for us to think of our relationships to community, and community-to-community relationships, as well as individual-to-community relationships, allowing for embodied knowledge and validity of this knowledge another entry point into our school spaces.

Conclusion

In this chapter, I hoped to aid in laying some of the groundwork that is needed to start looking at and bringing awareness to what is going on in the intersections of Blackness and disability. Understanding Blackness, disability, and where the overlaps are and what goes on in the overlap is not only "recovery work, but work that requires a willingness to deconstruct our systems" (Bell, 2011, p. 3). While identity and having a Black identity have been socially constructed, this social construction has created an environment outside and inside our schools that normalizes and reproduces White domination and power. Special education within our schools, as previously stated, runs on the underlying notions of the medical model of disability that places the problem within the individual, separating the individual and the problem from the community, while simultaneously limiting any cohesion and support for this individual. Special education classrooms are looked at either as temporary sites or as spaces filled with bodies with limited possibilities. Ultimately, special education classes and their students are treated as second thoughts in the current education system. Disability education, through its current policies and procedures, creates an atmosphere where two marginalized groups are positioned against each other in competition through comparison. The outcome is that one is reduced to favor the other, a balancing act colonialism thrives on, as it denies the existence of individuals belonging to both groups (Dunhamn et al., 2015). In following Paul Gilroy's (2000) notion of anti-racism work in *Against Race: Imagining Political Culture beyond the Color Line,* anti-racist work in disability education lies within the practices that enable systems of oppression to exist. Consequently, this requires intersectional disability education through the foundation and principles of Afrocentric education so that special education classes (and education systems at large) can begin to "challenge rather than further perpetuate [e]xisting negative constructs regarding multiple identities including disability itself" (Mitchell, 2013, p. 233). Continuing in the current manner will continue to silence Blackness in special education spaces while also leaving the futurity of Blackness and Black bodies in question.

References

Annamma, S. A., Jackson, D. D., & Morrison, D. (2017). Conceptualizing Color-Evasiveness: Using Dis/ability Critical Race Theory to Expand a Color-Blind Racial Ideology in

Education and Society. *Race Ethnicity and Education, 20*(2), 147–162. doi:10.1080/13613324.2016.1248837

Bell, C. (2011). *Blackness and Disability: Critical Examinations and Cultural Interventions.* East Lansing: Michigan State University Press

Brown, R., & Parekh, G. (2010). Special Education: Structural Overview and Student Demographics. *Toronto District School Board.* Retrieved from http://www.tdsb.on.ca/Portals/0/Community/Community%20Advisory%20committees/ICAC/research/SpecEdStructuralOverviewStudentDemo.pdf

Carbado, D. W., Crenshaw, K. W., Mays, V. M., & Tomlinson, B. (2013). Intersectionality: Mapping the Movements of a Theory. *Du Bois Review: Social Science Research on Race, 10*(2), 303–312. http://doi:10.1017/S1742058X13000349

Community Living Ontario. (2018). Ontario's Education System is Failing Students with Disabilities. *Community Living.* Retrieved from https://communitylivingontario.ca/en/ontarios-education-system-is-failing-students-with-disabilities/

Connor, D., & Ferri, B. (2005). Tools of Exclusion: Race, Disability, and (Re)segregated Education. *Teacher's College Record, 107*(3), 453–474.

Daaisma, M. (2017). Black Students in Toronto Streamed into Courses below Their Ability, Report Finds. *CBC.* Retrieved from http://www.cbc.ca/news/canada/toronto/study-Black-students-toronto-york-university-1.4082463

Dei, G., & Kempf, A. (2013). *New Perspectives on African-Centered Education in Canada.* Toronto: Canadian Schlor's Choice.

Dunhamn, J., Harris, J., Jarrett, S., Moore, L., Nishida, A., ... & Schalk, S. (2015). Developing and Reflecting on a Black Disability Studies Pedagogy: Work from the National Black Disability Coalition. *Disabilities Study Quarterly, 35*(2). Retrieved from http://dsq-sds.org/article/view/4637/3933#top

Gilroy, P. (2000). *Against Race: Imagining Political Culture beyond the Color Line.* Cambridge, MA: Harvard University Press.

Gordon, A. (2017, April 24). Black Students Hindered by Academic Streaming, Suspensions: Report. *The Star.* Retrieved from https://www.thestar.com/yourtoronto/education/2017/04/24/Black-students-hindered-by-academic-streaming-suspensions-report.html

Kelly, J. (1998). *Under the Gaze: Learning to be Black in White Society,* Halifax: Fernwood.

Leonardo, Z. & Broderick, A. (2011). Smartness as Property: A Critical Exploration of Intersections Between Whiteness and Disability Studies. *Teachers College Record, 113*(10), 2206–2232.

Mitchell, D. (2013). Disability in the Context of Blackness: Is It a Manifestation of Past Sins or a Blessing in Disguise? *Religion & Education, 40*(2), 221–235. doi:10.1080/15507394.2013.786630

Moore, J., & Lewis, C. (2012). *African American Students in Urban Schools.* New York, NY: Peter Lang.

Massoumeh, Z., & Leia, J. (2012). An Investigation of Medical Model and Special Education Methods. *Procedia – Social and Behavioral Sciences, 46,* (pp. 5802-5804). Retrieved from https://www-sciencedirect-com.myaccess.library.utoronto.ca/science/article/pii/S1877042812022549

Ontario Ministry of Education. (2018). *Special Education.* Retrieved from http://www.edu.gov.on.ca/eng/parents/speced.html

Sium, B. (2014). *How Black and Working Class Children Are Deprived of Basic Education in Canada.* Toronto: Sense Publishers.

Titchkosky, T. (2003). *Disability, Self, and Society.* Toronto, Canada: University of Toronto Press.

Walcott, R. (1997). *Black Like Who?: Writing Black Canada.* Toronto: Insomniac Press.

CHAPTER 10

Prisoners of a Skin Color: The Criminalization and the Social Construction of Blackness in Risk Assessment of Black Youth

Dr. Paul Banahene Adjei and Harriet Akanmori

In Shakespearean's *Henry II*, readers were introduced to the frustration of King Henry II about the Archbishop of Canterbury, Thomas A Becket, who despite being appointed the Lord Chancellor of the King was still more loyal to the Pope than to the King. In his frustration, King Henry proclaimed, "Who will rid me of this meddlesome priest?" The next day, the Archbishop was murdered by four knights. *Henry II* reminds us of the frustration of dealing with an issue that poses permanent difficulty for one's well-being.

Writing under "the fact of Blackness" in the *Black Skin, White Masks*, Frantz Fanon (1967) similarly expressed frustration about his own skin color—Blackness—which appeared to affect his ontological status as a human being with a self-consciousness of a normative being like a European man. According to Fanon, there is an emotional and physical cost in showing up Black in an anti-Blackness world that the possessor of a Black skin often gets infected with "corporeal malediction" through "historico-racial schema" (p. 111) in which the bearer of the Black skin feel imprisoned by "white glancers." As Fanon puts it,

> 'Dirty nigger!' Or simply, 'Look, a Negro!' I came into the world imbued with the will to find a meaning in things, my spirit filled with the desires to attain to the source of the world, then I found that I was an object in the midst of other objects. . . . And then the occasion arose when I had to meet the white man's eyes. An unfamiliar weight burdened me. The real world challenged my claims. In the white world the man of color encounters difficulties in the development of his bodily schema. Consciousness of the body is solely a negating activity. It is a third person consciousness. (pp. 109 - 110)

Fanon describes such experience as a form of imprisonment, one in which progress can only be gained either "by crawling" (p. 116) or "an amputation, an excision, a hemorrhage" that will spatter the whole Black body and fill it with white blood (p. 112).

In this chapter, we draw on Fanonian racial interpellation, online publications, scholarly research, and institutional reports from the United States and Canada to critically examine the social construction of Blackness in risk assessment of Black youth. Though a small minority of the Canadian population—815,000 in 2006 Canada population census and projected to increase to 1,809,000 by 2031 (Statistics Canada, 2012a)—Black people represent the second highest percentage of incarcerated persons in the Canadian prison system, closely following Indigenous peoples of Canada. In the United States, the three-strikes law has had cumulative effects on racial minorities. In California, for instance, over 150,000 Blacks have been incarcerated (Brewer & Heitzeg, 2008; Foster & Hagan, 2009). Further, anti-social lobbying projects—which are sometimes disguised as gentrification projects—have also marked vulnerable groups such as the homeless, the poor working-class Blacks, and welfare recipients as disposable and unnecessary burden on states coffers (Giroux, 2006; Kempa, Stenning, & Wood, 2004). In Toronto, Canada, for instance, entire communities such as Jane and Finch—mostly dominated by Blacks—have been branded "risky" areas, and in agreement with "the risk" rhetoric, the local law enforcement officers have intensified policing practices in these communities. In Tanner and Wortley's (2002) survey of over 3,400 Toronto high school students, 74 percent of Black youth in comparison with 31 percent South Asians, 27 percent Asians, and 13 percent Whites were found to be unfairly stopped and questioned by police. Black youth were also much more likely to report being physically searched by police (40 percent) compared to 17 percent White and 11 percent Asian students.

In the United States, any routine traffic stops involving a young Black driver carries the potential of tragedy for the young driver—either being shot by the police or being arrested and criminally charged (Crockett, 2015). The untimely death of Sandra Bland in July 2015's routine traffic stop in Waller County, Texas, is a critical reminder of the fragility of Black lives in the United States as the federal statistics indicate that the police are

31 percent more likely to pull over a Black driver than a White driver in the United States (Crockett, 2015; Goodman & González, 2015). In fact, a study published by Malcolm X Grassroots Movement shows that in 2012 alone, of the percentage of general people killed by either the police, security guards, or vigilantes in five cities in the United States, Blacks constitute 91 percent killed in Chicago, Illinois; 48 percent in Houston, Texas; 87 percent in New York; 100 percent in Rockford, Illinois; and 100 percent in Saginaw, Michigan (Eisen, 2014). Arguably, those who argue crime has no color have not paid attention to how statistics of victims of police brutality discount non-White bodies. What do these statistics mean for unmasking race and crime in the United States and Canada? What then does this mean for the embeddedness of race in risk assessments? The rest of the chapter examines these questions.

The Embeddedness of Race and Racialization In Risk Assessments: A Conceptual Thinking

More than a century ago, W.E.B. Du Bois, on launching his groundbreaking 1903's treatise *The Souls of Black Folk*, noted with certainty these memorable words:

> Herein lie buried many things which if read with patience may show the strange meaning of being Black here in the dawning of the Twentieth Century. This meaning is not without interest to you, Gentle Reader; for the problem of the Twentieth Century is the problem of the color-line. I pray you, then, receive my little book in all charity, studying my words with me, forgiving mistake and foible for sake of the faith and passion that is in me, and seeking the grain of truth hidden there. (p. 3)

While many had hoped that Du Bois's color line would fade away before the end of the 20th century, the color line problem unfortunately has followed us into the 21st century. Nowhere is the problem of Dubois's color line more visible than the recent racially unjustified slayings of unarmed young Black men and women in Canada and the United States—Michael Brown, Tamir Rice, Travyon Martin, Eric Garner, Freddie Gray, Renisha McBride, Aiyana Jones, Philando Castile, Deravis "Caine" Rogers, and Sakia Gunn of the United States; Michael Wade Lawson, Eric Osawe, Andrew Loku, and Jardine-Douglas of Canada to name a few—by mostly White killers, and in each case the assailants claimed they felt their lives were in danger by their unarmed Black victims. Henry Giroux (2015) describes this phenomenon as "the new totalitarianism of the boot in your face racism, one in which the punishing state is the central institution for both controlling poor minorities of race and class and enforcing the rules of the financial elite" (p. 1). The experience of being Black in the United States and Canada is best captured in the words of James Baldwin (1985), the African American literary writer: "It comes as a great shock to discover that the country [the United States or Canada] which is your birthplace and to which you owe your life and identity has not, in its whole system of reality, evolved any place for you. The disaffection and the gap between people, only on the basis of their skins, begins there and accelerates throughout your whole lifetime" (p. 404). Despite this reality that racism is the hydra-headed issue that refuses to die in Euro-American/Canadian society, there are those who think that by denying, rejecting, trivializing, rationalizing, and distancing themselves from the color line problem, they will somehow wish the color line away (see Allahar, 2006; Gilroy, 2000; Hall, 1996, 1997; Hier & Bolaria, 2006; Lopez, 1995; Miles, 1980; Miles & Brown, 2006). The racial distancing reached an absurd point after President Obama won the United States presidency, with the emergence of a post-racialist discourse that suggested now that a Black person had been elected into the highest office of the United States, racism had been transcended, and therefore race is no longer a relevant issue (Cho, 2008; Goldberg, 2009, 2012; Howard, 2014). What post-racialism discourse hopes to achieve is for society to forget or ignore the scars and legacies of racism even though the historical ramifications of racism are still being felt today (Goldberg, 2009). One can therefore argue that this silencing of racism in post-racialist discourse while racial arrangements continue is the strategy of Whiteness to reap the benefits of racism while at the same time branding accusations of racial injustices as spurious (Cho, 2008; Goldberg, 2009; Howard, 2014).

In *Against Race: Imagining Political Culture beyond the Color Line,* Paul Gilroy (2000) writes about the spuriousness of race by rejecting Frantz Fanon's epidermization of skin color on the grounds that skin color pigmentation is no more significant at the threshold of identity. Gilroy calls on society to move past "raciology"—the study of race as a scholarly discipline—because raciology focuses on the old irrelevant differences that exist between Whites and non-Whites. Gilroy, however, admitted in the latter part of the book that the utopian project of getting rid of race hinges on unstable conditions he describes as "a crisis of raciology" (p. 265). For Gilroy, the "crisis of raciology" demands critical action: First, either humanity stands aside to allow raciological regimes to reconfigure around genomic or gene-centered determinism, or, second, society sees to it that the new technologies of imagining bodies and coding differences destabilize those "truths" of race based on morphological and epidermal differences (also see Adjei, 2013).

The limitation in Paul Gilroy's analysis of raciology is that he fails to adequately distinguish the "representation of race" from the "lived experience of race." Although the representation of Blackness in North American culture may be shifting as "Black culture" has today become a billion dollar industry in the mainstream American-Canadian society (Cashmore, 1997; Hart, 2009; Tomlinson, 2016), the popularity of Black culture does not remove nor negate the threat of showing up Black in the United States and in Canada. In fact, a Black person gets killed every 28 hours in the United States by either the police, security guards, or vigilantes (Eisen, 2014). To put it differently, the popularity of Black culture in North America does not make it anymore safe than it is for Blacks in the United States and Canada. What does this revelation say about Paul Gilroy's analysis of raciology? Frantz Fanon (1967), using his own life example, warns us against the danger of engaging in this highly intellectual abstract discussion of race. Fanon argues that the knowledge that comes with experiencing racism is entirely different from the knowledge that comes with reading or writing about racism. Although Fanon has an intellectual knowledge of race and on many occasions had joined force with others to resist racial injustice, it appears his intellectual knowledge of racism could not prepare him adequately for the day he experienced racism in the flesh:

> I have talked about the Black problem with friends, or, more rarely, with American Negroes. Together we protested, we asserted the equality of all men in the world.... But I was satisfied with an intellectual understanding of these differences. It was not really dramatic.... And then the occasion arose when I had to meet the white man's eyes. An unfamiliar weight burdened me. The real world challenged my claims. (p. 110)

Arguably, Fanon was neither against an intellectual knowledge of race, nor was he suggesting only people with an experiential knowledge of race should be allowed to discuss racism. Instead, he argues that an intellectual knowledge of race must be considered limited in order to understand the real experience of racism. Fanon (1967) therefore calls for a broad theoretical elucidation of race in order to understand and unpack the existential threat of showing up Black in anti-Black racism contexts (see also Adjei, 2013).

Unlike other forms of identity such as class, sexuality, gender, religion, nationality, and disability that, arguably, could be hidden or temporary, there is no temporal concealment for the one who shows up Black in anti-Black racism contexts. Instead, the Black person is immediately caught up in what Ralph Ellison (1952) describes in his novel as the invisible man: "I am invisible, understand, simply because people refuse to see me. Like the bodiless heads you see sometimes in circus sideshows, it is as though I have been surrounded by mirrors of hard, distorting glass" (p. 3). Thus, when racial identity becomes an important category that informs the risk assessments and criminalization of people, bodies already deemed social threats because of their Blackness easily become the targets.

Relatedly, Adjei (2013), using the murder of Travyon Martin by George Zimmerman as a case in point, discusses how public spaces are socially and politically constructed to determine which bodies are worthy to inhabit certain spaces and which bodies are deemed intruders once they enter into certain spaces. Adjei argues that Travyon Martin's death has little to do with the obnoxious Florida "stand your ground" law and gun proliferation in the United States, but more to do with the racial spatial rules that exist in the United States. Adjei further argues that the crime of Travyon Martin, contrary to the claim of his "innocence," is that he broke racial spatial rules by moving his Black body from a space of degeneration into a space of respectability—an adventure that is reserved for only Whites because they alone possess an unquestioned right to go anywhere they want. Thus, when George Zimmerman said Travyon Martin looked "real suspicious" when he was seen at the Retreat at Twin Lakes in the city of Stanford, Florida, he was invariably saying Martin was "out of place" and therefore deserved to be followed, questioned, and if possible stopped. Adjei concludes that the encounter between George Zimmerman and Travyon Martin is a reenactment of racist imperial history that creates, regulates, and reminds Black people of their "limited place" in the larger American society.

In examining how a place becomes race, Sugrue (1996) notes the significant roles local politicians, real estate agents and developers, and community-based neighborhood preservationists play in discouraging Blacks from moving into White neighborhoods. Sugrue argues that in a postwar city, "Blackness and whiteness assume a spatial definition" (p. 9). Blacks who tried to break the racial spatial rules by buying homes in White neighborhoods were met with violence and intimidation (Bass, 2001). For example, between 1945 and 1960s, over 200 incidents of White antagonism toward Blacks for moving into White neighborhood in Detroit—harassment, mass demonstrations, picketing, effigy burning, window breaking, arson, vandalism, and physical attacks—were recorded (Sugrue, 1996). In Chicago alone, 58 Black homes were bombed between 1917 and 1921 (Bass, 2001). In one particular case, a Black real estate agent's home and office in Chicago were bombed seven times in just one year (Massey & Denton, 1993).

The point we want to establish is that the social construction of Blackness as quintessential evil, no doubt, has material, psychical, and tangible effects on how Blacks are policed and regulated in Canada and the United States. Although Anthony Platt and his colleagues (2010), authors of the book, *The Iron Fist and the Velvet Glove,* want readers to believe that police brutality against racialized groups is a reflection of a broader capitalist repression of the working class, the important role of racism in policing cannot be easily dismissed. In fact, Myrdal (1944) argues that racism in policing helps creates "an artificial city" (p. 619) devoid of any politeness and civility where the rules of law appear to have little to no bearing over police activities, and all manners of police violence against Blacks are permitted and sometimes encouraged. McCulloch (2001) emphasizes that the social construction of bodies deemed a threat to society usually has a logic to it: There is usually an ulterior motive underlying this move, and it gradually becomes normalized and accepted as part of the system. As William and Murphy (1990) rightly note:

> The fact that the legal order not only countenanced but sustained slavery, segregation, and discrimination for most of our nation's history and the fact that the police were bound to uphold that order—set a pattern for police behavior and attitudes toward minority communities that has persisted until the present day. That pattern includes the idea that minorities have fewer civil rights, that the task of the police is to keep them under control, and that the police have little responsibility for protecting them from crime within their communities. (p. 2)

Thus, the current rhetoric of risk and national security, and the resulting penal excesses in North America today, when considered from the point of view of the racialization of risk, have been seen from one perspective as a mask for racial targeting and profiling. The risk assessments contain racist prejudice, especially when the statistical associations made from data gathered from them are analyzed and employed to generate risk in a self-fulfilling prophecy; anti-crime policies and practices intentionally target communities masked as "criminals," which results in a high level of incarcerations among the targeted communities. The high numbers of incarceration among the targeted communities then become statistics that justifiy their over-policing. This vicious cycle of risk management has become a worrisome issue for fear that these frenetic measures do not commensurate with the actual realities of crime and crime control statistics, but rather seem to resonate with certain political and ideological priorities that raise serious questions about identity and issues of national security. The discussion that follows elaborates on this issue.

Race and Risk Assessments: The Social Construction of "At Risk" Populations

The social construction of race has been essentially defined as the "Othering" of non-Europeans as degenerates in order to rationalize their violent experiences—what Aimé Cesairé (1955) describes as "thingification" (p. 6). There cannot be any doubt that race is a salient factor in the victimization and criminalization of racial minorities (Bosworth, 2012). The irony is that racism has been "overtly" eliminated from the letter of the law, but somehow it continues to be active covertly in the spirit and the practice of the law (Aberson & Gaffney, 2009). As already demonstrated, statistics from both Canada and the United States suggest that the criminal justice system is being used as a form of racist agenda to re-inscribe the superiority of Whiteness, and in the process, racialized people like Blacks, Aboriginals, and Muslims have been pathologized as criminals and degenerates.

The United States and Canada have a settler history-based phenomenology of racial relations with Indigenous peoples, people of African descent, and Latinos. This has greatly impacted present-based epistemologies of race in Canada and the United States. In fact, there are research works in the United States that argue that the "slave-catching patrolling" in the United States is a precursor to modern systems of policing (David, 2015; Hadden, 2001; National Constables Association, 1995; Reichel, 1988; Turner, Giacopassi, & Vandiver, 2006; Walker, 1992). W.E.B Du Bois (1904) also writes, "A system of rural police" was formed to control slaves (p. 3). Turner, Giacopassi, and Vandiver (2006) also write:

> The literature clearly establishes that a legally sanctioned law enforcement system existed in America before the Civil War for the express purpose of controlling the slave population and protecting the interests of slave owners. The similarities between the slave patrols and modern American policing are too salient to dismiss or ignore. Hence, the slave patrol should be considered a forerunner of modern American law enforcement. (p. 186)

Victor Kappeler (2014), tracing the history of American policing to slavery in the United States, also echoes:

> The birth and development of the American police can be traced to a multitude of historical, legal and political-economic conditions. The institution of slavery and the control of minorities, however, were two of the more formidable historic features of American society shaping early policing. Slave patrols and Night Watches, which later became modern police departments, were both designed to control the behaviors of minorities. (para. 1)

Suffice to say, the abolition of slavery did not result in the abolition of essentialist racism in law and the manner of policing; if anything, the manner of enforcing criminal laws in the United States has become a legitimate method of "lynching" young Black men and women while upholding the interests of Whiteness (Brewer & Heitzeg, 2008). Are we then surprised when we hear stories of members of Ku Klux Klan in the police force in the Unites States as in the case of Williamson County, Texas, where two police officers were fired for being members (ABC News 2017), or the case of Florida, where a deputy police chief was forced to resign after being exposed as a member of KKK in 2014 (Gardner, 2015)? There is more. In September 2015, a Louisiana police detective was caught in a photo giving a Nazi salute at a KKK rally (Rivas, 2015). Similarly, in Alabama, an Anniston police officer was exposed for speaking at a rally of a League of the South—a known Southern nationalist organization (Gardner, 2015). In Los Angeles, a United States district judge, Terry J. Hatter Jr., described police deputies at the Lynwood Sheriff's station as a "neo-Nazi, white supremacist gang" (Tobar, 1991, para. 3), who, according to civil rights lawsuits filed by 70 residents of Lynwood, allegedly engage "in systematic acts of shooting, killing, brutality, terrorism, house-trashing, and other acts of lawlessness and wanton abuse of power," especially against Latinos and Blacks (Tobar, 1991, para. 5). Further, Larissa Moore, in her investigation of unsolved civil rights murders between 1946 and 1969, including suspicious cases that involved police officers pulling the trigger, notes that members of the KKK have infiltrated police departments "because the laws don't apply to [police] if they are the law (as cited in Rivas, 2015, para. 10). Larissa Moore further argues, "If you think about the history with the police department, they were pretty much set up to continue white supremacy" (para.11). Arguably, when Angelia Williams Graves, the Norfolk City council woman said, "More than 200 have taken off their white hats and white-sheeted robes and put on police uniforms. Some of them have put on shirts and ties as policymakers and some of them have put on robes as judges" (as cited in Wootson, 2016, para. 2), she was not engaging in incendiary talks but rather speaking to what many studies on racism and policing have noticed. What then does this mean for the social construction of at-risk populations? If criminal laws and enforcement of laws have been used historically as a method to oppress Blacks, can we fully trust racist police officers to be unbiased when assessing risk in Black communities?

The implications of race do not only stop at risk assessments and their impact on the criminalization of racialized peoples, but also contributes to the police profiling of racialized groups as the quintessence of evil and the carriers of deviancy and degeneracy. The social construction of Blacks and Latinos in the United States, and Blacks and Aboriginals in Canada, as the "usual suspects" has produced a form of self-fulfilling prophecy in police practices, and in the process compromises the image of the police as fair and unbiased law enforcement units in the justice system (Wortley & Tanner, 2006). The Ontario Commission on Systemic Racism (1995) declared that Black youth were less likely to be allowed pre-sentencing release by the police and more likely to be detained until a hearing, while, conversely, White youth were more likely to be detained on sentencing rather than on remand. Statistics Canada (2012b) states that Aboriginal youth are overrepresented in the correctional system in all reporting provinces and territories, except Newfoundland and Labrador where only 26 percent of youth on admissions are Aboriginal. In Manitoba, Aboriginal people account for 71 percent of sentenced admissions in 2005/2006, although Aboriginals only make up 16 percent of Manitoba's population. In Saskatchewan, Aboriginal adults make up 79 percent of the total prisoner population, although they make up 15 percent of Saskatchewan's population. And these figures are in spite of changes to the criminal code in Canada to address the overrepresentation of Aboriginals in prisons in Canada (Chura, 2014).

The rhetoric of "war on" is apparently impacting differently on certain racial and ethnic groups in the United States and Canada. For example, the war on drugs has become a notable war on Blacks—Blacks comprise 62 percent of drug offenders sent to state prisons, yet Blacks represent only 12 percent of the United States population (Watkins, 2011). The war on terror has also become a war on Arabs, Persians, and Muslims (Powell, 2011). Even youth gangs from Arab, Persian, and Muslim backgrounds are now a subject of anti-terrorist scrutiny and are considered a threat to national security (Bleich, Nisar, & Abdelhamid, 2016). In fact, Blacks, Arabs, Persians, and Muslims have been targeted as potential penal subjects that need scrutiny, and should they be found foul of the law, deserve to be treated as rational actors who have chosen to commit crime and therefore must be punished and not reformed (Bosworth, 2012). Despite the apparent racial profiling in risk assessments, there are those who are reluctant to acknowledge the saliency of race as a category in risk assessment. This refusal to acknowledge the embedded racism within risk assessments has resulted in high incidents of racial biases in policing, legal procedures, sentencing, and incarceration. Within this context, Hannah-Moffat and Marrutto (2010) and Garland (2003) have argued against the exclusive use of risk assessment tools to define at-risk populations.

Risk assessment and the Racial Masking of at-Risk Population

In Foucault's (1980) theory of discourse analysis, he explains that it is important to look at text to discern what it does and does not say. He further posits that language and the power therein are not neutral. With this in mind, it is imperative to scrutinize how risk assessments have been employed to reinforce the creation of the "Other" as subordinate and different. Risk assessments are tools that were initially built for use by Eurocentric societies, but were also embedded with discriminatory features when used on other racialized groups. The use of language within them reinforces discriminatory policing and practices and indeed shows clear patterns of exclusion (Zedner, 2009). They have become an integral part in actuarial crime control and are now used internationally. Originally developed in Canada by two psychologists, Andrews and Dowden (2007), these assessments target the revealing factors that indicate criminogenic settings or environments such as family background and peer relations and how this further relates to criminogenic behaviors. They were intended to reinforce rehabilitative models of penology through a behavioral cognitive approach but have now become restructured and adapted for supporting risk management and control. These assessments now include a mélange of actuarial and cognitive risk tools, some designed for specific target groups (Pratt, 2010).

The appeal of risk assessments to law enforcement agencies and the criminal justice system lies in their ability to assess how risky an offender is to others. They are used to track patterns in groups or categories of people in order to predict or anticipate certain criminogenic behavior. They claim a level of standardization in order to achieve consistency and lack of bias, but this claim to equity remains highly debatable. In an era of actuarial penology and criminology, these assessments have replaced the subjectivity and expense of employing clinical psychologists and aim at applying the same criteria to everyone who takes the assessment to ensure validity and defensibility of the results. This claim to accountability has promoted its appeal to legal practitioners such as probation officers, courts, as well the neoliberal agenda for actuarial efficiency and cost-effective management. Thus, though they were initially developed to assist prison classifications to determine rehabilitation programs for inmates, they have now progressed to other levels of use, such as determining parole in courts, assisting frontline officers to make on-the-spot decisions, and informing immigration and customs officers in their decisions at the borders of the country. Therefore, assessment tools have graduated from their original purpose of enabling correctional service workers to draw up profiles of criminogenic persons and to determine which programs to allocate resources to in order to effect change in their lives (e.g., drug or alcohol addictions) and are now performing multipurpose functions in crime, crime control, and national security (Marutto & Hannah-Moffat, 2006).

The risk assessment tools are made up of static factors such as information on age, criminal history, mental health, and abuse history; then also they contain dynamic factors such as family and marital history, employment and education history, and information on substance abuse. Often, the static factors are of secondary importance in these assessments; it is the dynamic factors that are the focus of scrutiny, and these lead to the identification and labeling of certain groups of people as "at risk" (Marutto & Hannah-Moffat, 2006). For example, accommodation or housing and financial status in real life are always closely correlated, but the assessment tools do not make this connection, and due to the absence of other such factors that are significant indicators of potential risk, what is in actual fact indicative of high violence in real-life terms may not show up as being high risk on the assessment tools. Thus, Aboriginal offenders who may exhibit high alcoholism recidivism rates may stand out as high risk on the assessments, yet this can in no way be correlated to mean they are highly violent. On the other hand, given the same assessment, the Sandy Hook shooter, who actually killed many, would have scored as very low risk and therefore low violence marks on these tools.

The main confusion has resulted because risk assessment tools were originally intended to measure potential for re-offense or recidivism to clinical psychologists, not as tools to measure potential for violence for court judges. This has resulted in the targeting and labeling of certain groups of people, especially Blacks and Aboriginal peoples, as high-risk offenders, when in actual fact many of those so labeled are nothing more than alcohol and drug abusers, who in most cases, need nothing more than clinical rehabilitation and not criminalization. In effect, the risk tools are more or less being used to put normal findings in society at a "risk of pathologization," raising the risk potential of issues that previously had nothing to do with social or national security and thereby elevating risk in society (Kemshall, 2003).

In Ontario, Canada, both the Correctional Services and the Ontario Ministry for Community Safety require the police to use these risk assessments in their work to process people of interest; however, interestingly, this is not reported in court as determining presentencing report results. However, it is more than apparent that these risk tools do affect sentencing significantly and contribute greatly to the decision to determine who goes through the court system and is eventually sentenced to imprisonment and who is diverted to alternate programs. These facts and state of affairs need to be transparently acknowledged (Harcourt, 2007).

As policy discussions become increasingly framed in neoliberal terms and emphasize the management of high-risk groups, Feeley and Simon (1992) point out that this intensification of actuarial criminology has led to a highlighting of the interaction of criminal justice institutions and *specific segments of the population*. The question is "Who has been characterized as specific segments of the population?" Wilson (1987) uses the term *underclass* to characterize a segment of society that is viewed as permanently excluded from social mobility and economic integration. He was referring specifically to a largely Black and Hispanic population living in concentrated zones of poverty in central cities of the United States, separated physically and institutionally from the mainstream of society. Without literacy, skills, or hope, Wilson characterizes this subset of people as a self-perpetuating and pathological segment of society, and concludes, "Conceived of this way, the underclass is also a dangerous class, not only for what any particular member may or may not do, but more generally for collective potential misbehavior. It is treated as a high-risk group that must be managed for the protection of the rest of society" (p. 34).

Within such minority communities in North America, and in the case of Canada, with the Aboriginal community on reservations, all the predictors of risk factors can be found. The males within a certain age bracket live in housing projects and are usually subject to varying degrees of poverty and deprivation. The youth from such marginalized communities and homes are usually assessed as being criminogenic and "at risk" of sliding into a pathological descent due to family structures that do not reflect the traditional Eurocentric normalized family, such as the lack of a father or a male role model and having little parent supervision. Other risk factors come from neighborhood influences from deviant peers and family members, potential for alcohol and illicit substance use, and delinquency and drop out, which affect measurements like educational performance and are significant indicators of risk in the assessment tools. Even immigration status and ethnicity or race within this context become red flags for risk. Eventually, it is these same criminogenic factors and markers of social alienation that drive the scores to high risk even higher.

In this case, for criminal elements apprehended from these communities at risk of poverty and multiple abuses, incarceration becomes best understood as a social management instrument rather than an institution for the mere process of criminal justice. Unfortunately, it is the youth who suffer the most casualties in these communities, and the National Crime Prevention Center (2012), Public Safety Canada, reported that youth crime continues to represent a small proportion of overall crimes. In 2010, of the 494,621 persons charged for criminal code violations (excluding traffic), 64,800 (13.1 percent) were youths.

That contemporary language of corrections reinforces a penal discourse saturated by risk and the principles of effective practice or risk classifications. These risk classifications identify high-risk offenders and those likely to re-offend and sort them to receive more intensive services while those classified as low risk require lower levels of intervention. This practice has fueled the development of "actuarially derived risk prediction instruments," which are now routinely used in the criminal justice system, and the correctional industry sorts offenders into categories, ostensibly with the intention of identifying individuals who will benefit from rehabilitative interventions. This risk-driven, differentiated approach also uses the logic of risk to determine the level of resources that will be appropriately allocated to individual offenders. Indeed, Robinson (2008) goes as far as to say that a "tiering framework" is embedded within this model, specifying four differential response interventions for allocating offenders' risk profiles: punish, help, change, and control. Thus, risk assessments play a central role in presentencing and sentencing (Robinson, 2008). Field and Nelken (2010), like many other critics of these actuarial risk assessment tools, conclude that there is bias inherent in these tools that construct young offenders into "little monsters," which in turn predispose judicial officials to making punitive sentencing decisions, leading to unintended high incarceration rates.

Conclusion

The notion of crime as risk, and the new paradigm of seeing crime as a social contingency that requires defensive action, has ensured that prison has become a warehouse for high-risk groups. To determine the decision between offering the offender the opportunity for custody or community-based sanctions or supervision, the criminal justice system relies on the technology of risk assessments to classify and sort offenders into groups in order to determine the degree of control according to their resulting risk profiles. Within this model, effective rehabilitation equals effective risk management, whether criminogenic people were warehoused in prison or under some form of community-based supervision (Robinson, 2008). Prison in this actuarial era is no longer a place for rehabilitation, but a place to warehouse individuals for extended times, to function primarily as punitive incapacitation of offenders.

Within risk-based actuarial management, the fundamental premise of risk theory is that risk probabilities are predictive and that anything and anyone can be seen as risky depending on how risk is framed and characterized. The ultimate aim of risk management is prevention of crime, and risk logic is based on rational assumptions, which rest on the premise that accidents, and therefore crime, are preventable. Thus, risk assessments, through the measurement of predetermined factors to measure the likelihood of offense, are used to predict the likelihood to commit crime, and risk assessment tools have become the trend to assess and determine who constitutes a risk and inform how to treat or process the "at risk" within the criminal justice system. The main principle guiding the treatment of "risky offenders" is to exclude and incapacitate them, leading to the criminalization of whole groups and categories of individuals (Douglas, 1999). Many criminological studies have shown that identified "risky populations" tend to be overrepresented by racialized minorities.

Actuarial forms of representation promote quantification and crime statistics as a way of visualizing populations. It is about identifying and managing unruly groups. It is concerned with the rationality not of individual behavior or even community organization, but of managerial processes (Feeley & Simon, 1992). Rather than extending the capacity of the prison system to rehabilitate or control crime, the correctional enterprise is increasingly interested in actuarial classifications, developing more cost-effective custody and control mechanisms and devising newer technologies and statistical techniques to identify and classify risk, as well as assessing and predicting risk and dangerousness (Kemshall, 2003; Robinson, 2008).

Risk assessments have been designed by academic experts and community, though they are administered by frontline staff such as probation officers and community and social workers. Though this should have ensured their objective usage, these tools are embedded with certain biases that have caused them to end up having racial implications, and though the measurement of these tools does not focus or openly address race, the factors that are employed to determine risk profiles are inherently racially implied (Douglas, 1999). In examining cultural theories of risk, Douglas points out that risk as a cultural factor can be framed multiple ways, and she identifies that in North America, risk is framed in a manner that has implications for race and that reflects the cultural dominance of "Whiteness" and the labeling of non-Whites as the "Other." Thus, risk assessment tools are calculated to incriminate the "Other."

The relationship between race and criminal punishment is a complex issue that should not be simplified by treating race as an objective factor. Obviously, much work needs to be done in terms of empirical study and police education to achieve the needed change in how actors in the criminal justice system think about and treat the relationship between race and criminal punishment in order to attenuate the disproportionate, discriminatory treatment of racial minorities within the criminal justice system. These developments, all in the name of greater security of the public and rhetoric of risk management, have become worrisome trends to observers of social equity and proponents of rehabilitation in punishment. There is a growing concern that all these frenetic measures are not commensurate with the actual realities of crime and crime control statistics, but rather seem to resonate with certain political and ideological priorities that are reflections of a neoliberalist agenda, an agenda that in an era of globalization raises serious challenges for questions of identity and citizenship and the matter of security.

Despite the fact that these assessment tools seem attractive to the neoliberal logic of institutionalized risk management, and present a fitting means of statistical analysis for justification and defense of correctional and criminal justice policies and practices, there is no doubt about the fact that there are obvious biases inherent in the risk assessment as they stand currently, and these constitute a serious limitation and challenge to their validity as universal assessment tools. This is especially so, as their statistical analysis reflects social values of the dominant society.

In conclusion, we would advocate for a renewed effort to render these risk assessment tools as racially specific as possible, informed by anti-racist research on various communities. This cannot be a difficult task, as within the academia there already exists a large body of sociological and sociolegal research literature on the various racial groups represented in the country (Crawford, 1998; Garland, 2001; Swift, 2006). Such anti-racist assessments are certain to yield more statistical credibility and therefore make more credible claims to risk rankings and identifications.

In greater society there needs to be an effort, starting especially within the educational system and reaching to institutional and systemic levels, for an improved history-based phenomenology of race through the continuity of the contextual importance of authentic historical narratives. When the public and criminal justice actors are educated to acknowledge the salience of race in the construction of criminal justice tools and outcomes through subjective, contextual information about race, and empirical evidence abundant in social science research, this will be beneficial for improving present-based epistemology of race in criminal punishment. Once there is understanding of the phenomenology of race when it comes to criminal punishment, and acceptance of race as a contextually inseparable subjective risk indicator in terms of the racialized offender, there is hope for change (*R. v. Gladue, [1999] 1 S.C.R. 688*); Loughran, Paternoster, Piquero, & Pogarsky, 2011). As to the use of risk assessments, we can only hope that the social scientists designed these assessments to construct socially in this manner, and future designers of such assessment tools will find a way to refine the use of statistical models to account for race in this way.

However, this chapter cannot end without reverberating the call from Cullen, Wright, and Chamlin (1999) for concern to be paid to social support for at-risk youth, families, and communities. Violence disproportionately occurs in socially disadvantaged communities where race, economic, and social deprivation intersect. The authors describe such support as "good policies because empirical evidence show[s] this is inversely related to individual offending and to macro-level crime rates" and also state that "it will improve the lives of [those] at risk for crime and thereby increase public safety at large. Such social support is the provision of affective and/or instrumental (or material resources . . . also the process of transmitting various forms of capital—human, cultural, social and material)" (Cullen et al., 1999, p. 190).

References

ABC News. (2017). *Texas Officers Fired for Membership in KKK.* Retrieved from https://abcnews.go.com/US/wireStory/officer-leave-apparent-klan-document-home-64879671.

Aberson, C. L., & Gaffney, A. M. (2009). An Integrated Threat Model of Explicit and Implicit Attitudes. *European Journal of Social Psychology, 39*(5), 808–830.

Adjei, P. B. (2013). When Blackness Shows Up Uninvited: Examining the Murder of Trayvon Martin through Fanonian Racial Interpellation. In G. J. Dei & M. Lordan (Eds.), *Contemporary Issues in the Sociology of Race and Ethnicity: A Critical Reader* (pp. 25–41). New York, NY: Peter Lang.

Allahar, A. (2006). The Social Construction of Primordial Identities. In B. S. Hier & B. S. Bolaria (Eds.), *Identity and Belonging: Rethinking Race and Ethnicity in Canadian Society* (pp. 31–42). Toronto, Canada: Canadian Scholars' Press.

Andrews, D. A. & Dowden, C. (2007). The Risk-Need-Responsivity Model of Assessment and Human Service in Prevention and Corrections: Crime-Prevention Jurisprudence. *Canadian Journal of Criminology and Criminal Justice, 49*(4), 439–464.

Baldwin, J. (1985). *The Price of the Ticket: Collected Nonfiction, 1948–1985*. New York, NY: Macmillan.

Bass, S. (2001). Policing Space, Policing Race: Social Control Imperatives and Police Discretionary Decisions. *Social Justice, 28*(1), 156–176.

Bleich, E., Nisar, H., & Abdelhamid, R. (2016). The Effect of Terrorist Events on Media Portrayals of Islam and Muslims: Evidence from New York Times Headlines, 1985–2013. *Ethnic and Racial Studies, 39*(7), 1109–27.

Bosworth, M. (2012). Subjectivity and Identity in Detention: Punishment and Society in a Global Age. *Theoretical Criminology, 16*(2), 123–140.

Brewer, R. M & Heitzeg, N. A. (2008). The Racialization of Crime and Punishment: Criminal Justice, Color-Blind Racism, and the Political Economy of the Prison Industrial Complex. *American Behavioral Scientist, 51*(5), 625–644.

Cashmore, E. (1997). *The Black Culture Industry*. New York, NY: Routledge.

Cesairé, A. (1955). *Discourse on Colonialism*. New York, NY: New York University Press.

Cho, S. (2008). Post-Racialism. *Iowa Law Review. 94*, 1589.

Chura, P. (2014). Report Flags 'Severe' Over-Representation of Aboriginals in Manitoba Jails. *Global News*. Retrieved from https://globalnews.ca/news/1618120/report-flags-severe-over-representation-of-aboriginals-in-manitoba-jails/

Crawford, A. (1998). *Crime Prevention and Community Safety: Politics, Policies and Practices*. Edinburgh, Scotland: Longman.

Crockett S. A., Jr. (2015). Sandra Bland Drove to Texas to Start a New Job, So How Did She End up Dead in Jail? *The Root*. Retrieved from https://www.theroot.com/sandra-bland-drove-to-texas-to-start-a-new-job-so-how-1790860528

Cullen, F. T, Wright, J. P., & Chamlin, M. B. (1999). Social Support and Social Reform: A Progressive Crime Control Agenda. *Crime & Delinquency, 45*(2), 188–207.

David, M. (2015). Police Originated from 'Slave Catching Patrols.' *Counter Current News*. Retrieved from http://countercurrentnews.info/2015/04/police-originated-from-slave-catching-patrols/

Douglas, M. (1999). *Risk and Blame*. London, UK: Routledge.

Du Bois, W. E. B. (1903). *The Souls of Black Folk*. Chicago, IL: A.C. McClurg & Co.

Du Bois, W. E. B. (1904). *Some Notes on Negro Crime, Particularly in Georgia*. Atlanta, GA: Atlanta University Press

Eisen, A. (2014). Operation Ghetto Storm: 2012 Annual Report on the Extrajudicial Killings of 213 Black People by Police, Security Guards and Vigilantes. Oakland, CA: Malcolm X Grassroots Movement.

Ellison, R. (1952). *Invisible Man*. New York, NY: Random House.

Fanon, F. (1967). *Black Skin, White Masks*. New York, NY: Grove Press.

Feeley, M. M. & Simon, J. (1992). The New Penology: Notes on the Emerging Strategy of Corrections and Its Implications. *Criminology, 30*(4), 449–474.

Field, S., & Nelken, D. (2010). Reading and Writing Youth Justice in Italy and (England and) Wales. *Punishment & Society, 12*(3), 287–308.

Foster, H., & Hagan, J. (2009). The Mass Incarceration of Parents in America: Issues of Race/Ethnicity, Collateral Damage to Children, and Prisoner Reentry. *ANNALS of the American Academy of Political and Social Science, 623*(1), 179–194.

Foucault, M. (1980). *Power/Knowledge: Selected Interviews and Other Writings, 1972–1977.* Colin Gordon (Ed.). New York, NY: Pantheon.

Gardner, J. (2015). The KKK Has Infiltrated U.S. Police Departments for Decades. *AlterNet.* Retrieved from http://www.alternet.org/civil-liberties/kkk-has-infiltrated-us-police-departments-decades

Garland, D. (2001). *The Culture of Control: Crime and Social Order in Contemporary Society.* Oxford, UK: Oxford University Press.

Garland, D. (2003). The Rise of Risk. In R. Erickson (Ed.), *Risk and Morality* (pp. 48–86). Toronto, ON: University of Toronto Press.

Gilroy, P. (2000). *Against Race: Imagining Political Culture beyond the Color Line.* Cambridge, MA: Harvard University Press.

Giroux, H. (2006). Reading Hurricane Katrina: Race, Class and the Biopolitics of Disposability. *College Literature, 33*(3), 171–196.

Giroux, H. A. (2015). Taking Notes 48: America's New Brutalism: The Death of Sandra Bland. *Philosophers for Change.* Retrieved from https://philosophersforchange.org/2015/07/28/taking-notes-48-americas-new-brutalism-the-death-of-sandra-bland/

Goldberg, D. T. (2009). *The Threat of Race: Reflections on Racial Neoliberalism.* Malden, MA: Blackwell.

Goldberg, D. T. (2012). When Race Disappears. *Comparative American Studies: An International Journal, 10*(2–3), 116–127.

Goodman, A. & González, J. (2015). Truthout's Maya Schenwar and Former Prisoner Jason Hernandez Speak out on Prisons and Policing. Retrieved from http://www.truth-out.org/news/item/31939-former-el-reno-prison-inmate-freed-by-obama-speaks-out

Hadden, S. E. (2001). *Slave Patrols, Law and Violence in Virginia and the Carolinas.* Cambridge, MA: Harvard University Press.

Hall, S. (1997). Representation, Meaning and Language. In S. Hall (Ed.), *Representation: Cultural Representation and Signifying Practices* (pp. 15–24). Thousand Oaks, CA: SAGE.

Hannah-Moffat, K., & Maurutto, P. (2010). Re-Contextualizing Pre-Sentence Reports: Risk and Race. *Punishment & Society, 12*(3), 262–286.

Harcourt, B. (2007). *Against Prediction: Profiling, Policing and Punishing in an Actuarial Age.* Chicago, IL: University of Chicago Press.

Hart, W. E. (2009). The Culture Industry, Hip Hop Music and the White Perspective: How One-Dimensional Representation of Hip Hop Music Has Influenced White Racial Attitudes [Master's thesis]. University of Texas, Arlington. Arlington, TX.

Hier S. P., & Bolaria, B. S. (Eds.). (2006). *Identity and Belonging: Rethinking Race and Ethnicity in Canadian Society.* Toronto, Canada: Canadian Scholars Press.

Howard, P. (2014). Drawing Dissent: Post-Racialist Pedagogy, Racist Literacy, and Racial Plagiarism in Anti-Obama Political Cartoons. *Review of Education, Pedagogy, and Cultural Studies, 36*(5), 386–402.

Kappeler, V. E. (2014). A Brief History of Slavery and the Origins of American Policing. *Eastern Kentucky University.* Retrieved from http://plsonline.eku.edu/insidelook/brief-history-slavery-and-origins-american-policing

Kempa, M., Stenning, P., & Wood, J. (2004). Policing Communal Spaces: A Reconfiguration of the 'Mass Private Property' hypothesis 1. *British Journal of Criminology, 44*(4), 562–581.

Kemshall, H. (2003). *Understanding Risk in Criminal Justice.* Maidenhead, UK: Open University Press.

Lopez, I. F. H. (1995). The Social Construction of Race. In R. Delgado (Ed.), *Critical Race Theory: The Cutting Edge* (pp. 191–203). Philadelphia, PA: Temple University Press.

Loughran, T. A., Paternoster, R., Piquero, A. R., & Pogarsky, G. (2011). On Ambiguity in Perceptions of Risk: Implications for Criminal Decision Making and Deterrence. *Criminology, 49*(4), 1029–1061.

Massey, D. S., & Denton, N. A. (1993). *American Apartheid: Segregation and the Making of the Underclass.* Cambridge, MA: Harvard University Press.

Maurutto, P., & Hannah-Moffat, K. (2006). Assembling Risk and the Restructuring of Penal Control. *British Journal of Criminology, 46*(3), 438–454.

McCulloch, J. (2001). Paramilitary Surveillance: S11, Globalisation, Terrorists and Counter-Terrorists. *Current Issues in Criminal Justice, 13,* 23.

Miles, R. (1980). Class, Race and Ethnicity: A Critique of Cox's Theory. *Ethnic and Racial Studies, 32,* 169–181.

Miles R., & Brown, M. (2006). Representations of the Other. In B. S. Hier & B. S. Bolaria (Eds.), *Identity and Belonging: Rethinking Race and Ethnicity in Canadian Society* (pp. 19–30). Toronto, Canada: Canadian Scholars Press.

Myrdal, G. (1944). *An American Dilemma: The Negro Problem and Modern Democracy.* New York, NY: Harper and Row.

National Constables Association. (1995). Constable. In W. G. Bailey (Ed.), *Encyclopedia of Police Science* (p. 114). New York, NY: Garland Press.

National Crime Prevention Center. (2012). *Guide to Select Promising and Model Crime Prevention Programs – 2012 Congress.* Retrieved from https://www.publicsafety.gc.ca/cnt/rsrcs/pblctns/gd-slct-prmsng-mdl-2012/gd-slct-prmsng-mdl-2012-eng.pdf

Powell, K. A. (2011). Framing Islam: An Analysis of Us Media Coverage of Terrorism since 9/11. *Communication Studies, 62*(1), 90–112.

Pratt, A. (2010). Between a Hunch and a Hard Place: Making Suspicion Reasonable at the Canadian Border. *Social & Legal Studies, 19*(4), 461–480.

R. v. Gladue. (1999). 1 S.C.R. 688 (Supreme Court of Canada 1999)

Reichel, P. L. (1988). Southern Slave Patrols as a Transitional Police Type. *American Journal of Police, 7,* 51–77.

Rivas, J. (2015). It's Time to Admit Police Have a History of Connections with the KKK. *Splinter News.* Retrieved from http://splinternews.com/its-time-to-admit-police-have-a-history-of-connections-1793853567

Robinson, G. (2008). Late-Modern Rehabilitation: The Evolution of a Penal Strategy. *Punishment & Society, 10*(4), 429–445.

Statistics Canada. (2012a). *Population.* Retrieved from http://www.statcan.gc.ca/pub/12-581-x/2012000/pop-eng.htm

Statistics Canada. (2012b). *2011 National Household Survey, 99-010- X2011026.*

Sugrue, T. J. (1996). *The Origins of the Urban Crisis: Race and Inequality in Postwar Detroit.* Princeton, NJ: Princeton University Press.

Swift, K. (2006, September). The Cultural Contradictions of Risk Assessment in Child Welfare. Paper presented at the XVI International Congress on Child Abuse and Neglect. York, UK.

Tanner, Julian, and Scot Wortley. 2002. *The Toronto Youth Crime and Victimization Survey: Overview Report.*Toronto: Centre of Criminology, University of Toronto.

Tobar, H. (1991, October 12). Deputies in 'Neo-Nazi' Gang, Judge Found : Sheriff's Department: Many at Lynwood Office Have Engaged in Racially Motivated Violence against Blacks and Latinos, Jurist Wrote. *Los Angeles Times.* Retrieved from http://articles.latimes.com/1991-10-12/local/me-107_1_deputy-county

Tomlinson, L. (2016). The Ongoing Economic Exploitation of Black Music. *Huffington Post.* Retrieved from http://www.huffingtonpost.ca/dr-lisa-tomlinson/Black-music-exploitation_b_8934870.htm
Turner, K. B., Giacopassi, D., & Vandiver, M. (2006). Ignoring the Past: Coverage of Slavery and Slave Patrols in Criminal Justice Texts. *Journal of Criminal Justice Education, 17*(1), 181–95.
Walker, S. (1992). *The Police in America: An Introduction.* New York, NY: McGraw-Hill.
Watkins, B. (2011). Jesse Jackson, Black Leaders Are Right About Ending the War on Drugs. *Huffington Post.* Retrieved from http://www.huffingtonpost.com/dr-boyce-watkins/jesse-jackson-Black-leade_b_883721.html
William, H., & Murphy, P. (1990). The Evolving Strategy of the Police: A Minority View. *Perspectives on Policing, 13,* 1–16.
Wilson, W. J. (1987). *The Truly Disadvantaged: The Inner City, the Underclass and Public Policy.* Chicago, IL: University of Chicago Press.
Wootson, C. R., Jr. (2016, October 11). Yesterday's Ku Klux Klan Members Are Today's Police officers, Councilwoman Says. *Washington Post.* Retrieved from https://www.washingtonpost.com/news/local/wp/2016/10/11/yesterdays-ku-klux-klan-members-are-todays-police-officers-councilwoman-says/).
Wortley, S. (2008). A Province at the Crossroads: Statistics on Youth Violence in Ontario. *Review of the Roots of Youth Violence, 4,* 1–64.
Wortley, S. (2002). The Depiction of Race and Crime in the Toronto Print Media. In B. Schissel & C. Brooks (Eds.), *Marginality and Condemnation: An Introduction to Critical Criminology* (pp. 55–82). Halifax, Nova Scotia: Fernwood.
Wortley, S., & Tanner, J. (2006). Immigration, Social Disadvantage and Urban Youth Gangs: Results of a Toronto-Area Survey. *Canadian Journal of Urban Research, 15*(2), 18–37.
Zedner, L. (2009). *The Semantics of Security and Governing Security.* New York, NY: Routledge.

CHAPTER 11

The Complexities of Race, Racialization, Blackness, and Africanness: Working to Decolonize my Teacher Education Program

Andrew M.A. Allen

Introduction

I LOCATE MYSELF socially and politically as an African who was born abroad in a colonized Caribbean country and is now living and working on Native, (Ab)Original or Indigenous peoples land in Canada. As a faculty member, I further situate my Africanness and Blackness in a Diasporic context as a way of making sense of the way race and in particular anti-Blackness and anti-Black racism continue to manifest themselves in schooling, education, and generally in society. I intend to seek out new ways that we can re-envision education that challenges and resist the current issues facing global anti-Blackness and anti-Black racism. As a teacher educator, my experiential knowing and being shapes my scholarship and my work with teacher candidates. The issues I intend to raise in this chapter seek also to bridge some of the gaps in my own research, writings, and professional experience. This introspection will be carried out for personal reasons, as well as academic and professional reasons. It will be a way of reflecting on the complex ways that claiming my own Blackness and Africanness shape my work as a faculty member and a continued attempt to work through the development of my own personal and professional identities.

This chapter must be read and interpreted as the actualization of my own experiences, which have been informed by my nested or layered personal and professional identities as a former elementary classroom teacher in Toronto and a faculty member in two different teacher education programs in Ontario. In addition, my own social, cultural, and personal identities as Black, male, middle class, and heterosexual intersect and are enmeshed within my professional and institutional identities and shape and frame my own commitment to challenging anti-Blackness and anti-Black racism. How has my understanding of the complexities of race and racialization helped to shape my personal and professional identities? How does reclaiming and mapping my own Blackness and Africanness affect the political agenda to my teaching? How can decolonization and anticolonial approaches be applied to my teacher education program?

I have structured my discussion of the issues into two sections: First, I set the context by highlighting some of the key arguments in looking at race, racialization, Blackness, and Africanness as understood and engaged in the cultural and racial politics of education. Second, I identify the major contributions of several scholars, particularly three key scholars in the field: Grace Edwards Galabuzi, Awad Ibrahim, and George Sefa Dei. I have chosen to highlight the influence of these scholars' work on my thinking because their conceptions of race, racialization, Blackness, and Africanness are most relevant to my work and have helped me name and locate the complexities of my identities. They also theorize about race from a Canadian perspective and speak with authentic voices as actual Black African scholars in Canada. All three scholars consider the concept of race to be problematic, and they have helped in my thinking of how race is taken up in Canada. Within this context of interrogating race, racialization, Blackness, and Africanness, I establish also how the contributions of these colleagues' work have informed the complex ways I attempt to map my interconnected identities. I will then offer examples of how my racialized identities have shaped and continue to shape my political and scholarly agenda as a teacher educator. I will suggest possibilities for developing a decolonized or anticolonial curricula in my teacher education program and particularly in the process of decolonizing my language and getting my teacher candidates to do the same.

Theorizing Race and Racialization

It is important to understand how I am using race in this text, as discussions about race are central to my experiences. Although I oppose race as any serious biological classification of humanity, I instead recognize and acknowledge that the concept of race is a social construct that operates in very real and powerful ways that affect our everyday lives as Canadians (Wright, 2004). However, Gloria Ladson-Billings & William Tate

(1995) argue that race can and perhaps should be used as a powerful tool for explaining social inequity. They say that discussions around race and critical examination of race in society rarely find their way into school curriculum and education.

> Our notions of race (and its use) are so complex that even when it fails to "make sense" we continue to employ and deploy it. I want to argue, then, that our conceptions of race, even in a postmodern and/or postcolonial world, are more embedded and fixed than in a previous age. (p. 51)

More specifically in the Canadian context, Backhouse (1999), in her study of the history of racism in Canada states that

> [t]he study of the concept of "race" through time illustrates beyond controversy that the very notion is built upon shifting sands. The impermanence and transmutability of "race" is never clearer than when examined against the backdrop of the past. (p. 22)

Discussions about race do not normally find their way into most of our classrooms, even at the university level. In attempting to raise issues around race with my students Dei (2017) argues that as Black and/or African scholars, our own academic work and politics are heavily intertwined with our experience. In that way, my own personal history and how I have come to be racialized as Black in Canada becomes the backdrop to my professional journey today as a teacher educator, as I never find myself either personally or professionally outside of issues of race. For example, I often bring issues of race and other forms of oppression and my own experience of racism into my teaching and encourage my students to speak about race and share stories of their experiences. The concept of racialization is not new and has been used as a way of shifting the focus of discussions about race to how race is taken up in society. For example, in his 1989 book, *Racism*, Robert Miles argued that race had no real scientific meaning and rather that racialization or the dialectical process of ascribing meaning to human beings based on particular biological features was the root of the problem in race relations.

Awad Ibrahim (2014) describes racialization for people of African descent as the processes of becoming Black in society. In other words, it is the processes of being constructed as Black because Black folks fall within the apparatus, gaze, and discourse of power, and at the same time, the processes by which they construct their own identities or own their own subjectivity. Grace Edward Galabuzi (2006) argues that being racialized also refers to all oppressed racial groups who are not seen as White in society. For Galabuzi, racialization is described as the social process by which certain groups of people are singled out for unique treatment on the basis of real or imagined physical characteristics of race (York University, 2011). Galabuzi argues that the use of the term *racialized* (as opposed to invalid terms such as *visible minority* or *people of color*) draws attention to the actual process that created disadvantage for groups in society on the basis of physical attributes. Racialization is a process that erroneously labels and stigmatizes groups who are not socially constructed or recognized as White. In addition, the use of *racialized groups* here and elsewhere suggests a discomfort with the official use of the term *visible minorities* because of its implication of permanence of the minority status that is imposed onto that population. *Racialized* denotes that process of imposition, the social construction of the category, and the attendant experience of oppression as opposed to the seemingly neutral use of the terms *visible minorities* or *racial minorities,* which have the effect of masking oppressions (Galabuzi, 2006; York University, 2011). I will use both Ibrahim and Galabuzi's idea of racialization as a way of framing my reflections on race and being racialized in Canada. And as discussed later, George Dei builds on both these ideas and argues that racialization is further realized through social action and leads to activism. In addition, I am further drawn to the way the term *racialized* is used as a verb to describe something that has been or is continually being done to me, and it also suggests that being racialized is something that I do not have control over.

Research Methodology

Methodologically and as a researcher, I keep extensive personal and professional journals, and I often write reflections of my experiences as a faculty member in order to make sense of those experiences and as part of my own professional development. For this chapter, I will use a narrative research methodology (Clandinin & Connelly, 2000) as a form of narrative inquiry that captures personal and human dimensions of an experience of phenomena over time. Narrative inquiry involves collecting data through storytelling, and I will present my accounts of my experiences as the subject under study (Creswell & Creswell, 2017). According to Creswell & Poth (2017), narrative studies may have a specific contextual focus, and I will use my experiences as a racialized professor teaching and working at a small comprehensive university in Ontario, Canada, as the contextual focus for this study.

Identifying African, Black, Canadian, Caribbean, and Mixed

Being a racialized person, I have been a faculty member and teacher educator for 20 years now and at times I encounter situations where I struggle to make sense of how race is operationalized. For example, a few years ago, I was invited to a community town hall meeting where some of my colleagues were sharing results of a study of with participants identified as African, Black, Canadian, Caribbean, and mixed youth in Ontario. After the presentation, I mused with the lead researcher on how I could argue that I personally identified with the individual identities that were the subject of this study. I wondered how the participants in that study were asked to choose to identify themselves and if they had to choose from just one of the listed categories. I also wondered if dividing predominantly Black communities into African, Caribbean, Black, Canadian, and mixed categories might be not only problematic on the surface, but part of a larger colonized way of thinking that we simply take for granted or fail to challenge. Inadvertently, we may have somehow intellectually "recolonized" the participants by categories based on geography. By geography, here, I mean as space, place, and location in our physical materiality and imaginative configurations (McKittrick, 2006). And relevant to my exercise in defining my own Blackness and Africanness, geography is also a metaphor for remapping and re-charting ourselves socially in relation to different land and land masses. That makes identification for someone like myself more difficult through my own transnational mobility as I have lived and worked on and identify with different lands, continents, and regions.

As a coprincipal investigator of a research grant with a similar focus on African Caribbean and Black (ACB) people, I acknowledge that much of these tri-council- or government-funded academic studies are based on the Ontario HIV/AIDS Strategy for African, Caribbean and Black Communities 2013–2018 and the African and Caribbean Council on HIV/AIDS in Ontario (2013) rather than being informed by academic definitions of Blackness and Africanness. These research projects were initiated and guided by the work of policymakers who were tasked with identifying communities most vulnerable to HIV and AIDS. The African, Caribbean, and Black (ACB) strategy was not meant to identify specific bodies per se, but communities in which people live. In other words, here I argue that identifying participants as any one of the categories of being African, Caribbean, Black, Canadian, or mixed can be misleading. The original policy was meant to describe communities that were most likely to have disproportionately larger populations of people with HIV and AIDS. Identity is not static or rigid and far more complex than checking off boxes. People or individual bodies can and should be able to identify with and move in between or among these communities and simultaneously be part of multiple communities. Moving away from the original definition of the policy from identifying communities to identifying bodies erroneously locks study participants into fixed categories. As another colleague in our faculty at the University of Windsor, Finney Cherian, so aptly pointed out, identifying oneself as either one of African, Caribbean, Black, Canadian, or mixed "would be like standing in#line with oneself." As racialized Black folks, we are part of and inseparable from the multiple definitions of Blackness and Africanness.

Consequently, and as a response to these categorizations, here is how I am mapping myself in terms of my own Blackness and Africanness: I am racialized or socially constructed in Canada as Black; I am of African ancestry as my forbearers or ancestors are from Africa; I was born in Jamaica; my lineage or lines of familial descent are both African and non-African (my mother was not of African descent); and, as an immigrant, my nationality is Canadian by legal relationship or through naturalization. Indeed, my charting my own Blackness and/or Africanness does not reveal a static or fixed categorization or label. I identify myself in very complex, fluid, and dynamic ways that call into play several nested, layered, and interconnected social identities. Wright (2004) describes Blacks in the Diaspora like myself as possessing an intimidating array of different historical, cultural, national, ethnic, religious, and ancestral origins and influences. Blackness and Africanness for those of us who were first brought to the "third space," in the Caribbean, in which neither Blacks nor Whites originally understood that space as their "home," positions us as immigrants in Canada as being in an in-between space (Ibrahim, 2014; Wright 2004). For example, I have lived for two-thirds of my life in Canada and still get asked, "So, where are you really from?" or "You don't sound Jamaican." (Whatever that means. The issue of language, dialect, and accent deserves an entire paper or study by itself.) So, to be clear, I am very proud of the complex constellation of identities by which I am charted, and I value the freedom to express all or parts of those identities as I please. I do not appreciate always or constantly being called out or asked to self-identify in order for my identity to make sense to someone else.

At the same time, I both embrace, and at the same time, challenge my Blackness. Wright (2004) argues that Blackness may have become a racial category with the forced removal of West Africans to the Western Hemisphere. As such "becoming Black" highlights the fluidity of Black identity in the West and our ever-evolving understanding of our Blackness and Africanness. Dei (2017), on the other hand, argues that Blackness has always been part of the Indigenous lexicon of African peoples. Black or Negro, as used by the Spanish colonizers in the Caribbean, was used as a negative connotation and a way of labeling Africans as the "Other," justifying mistreatment by stripping them of their identity as Africans. In addition, unlike Ibrahim (2014) and the participants in his study who identified as continental Africans and who only reported becoming Black when they arrived in Canada, I (like Dei) had identified as being Black long before I came to Canada. Race openly played out politically and socially in Jamaican culture for me as a child because of our history/legacy of colonization, African enslavement, the resistance and awareness of reggae music culture, and Jamaica's proximity to the United States. Growing up, my exposure in Jamaica to American television programs and movies, particularly the television series *Roots*, also played a key role in my identity formation. In addition, Bob Marley and the reggae music culture in Jamaica had lyrics that were very politically charged with issues of Black and African identity and dreams of "going back to Africa" and Black and "African unity." In high school in the 70s we wore Afro hairstyles and imitated American slang and mannerisms. Subsequently, my objectified "Otherness" of Africa was strongly influenced by my Jamaican perceptions of the imaginary of Africa as a home that we had been separated from through enslavement, and at the same time, also influenced by textbook and media images of the Africa where we were brought from and of Africans who were brought to Jamaica. When I was growing up, Africa was a place of desire, romance, fantasy, imagination, or the great aporia at the center of my identity (Ibrahim, 2014). So, my body as a Black person and my identities are mapped in multiple ways, although I am forced to fit racially into only one category as simply a part of homogenous Black. However, as the next examples illustrate, my experiences in eventually traveling to the continent of Africa made me realize just how complex the issues around my identity could be.

My Experiences of Being Reidentified and Disidentified in Africa

In exploring the issues of my own Blackness and Africanness, over the years as a faculty member I have traveled to the four corners of the continent of Africa, and the ways in which I am identified in countries there were quite different from what I had expected. For example, in Tanzania I was told that I spoke Kizungu or the colloquial for a White, European, or global North–sounding speaker. Similarly, in Nigeria, I have been referred to an "Oyibo," meaning a person who is White or of European descent. So, in Tanzania, they recognize me as an African born abroad who sounds White and other times I am even mistaken as an American Black tourist. In Nigeria, I was told that the way that I walked and carried myself, "as if I owned the place," made me not look like a local. Even when I return to Jamaica to visit, I soon get spotted by the locals as somewhat of an outsider. After all, I have been away for almost 40 years and I do not speak or sound quite the same as the locals anymore.

I see this also as an in-between space and as feeling like an insider and outsider at the same time in all these different spaces. In one moment I can identify with being African, Caribbean, Black, or Canadian, and in another moment I feel like I can somehow slip between identities. Ibrahim (2014) refers to this experience in Canada as a slippage in and out of Black and Africanness into mainstream culture, and perhaps in my complex intertwined identities my experience of a slippage is far more nuanced. For example, I had never been identified as Caribbean before I came to Canada. Somehow I also always assumed that I could simply go to any predominantly Black country and just fit in or "pass" as a local. Being disidentified in Africa was quite troubling at first for me, as I had a great desire to reconnect with my West African "roots." I had to reframe and recast my own identities as a Black man in Africa.

I was in a constant repositioning of myself as an insider and an outsider at the same time and re-identifying sometimes within the moment as I interacted with local people in Africa or the Caribbean. I also felt like an imposter going around and not speaking in order to somehow "pass" as a local. This is the process of disidentification or becoming either increasingly or dramatically less identified with one's own familiar social and cultural norms and ways of seeing and identifying oneself with the ways one is been seen and identified (Britzman, 1991). The paradox here is my desire to be able to exert control over that slippage. That is, I had a desire to be identified as Canadian in Canada and identified as African (or Nigerian) in Africa (or Nigeria). My journey into the exploration of the complexity of my racial identities is not just an exercise in the discovery of self, but also an intellectual one.

The Significance to Me as a Faculty Member

I have learned a lot about my Blackness and Africanness from my experiences of being in different spaces in North America and in Africa or the Caribbean. The question of race and my racial identity becomes important in my experience as a faculty member in Canada. As someone who is racialized Black in Canadian society, I simultaneously challenge and fiercely embrace the label "Black" in describing my racial identity. In my writing, I often politicize the term and I still see it as a term worth further problematizing. For example, as a Canadian of African descent, I am always trying to reframe and recast my Blackness as different from the popular narrative dictated by the mainstream media; much of that we get from the United States. Most of the discussion also is dominated by the hip-hop or African American Blackness discourse and a homogenization of the experiences of all peoples of the African Diaspora. At the same time, I realize how Canadian society sees me and objectifies me in the larger narrative of being identified as Black. In Canada too, identity politics and the politics of identity play out in the use of hyphens (e.g., African-Canadian or Jamaican-Canadian), and it evokes this dual consciousness for Black folks living in North America. In addition, and as mentioned before, these categories assume that identity is universal and static and not fluid and dynamic.

For example, I tend to define myself depending on the context that I am in and my multiple and nested identities might change over time or even in the moment. For example, I might identify African when in a group of Africans or Caribbean in a group of Caribbeans. Similarly, I can also identify as Black in a mixed group of other Black folks or if I am uncertain of the group that I am in. As a racialized person, I am acutely aware of race and racial categorization and I am always being positioned, constrained, and reshaped through categories of race. I am always reacting to how we are perceived in society and, in essence, I am forced to carry the burden of race. At the same time, I realize how my African heritage has been reshaped through a Caribbean immigrant perspective in North American society, and uniquely in Canada, and sustained and reproduced through my various social, institutional, and personal identities and identifications (see Henry, 1992, 1993, 1998). Again, I see myself caught in a paradox of a sliding scale of shifting identities. I am not quite Black, African, or Canadian, but at the same time uniquely Black, African, and Canadian.

Racial Identity and Activism in the Diaspora

When my family migrated to Canada in 1980, it was difficult identifying as Jamaican. As the largest population and probably the newest group of Black immigrants, Jamaicans were stigmatized and blamed for all the woes of Canadian society, particularly in Toronto. It is interesting to see how those labels are now being pinned on other groups like Somalis. I remember Trinidadian-born activist Lennox Farrell at that time coming on television to assert that we as Black people in Toronto "[a]re all Jamaicans." He was reacting to police brutality of Blacks in Toronto and the ways that the media was subtly suggesting that non-Jamaicans were the model Black immigrants and pitting them against Jamaicans. We still see this type of ugly and divisive identity politics being played out in the mass media today. Perhaps I can also make a claim today that we are all Somalis. Ibrahim, Galabuzi, and Dei all argue that nothing or not much has changed for the Black or African, racialized, working-class, immigrant today. For example, Dei (2017) states that in the political economy of globalization, the vast majority of racialized migrants from the global South nations are involuntary migrants or those forced to leave their own lands and home. Similarly, in 2008, John Ogbu identified the voluntary and involuntary minority caste status faced by Blacks and other racialized groups in North America. I agree with Dei (2017) and Ibrahim (2014) that Blackness is indeed very complex, and it is an endlessly ongoing process of individual as well as collective becoming. According to Ibrahim, our identities of being and becoming Black can be described as rhizomes or uniquely branched or connected and at the same time emerging new identities. He says that our rhizomatic identities of becoming Black can be imagined as "multiple, multiplying, complex, complicated, fluid, and infinite lines of flight and possibilities of identities and becomings" (p. 51).

Building on Dei's understanding of becoming Black, Ibrahim argues that it is also a process of becoming socially and politically aware or becoming a part of the accumulative memory and accumulative narrative of Black sensibilities. So, identifying and becoming Black is not neutral or a neutral act. It is a call to activism and struggle for change. So, in a sense, I have been created through my Blackness and in the choice of work that I do. If my body or identities were mapped in a different way, perhaps I would have been doing different kinds of work. Dei further defines Blackness and African (inter)subjectivity as an exercise of academic and political decolonization. He says that a key component of understanding Black/African identity and Blackness is Black agency and resistance to colonial subjugation. Much of his work for years has been grounded in antiracism, decolonization, and anti-colonial theories and pedagogies. In this way, reclaiming Blackness is reclaiming a "living knowledge" about ourselves and our histories, cultures, and identities. Blackness and by extension Africanness is about knowledge (re)production, reconceptualization, representation, and politics centered on race, Indigeneity, culture, and history. Situating oneself in a "Black" or "- African" identity is claiming an identity that is synonymous with struggle, politics, oppression, and resistance (Dei, 2017).

In her 1992 book, *Black Looks: Race and Representation*, bell hooks refers to the "pain of awareness" in identifying and naming social injustices and the difficulty in challenging oppression. As a result, she says that we are often forced to chose "militancy [as] an alternative to madness" (p. 6). In trying to situate and locate myself as a scholar and faculty member, I have chosen militancy as an option over madness. I have been drawn to the scholarship rooted in activism and resistance. This is evident through my research scholarship and teaching. My Blackness was developed first through deep pain and introspection in becoming aware of inequities and injustice in schooling and society. Then, through a desire to challenge anti-Blackness and anti-Black racism and the ways that they manifest themselves in contemporary social structures, systems, and institutions, I decided to teach for equity and social justice. My resistance and responses to a racist educational system and society have always been to find ways to come up with productive and constructive strategies of change (see Allen, 1997). In addition, in claiming my Africanness as activism, I contest the current school curriculum and the attempts to keep hidden the history, culture, and identity of African peoples and to resist dominant constructions of Black identities (Dei, 2017). In the next section, I will describe how my identities shape and, in turn, are being shaped by the work that I do in a faculty of education in Ontario and how I help my students come up with their own strategies for change (Solomon & Allen, 2001; Solomon, Allen, & Campbell, 2005; Solomon, Allen, Campbell, & Singer, 2011).

Enacting Blackness and Africanness as Decolonization

Dei (2017) argues that "a critical scholarship on Blackness is, and must be, about anti-racist practice, and particularly resistance to anti-Black racism, as well as, the pursuit of decolonial and anti-colonial praxis" (p. 3). Since naming, claiming, or locating my Black or African identity and Blackness is a political act as a faculty member, my call to activism has helped to shape my passion in teaching. My passion is grounded in several key critical theoretical frames like critical race theory, anti-racism, and decolonization. Ladson-Billings and Tate (1995) argue that critical race theory is based on the premise that race is salient in North American society and racism is not exceptional or aberrant but normal and prevalent, pervasive, and endemic in all our social structures, customs, and norms. I also build on and draw broadly from other related fields of cultural studies (Storey, 1996), gender studies and feminist pedagogy (Collins, 2000), critical pedagogy (Aronowitz & Giroux, 1993), and antibias and anti-discriminatory pedagogies (James, 1995; Solomon, 1995). Many of those theories point to the way working-class, racialized, and immigrant populations are disproportionately streamed into general and vocation classes and end up trapped or unable to escape their class origin (Curtis, Livingstone, & Smaller, 1992)

Over the years, I have been involved in several programs that highlight this political agenda. I have coordinated an urban education program in Windsor and Toronto, I have taken teacher candidates to practice teach in Tanzania, East Africa, and I have worked to develop the Africentric curriculum with the Toronto District School Board. Central to these service-learning initiatives and my community work is a decolonization and anti-colonial agenda. For example, I am very much influenced by Drs. George Sefa Dei (1996a) and Molefe Kete Asante (1991) and their work on both the Africentricism and Afrocentrism in Canada and the United States. An important part of the decolonization and anti-colonial work is the working inside and through discourse and questioning or challenging the values, practices, and codified way of organizing knowledge and language of the discourse (Bourdieu, 1973; Rorty, 1991). In my work with beginning teachers, I often start with identifying challenging, and decolonizing oppressive language that we find in our curriculum. Driving my work is "unoppressing the oppressed" and rethinking and reframing my language to get rid of oppressive language or language that continues to oppress.

For example, when I first heard Molefi Kete Asante speak in person on a visit to Toronto, he challenged the use of the term *tribes* to refer to Indigenous peoples in Africa. I first began to question language and the colonial legacy of language. I encourage my teacher candidates to interrogate the language used in the school curriculum and to question for themselves the colonized language they encounter in teaching. In speaking about the power and influence of language, Judith Butler (2013) states, "We do things with language, produce effects with language, and we do things to language, but language is also the thing that we do. Language is a name for our doïng: both 'what' we do (the name for the action that we characteristically perform) and that which we effect, the act and its consequences." I believe that it is also important to introduce my students to the idea of colonized thinking and decolonization through the works by Frantz Fanon (2007), Lee Maracle (2006), Linda Thuwai Smith (2013), Taiaiake Alfred (Alfred & Corntassel, 2005), Andrea Smith (2010), Haunani-Kay Trask (1991), and Ngugi Wa Thiong'o (1986). I want all my students to question not just the way things are, but how they became that way in order for them to come up with ideas or possibilities for the ways that things could have been or perhaps should be.

Another example of colonized language in the curriculum is the use of the term *jungles* and the distinction between a jungle and a rainforest. There are no clear distinctions of the difference between the two terms other than geographical location where jungles are meant to be a negative connotation to denote the global primitive or uncivilized. In addition, in my travels all across the African continent, I have never seen any jungles. One of our most endearing stereotypes of the continent has its roots in fiction from the Tarzan myth (Asante, 1991). Perhaps the most troubling of all colonized terms used is that of *slaves* brought to the Americas. As a way of addressing this issue, several years ago as a classroom teacher I had encouraged my fifth-grade students to imagine they could go back in time and interview people during the time of African enslavement to envision how the Africans would have described themselves. In one lesson with my fifth graders, I had one student who had an epiphany during one of our language lessons, and he explained his discovery to the class that the word *trade* was inappropriate. He said that trade implies the exchange of things of equal value and that he believed that nothing at any point in history can be equal to the value of human life. The original purpose of the lesson was for my students to identify biased language in reading materials and to look particularly for gender and social class bias. I had originally believed that the students were only able to handle so-called softer issues of social injustice and bias. They surprised me and although the students were not able to come up with a term to replace the erroneous use of the term *slave trade* in most of the books that they could find in the library, we decided as a class that there is perhaps no term that is suitable. Perhaps, for my fifth graders, the exercise of naming and identifying bias is the most powerful part of the lesson. I was able to allow my students to think critically about history and to, as one student put it, "to see the world with different eyes." Based on their own initiative and words, students named and called out the describing of the kidnapping and enslavement of people as not being a trade. I share stories of my work with my students as a classroom teacher with my groups of teacher candidates to get them to reimagine their roles as teachers themselves. I want to present a range of possibilities for my beginning teachers to understand their roles as critical educators.

Decolonizing the Canadian History Curriculum

Wright (2004) argues that although Blackness and Africanness have been reimagined and reproduced in contradiction to or in opposition to Whiteness by Western discourses, those discourses continue to still locate Black folks as the "Other" to the Western imaginary. Teachers and teacher candidates still face the challenge of getting their students to think critically about the world around them. As a teacher educator now, I also encourage my beginning teachers to get their own students to critically question what they read, view, and hear. I believe that we have a responsibility to help equip students with the ability to think critically and to question what they are exposed to in school and in the media. For example, much of African history as it is taught in schools uncritically presents the Underground Railroad and African enslavement as mere events in history and some form of odd historical tragedy. I challenge my education students to think about how much of the history of African enslavement could or should also be considered European history. The effort that went into building ships, sailing across the Atlantic and capturing people, taking them to over-cultivate sugar, banana, and coffee in the Caribbean is rarely highlighted in textbooks as specifically European history. I encourage my teacher candidates to focus also on how African history began way before

America or Canada were even words. Another way of decolonizing our language with respect to the narrative around the Underground Railroad to Canada is to rethink Africans not as "runaways" or "fugitives." Those terms suggest the idea of "escapees" running away from the law or some other form of authority. Implied in those meanings are the notions of an illegal act of escaping or running away. Although leaving their oppression was an illegal act, what is missing is an explicit discussion of oppression and how laws can be unjust. The lack of an open discussion of oppression again tacitly absolves the oppressors' wrongdoing. Rather, the curriculum should present Africans as their own liberators who made a conscious and just choice to free themselves from oppression. I would like to think that those ancestors walked away in defiance of those unjust laws. One unexpected result of my activism in teaching has to do with the ways that the work that I choose to do reconnects with the ancestors in fighting against injustice.

In addition, given that much of the images we see of Africa and Africans in the media today continue to be maligned, and given also the difficulties African Canadian students continue to encounter in our schools system for years, these concerns about the present curriculum are real (Brown & Sinay, 2008; Codjoe, 2001; Dei, 1996ab, 2003; James & Brathwaite, 1996; Lewis, 1992; Royal Commission on Learning, 1994; School Community Safety Advisory Panel, Falconer, Edwards, & MacKinnon, 2008; Solomon, 1992; Toronto Board of Education, 1993; Working Group, 1992). Indeed, Black students continue to feel alienated, disconnected, and even disengaged from the curriculum. There is a definite lack of an African perspective in the curriculum. Furthermore, the African perspective is absent in the texts, in learning materials, the curriculum, or any recorded history. The current curriculum in schools is Eurocentric and tends to focus on the contributions of Whites to the development of civilization (see Dei, 1994, 1995, 1996ab; Asante, 1991). This European perspective and worldview is so entrenched in our curriculum and in the practices and policies of our schools that it has become taken-for-granted knowledge and a way of coming to know. An example of Eurocentrism in society is the idea of the two European founding fathers of Canada, even within a multicultural context. This lends the questions as to who is Canadian and what our national identity is as Canadians. Who is included and who is left out? Where do Africans and other underrepresented groups fit into this notion of Canada? How do students see themselves and particularly how do Black or African students understand their histories? Often times, they are led to believe that they were either brought here during enslavement or escaped from the United States to freedom in Canada. Surely, the history of Africa and Africans is far more complex than students come to understand.

Conclusion

Whenever I am asked to define African-centered thought in education or to justify the need for invoking race as a crucial component of connecting students and particularly

Black students to their learning, I argue that we are never outside discussions of race. I also have to try to explain to people outside my experience as an African in the Diaspora how Africans experience the current curriculum in Ontario, what a curriculum inclusive of Africa and Africans might look like, and why we need it. We experience the curriculum differently, and when students feel that they are outside of curricular knowledge, they struggle to find relevance and to make connections. It is also troubling that those who are in positions of privilege and power are least likely to be aware of the situation of Blacks and Africans in the curriculum. Reclaiming our Blackness and Africanness in the curriculum is a process of becoming Black and also a process of becoming politically conscious (Dei, 2017). It is important to note that claiming my Blackness and Africanness is not anti-White. It is a process of reclaiming and reinfusing what is currently missing. We are all miseducated if any piece of our complete history is missing.

One way of understanding the Blackness and Africanness as it relates to my teaching and the curriculum, what it is and why we need it, is to examine what it is not and what the current curriculum looks like without it. Our curriculum has a Eurocentric legacy and in its current state omits or excludes information by and about Africa and Africans. Or it gives some kind of cursory mention of Africa or Africans, and it does not see this information as being relevant or needed in schools. Africans are seen as being passive and being acted upon and never active agents in their own struggle for social justice. Our curriculum misinforms or disparages both African peoples and the continent of Africa. It continues to stereotype and treat the entire continent as one undifferentiated unit. It tends to focus on the negative or the exotic and fails to connect students of African descent to the curriculum. It fails also to challenge and address the misrepresentation of Africa and Blacks in the media. A closer examination of the curriculum from an African-centered perspective reveals a curriculum that leaves all students learning the wrong information about the history of African peoples and the African Diaspora.

According to Dei (2017), my Blackness and Africanness mean becoming an embodiment of struggle and resistance and challenging White supremacy and dominance. He says calling oneself "Black" or "African" is claiming an identity that is synonymous with struggle, politics, oppression, and resistance. In this chapter, I have shown how a reclaiming of my Blackness and Africanness was a reclaiming also of my academic self as an activist and scholar. I looked specifically at race and racialization and the processes of becoming Black as understood and engaged in the cultural and racial politics of education in Ontario. I have argued that my Blackness and Africanness have informed the complex ways I attempt to map my interconnected social, cultural, political, professional, institutional, and personal identities. I provided examples of how my racialized identities have shaped and continue to shape my political and scholarly agenda as a teacher educator. I then used critical race theory, antiracism, decolonization, and an anticolonial curriculum in my teacher education program to model a process of decolonizing my language in looking at and rethinking key events and terms in the curriculum related to Africa and Africans. I provided concrete classroom examples and shared stories of my experiences with my students. I then suggested how this model of working in a teacher education program might reveal benefits of getting my teacher candidates to interrogate the curriculum with their students and work to decolonize their own language. I do this to provide a model for what curriculum can and should be. I do this also because Dei (2017) challenges us to reinvent our Africanness in a Diasporic context and in doing so we do it the spirit of healing, transformation, critique, and resistance. Blackness and Africanness is a way of coming to a critical self-awareness and critical self-consciousness and finding an authenticity through the participation in decolonization and anti-racist and anti-colonial struggles.

Cartography is the art and science of making and using maps and charts. Mapping my journey has opened an understanding of myself as a faculty member of African descent in ways that have been enlightening both personally and professionally. The implications of exploring my personal and professional cartographies of Blackness and Africanness are varied. Blackness and Africanness are interrelated, separate and different at the same time. Whereby, my Africanness is based on my lineage and the people I am descended from, my Blackness is a process of being categorized and racialized in North America (Galabuzi, 2006; Ibrahim, 2014). In addition, my Blackness is also an active process or naming and claiming an identity as a political act (Dei, 2017). This kind of retrospection has given me the opportunity to understand how I came to the kinds of research and scholarship that I am drawn to and the work that I do as a faculty member. Race and racialization were central to helping me reflect on how I navigated my journey as an academic based on my experiences and my multiple identities. I am not just interested in scholarship on race and racism; I am also committed to helping to address issues of race and racism in schools. This commitment is reflected in my teacher education program and my work with teacher candidates. I now see how my Blackness and Africanness are mapped out on my journey as a racialized faculty member. I write this chapter not only as a way of mapping or making sense of my journey, but with the hope that it also might inspire others to do the same.

References

African and Caribbean Council on HIV/AIDS in Ontario. (2013). *Ontario HIV/AIDS Strategy for African, Caribbean, and Black Communities 2013–2018*. Retrieved from: https://www.catie.ca/en/resources/ontario-hivaids-strategy-african-caribbean-and-black-communities-2013-2018

Alfred, T., & Corntassel, J. (2005). Being Indigenous: Resurgences against Contemporary Colonialism. *Government and Opposition*, 40(4), 597–614.

Allen, A. M. A. (1977). Creating Space for Discussions about Social Justice and Equity in an Elementary Classroom. *Language Arts*, 74(7), 518–524.

Aronowitz, S., & Giroux, H. (1993). *Education Still under Siege* (2nd ed.). Toronto, Canada: OISE.

Asante, M. K. (1991). The Afrocentric Idea in Education. *Journal of Negro Education, 60*(2), 170–180.

Backhouse, C. (1999). *Colour-Coded: A Legal History of Racism in Canada, 1900–1950.* Toronto, Canada: University of Toronto Press.

Bourdieu, P. (1973). Cultural Reproduction and Social Reproduction. In R. Brown (Ed.), *Knowledge, Education, and Social Change* (pp. 71-84). London, UK: Tavistock.

Britzman, D. P. (1991). *Practice Makes Practice: A Critical Study of Learning to Teach.* Albany, NY: SUNY.

Brown, R., & Sinay, E. (2008). *Summary of Student Achievement and Its Relationship to Demographic Variables.* Toronto, Canada: Toronto District School Board and Organizational Development/Research and Information Services.

Butler, J. (2013). *Excitable Speech: A Politics of the Performative.* New York, NY: Routledge.

Codjoe, H. M. (2001). Fighting a "Public Enemy" of Black Academic Achievement: The Persistence of Racism and the Schooling Experiences of Black Students in Canada. *Race, Ethnicity and Education, 4*(4), 343–375.

Collins, P. H. (2000). Gender, Black Feminism, and Black Political Economy. *Annals of the American Academy of Political and Social Science, 568*(1), 41–53.

Clandinin, D. J., & Connelly, F. M. (2000). *Narrative Inquiry: Experience and Story in Qualitative Research.* San Francisco, CA: Jossey-Bass.

Creswell, J. W., & Creswell, J. D. (2017). *Research Design: Qualitative, Quantitative, and Mixed Methods Approaches.* Thousand Oaks, CA: SAGE.

Creswell, J. W., & Poth, C. N. (2017). *Qualitative Inquiry and Research Design: Choosing among Five Approaches.* Thousand Oaks, CA: SAGE.

Curtis, B., Livingstone, D., & Smaller, H. (1992). *Stacking the Deck: The Streaming of Working-Class Kids in Ontario Schools.* Montreal, Canada: Our Schools/Our Selves Education Foundation.

Dei, G. S. (1994). Anti-Racist Education: Working Across Differences. *Orbit, 25*(2), 26–29.

Dei, G. S. (1995). Integrative Anti-Racism: Intersection of Race, Class, and Gender. *Race, Gender & Class, 2*(3), 11–30.

Dei, G. S. (1996a). *Anti-Racism Education: Theory and Practice.* Halifax, Nova Scotia: Fernwood.

Dei, G. S. (1996b). Rethinking 'African-Centred" Schools in Euro-Canadian Contexts. In K. S. Brathwaite & C. E. James (Eds.), *The Education of African Canadians: Issues, Contexts, Expectation* (pp. 295–301). Toronto, Canada: James Lorimer & Company.

Dei, G. S. (2003). Schooling and the Dilemma of Youth Disengagement. *McGill Journal of Education, 38*(2), 241–256.

Dei, G. S. (2017). *Reframing Blackness and Black Solidarities through Anti-Colonial and Decolonial Prisms.* New York, NY: Springer.

Fanon, F. (2007). *The Wretched of the Earth.* New York, NY: Grove.

Galabuzi, G. (2006). Race, Racialization and Multiculturalism. *Canadian Diversity, 5*(2), 29–31.

Henry, A. (1992). African Canadian Women Teachers' Activism: Recreating Communities of Caring. *Journal of Negro Education, 61*(3), 392–404.

Henry, A. (1993). Missing: Black Self-Representations in Canadian Educational Research. *Canadian Journal of Education, 18*(3), 206–222.

Henry, A. (1998). *Taking Back Control: African Canadian Women Teachers' Lives and Practice.* Albany NY: SUNY.

hooks, B. (1992). *Black Looks: Race and Representation.* Boston, MA: South End Press.

Ibrahim, A. (2014). *The Rhizome of Blackness: A Critical Ethnography of Hip-Hop Culture, Language, Identity, and the Politics of Becoming*. New York, NY: Peter Lang.

James, C. E. (1995). Multicultural and Anti-Racist Education in Canada. *Race, Gender & Class*, 2(3), 31–48.

James, C. E., & Brathwaite, K. S. (1996). The Education of African Canadians: Issues, Contexts, Expectations. In K. S. Brathwaite & C. E. James (Eds.), *Educating AfricanCanadians* (pp. 13-31). Toronto, Canada: James Lorimer & Company.

Ladson-Billings, G., & Tate, W. (1995). Toward a Critical Race Theory of Education. *Teachers College Record*, 97(1), 47–68.

Lewis, S. (1992). *Stephen Lewis Report on Race Relations in Ontario*. Toronto, Canada: Government of Ontario.

Miles, R. (1989). *Racism*. London: Routledge

Maracle, L. (2006). Decolonizing Native women. In B. A. Mann (Ed.), Daughters of motherearth: The wisdom of Native American women. (pp. 21-51). Westport, Conn.: Praeger.

McKittrick, K. (2006). *Demonic Grounds: Black Women and the Cartographies of Struggle*. Minneapolis, MN: University of Minnesota Press.

Ogbu, J. U. (Ed.). (2008). *Minority Status, Oppositional Culture, and Schooling*. New York, NY: Routledge.

Rorty, R. (1991). *Objectivity, Relativism, and Truth: Philosophical Papers*, Vol. 1. New York, NY: Cambridge University Press.

Royal Commission on Learning. (1994). *For the Love of Learning: Report of the Royal Commission on Learning*. Toronto, Canada: Ministry of Education.

School Community Safety Advisory Panel, Falconer, J., Edwards, P., & MacKinnon, L. (2008). *The Road to Health: A Final Report on School Safety*. Toronto, Canada: Toronto District School Board.

Smith, A. (2010). Queer Theory and Native Studies: The Heteronormativity of Settler Colonialism. *GLQ: A Journal of Lesbian and Gay Studies*, *16*(1–2), 41–68.

Smith, L. T. (2013). *Decolonizing Methodologies: Research and Indigenous Peoples*. London & New York: Zed Books.

Solomon, R. P. (1992). *Black Resistance in High School: Forging a Separatist Culture*. Albany, NY: SUNY.

Solomon, R. P. (1995). Why to Teach from A Multicultural and Anti-Racist Perspective? *Race, Gender & Class*, 2(3), 49–66.

Solomon, R. P. & Allen, A. (2001). The Struggle for Equity, Diversity and Social Justice in Teacher Education. In J. Portelli & P. Solomon (Eds.), *The Erosion of the Democratic Tradition in Education: From Critique to Possibilities* (pp. 217–244). Toronto, Canada: Detselig/Temeron Books.

Solomon, R. P., Allen A. & Campbell, A. (2005). The Politics of Advocacy, Strategies for Change: Diversity and Social Justice Pedagogy in Urban Schools. In R. P. Solomon (Ed.), *Preparing Teachers for Urban Schools*. Toronto, Canada: Lawrence Erlbaum.

Solomon R. P., Allen, A, Campbell, A., & Singer. J. (2011). *Brave New Schools [The Urban Diversity Phenomenon]: Equity, Diversity and Social Justice Teacher Education*. Toronto, Canada: Canadian Scholars Press.

Storey, J. (Ed.). (1996). *What Is Cultural Studies?: A reader*. London, UK: Arnold.

Toronto Board of Education. (1993). *Report on 1991 Toronto Every Secondary Student Survey* Toronto, Canada: Author.

Thing'o, N. A. (1986). *Decolonizing the Mind*. London, UK: James Currey.

Trask, H. K. (1991). Natives and Anthropologists: The Colonial Struggle. *Contemporary Pacific*, 3(1), 159–167.

York University. (2011). *Racialization: The Racialization Process.* http://www.yorku.ca/lfoster/2011-12/HRES3890/lectures/RACIALIZATION_THEPROCESSOFRACIALIZATION.1.htm

Working Group. (1992). *Towards a New Beginning: The Report and Action Plan of the Four Level Government/African Canadian Community Working Group.* Toronto, Canada: Metropolitan Toronto Government.

Wright, M. M. (2004). *Becoming Black: Creating identity in the African diaspora.* Durham, NC: Duke University Press. </ref>

CHAPTER 12

Black Theorizing in Academia: Toward an Anti-Colonial Reading

A Response to George J. Sefa Dei

Jennifer Mills[1]

Introduction

"Black Theorizing in Academia: Toward An Anti-Colonial Reading: A Response to George J. Sefa Dei" evolved from my response to his African Liberation Month lecture, where I attempted to critically engage what I understood to be Dei's contribution to the discourse and development of an African or Black Canadian tradition of critical theory. As I was researching and writing the chapter, I developed an intense affinity with Dei's intellectual legacy, as one that I have now come to see as a major shift in my intellectual political development. Dei offers continental and Diasporic African Canadian scholars an African Indigenous tradition of critical theory, not as a critical theoretical point of departure, but also along the lines of W.E.B Du Bois, Frantz Fanon, and Amíl Cabral, among others. In his academic career, he has contributed a treasure trove of innovative ideas and critical theories that extend beyond the borders of anti-Black racism,

[1] Correspondence should be addressed to Jennifer Mills, Institute for Social Research, Dahdaleh Building, York University, 4700 Keele Street, Toronto, Canada, M3J 1P3. Email: jpmills@yorku.ca.

education, colonialism, and sexism, and he consciously developed his African Indigenous perspective in the interest of continental and Diasporic African peoples.

When Dei (2018a) critiques Western epistemologies, anti-Black racism is brought into the context of an emerging Black critical theory (BCT) tradition in Canada. His goal is to "challenge Black and Indigenous exclusions from canonized theorizing and re-envision a different world through the power of ideas." To do so, Black theorizing in academia entails a decolonization of the inherited Western epistemologies that exist as established knowledge as well as an excavation of the structuring power in the formation of theories, methods, and methodologies and teaching and learning practices and thus ways of thinking. Drawing on his discussion, this chapter argues that Black theorizing in academia emerges against the distinct epistemology of colonial modernity. Colonial modernity is a discursive term to encompass the way ideas, ideologies, and knowledge systems are organized, as well as to splinter and attempt to erase the modern contours of the everyday experiences of non-Western people. Black theorizing becomes a way to reenvision academia as existing with multiple epistemologies.

To this end, this chapter utilizes four concepts: *multicentricity, epistemic saliency, subversive inclusion,* and *African Indigeneity* to shape Black Canadian theorizing. The goal is to use a Deisian perspective to construct the conditions that allow for Black theorizing in academia while learning from Black Canadian knowledge. In offering a Deisian perspective, this chapter presents his lens as a challenge to academia to reintegrate African Indigenous perspectives. This chapter acknowledges that Black theorizing is multi-centric, thus it presents an overview of a Deisian perspective that is not meant to represent all Black Canadian scholars, as they are a diverse group. While this perspective is grounded in the specific Canadian context, this chapter encourages Black scholars to engage Dei's scholarship, noting its relevance to various African Indigenous peoples locally, provincially, nationally, and internationally, as issues faced in the academy that involve Black Canadians are often similar.

This chapter is divided into four parts. Part 1 locates Dei's Black theorizing within a tradition of Black radical intellectual theorization. Part 2 briefly describes Dei's four conceptual framings to argue that his work places on the scholarly agenda questions about Black theorizing that have received much attention in the Western academy. Part 3 argues that his model alone cannot adequately address the concerns of Black theorizing, as his perspective in rejecting colonial modernity abandons the very tools that may assist his thinking: *critical reflection.* Part 4 will take on the task to briefly sketch a Deisian perspective as an example of what Black theorizing in academia looks like to the author in the Canadian context.

Part 1: Black Critical Theory (BCT)

This section locates Dei's Black theorizing within what he calls a radical intellectual tradition that speaks to a critical sociology of knowledge or Black critical theory (BCT). BCT is a term that covers a wide range of intellectuals working in disciplines as diverse as sociology, social justice education, Caribbean studies, Pan-African studies, and of course, Black studies. Much of their Black theorizing is in response to calls from scholars for culturally specific knowledge production, which has led to an increase in continental and Diasporic thought within the academy. Derived from this BCT tradition, a Deisian lens offers distinct epistemic insight: a way of theorizing that seeks an ongoing synthesis of the most emancipatory elements of a wide range of theories in the interest of African peoples. Thus, the Deisian perspective is about offering alternatives of what ought to be and what can be—human liberation and societal transformation.

Deisian theory is not a critical theory. The term *critical theory* has its origins in the work of scholars known as the Frankfurt school. German scholars of Jewish descent used the term *critical theory* to designate a specific approach to interpreting Marxist theory (Bernstein, 1995). But the term has taken on new meanings in the interim and cannot be exclusively identified with the Marxist tradition from which it has originated given the new iterations outside of the original German context. Therefore, this section does not limit the term to refer only to the Frankfurt school's meaning, a theory critical of forms of domination. In the social sciences, critical theory can (1) continuously allow for an epistemic openness that embodies the historical and emancipatory alternatives of a historical context; (2) not be tied only to the Marxist tradition (for a history of the Frankfurt school (see Bernstein, 1995; Held, 1980); and (3) can embody a critical reflective capacity to reconceptualize a range of continental and diasporic BCT and praxis.

In order to understand Dei's contribution to BCT and Canadian theorizing specifically, this section briefly engages the discursive formations of his intellectual influences. Why? Well, this section argues that Dei's thought and texts prefigure and continue to contribute to virtually every area of critical inquiry in Black thought in Canada, from education, social sciences, and the humanities, African Indigeneity to Black Lives Matter. Therefore, to get a grasp of Dei's thought, let alone seriously grapple with the issues he addresses, we have to critically engage the classical thought traditions that fueled his ideas and lay a foundation for his thought to develop. This section will now briefly return to three of many intellectual sources of Dei's African Indigenous perspective: W.E.B Du Bois, Frantz Fanon, and Amíl Cabral.

William Edward Burghart (W.E.B.) Du Bois is an important African-American thinker in the radical intellectual tradition. In *The Souls of Black Folks*, Du Bois (1994) develops his central philosophical concept, the concept of *double consciousness*. African Americans have an epistemological perspective that allows them to understand the White world and yet have a perspective that is different from it. They feel this dual self-perception as double consciousness. Du Bois's (2001) concept of double consciousness has contributed significantly to theories about race, that there is real meaning to it.

In Dei's (2018a) lecture, he finds parallels in Du Bois's conception of double consciousness. The idea is that African Diasporic people are within Canadian culture and are at the same time able to stand outside of it. Dei develops his theory within the concept of African Indigeneity to affirm our human condition and make others see us as we see ourselves. Taking his cue from Du Bois's conceptualization of double consciousness and theory as a weapon that can be used to dismantle anti-Black racism, Dei's Black theorizing confronts race, class, and gender oppression while maintaining conceptual political linkages between the struggles to end it. In the same view, Dei's and Du Bois's thought examines the power of men and women to be human, a struggle attributed to the horrible crimes against humanity due to the historical legacy of colonialism, racism, and anti-Blackness. The double consciousness plays itself out in a number of ways historically: slavery; police violence; creation of poverty in Black communities; women's lived experiences in a racist, sexist, capitalist, White patriarchal society and their relations among themselves and to men—always with the same effect: the compromising of identity and yet with a new identity that is forming and emerging. Dei's Black theorizing encourages African Canadian men and women to remove their veil and use their epistemological perspective to be themselves.

Du Bois's work has also been essential for a Black radical intellectual tradition (Rabaka, 2007, 2009, 2014) and Deisian theory and he is located among the early pioneers in this tradition (Anton Wilheim Amo, Sojourner Truth, Thomas Nelson Parker, Gilbert Haven Jones, Jean Slappy, Charles Leander Hill, William Fontaine, Kwame Nkrumah, C.L.R. James, etc.). This analysis compares Dei's work to Du Bois's work in their call to overcome global anti-Blackness. In the Canadian context, Dei's thought is influenced by Du Bois's commitment to tell the truth about the African Canadian experience and history. In this sense, Du Bois's theory and Dei's African Indigenous perspective amount to a programmatic shift away from abstraction and toward engaged social criticism. In affecting this change in BCT, especially on behalf of African Americans and pertaining to the issue of race, Du Bois adds concrete significance and urgent application to African American analysis of race. However, Du Bois's philosophy is significant today because it addresses what Dei and many argue is the real-world problem of White domination. Dei's lecture argues that as long as White privilege exists and suppresses the freedoms of human beings, Du Bois will remain a relevant thinker, for he, more than almost any other, employed thought in the service of exposing this privilege and worked to eliminate it in the service of a greater humanity.

Born in the French Caribbean colony of Martinique, Frantz Fanon is another important intellectual influence in Dei's work. In Fanon's (1967) book, *Black Skin, White Masks,* he challenges the abstract universalism of Western epistemologies by showing how colonial modernity serves to structure a hierarchical relationship between the colonizer and colonized. Fanon's anti-colonial theory contests the assumption that European notions of progress truly advance justice and secure mutual benefit. His intellectual focus is to show that resistant subjects can work to articulate a de-colonial, anti-racist philosophy. Fanon focuses on the development of Black consciousness by exploring the psychological alienation and displacement caused by colonial domination. He describes a fractured self who identifies with French culture even while experiencing exclusion from the ideals of universalism, equality, and reason.

In his lecture, Dei (2018a) draws on Fanon's ideas presented in *Black Skin, White Masks*. Inspired by Fanon's reflection on the need to decolonize our national consciousness, Dei talks and writes about the need to get beyond our intellectual enslavement that occurs when using Western epistemologies. Like Fanon, Dei recognizes that Western epistemologies have a dual character. It colonizes in the sense that it has the power to conceal how theory is used to maintain systems of domination, but it can also be adapted to our subject position as a means by which we liberate ourselves. Dei's lecture and writings are his official renunciation of the colonizer's theories in favor of other perspectives. His account of the African Indigenous subject position and development of a literature can fruitfully be read as an illustration of the abstract claims Fanon makes about culture in *Black Skin, White Masks* (Dei, 2015b, 2016e, 2016h, 2017a, 2017c, 2018a, 2018b).

Dei takes up Fanon's call for intellectuals of decolonizing societies to create new literatures and new cultures for their liberating nations. Applying Fanon's call to his own context, Dei has produced literature that reflects and supports continental African and Diasporic peoples. Inspired by Fanon's call to voice, he has contributed scholarly work to the *Handbook of Indigenous Education* (2018c)*, Indigeneity and Decolonial Resistance* (2018a) *and Anti-Colonial Theory and Decolonial Praxis* (2016d), books that interrogate the way research has been used by anti-colonial researchers to empower African Indigenous peoples and that lay out methodological principles for their research agendas that will not reproduce the same dehumanizing results for which colonial knowledge production has been responsible.

Amíl Cabral was an intellectual of Bissau-Guinean descent and one of Africa's foremost anti-colonial thinkers. In his "Brief Analysis of the Social Structure in Guinea"and "The Weapon of Theory" (1979), Cabral departs from the Marxist discourse at the time and it is derived from a specific African ontological lens. Cabral (1979) argues that "the true motive force of history is the mode of production" (p. 124). The mantra of class struggle not only runs against the grain of observed historical patterns, it produces "for some human groups in our countries . . . the sad position of being people without history . . . (and negates) the inalienable right of every people to have its own history" (pp.125).

Cabral argues that colonial modernity attempted to erase the history of Africa and associated Africans in the 15th century with the transatlantic slave trade in the Americas, the Caribbean, and elsewhere. The transatlantic slave trade and slavery were the cornerstones of capital accumulation that gave birth to capitalism, as were the genocides of Indigenous populations of Africa and the Americas. The systematic anti-Black racism, seizure of land, forced labor, and destruction of societies and culture was intimately intertwined with the birth, growth, and continued expansion of capital and remains the hallmark of its development. Cabral understood that separating Africa and Africans from the general flow of common human experience could only lead to the action of slowing social processes on the continent.

This attempt to erase African culture and history is a colossal failure, for while the forces of liberalism interrupted their social structures on the continent, the people's memories of their material culture remained alive and they were carried across on the slave ships to where enslaved Africans found themselves, where that culture evolved in their new material conditions to become a basis for resistance. For Cabral, the national liberation of a people is the regaining of the historical personality of that people; it is their return to history through the destruction of the imperialist domination to which they are subject.

Drawing on Cabral's anti-colonial perspective, Dei argues that the response to the transatlantic slave trade is to claim the identity of African as a positive, liberating definition of a people who are part of humanity, "who belong to the whole world," as Cabral (1979) articulates it (p. 80). As in the struggles of the oppressed throughout history, a transition occurs in which terms used by the oppressors to other people are eventually appropriated by the oppressed and turned into terms of dignity and assertion of humanity. His theorizing ties the concept of being African and Indigenous with the concept of freedom and emancipation. Continental and African-descended peoples "have kept their culture alive and vigorous despite the relentless and organized repression of [their] cultural life," writes Cabral (pp. 139-140). Cultural resistance is the basis for the assertion of people's humanity and the struggle for freedom.

For Dei, Cabral is an organic intellectual whose anti-colonial perspective lays the foundation for his theorizing. First, Cabral's writings and reflections provide Dei with a series of publications to critique about the incessantly overlapping, interlocking, and intersecting nature of racism, sexism, capitalism, and colonialism in contemporary society. Second, Cabral's ideas lead to action—actual cultural, historical, and political transformation, ultimately revolutionary decolonization and national liberation movements—and therefore represent the zenith of 20th-century Black radical intellectual theory and praxis (Rabaka, 2007, 2009, 2014). Third, Dei is creating a body of work on issues concerning the course of social transformation, Indigenous education, Black theorizing, identity, anti-racism, de-colonial politics, history, an anti-colonial lens, and liberation (2015b, 2016e, 2017c, 2018a; Fanon & Lordan, 2017).

What is significant for Dei's theorizing is that he builds on Du Bois's concept of double consciousness, Fanon's concept of decolonization, and Cabral's anti-colonial perspective. These concepts provide him with a point of departure to develop an African Indigenous theory and praxis that simultaneously contribute to Black Canadians, national struggles and the broader international struggles against global anti-Blackness. Part of the key to understanding Dei's African Indigenous theory is the synthesis of ideas and actions of the many who came before him including Du Bois, Fanon, and Cabral, among others, especially in terms of their critique of theory, anti-Black racism, and colonialism.

Dei's Black theorizing in the academy shows that we are in the midst of a moment. The moment is evident by the proliferation of epistemologies by African, African Canadian, and other scholars. These epistemologies are forms of critical pedagogy; that is, they embody a critical politics of representation that is embedded in African-descended communities. Continental and African-descended scholars are leading the way on this front. They have launched a full-scale critique of Western epistemologies and methodologies. Black scholars demonstrate how the academy can decolonize its Western practices. At the same time, Dei seeks to disrupt the tradition's ways of knowing, while developing theories to research that privilege Black voices, Indigenous knowledges, and experiences.

Today, Black scholars are building these connections, learning how to dismantle, deconstruct, and decolonize traditional ways of doing research that are always both moral and political. In the North American context, the literature review cuts across several historical moments. These moments are operant in the present. This literature reviewed them in terms of the radical intellectual tradition offered by Du Bois, Fanon, and Cabral.

Part 2: Dei's Four Conceptual Framings

Dei argues that academia sustains colonial structures that create hierarchies and colonial relations of production. In order to subvert these European structures, an anti-colonial lens is required. He contends that an African Indigenous orientation can counter and provide an oppositional model for a community of Black scholars that makes a difference to the nature of knowledge production and thus to academia. In this regard, Table 12.1 presents his four concepts for thinking about an African Indigenous perspective or what he calls multicentricity, epistemic saliency, and subversive inclusion and African Indigeneity.

Table 12.1

FOUR COMPONENT PARTS OF DEI'S PERSPECTIVE

Multicentricity	**Creating spaces for multiple centres of knowledge to exist** (Dei, 2018a)
1. Epistemic saliency	Allowing for the subjective voices of the oppressed in understanding their oppression to be heard
2. Subversive inclusion	Rethinking the notion of inclusion as beginning anew
3. African Indigeneity	An international category that supports African peoples on multiple lands and spaces

His perspective includes the concept of *multicentricity* to "create spaces for multiple centres of knowledge to exist." Sustaining the autonomy of multicentric knowledge depends on the existence of a community of scholars. Multicentric or critical knowledge is the conscience of the community; it is an interrogative process that acknowledges that "one standard of knowledge is not better than another and all knowledge systems must be assessed in their own right." Multicentric knowledge is the conversation between scholars about the broad direction of society and the consequences that might follow. In this perspective, there is an intersection of critical and multicentric knowledge as each infuses the other with a discussion of values.

Using African Indigenous research is an approach to decolonize knowledge and is based on the acceptance of a multicentric knowledge base as relevant to the academy. "As an entry point, the Black scholar seeks to Indigenize the academy, and use the local resources in the search for knowledge." This is a call to the academy to reimagine itself in relation to African Indigenous knowledge and researching becomes a project of decolonization. According to Asante (2007), "[D]ecolonizing and Indigenizing the modern university is not just de-Westernizing but a total reassertion of Indigenous peoples and their knowledges at the center of the process of knowledge discovery and dissemination" (p. 3). In the Canadian context, this means that the African Canadian Indigenous voice is affirmed and the epistemic saliency of African Canadian experiences are emphasized.

Affirming the *epistemic saliency* of African Canadian experiences or the self-defined experiences of Black scholars allows for "the subjective voices of the oppressed in understanding their oppression" to be heard (Dei, 2018a). For Dei, a truly African Indigenous framework must seek to capture the "lived experiences, institutional practices and resistance of the scholars with implicit or explicit perspectives to articulate them." By using the epistemic saliency of African Indigenous voices in research, Black scholars have a valuable mechanism for social change in a colonial and anti-Black Canadian society. The Indigenous perspective allows them to construct a view of themselves that is different from the established colonial structure and enact the resistance to follow. More importantly, this perspective creates a community of discourses that "involves them as active subjects playing significant decision-making roles in research projects involving their own communities" (Dei, 2018a).

Sustaining multicentricity and epistemic saliency is the role of *subversive inclusion* that depends on "rethinking the notion of inclusion as beginning anew" (Dei, 2018a). How does the Black scholar in the academy begin anew? What Dei is redefining as the academy gives weight to African Indigenous knowledge and recognizes its interdependence with other epistemologies within academia. This framework can be extended to teaching, recognizing that pedagogy comes into play with his concepts: Professors impart to students the African Indigenous knowledge that defines a discipline, social sciences, and critical teaching that examines the foundations of knowledges and their existence and teaching as a public engagement. Within this perspective, students are not regarded as *tabula rasa*, but as members of a public within their own interests and experiences that are elaborated through pedagogical dialogue based in different disciplines. Therefore, this research has to be Indigenous because it provides for the active engagement with scholars, students, staff, and university communities and research participants to create new knowledge both for and by them.

African Indigeneity has been implicated in the project of colonial modernity and colonialism in the way the ideas, ideologies, and knowledge systems are organized to refract and make invisible the everyday experiences of the people who are colonized. In this respect, the European narrative made Europe the center of the world and Africa the periphery. This historical argument regarding Eurocentrism is extended by Dei (2018a) when he suggests that Eurocentrism is an epistemology or a key element in managing the reproduction of colonial modernity, and the end result is the

> devaluation of the knowledge systems, cultures, history, and identities of Indigenous peoples. By distorting histories and cultures, the Euro-colonizers succeeded in sowing an inferiority complex in the African mind such that as Africans we shunned our cultures, histories, heritages, and knowledge systems in favor of the colonizers. By not defending their cultural values and knowledge systems, colonized bodies have since been implicated in the colonizer's oppression.

For Dei (2018a), African Indigeneity is "an international concept that supports African peoples on multiple lands and spaces." The concept incorporates the "body of local, cultural knowledge that comes with understanding and experiencing African social, physical, and metaphysical worlds. We cannot claim that there is not African knowledge. African knowledge is related to the land, cultures, identities, spirituality, histories, and local communities of Africans." The Black scholar theorizing in academia therefore must "insist on the validation, legitimation, and acceptance of such knowledges on their own merits and rights. The starting point is to respect all knowledges worthy of academic inquiry and to raise questions that allow knowledges to contest each other in the search for the answers to global challenges." Indigenous knowledge is part of the academic discussions, not a backdrop to them.

In order to understand Dei's process of Black theorizing in academia, this section started by briefly outlining his four conceptual framings. Part 2 shows thsat in many ways his work presents an outline to understand the experiences of Black Canadian scholars and their communities. In the process, he conceives of a theory to counter colonial ones. In the next section, this analysis engages his perspective and critiques it.

Part 3: Toward A Critique Of Dei's Four Concepts

According to a Deisian perspective, it should be quite obvious by now that we are fundamentally epistemological beings. By taking up the African Indigenous perspective, or the body of the knowledge producer, politics, place, and contexts in which knowledge is produced, we can comprehend the epistemic saliency of our Black Canadian experiences. But to what extent is this process possible? That is, how does a Black scholar move beyond the specific social concerns of colonial modernity? How can Black scholars, who as human beings are embedded in their own lived reality, get outside of this historically constituted linguistic reality? Dei seems to think that in the move to the African Indigenous perspective, academic warriors can put aside their own taken-for-granted assumptions and take up a position beyond them. Black scholars must then formulate an ideal description, which must be understandable to the scholars themselves in terms of their diverse experiences. Is this possible? A Deisian perspective through its four conceptual framings can account for rationality, as it explores those features of Black theorizing which are trans-subjective, in that they would have the same meaning for all Black scholars and observers of that social action regardless of their geohistorical location. But what if such a move is impossible? What if the Deisian perspective, like Western epistemologies, is always implicated in a tradition constituted by the sociolinguistic community in which the Black scholar resides? Does this delegitimize the Black scholar's findings?

To a large extent, the Deisian perspective rotates around the problems of epistemological skepticism where nothing is fixed, where one cannot touch bottom, nor have support on the surface (Bernstein, 1995). The Deisian perspective has left us without those features of human life that provide us with a permanent matrix through which we can ultimately appeal in determining the natures of rationality, knowledge, truth, reality, or rightness. A Deisian perspective falls victim to all the problems of the philosophy of subjectivity. How do we attempt to address the perspective's weakness?

A Deisian perspective can provide Black scholars with an understanding of their own lived experiences in which the essential features of social reality are de-reified as human subjects, praxis, and communication. As such, his conceptual framings can at last fulfil the conditions of Black theorizing in academia. But what about applying the perspective to develop a methodology or rationalization? Why would the Deisian perspective need a theory of rationalization? As this chapter sees it, unlike premodern societies, Black scholars are knowledgeable of the historical character of their consciousness. As such, we can only conceptualize our present historical consciousness in each and every Black theory we formulate. And it is for this very reason that a Deisian perspective is problematic. In other words, a Deisian perspective can only access the sociohistorical context of the present. Therefore, although his insights inform us of who we essentially are in our epoch, the perspective itself does not constitute the basis for a social science but a de-reified historical understanding of our humanness, which can clear the path to a developing itself as a critical perspective and a legitimate African Indigenous social science. Here, we need to explore the possibility of drawing insights from Dei's discussion.

From his viewpoint, the fundamental importance of being academic warriors is to allow us to develop a reflexive methodology, which would facilitate our development of a critical Deisian theory. Drawing on Dei's discussion, a reflexive African Indigenous methodology would facilitate Black scholars' development of their own theorizing in the academy. This section argues that a reflexive Deisian methodology is not context dependent. The reflexive Deisian methodology allows Black scholars to engage in a process of critique so that they can understand, critique, and reflect on their experiences in Canadian society.

The substantiality of what is historically pre-given does not remain unaffected when it is critiqued by reflection. Western scholarship has been rendered transparent and can no longer function as universal. But this is precisely what Dei (2018a) claims: "[T]he complex challenges facing the world today defy universalist solutions and calls for multicentric ways of knowing/doing/acting," which deny the power of reflection. Reflection proves itself in being able to reject the claims of modernity, tradition, and Western science. To be sure, knowledge is rooted in a Western tradition and it remains bound to contingent conditions. But reflection is not exhaustible; it emerges after the fact, in glancing back it develops its critical power. We can engage in subversive inclusion, but only after we have learned through hegemony to follow them blindly. Reflection recalls that Western knowledge systems are inculcated as universal laws for interpreting the world and for action. In this way, as Dei (2018a) writes: "[T]he violence of the [Western] academy reveals itself in the myriad of manifestations of anti-Blackness and anti-Indigeneity; the negation and devaluation of Black/Indigenous scholarship and the prevailing codes of global anti-Blackness" can be stripped away and dissolved into the less-violent forms of insight and rational decision. A Deisian perspective seems to imply the denial of the power of reflection. In other words, Dei's desire to eradicate the demons of Western knowledge systems and the philosophy of subjectivity from our thinking has rejected the critical reflexive methodology that can critique domination, anti-Black racism, and anti-Indigeneity.

This chapter argues that due to the historically situated character of reflection, it cannot be considered absolute, but instead is always rooted in the complexity of tradition. However, this does not mean that a critical reflexive methodology should be accepted totally. But, Dei's rejection of the power of reflection leaves him unwittingly committed to whatever dominant truth claims a tradition provides the Black scholar. Voiced another way, while this chapter agrees with Dei that the violence of the Western academy reveals itself in the myriad manifestations of anti-Blackness and anti-Indigeneity, this does not mean that we should reject the critical reflexive methodology in the tradition, or at least one tendency within the tradition, that provides us with the critical reflexive methodology with which we can criticize dominant and oppressive epistemologies, institutions, and social structures. The Deisian perspective, in rejecting the role of critical reflection, unwittingly rejects the very tools that help Black scholars to critique institutions and is again assisting us to decolonize oppressive institutions and prevailing codes of global anti-Blackness. On the other hand, infusing a Deisian perspective with a reflexive African Indigenous methodology attempts to undermine the forms of domination in Canadian society, thus providing insight and revealing the forms of power that exist in academia.

A Deisian perspective informed with a theory of rationalization can assist the Black scholar in developing an adequate theory. In this sense, a Deisian perspective can play an important part in providing us with insights into the experiences of Black scholars and their communities (rationality), while our theory of rationalization, along with a critical reflexive methodology, can provide the tools for ideology critique. Using an ideological critique of Western knowledge systems, the Black scholar is encouraged to reflect on the traditions of domination that are historically established in our tradition.

In the next section, this chapter takes on the task to briefly sketch a Deisian perspective and examine its applicability to the Canadian context.

Part 4: Black Theorizing In The Canadian Academy: Toward A Deisia Perspective

As an Irish, Kittian, Canadian, Deisian feminist scholar, Dei's four concepts offer a useful starting point in reframing theory in the Western academy. His perspective encourages us to document "our history, culture and tradition as a necessary exercise in our own decolonization and to . . . place our cultural frames on a level footing with other ways of knowing" (Dei, 2012, p. 109). My engagement with a Deisian perspective is linked to the scholarly work he is initiating in Canada on the nature of being African Canadian and Indigenous. Therefore, this part of the chapter claims that Dei is the father of African Indigenous research in the Canadian academy. His work contributes to scholarly work that is establishing an African-Canadian literature to examine our understandings of the relationship between African Canadians and their communities. Table 12.2 provides an outline of the Deisian perspective to apply to my Deisian feminist theorizing in academia.

Table 12.2
A DEISIAN PERSPECTIVE

Five theoretical framings		Five core concepts	
1. Multi-centricity	Creating spaces for multiple centers of knowledge to exist	**1. Spirituality**	Subjectivity that is not colonized and is vital for anti-colonial resistance
2. Epistemic saliency	Allowing for the subjective voices of the oppressed in understanding their oppression is heard	**2. Land**	One is responsive to the land dimension, a uniting force that gives people their identities
3. Subversive inclusion	An international category that supports Indigeneity on multiple lands and spaces	**3. Identity**	Indigeneity or Indigenous identity is about the process groups share with their experiences of exclusion and liberation
4. African Indigeneity	An international category that supports Indigeneity on multiple lands and spaces	**4. Communities**	Engagement with one's community within or outside academia and responsibility to the community in which it is produced
5. Critical reflection	Black theorizing gleaned through an inter-subjectively constituted world	**5. Local histories/cultures**	Indigenous knowledge supporting the histories, cultures, and languages of African people

Toward a Critical Reflexive African Indigenous Methodology

How is a Deisian perspective applicable to the Canadian context? Using his perspective, Black scholars enter into the Canadian academy in a way that is customary for African/Black and Indigenous peoples by locating themselves to share their knowledge and experiences. I am indebted to God who sustains us, and for the land that I inhabit as an Irish, Kittian, Canadian woman who emigrated to the ancestral home of the Indigenous peoples of Turtle Island. Like Dei (2017a), my presence here is due to the reality of colonization, land seizure, colonial structures, enslavement, and violence done to Indigenous and African Indigenous peoples and to this land. Dei (2018a) correctly states that

> a Land acknowledgement is meaningful only if we hold ourselves and each other collectively accountable to the Indigenous and African peoples of this Land. There are many lessons to guide the past and present, onto the future. The Land is a place of spiritual, emotional, psychological, material, economic, and political attachment, for all, albeit in different ways.

Therefore, the purpose of my theorizing is to, as Dei says, "place our cultural frames on a level footing with other ways of knowing" so that new knowledge is created and transformed both for and by African Canadian peoples.

Spirituality And Land

In the African Indigenous perspective, spirituality and land are interconnected. Dei (2018a) defines spirituality as a "subjectivity that cannot be colonized because it is vital for anti-colonial resistance." Land embodies the individual's place of long-term occupancy. He argues that colonizers have interrupted Indigenous people's connection to the land and their spirituality. For example, Mensah (2010) says that the African Canadian population exhibits diversity in origin, with some coming from continental African, the Caribbean, the United States, and Europe, while others trace their history to Canada as Indigenous Black Canadians. Despite this diversity, Black Canadians exhibit a range of knowledge bases emanating from their relationship to the land, which are held within the spiritual union with human beings and include their contemporary lived experiences within the academy.

In a Deisian perspective, spirituality is the nodal point that connects "the body, mind, soul and spirit" (Dei, 2018a). Within the Canadian context, spirituality and land are cosmologies or principles that bring order to the universe. In its religious sense, spirituality represents the moral and ethical principles that Black Canadians are expected to embody in their daily actions toward their families, communities, state, land, and God. As Black Canadian scholars exhibit diversity in origin, this concept will be applied to their different belief systems, as a Deisian perspective allows for multicentricity or multiple centers of spiritual knowledge to exist. The broad application of spirituality and land within the Canadian context is that it embodies the cosmic, ethical, earthy, and social laws that invisibly guide the heavens and the earth, like the Egyptian principle of

"Ma'at it is the way of harmony, truth, justice balance and right order" (Perry & Delpit, 1998, p. 106).

Within a Deisian perspective, spirituality represents the opportunity to subvert and reject Western modernist claims of neutrality, objectivity, rationality, and universality of science and knowledge, with an alternate version of reality more rooted in the lived experiences of Black Canadian people. An anti-colonial epistemology is suggested by the Deisian perspective, which is grounded in the equality of all peoples, male and female, and so on. It is in the area of gender and ethnicity, then, that the Deisian perspective offers a valuable contribution to my Deisian feminist theorizing in academia. It encourages the recognition of gender and racial equality and a realization of the critical importance of women in Canadian society and transformative praxis.

Identities

Identity includes both an individual and collective component. My Deisian feminist identity is ultimately tied to the collective identity of Black Canadian communities and the nation state. Conversely, in order to understand myself, to identify myself, the group from which I emerge must have an identity as well. Black Canadian scholars will draw on their shared identities, cultural knowledge, and the deployment of that knowledge within the academy to constitute themselves in their own terms. Black Canadian identities are diverse and will only strengthen the Diasporic connections.

In the 21st century, a Deisian perspective serves as a call for us to theorize. Our identities as Black Canadian scholars are steeped in our understanding that we are tied to diverse continental and African-descended Indigenous communities, which inform our experiences. That understanding compels us to place ourselves in a relationship to African peoples globally by theorizing and mobilizing to uproot and dismantle oppression that is found in the Canadian context. Black theorizing in the academy serves as an indicator of the self-perception of our ancestors and forebears of that period. While the term *African* is used to define Black Canadian communities in the academy, a Deisian perspective is not just based on an individual or group identity; it is also determined by the meaning the group gives the name as it exists and comes to be known by itself and others. Black Canadian identity within the academy is determined by the behaviors of Black Canadians who claim this name. The Deisian perspective argues that our issues in the academy are tied to our identities and must continue to develop our theories that are self-defined and that resist and defy our dehumanization.

Exploring continental and Diasporic African identities within the Canadian academy, an institution structured by a history of racism affecting Black Canadian scholars, is important. While critical friends have been instrumental in what Immanuel Wallerstein (1996) described as advocating for the academy and the discipline of social sciences to "open" itself to incorporate the challenges from interdisciplinary social sciences. This call leads to the development of new theories to incorporate the challenges from interdisciplinary social sciences, such as gender studies, environmental studies, cultural studies, and race and ethnicity studies.[2] The next step is for Canadian universities to institutionalize diverse approaches in their structures. The goal is not to interrogate merely the silences of race, gender, ethnicity, and other identities within Canada, its provinces and cities; the goal is to use Dei's perspective to reframe the academy itself and work with our critical friends to incorporate African and Indigenous perspective on the same footing as other epistemologies (Dei, 2018a).

Local Communities

According to Dei (2018a) "The Black scholar must be an academic warrior working with facticity and possibility and understanding that the pursuit of knowledge should make a concrete difference in the lives of communities." Black Canadian scholars in academia are charged with a dual responsibility of academic intellectuality and social responsibility. As academic warriors, they are expected to commit themselves to using their knowledge and training to improve their communities. The conception of community varies, and Black scholars may perceive themselves as being part of diverse Black communities, scholarly communities, or may analyze their multiple experiences of community. The Deisian perspective allows scholars to cater to more than one ethnic group and therefore there are multiple communities with which to communicate. For example, in academia, Dei's perspective encourages Deisian feminist researchers to engage and relate to a number of discrete communities: Black Canadian feminist, African Caribbean, Ghanian, and so on. In this instance, there is interaction between the community of scholars and African Canadian communities to recognize their struggles and to resist the colonial divide tactics by colonial structures and dominant groups.

W.E.B. Du Bois recognized the comprehensive responsibility and role of Africana scholars to confront White superiority and Black inferiority. Yancy (2005) recognizes this responsibility and writes that "Black life (in the academy) constitutes a "counter-white episteme, a mode of knowing and being that is deconstructive, reconstructive, and transformative of what it means to be a Black scholar in contemporary times" (p. 51). In this

[2] Black theorizing is located within a radical intellectual tradition that speaks to a critical sociology of knowledge. Some of the early pioneers of Black radical thought that Dei mentions are Anton Wilheim Amo, Sojourner Truth, Thomas Nelson Parker, Gilbert Haven Jones, Jean Slappy, Charles Leander Hill, William Fontaine, Marcus Garvey, Kwame Nkrumah, C.L.R. James, and W.E.B. DuBois.

At the same time, over the years, Dei (2018a) says that "Black theorizing has revolved around contested conceptions of Negritude Philosophy; Pan Africanism; Black Nationalism; Fanonian Anti-Colonialism; Postcolonial and Diasporic Literature Theories; Afrocentrism and African-Centered Thought; Black Feminist Thought; Intersectional Theory; Critical Race Theory (CRT); and Critical Anti-Racist Theory (CART).

In his presentation Dei (2018a) says, "We are entitled to a degree of self-centrism." However, the question is not whether nondominant thinking (bodies of knowledge) can reach a self-consciousness and evident neutrality, but rather engaging such knowledge as intellectual resistance and subversion for the main purpose of offering alternative (complementary or contradictory) visions of reality are more rooted in the lived experiences of Black and African peoples.

manner, a Deisian perspective increases its potential as instrument for transformation: As a theory and movement, challenges colonial modernity African Indigeneity and is continually about remembering, connecting, emancipating, and reflecting our experiences. In particular, it focuses on the liberation of spaces and information, images, concepts, definitions, and symbols from European hegemonic control. A Deisian perspective affirms the importance of African Indigeneity, asserting that it is characterized by its commitment to a political program in conformity with the idea that theory is not disconnected from practice.

Local Histories And Cultures

A Deisian perspective pioneers an African Indigenous lens for understanding Black Canadian communities, histories, and cultures that is rooted in our own cultural perspectives. He urgently calls for the growth of a critical analysis of Black Canadian women and men, which allows for new scholarship on African Indigenous communities to flourish. For example, Black Canadian theorizing in the academy draws from a set of ideas basing itself on the history and culture of the local people, as well as African wisdom. Dei (2018a) writes, "[T]here is an Akan Ghanian proverb that says, 'If you want to know how heavy a bag of salt is, ask the one carrying it.'" This assumption has influenced the formation of a discursive approach elaborated by Dei that argues that Black theorizing in the academy needs to reflect the values of the land, region, and communities. Within the academy, he is putting together an African Indigenous perspective that is "intimately connected to decolonization and by implication, decolonization cannot happen solely through Western science scholarship" (Dei, 2018a). The analysis of Black Canadian communities can posit that local history and communal life is based on the common good and is *sui generis* in the existence of the individual.

His five conceptual framings and five core concepts advance our own theorizing about our Black Canadian history and culture to become self-knowing reflexive subjects; redirect Black Canadian scholars toward their cultural center; convert African Canadian history and culture to draw on our values and spirituality; and analyze our context from a Deisian perspective. Black scholars will analyze the social conditions, determining our possibilities, reorienting, if necessary, the quest for definitional and textual power. Dei emphasizes the primacy of the African Indigenous worldview, values, and perspectives to predominate. As a perspective, Indigeneity can be seen to have five elements: African Indigeneity, epistemic saliency, multicentricity, subversive inclusion, and reflection. Indigeneity focuses on African history, culture and experiences; epistemic saliency on the needs and concerns of African-descended people; multicentricity on the emancipation and empowerment of African-descended people, and subversive inclusion and reflection on beginning anew.

The purpose of this section was to initiate a discussion about how to apply a Deisian perspective to the Canadian context. Briefly, to reiterate, central to a Deisian perspective are the concepts of spirituality, land, identities, local communities, and histories/cultures. These five concepts are important in the process of knowledge production, and Black theorizing in the academy is about knowledge creation. In this case, my Deisian feminist theorizing is about engaging the myriad identities as an Irish, Kittian, Canadian scholar and the local Black Canadian communities who are partners in my knowledge production.

Where Do We Go From Here?

Dei's Black theorizing in the academy provides us with a call to action, to become academic warriors. His vision for the academy is relevant for different local, provincial, and national contexts and potentially for a global context, which has to counter the pressures of global anti-Black racism to which the academy is also subjected. Critical engagement and reflection and critical friends are central to this vision of redefining our Black theorizing in the academy. The academy is therefore an institutional space that can allow for multicentric ways of thinking. Black theorizing in the academy can be reinserted as an anti-colonial perspective, drawing on the five conceptual framings and five core concepts.

Against this backdrop, Black scholars in academia have to formulate anti-colonial perspectives or Black theorizing in this institution. As Dei (2018a) says, "[T]he academy should be viewed as a critical sphere where multicentric knowledge can exist, where there is indeed discussion among Black scholars and critical friends about the nature of the academy and its place in Canadian society." The recent scholarship on Black Canadian communities, discussions, and conferences about Blackness in the academy suggest that there is a lively debate about the fate of the academy, but it also has to happen across disciplines.

If Black theorizing in the academy provides an anti-colonial model, an African Indigenous perspective, or what this chapter is calling a Deisian perspective, the academy has to be regarded as part of the discussion about the direction of the literature. As more Black scholars are engaged in critical scholarship, there is a need to encourage them to use the perspective, build the literature, and critique it for omission, errors, and faulty parallels. Scholars in the cities across Canada have to contribute to this call to action and engage in their own Black theorizing in academia.

Acknowledgments

Dei's stimulating African Liberation Month Lecture at the Ontario Institute for Studies in Education (OISE) during the 2017–2018 academic year encouraged this chapter through the months of excellent conversation and important feedback. I want to sincerely thank George Dei for his Black theorizing in academia and facilitating the progress of this chapter.

I want to thank the anonymous reviewers for their comments on a previous draft of this chapter. I want to thank my sister, Jacqueline Mills, and my nephew, Elliott Mills, for their support.

References

Asante, M. (2007). *An Afrocentric Manifesto: Towards an African Renaissance*. Cambridge, UK: Polity Press.

Bernstein, R. (1995). *Habermas and Modernity*. Cambridge, MA: MIT Press.

Cabral, A. (1979). *Unity and Struggle*. New York, NY: Monthly Review Press.

Dei, G. (2012). Indigenous anti-colonial knowledge as 'heritage knowledge' for promoting Black/African education in diasporic contexts. *Decolonization: Indigeneity, Education & Society, 1*(1), 102-119.

Dei, G. (2015b). The African Scholar in North America. In M. J. Shujaa & K. L. Shujaa (Eds.), *Encyclopedia of African Cultural Heritage in North America*, Vol.1 (pp.139–141). Thousand Oaks, CA: SAGE.

Dei, G. (2016d). Anti-Racist Theory. In B. S. Turner, C. Kyung-Sup, C. Epstein, P. Kivisto, W. Outhwaite, & J. M. Ryan (Eds), *Wiley Blackwell Encyclopedia of Social Theory*. Chichester, UK: Wiley.

Dei, G. (2016e). Indigenous Philosophies, Counter Epistemologies and Anti-Colonial Education. In W. Lehman (Ed.), *Education and Society* (pp. 190–206). London, UK: Oxford University Press.

Dei, G. (2016h). Anti-Racist Educational Leadership. In D. Griffiths & J. Portelli (Eds.), *Key Questions for Educational Leaders* (pp. 99–103). St. Thomas, ON: Word and Deed.

Dei, G. (2017a). *Reframing Blackness and Black Solidarities through Anti-Colonial and Decolonial Prism*. Cham, Switzerland: Springer.

Dei, G. (2017d). Foreword. In A. Abdulle & A. N. Obeyesekere (Eds.), *New Framings on Anti-Racism and Resistance*, Vol. 1 (pp. ix–xiv). Rotterdam, Netherlands: Sense.

Dei, G. J. (2018a). *Black Theorizing in Academia: Towards an Anti-Colonial Reading* [Lecture]. Ontario Institute for Studies in Education (OISE), University of Toronto. Toronto, Canada

Dei, G. J. (2018b). Black Like Me: Reframing Blackness for Decolonial Politics. *Educational Studies: A Journal of the American Education Studies Association, 54*(2), 117–142.

Dei, G. J. (2018c). Indigenous Governance for Africentric School Success. In McKinley & T. L. Smith (Eds.), Handbook of Indigenous Education. New York, NY: Springer. Retrieved from https://link-springer-com.myaccess.library.utoronto.ca/content/pdf/10.1007%2F978-981-10-1839-8_27-1.pdf

Du Bois, W. E. B. (1994). *The Souls of Black Folk*. New York, NY: Dover.

Du Bois, W. E. B. (2001). The Conservation of Races. In R. Bernasconi (Ed.), *Race* (pp. 84-91). Oxford, UK: Blackwell.

Fanon, F. (1967). *Black Skin, White Masks*. C. L. Markmann (Trans.). New York, NY: Grove.

Held, D. (1980). *Introduction to Critical Theory*. Berkeley, CA: University of California Press.

Mensah, J. (2010). *Black Canadians: History, Experiences, Social Conditions* (2nd ed.). Halifax, Nova Scotia: Fernwood.

Perry, T. and Delpit, L. (Eds). (1998) *The real ebonics debate : power, language, and the education of African-American children* . Boston: Beacon Press.

Rabaka, R. (2007). *W. E. B. Du Bois and the Problems of the Twenty-First Century: An Essay on Africana Critical Theory*. Lanham, MD: Lexington Books.

Rabaka, R. (2009). *Africana Critical Theory Reconstructing the Black Radical Tradition from W. E. B. Du Bois and C. L. R. James to Frantz Fanon and Amilcar Cabral*. New York, NY: Lexington.

Rabaka, R. (2014). Concepts of Cabralism Amil Cabral and Africana Critical Theory. New York, NY: Lexington.

Wallerstein, I. (1996). *Open the Social Sciences: Report of the Gulbenkian* Commission on the *Social Sciences*. Stanford, CA: Stanford University Press.

Yancy, G. (2005). *White on White/Black*. Oxford, UK: Rowman & Littlefield.

CHAPTER 13

Black Graduation at the University of Toronto: A Case for Placemaking as Liberation Praxis

Jessica P. Kirk

On June 22, 2017, Black students across the University of Toronto at the undergraduate, graduate, and doctoral level who had or would be graduating that year attended the first ever recorded Black graduation ceremony in Canada. While it functioned as a space of collective healing and presented an opportunity for Black students involved and watching to shift their self-concept in academia, Black graduation may also have invited implications of neo-liberalizing anti-Black resistance work at the postsecondary level. This leads to the questioning of whether spaces like Black graduation strengthen, nullify, or perhaps shift the ability for university administrators and/or other relevant bodies to respond to demands put forth through more direct action-oriented organizing. This chapter seeks to interrogate the conditions in which Black students are expected to learn and speaks to the ways in which they have and continue to resist through organizing Black graduation and engaging in other forms of campus activism (Calliste, 2000). It also invites us to engage with different strategies that can be used to avoid the appropriation of Black liberation praxis. How do we rationalize carving out spaces for some Black students to experience pride and joy surrounded by members of their community when it happens at the expense of pressing issues impacting other Black students being willfully overlooked by administration? How do we grapple with the institution hiding behind particular projects concerning Blackness as a means to shield itself from exposures of anti-Black violence toward its students, staff, and faculty? This chapter invites a discussion on how these questions and the implications for Black student organizing at the University of Toronto functions as a form of antiracism education in and of itself. Relying on both Black feminist theory (hooks, 1989) and critical anti-racist theoretical framework (Dei, 2013), I intend to critically analyze the experiences of Black students in postsecondary educational spaces and use Black graduation as a case study to consider the ways in which postsecondary institutions capitalize off diversity because it has what Sara Ahmed (2006) considers "economic value" (p. 120). I nonetheless address the functionality of Black student organizing in the institution as an invitation to explore possible futurities for Black people to "come to voice" (hooks, 1989, p. 13) and claim space in academia.

While I offer slight caution toward the implications of Black graduation as a cofounder of the ceremony at the University of Toronto, I also come to my understanding of a Black student experience as a learner who, like so many others, has had to navigate my general academic (and personal) journey with a White supremacist backdrop actively working against me. I am a Black woman who was raised being taught to assert pride in my Blackness, and I am grateful to have been offered at least some context behind the importance of affirming a proclamation of that nature, as well as its rootedness in resistance. Nonetheless, living in the Diaspora—the Black Diaspora in particular—presents a very specific form of disconnectivity with respect to charting Black geographies on Indigenous lands because of our own ancestral histories of being colonized and being forbidden from learning our Indigenous languages and cultures, through forced displacement and due to enslavement.

On the topic of disappeared histories, that disconnectivity extended beyond the individual experiences since there was also an absence of teachings on the history of Black Canadians throughout my schooling experience. Nonetheless, being enrolled in a variety of educational spaces offered me diverse experiences during my schooling career. Throughout my own upbringing, I was fortunate enough to have immersed myself with a variety of cultural and religious knowledges that youth who surrounded me had learned from ancestral teachings of communities, while all were intentionally left out of the traditionally Eurocentric curriculum. Incidentally, these playground teach-ins were offered during my time attending under-resourced schools in Scarborough, where the demographic make-ups were predominantly low-income Black and Brown children of immigrants. Contrastingly, my experience attending a high school located in a relatively upper-class, predominantly White neighborhood in Toronto presented much fewer opportunities to meaningfully connect with my classmates' cultural teachings, insofar as many of their histories were already situated within the curriculum.

My range of schooling experiences have served as visceral reminders that students from particular geographic areas are simply better supported than others, more specifically that resources for students vary drastically depending on the neighborhood in which the schools are situated. In 2017, Dr. Carl James, Jean Augustine Chair in Education,

Community, and Diaspora at York University, in collaboration with the African Canadian Legal Clinic (ACLC) and the Ontario Alliance of Black School Educators (ONABSE), developed a report on Black students and schooling in the greater Toronto area, whereby the participants interviewed also spoke to the challenges that came with navigating inequitable resource distribution. Similar to my personal experiences and observations, the participants "contend that schools in low-income neighbourhoods with a significant population of racialized and predominantly Black residents [are] not set up to support these students to take Academic courses and go on to university" (James & Turner, 2017, p. 42). During my own schooling experiences in Scarborough, I noticed that those who were more "difficult" to support were given up on much too soon, and these children were often the ones who lived on the intersection of racial and classed marginality. While I am Black and was raised in and out of income insecurity during my childhood, I was privileged to have been raised by a family who had the capacity to encourage and support my academic pursuits. However, due to the ways in which racism and classism intersect, some of my Black and Brown friends were raised in single-parent households, and most of their parents were not afforded the time to support their kids with homework. These were parents who were simultaneously working two to three jobs to keep a roof above their family's heads. While most of the students I went to Leaside High School with were supported by teachers in their pursuit to attend university, many of the friends I grew up with in my earlier childhood were encouraged to either pursue college or head straight into the workforce. Some were repeatedly told by guidance counselors and teachers that they weren't smart enough for university. In many ways, my personal engagements with racially informed selective supports speak to what George Dei (1997) refers to as a "failure of the educational system" (p. 84). In order to open a discussion about Black graduation at the University of Toronto, the following seeks to further contextualize the Black student experience in Toronto, Canada. This discussion will lead to an intervention with the ways in which political climate has historically and continues to inform the intensity with which Black students organize and actively resist White supremacist violence on campus grounds.

While we know that Black students are just as bright and capable and offer just as much critical insight to the academy as their non-Black counterparts, research demonstrates that the Black student experience at the primary, secondary, and postsecondary level are all often met with irremediable violence. With the basis of our discussion rooted in a call for attention toward the creation of spaces to celebrate the resilience of Black postsecondary graduates and their role in amplifying Black student demands, this comes with a requirement to set the context of the Black student experience. For starters, as much as there is a need to address the structural barriers being challenged through student organizing and placemaking in universities, it is imperative to acknowledge that so many Black youth do not even make it to the postsecondary level for reasons beyond their control. Drop-out rates are persistent among the community; Black youth are pushed out of school at exponential rates, and in some cases they become victims of the school-to-prison pipeline (Crenshaw, 2015). Though Kimberlé Crenshaw's findings are drawn from research within the U.S context, George Dei's (1997) research demonstrates that punitive measures are disproportionately inflicted on Black students north of the colonial border as well. This conversation is limited, however, in the sense that research pertaining to drop-out rates among Black students pursuing their postsecondary education in Canada is virtually nonexistent. The University of Toronto has only recently committed to race-based data collection in response to demands put forth by the Black Liberation Collective (BLC) Toronto (Reynolds, 2016), which could lead to easier access to drop-out trends across different racial demographics pursuing PSE. Nonetheless, alarming streaming processes are one of many ways our education system fails the students it is meant to support.

Beside the active absenting of Black students pursuing schooling vis-à-vis the "drop-out problem" (Dei, 1997, p. 84), the absence of Black critical thought and Black history in the curriculum is yet another example of anti-Blackness in the classroom. At all levels of schooling, research and reports have proven time and time again that "poor outcomes for Black students [are] partly a reflection of a curriculum that is not responsive to their needs and interests, nor culturally relevant to, or reflective of, their cultural worlds" (James & Turner, 2017, p. 55). While there have been tremendous strides toward culturally responsive curriculum development and implementation through both TDSB's Afrocentric school and Black Lives Matter, Toronto's Freedom School, the reality is that access to non-Eurocentric curriculum should not be solely reliant on alternative educational spaces. Rather, theoretical, political, and cultural teachings about Black thought and Black history should *also* be integrated into general curriculum at all levels of schooling. While integration alone should by no means stand in as the ultimate solution for meaningfully supporting a Black student's educational journey, avoiding the approach in its entirety cultivates a risk of students at all levels of mainstream schooling who continue to experiencing intellectual exploitation, with being called on to offer the "Black perspective" in the classroom. White supremacist logic is such that Black and Indigenous people are "'naturally' resource people" (Calliste, 2000, p. 156), who are supposedly meant to unquestionably work toward serving others. In an interview, a Black sophomore from Yale spoke to the frustration of being subjected to the aforementioned experiences, mentioning that they are "tired of being an unpaid, untenured professor teaching these guys the elementals of humanity" (Biondi, 2012, p. 21). This is not to say that all students do not have a responsibility to intellectually engage with classroom material, but rather an argument that points to the ways in which Black students being the only source of Black thought in educational spaces is deeply problematic. This is particularly true since the curriculum built into the public schooling system is such that it fails to offer teachers the tools to meaningfully integrate racially responsive material into the classroom. While part of anti-racist education involves alternative approaches to classroom engagement, including opportunities for students and teachers to engage in "collaborative learning" (Crozier, 1994, p. 221), leaving Black students unsupported as the only voices offering alternative perspectives on any/all classroom material is, at its core, an exploitation of labor.

Beyond the inescapable experience of being a resource for all things related to Blackness, Black students also undergo a coinciding process of being Othered in postsecondary education. When describing what it feels like when Black, Indigenous, and racialized people are made to feel like they don't belong in academia, Sara Ahmed (2006) borrows from what Nirmal Puwar best describes as being treated like "space invaders" (p. 110). Meaning, non-White postsecondary students are made to feel as though they are invading places, since they were not fundamentally designed for them in the first place. In the case of Black students in particular, students who were interviewed across multiple studies cite their experiences responding to folks being "shocked to see Black students in university" (Codjoe, 1997, p. 353). Many instances go beyond others' surprise, as students have also described occurrences of students, staff, or faculty acting on their discomfort. For example, following an earlier tweet linked to the ongoing #BlackOnCampusUofT campaign, Black undergraduate University of Toronto student Bosi Moragia tweeted the following: "@Trinity_College Myself and other black [sic] trinity students are harassed whenever we use college facilities. We are told time and time again it's because we 'look unfamiliar.' With that logic, white nonresident members of college would be stopped also. I've asked them. They don't." (bosiburrito, 2018). Moragia is making explicit the inequitable treatment experienced by them and other Black students on campus, indicating the ways in which they are continuously made to feel like outsiders even though they too are members of the university. While the #BlackOnCampusUofT hashtag will be further explored later in the chapter—along with other social media campaigns responding to the dehumanizing experiences of Black people on campus and in our society—it is important to note here that Moragia's anecdote is far from a one-off experience. In a journalistic video segment on Black graduation at U of T, Matthew Campbell-Williams reveals the following: "I've had people tell me they want to sick dogs on me. I've had people tell me there should be more cases like Michael Brown" (Francis, 2017). Neither racially motivated threats of physical violence, nor the normalization of state-sanctioned police violence, should be treated lightly. Nonetheless, both Moragia and Campbell-Williams's stories are signifiers for the conditions under which Black students are expected to learn. They demonstrate the harsh realities that students should expect to be met with resistance while pursuing their postsecondary education, either by being Othered or by being subjected to other forms of anti-Black violence. That said, in instances where Black students and faculty alike are made to feel like invaders at any stage along their academic journey, it is always helpful to be reminded to "assume you don't belong" (Ferguson, 2017, p. 92). While we know self-determined places organized by and for Black people in academic institutions are critical for keeping folks grounded in the academy, we should also remind ourselves that we are "*in* the university but not *of* the university" (Kelley, 2016).

In effort to offer a more expansive perspective on the experiences of Black students pursuing postsecondary education, it is critical that an intersectional (Crenshaw, 1989) lens be applied to the discussion. In instances of sexual assault, not only are Black women perceived as more blameworthy than non-Black women in the courts and on campuses (Donovan, 2007; Ruparelia, 2012), Black women are also less likely to report their cases of sexual assault (Fisher, Daigle, Cullen, & Turner, 2003) due to Black peoples' general mistrust in the systems that criminalize them rather than offer justice. While we are unable to draw on race-based student data since it is not collected in postsecondary institutions across Canada, we can still deduce a prevalence of misogynoir on campus grounds (Morrison, 2016) due to researchers like Robyn Maynard (2016) who reminds us of state-sanctioned processes that "reinforce both racial and gendered hierarchies" (p. 156). Further, class and race intersect in structurally detrimental ways, impacting the experiences and outcomes of low-income Black students pursuing any and all stages of education. When interviewed, parents expressed frustration, contending "that schools in low-income neighbourhoods with a significant population of racialized and predominantly Black residents were not set up to support these students to take Academic [sic] courses and to go on to university" (James & Turner, 2017, p. 42). As noted earlier, resources and supports are disproportionately distributed to students across the city of Toronto, leading to inequitable outcomes for those who might have hoped to pursue undergraduate studies. Across the board, it is apparent that the Black student experience is layered with racialized violence. While some discussions were drawn from American scholars and perspectives, we are often reminded that anti-Black violence transcends borders. Next, we will explore the intimacies between resistance work on campus and in the community, unearthing the historic and contemporary overlapping responses to White supremacist violence. Tracing the patterns of resistance allows for more clarity around a more particular discussion on Black graduation at the University of Toronto and its function as both a celebratory occasion and a tactical platform used to open a public dialogue around critical issues faced by Black students in postsecondary education.

Much like other forms of social justice-oriented resistance work, intimate connections exist between freedom fighting for Black liberation within postsecondary education institutions and in our general society. In thinking about the transformative changes we'd like to see for Black students in postsecondary education, it is important that we draw associations with the patterns of resistance work that have been organized in response to anti-Black violence on campus and in our communities. For example, strategies used to organize direct actions on the streets during the Black power and civil rights movements were replicated by Black students in the 1960s to organize boycotts, strikes, sit-ins, violent and nonviolent confrontations, and other strategies (Morris, 1984). Similarly, in more recent years the movement for Black liberation on campuses has been influenced by organizing in the city—notably, the work of Black Lives Matter, Toronto (BLM-TO). BLM-TO was founded in November 2014, their first action being one in solidarity with folks responding to the murder of Mike Brown in Ferguson, Missouri, a Black boy who was killed by police officer Darren Wilson a few months prior. The action in November was also organized in response to the murder of 33-year-old Jermaine Carby, a Black man who was killed by Brampton Police that September (Battersby, 2016). In the few years that followed Black Lives Matter, Toronto's inception, Black students across the city have become subjected to a cultural shift toward more transformative social consciousness. The parallel waves of political consciousness raising have even intersected, in that the second annual "Black on Campus U of T" teach-in organized by the Black Liberation Collective was hosted at #BLMTOtentcity, a 15-day encampment set up outside Toronto Police Headquarters between Sunday, March 20, 2016 and continuing through to Monday, April 4, 2016. At "Black on Campus," Black student organizers discussed the demands that had been put forth to the University of Toronto by the Black Liberation Collective just months prior and updated attendees on progress that had been made since the release of the demands. Demands included, but were not limited to, stopping the funding freeze to the Transitional Year Program, increasing the percentage of Black faculty and staff to be proportional with the population of Black people in Toronto, and establishing culturally appropriate mental health services (Black Liberation Collective, 2014). Energized by the work of Black Lives Matter, Toronto, the BLC was able to garner a victory, as the University of Toronto responded to one of their remands by committing to race-based data collection (Reynolds, 2016). Ultimately, it is critical that we trace patterns of resistance that are rooted in connections made across struggles. Audre Lorde (2007), for example, points to legacies of feminist organizing as being instructive toward contemporary efforts to connect and build solidarities across struggles in her essay "Learning from the 60s": "Each one of us here is a link in the connection between antipoor legislation, gay shootings, the burning of synagogues, street harassment, attacks against women, and resurgent violence against Black people" (p. 139). Anti-Blackness is woven into the fabric of our society; it certainly exists beyond the walls of academic institutions, and, further, struggles for justice overlap. That said, all resistance work related to challenging that oppression at any level must actively speak to each other in an effort to strengthen our political practice.

Counter-storytelling is at the root of historic and more recent Black liberation work, a tool historically used by communities of color to vocalize struggles that have often gone unaddressed (Calliste, 2000). Hashtag activism has proven to be an effective tool of engaging in counter-storytelling, proven by the inception of Black Lives Matter as a global movement created through the #blacklivesmatter hashtag, and more relevantly by the Black Liberation Collective garnering student support through their #BlackOnCampusUofT hashtag. It should be noted that the second hashtag is a spinoff of a response to racially motivated death threats and nooses being hung across Mizzou University in November 2015. Put simply, the use of hashtags on what is referred to as "Black Twitter" (a digital community of Black people on Twitter, where they are able to speak about the everyday experiences of being Black), "prompts the Black social media community to recognize issues and respond to them" (Williams, 2015, p. 343). Though Williams writes within the context of sexualized violence against Black women, the author draws attention to social media as instrumental in amplifying instances of racial discrimination, anti-Black violence, and even Black death. When traditional mainstream media outlets ignore injustices inflicted on Black people, Black Twitter works to influence what stories media outlets should prioritize. Both tracing the influence of progressive political movements on postsecondary students and reinforcing the power of counter-storytelling online and on the ground shed lights on the impact of direct confrontation with experiences of racialized violence. Further discussions on Black graduation at the University of Toronto will demonstrate that resistance work manifests itself in creative ways, many of which remind us that "coming to voice" is, in and of itself, "a gesture of resistance, an affirmation of struggle" (hooks, 1989, p. 18).

Tracing the conditions of the Black student experience and a brief history of parallel efforts to organize against anti-Black racism on campus and in surrounding communities ground us with critical perspective on the importance of curating spaces that positively influence the emotional well-being of Black students. Further, it allows us to investigate our initial inquiry into whether these spaces strengthen, nullify, or shift the university's ability to adequately respond to demands put forth by Black students. Beyond the challenges that come with being made to feel like a space invader in academia, being intellectually exploited due to a shortage of Black theoretical classroom material, and experiencing a shortage of educational resources, Black students are also at higher risk of "stereotype vulnerability" (Steele & Aronson, 1995, p. 74). Social psychologists like Claud Steele and Joshua Aronson have conducted empirical research that demonstrates societal stereotypes of Black people and intellectual ability impact Black students' capacity to perform to the best of their ability. Without active effort put toward self-assurance or external validation, Black people are implicitly impacted by negative and false depictions of Black people as unintelligent and lazy. Within the context of schooling, George Dei (1997) warns that "a diminished sense of confidence in one's ability, can therefore lead to a sense of fatalism in which . . . students begin to internalize negative self-concepts and feel that the demands of schooling are beyond their capabilities" (p. 68). Luckily, prior to and through Black graduation at U of T, Black students have and continue to engage in active efforts to create spaces that remind us of our humanity. Through cultural celebrations, panels of discussion, documentary screenings, and facilitated discussions, Black students have historically and continue to carve out spaces and redefine community healing. With respect to a specific discussion on Black graduation, Aniyka Mark, the 2017-2018 president of the Black Students Association at the University of Toronto, was interviewed for a video-journalistic piece on the ceremony, speaking to its impact on Black students' livelihood: "It reminds them of who they are, and that they matter. Black Lives Matter, literally" (Francis, 2017). Ron from Main University reinforces Mark's proclamation in favor of confronting anti-Black racism through the more general practice of placemaking, stating that it's "really about making a change to make where we live more welcoming for ourselves, the place we pay to go to more welcoming" (Reynolds & Mayweather, 2017, p. 294). While Ron seems to have been commenting more generally on advocacy work that, if successful, allows for structural changes that in turn create more, accessible conditions for Black student learning, I argue that Black graduation celebrations have the capacity to do so as well, and further that placemaking is a means through which Black Diasporic students are able to be re-grounded, resisting histories of being forcibly uprooted.

Actively citing our inspiration drawn from the activism of the Black Liberation Collective(BLC) and Black Lives Matter, Toronto, as a founder of Black graduation at the University of Toronto organizer I consecutively spoke to the lack of Black faculty, the low number of Black students being accepted at graduate and doctoral levels across academic disciplines, and, further, the shortage of curriculum that includes the Black perspective when I was interviewed by major media publications (Francis, 2017; Gordon, 2017; Massa, 2017). These issues run parallel with some of the demands put forth by the Black Liberation Collective in fall 2016 that have yet to be addressed by the University of Toronto, which is why it was and is so critical to spark a public dialogue about those matters. Since the university's priority is its public perception, our organizing efforts focused on utilizing this platform. We targeted the University's purported commitment to responding to, and amplifying, the challenges faces by Black students at the postsecondary level, through both awareness and financial commitments. We aimed to hold them accountable for offering concrete solutions and economic support. Returning to hooks (1989), we are reminded that when "we end our silence, when we speak in a liberated voice, our words connect us with anyone, anywhere who lives in silence" (p. 18). Black graduation was a tactic, but the goal has always been liberation.

In addition to placemaking, giving Black students the capacity to shift their self-concept and using it as an entry point to demand racial justice, Black graduation acted as a sanctuary of emotional support for the Black community. Commonly referred to as Kente graduations, Black graduation ceremonies have become much more common in the United States since the 1990s, spanning from celebrations at the University of California in San Diego, University of Washington, Loyola Marymount University, and California State University, Long Beach, to name a few. These are some of many universities who influenced us to create an additional graduation ceremony to specifically celebrate Black graduate achievement. To quote a Black grad attendee who was live tweeting during the first Canadian ceremony of its kind, Cornel Grey tweeted the following: "Many of us don't know these graduates personally but we sending them love and praise like we fam #UofTBlackGrad" (holyblackness, 2017). The beauty of Black spaces organized for Black students (alongside their family, friends, and the broader Black community) by Black students, is such that it functions as a platform that grounds us in a reminder that we are stronger as a community when we are united.

It is helpful to remind ourselves of the positive influence that Black graduation has had on Black students in the following ways: shifting toward a more positive self-concept, encouraging Black youth to pursue their postsecondary education by allowing them to see themselves reflected among Black graduates at the ceremony, and opening up a public dialogue about the structural issues faced by Black students in efforts to find solutions. Nonetheless, we owe it to ourselves to be attentive, even during moments of positivity. There are critical conversations to be had about the gray areas regarding the impact that organizing the graduation ceremony could have had on Black students and Black liberation work at the University of Toronto. While it goes without being said that students resisting structural anti-Black violence will inherently be met with some resistance, the safety of Black graduation attendees was of particular concern leading up to the event. In fall 2016, the University of Toronto's very own Jordan Peterson sparked an international debate about gender identity, antiracism organizing, and political correctness, which was followed by Donald Trump's inauguration as the 45th president of the United States. Finally, the "Unite the Right" rally in Charlottesville took place just months after Black graduation in August 2017. While the resurgence of White supremacy is of international concern, mainstream national and Western coverage has focused on the United States. Nonetheless, community activists have made it clear that this resurgence is of grave concern in Canada as well. In particular, the "lack of critical engagement of race relations in Canada" (Khan, 2017) (and willful ignorance, quite frankly) explains the stark opposition to Black graduation, which is why some oppositional responses on *Reddit* and coverage in alt-right media publications left the organizers with mounting safety concerns. We recognized, however, that implementing extensive security measures by allowing campus police presence would not have created a warm environment for Black graduates, since some folks may have endured hostile interactions with campus police. Ultimately, no physical protests were organized in opposition to the Black graduation ceremony, and disdain from White supremacists did not pick up as much publicity as the organizers expected.

In addition to safety concerns, another implication I and other Black graduation organizers had to work through was the University of Toronto's administration appropriating the fruits of Black student labor. While we were the ones having to deal with the "whitelash" (Jones, 2016) that came with being at the frontline of curating a space to celebrate Black students' accomplishments—in addition to organizing a nationally recognized event without being financially compensated—the university was able to avoid any real accountability as it pertains to structurally improving the Black student experience. I say this as a means to acknowledge "racial and gender ideologies and racist logic [are such that] Black and Aboriginal [sic] peoples are 'naturally' resource people just as white people are " 'naturally' experts" (Calliste, 2000, p. 156). The implicit presumption that we are "resource people" was addressed much earlier, in relation to the classroom experience of Black students being expected to be the expert of all things Black without any intellectual labor being shared between them and faculty. However, this form of exploitation also translates to engagement between Black graduation organizers and university administration, since they were much more willing to provide us with the financial resources so that we could run the event than they were to take up the calls to address structural challenges that informed our motivation behind organizing Black graduation to begin with. The university endorsing the project in isolation of their complicity toward the calls to action of Black student graduates is, in effect, an "appropriation of the marginal voice [that] threatens the very core of self-determination and free-expression for exploited and oppressed peoples" (hooks, 1989, p. 14). I do not seek to undermine the ways in which Black students have and continue to make use of resources to suit the needs of our comrades. In fact, even in instances of apprehension toward their financial support for Black graduation, we must also remind ourselves of the longstanding history of "black activists repurposing university resources to instruct themselves and one another—to self-radicalize, in effect" (Kelley, 2016). Ultimately, in thinking about organizing the Black graduation ceremony and its influence on energizing the maintenance of Black liberation on campus, it is always the right time and place to meaningfully take up the demands put forth by Black students in their entirety.

This chapter has examined the ways in which anti-Black structural inequities impact the Black student experience, inviting us to explore historic and contemporary responses to those inequities through student-led Black liberation work on campuses. Verbal accounts of being intellectually exploited in response to a lack of incorporating Black scholars into curriculums as well as experiences of unbelonging on their campus are a few of many examples that were explored. Moreover, the intimacies between the political climate in our society and that which transmits onto campus were investigated, demonstrating their role in both strengthening and nullifying progressive resolves. Further, Black students, the university, and societal engagement with Black graduation as a concept was investigated, showing the opportunities—and sometimes the repercussions—that come with curating a politically rooted event at the University of Toronto. While these spaces were briefly mentioned earlier within the context of academics and activists creating culturally responsive curriculum and schools, I would like to reinforce the importance of Black liberation praxis having "multiple centers" (Dei, 2018). Similar to class discussions on the capability and need for antiracism education to exist both through alternative educational spaces and being inserted into traditionally Eurocentric curriculum, we should borrow this theoretical repositioning to confront how we think through Black Diasporic student placemaking in postsecondary education. Whether it is a sit-in, a teach-in, a slam poetry night, or a Black graduation ceremony, organizing efforts curated by Black students should and have been inherently connected through concentrated efforts that respond to structural inequities in academia and in the community. Lastly, while the focal point of discussion was the Black graduation ceremony, it is imperative that we redefine excellence and success in academia. Black people are also thriving outside/without/in spite of formal postsecondary educational schooling. Rather than admiring the students who crossed the stage on June 22, 2017, Black graduation should serve as a reminder to celebrate the everyday accomplishments within the Black community. Given the fact that we are confronted with traumatic structural violence every day, the resilience exhibited among Black people in our general society should also be held at high regard. Within the context of Black brilliance, Duwain Pinder, a Black graduate who participated in Harvard's first ever

Black graduation the same year as the ceremony at the University of Toronto, reminded his fellow classmates that they "are not the exceptions" (Levenson, 2017). Rather than exceptions, brilliance, excellence, and success are all the resulting manifestations of the everyday survival tactics employed by Black students and Black people outside of the academic institution.

References

Ahmed, S. (2006). The Nonperformativity of Antiracism. *Meridians, 7*(1), 104–126. Retrieved from https://www.jstor.org/stable/pdf/40338719.pdf?refreqid=excelsior%3A12c1c7e866c3bd14ce771f50484f48eb

Battersby, S. (2016, April 20). For Black Lives Matter, Some Long-Sought victories. *The Star*. Retrieved from https://www.thestar.com/news/gta/2016/04/20/for-black-lives-matter-some-long-sought-victories.html

Biondi, M. (2012). *Black Revolution on Campus*. Berkeley; Los Angeles; London: University of California Press. Retrieved from http://www.jstor.org.myaccess.library.utoronto.ca/stable/10.1525/j.ctt1ppfmn

Black Liberation Collective. (2014). Our Demands. Retrieved from http://www.blackliberationcollective.org/our-demands

bosiburrito (2018, March 1). @Trinity_College Myself and other black trinity students are harassed whenever we use college facilities. We are told time and time again it's because we "look unfamiliar." With that logic, white non resident members of college would be stopped also. I've asked them. They don't [Twitter post]. Retrieved from https://twitter.com/bosiburrito/status/969391360074711040

Calliste, A. (2000). Anti-Racist Organizing and Resistance in Academia. In M.Aguiar, A. M. Calliste, & G. J. S. Dei (Eds.), *Power, Knowledge and Anti-Racism Education: A Critical Reader* (pp. 141-161). Halifax, Nova Scotia: Fernwood Publishing.

Codjoe, H. M. (1997). Black students and School Success: A Study of the Experiences of Academically Successful African-Canadian student graduates in Alberta's Secondary School [Doctoral dissertation]. University of Alberta. Edmonton, Alberta.

Crenshaw, K. W. (1989). Demarginalizing the Intersection of Race and Sex: A Black Feminist Critique of Antidiscrimination Doctrine, Feminist Theory and Antiracist Politics. *University of Chicago Legal Forum, 1*(8), 139–167. Retrieved from https://chicagounbound.uchicago.edu/cgi/viewcontent.cgi?article=1052&context=uclf

Crenshaw, K. W., & Ritchie, A. J. (2015). Say Her Name: Resisting Police Brutality Against Black Women. *African American Policy Forum*. Retrieved from http://static1.squarespace.com/static/53f20d90e4b0b80451158d8c/t/560c068ee4b0af26f72741df/1443628686535/AAPF_SMN_Brief_Full_singles-min.pdf

Crozier, G. (1994). Teachers' Power, Anti-Racist Education and the Need for Pupil Involvement. *International Studies in Sociology of Education, 4*(2), 213–228. doi:10.1080/0962021940040205

Dei, G. J. S. (1997). *Reconstructing "Dropout": A Critical Ethnography of the Dynamics of Black Students' Disengagement from School*. Toronto, Canada: University of Toronto Press.

Dei, G. J. S. (2013). Chapter One: Reframing Critical Anti-Racist Theory (CART) for Contemporary Times. *Counterpoints, 445*, 1–14.

Dei, G. J. S. (2018, April 8). *SJE1921Y: The Principals of Anti-Racism Education* [Lecture]. Ontario Institute for Studies in Education of the University of Toronto. Ontario, Canada.

Donovan, R. A. (2007). To Blame or not to Blame: Influences of Target Race and Observer Sex on Rape Blame Attribution. *Journal of Interpersonal Violence, 22*(6), 722–736. doi:10.1177/0886260507300754

Ferguson, R. (2017). *We Demand: The University and Student Protests*. Berkeley, CA: University of California Press.

Fisher, B. S., Daigle, L. E., Cullen, F. T., & Turner, M. G. (2003). Reporting Sexual Victimization to the Police and Others: Results from a National-Level Study of College Women. *Criminal Justice and Behavior, 30*(1), 6–38.

Francis, A. (2017, June 29). University of Toronto Students Host Canada's First Black Graduation [Video file]. Retrieved from https://youtu.be/KMrnBFuU6No

Gordon, A. (2017, June 19). University of Toronto Gets Ready for First-Ever Black Graduation Ceremony. *The Star*. Retrieved from https://www.thestar.com/yourtoronto/education/2017/06/19/university-of-toronto-gets-ready-for-first-ever-black-graduation-ceremony.html

holyblackness. (2017, June 22). Many of us don't know these graduates personally but we sending them love and praise like we fam #UofTBlackGrad [Twitter post]. Retrieved from https://twitter.com/holyblackness/status/878050351911456772

hooks, b. (1989). *Talking Back: Thinking Feminist. Thinking Black*. Boston, MA: South End Press.

James, C. E. & Turner, T. (2017). *Towards Race Equity in Education. The Schooling of Black Students in the Greater Toronto Area*. Retrieved from http://edu.yorku.ca/files/2017/04/Towards-Race-Equity-in-Education-April-2017.pdf

Jones, V. (2016, November 9). Van Jones on a Trump Win: This was a White Lash [Video file]. Retrieved from https://www.youtube.com/watch?v=MA9aSvHzEIU

Kelley, R. D. G. (2016, March 7). Black Study, Black Struggle. *Boston Review*. Retrieved from http://bostonreview.net/forum/robin-d-g-kelley-black-study-black-struggle

Khan, J. (2017, August 15). Don't Kid Yourself, White Nationalism Is on the Rise in Canada Too. *Flare*. Retrieved from http://www.flare.com/news/janaya-khan-white-nationalism-on-rise-in-canada/

Levenson, M. (2017, May 23). "We Have Survived; Just Look at Us." *Boston Globe*. Retrieved from https://www.bostonglobe.com/metro/2017/05/23/black-students-gather-celebrate-their-harvard-graduation/x7hNzfxRtxCtgvl4IAhYzH/story.html

Lorde, A. (2007). *Sister Outsider: Essays and Speeches by Audre Lorde*. Berkeley, CA: Crossing Press.

Maynard, R. (2016) *Policing Black Lives*. Winnepeg, MA: Fernwood Publishing

Massa, G. (2017, June 22). Historic Graduation Ceremony at U of T [Video file]. Retrieved from https://www.youtube.com/watch?v=Y5oi1mosb6Y

Morris, A. D. (1984). *The Origin of the Civil Rights Movement*. New York, NY: Free Press.

Morrison, J. (2016) Let's Put an End to Sexual Violence on Campus. *The Star*. Retrieved from https://www.thestar.com/opinion/commentary/2016/03/08/lets-put-an-end-to-sexual-violence-on-campus.html

Reynolds, C. (2016). U of T to Track Race-Based Data of Its Students. *The Star*. Retrieved from https://www.thestar.com/news/gta/2016/02/22/u-of-t-to-track-race-based-data-of-its-students.html

Reynolds, R., & Mayweather, D. (2017). Recounting Racism, Resistance, and Repression: Examining the Experiences and #Hashtag Activism of College Students with Critical Race Theory and Counternarratives. *Journal of Negro Education, 86*(3), 283–304.

Ruparelia, R. (2012). All That Glitters Is Not Gold: The False Promise of Victim Impact Statements. In E. Sheehy (Ed.), *Sexual Assault in Canada: Law, Legal Practice and Women's Activism* (pp. 665–700). Ottawa, Canada: University of Ottawa Press. Retrieved from https://ruor.uottawa.ca/bitstream/10393/19876/12/Sexual_Assault_in_Canada.pdf

Steele, C. & Aronson, J. (1995). Stereotype Threat and the Intellectual Test Performance of African Americans. *Journal of Personality and Social Psychology, 69*(5), 797–811.

Williams, S. (2015, February 19). Digital Defense: Black Feminists Resist Violence with Hashtag Activism. *Feminist Media Studies, 15*(2), 341–344.

CHAPTER 14

A Spiritual Call for Afrocentric Learning Spaces and a Reflection on the Current state of Afrocentric Education in Toronto

Kimbra Yohannes Iket

Introduction

Racism manifests itself in our everyday encounters, whether it be health care, education, workplace, and all other daily interactions. African peoples continue to experience oppression. It is not surprising that African children are not immune to forces of White supremacy. The usage of the term *African peoples* in this chapter refers to people in Canada who occupy a Black identity. The diverse histories of Black people in Canada is important to centralize and should not be confined to a singular definition. Black people in Canada come from diverse geographic and historical origins; Blackness is multifaceted. The term *African peoples* is also an ontological reference point for Black people that transcends location, nationality, and citizenship status. The objective of employing the term African *peoples* is a political one; it is a calling for a Pan-African intellectual revolution. The call for a Pan-African intellectual revolution is most importantly a recognition and a centralization of African Indigeneity. It is a recognition that African Indigeneity encompasses a spiritual connection to the land that continues to be under attack by the forces of White supremacy and anti-Black and anti-African racism. George Dei (2018) argues that Blackness cannot be understood in isolation to Africanness; we must go beyond a fixed racial ideology. Dei argues:

> Hence in celebrating our uniqueness, nuances and complexities, what role does a Pan-African lens brings us in order to dream and futurize intimately closer? If we see each other as connected as one, how do we move forward acknowledging our multifaceted identities of privilege, power, oppression, skin markers, class, gender, sexual orientation, etc.? How does this reframing of Blackness permit brighter futures to (re)imagine what and how we can work on things together while still being responsible and accountable to each other and ourselves? (p. 121)

Moving forward, education is not neutral; rather, it is a state apparatus, with political implications, and as such it must be examined as having political force (Schick, 2010). It is our duty and responsibility as anti-racist educators to expose this reality. What we know today as Canada is a White settler colonial state founded on the genocide of the Indigenous people of this land, a state that consequently embodies Eurocentric values and reinforces a hegemonic structure, which works to oppress African people. The educational system is one the most insidious forms of colonial propaganda and its perpetuation of the status quo—a system that embodies hegemonic Eurocentric cultural values, political and economic systems, and social norms as the normative. The system works to legitimize a singular history that, in turn, works to universalize these values, histories, systems, and norms as the ultimate human reality (Asante, 1991). Within this process, Whiteness becomes the norm and Blackness becomes the default. African students in the classrooms internalize pathological perceptions of themselves and their culture through negative imagery of Blackness and Africanness. Often the invisibility and hyper-visibility of Blackness within public education in turns gives a falsified imagery of Blackness. Blackness in the classroom is simultaneously pathologized and erased. African students begin to disassociate themselves from our ancestral roots; this has lifelong devastating effects on our spiritual soul and mental well-being. The White gaze works to make Black bodies feel inadequate, and as a result produce a need to achieve success through proximity to Whiteness. Similarly, Philip Howard (2013) argues:

> However, what is less often identified in the context of the violence of schooling is the violent process of white identity construction on the back of Blacks, for it is through outright mistreatment, as well as the denial and negation of Black (and other non-white experience, that race discourse is managed in school contexts such that local and national mythologies and racial hierarchies are perpetuated. (White) Canadians in general, and white students and teachers in particular, can then know themselves as superior

> in contrast to abject negativity of Blackness constructed through relations of schooling. (p. 61)

To simply claim that the philosophical frameworks embedded within educational institutions are not political or cultural is to be intellectually dishonest. Euro-Western norms dominate the cultural, social, political, and economic system that exists within the classroom; Whiteness is centralized as the rubric for human progress. Education is a critical sector of this broader colonial system. White supremacy is not simply an attitude; it is institutionalized within this broader colonial system, which, in turn, takes a central role in public education.

The challenge for anti-racism educators is the concealing nature of White supremacy within education. As Michael Apple (1999) reminds us, "Race as a category is usually applied to 'non-white' peoples. White people are usually not seen or named. They are centered as the human norm" (p. 14). This speaks to the insidious nature of the historical and present-day power that exists within the classroom. Whiteness is humanized, and Blackness is subjugated to a subhuman status.

Carol Schick (2010) argues that school discourses are not neutral; rather, they are social entities that work to reproduce and normalize racism. Education played a significant role in European colonialism, forcing assimilation on colonized people. For African people in Canada, education has been a site for oppression and forced cultural integration.

Afua Cooper (2016) illustrates a general history of enslavement and education in the Western hemisphere during the 19th century:

> But with the coming of the nineteenth century, which with it the industrial revolution, a harsher form of slavery was ushered in. In this new period, enlightened slaves were viewed as dangerous and were feared because they had the ability to read "abolitionist" literature. (p.20)

Moving into the Canada of the 20th century, African people living and attending public schooling in Halifax, Nova Scotia, experienced what Bernice Moreau (1997) calls educational violence. In the article, "Black Nova Scotian Women's Experience of Educational Violence in the Early 1900s: A Case of Colour Contusion," Moreau writes on the lived experience of African women in Halifax's public schools:

> [A]ll black girls, including those who were privilege[d] to attended white schools were expected to be poor domestic servants. It can be argued that these were schooled for the specific positions of servitude in that society. Needless to say, the women resisted that expectation of themselves, and as a consequence, met with opposition from white educators and others in the educational system and society at large. (p. 184)

Moreau (1997) reminds us of the ways education in 20th-century Canada was used to deflect African people away from self-determination toward fulfilling the needed under-class labor for the growing capitalist economy.

This chapter calls for a serious interrogation of the continuous presence of colonialism and White supremacy in public education. The focal point of this chapter will be the Toronto District School Board (TDSB). It will outline the systemic marginalization of African students through forms of policing, academic streaming, and Eurocentric intellectual assimilation. The lived experience of African students enrolled in public schools throughout the city of Toronto reveals the continuous legacy of colonialism and White supremacy. The second half of the chapter calls for a serious investment from anti-racism educators in creating Afrocentric learning spaces. The chapter will mark out the fundamental principles of the Afrocentric paradigm; in addition, I will be engaging with seven important themes of Afrocentric pedagogies. The themes that will be discussed are representation, language, family/community, cooperative education, equity, Indigenous/community knowledge, and spirituality.

Locating myself in my work is key to understanding my entry point in this work. I am a continental African, born in Canada, a first-generation child. My parents migrated from Eritrea in the summer of 1990, and I was born few days after arrival. Growing up, the people in my community, mostly East African immigrants, believed that good education would lead to a better livelihood. Through European colonialism and Western propaganda, the imposition of Western values through violence had led to the internalization of capitalism and Western ideals of success. The impact of a global spread of neoliberal policies in the 21st century had led to the displacement and forced migration of racialized people. Within that process colonialization had deeply affected the ways in which we have come to view success and excellence. Ama Mazama (2001) reminds us of the psychological impact colonialism had on the minds of racialized people: "[C]olonization was not simply an enterprise of economic exploitation and political control, as it was commonly held, but also an on-going enterprise of conceptual distortion and invasion, leading to widespread confusion and ultimately, 'mental incarceration'" (pp. 3-4). The psychological displacement I experienced hurt my self-esteem by disconnecting me from my African ancestral roots. I was lucky to have dedicated Black educators in my life, who were committed to blossoming my revolutionary spirit. We African people are educated to wholly disconnect from Africa. Performing for the White gaze during my adolescence years meant subscribing to Western values of success via achieving academic excellence and distancing myself from everything associated with Blackness and Africanness. It included aesthetics, language, communal ties, spirituality, identity, political position, and cultural values. We are constantly expected to perform for the White gaze, to never work toward Black self-determination, to never be political, and to never mobilize as a community. However, today, the work I do within my community as a mentor, writer, student, and activist educator only exists because of the support I receive from my community. I do not exist outside of my community; I write using the intergenerational knowledge of my community.

The Pathologization of African People in Colonial Educational Spaces

The public school systemically worked to marginalize African students through forms of institutionalized racism, anti-Black racism, colonial education, and the militarization of learning spaces.

TDSB, operating within the city of Toronto, has the highest population of African students than any other board in Canada. It is also important to note that the province of Ontario has the highest population of African people, in comparison to all other Canadian provinces and territories. Statistics Canada (2017) reported that 52.3% (627,715) of Canada's African population resides in Ontario. The largest proportion of African people in Ontario live in the greater Toronto area: 38.21 % (239,850) of Ontario's African population currently live in Toronto, while another 20.87% (131,060) live in the Peel region.

Suspension/Expulsion and the Policing of African Students

In 2017 Carl James and Tana Turner assembled a report entitled "Towards Race Equity in Education" to expose the systematic marginalization of African students enrolled in TDSB. The researchers were able to conduct a series of race-based data collection and take testimonies from African students enrolled in TDSB as well as African educators and community members living and/or working within Toronto. The report exposed that African students were systemically discriminated against by teachers, guidance counselors, and school officials. This section focuses on some of the critical data, suspension rates, and expulsion and academic streaming.

According to the report, from the period of 2006–2011, African students made up 12% of the TDSB high school population. White students were in the majority and made up 35% of the student population, while non-African racialized students made up 53% of the remaining population (James & Turner, 2017). From the years of 2006-2011, 42% of African students enrolled in TDSB high schools were suspended at least once during high school. On the other hand, only 18% of White students and 15% of non-African students were suspended at least once during high school. In the same report, James and Turner lay out the distribution of expulsion rates by students' ethno-racial backgrounds. According to the data, out of all the students who were expelled in the period of 2010-2012 to 2015-2016, 48% of those students were African. In comparison, only 10% of the students were White, 2% were Southeast Asian, and 13% were South Asian. The data indicates that while African students only made up 12% of the high school population, they were disproportionately targeted for suspensions and expulsions. Through their observation,

James and Turner argue that many of the suspensions given for minor infractions lead to African students being pushed out of schools. It is also important to mention how the data is limiting, as ethno-racial categories simply do not take into consideration the multiple intersectionalities of African students. We cannot come to understand these trends without including the multiple identities and oppressions we encounter as African people living in a settler-colonial state. Our race, genders, sexualities, class, and disabilities are intertwined in how we experience anti-Black racism and colonialism. Furthermore, to contextualize and critically interpret the data, we must also understand how we as African people have been presently and historically over-policed and criminalized in public schools.

The History and Politics of Zero-Tolerance Policies

By the mid-1990s, the Ontario government, under the leadership of the Progressive Conservative Party, pushed for a zero-tolerance approach to dealing with disciplinary matter in schools. In September 2001, under the Mike Harris government, the Ministry of Education implemented the Safe Schools Act (Ontario Human Rights Commission, 2003).

The Safe Schools Act allowed for the expansion of authority; more power was given to school officials to suspend and expel students. However, the biggest impact the legislation had was the provision for mandatory suspension, expulsion, and police involvement. School officials were more likely to involve police when dealing with African students, even for minor infractions, whereby non-African students would experience less consequences for the same action. With the implementation of the Safe School Act, the African community has been adamant that this act has been used as a tool to discriminate against Black students. Although the zero-tolerance policy was removed by the liberal Ontario government in 2008, it cannot be denied that it still is being reinforced in school today (James & Turner, 2017).

How is racism embedded in these zero-tolerance approaches? How is the policing and criminalization of African bodies in schools part of larger societal patterns rooted in a history of colonialism and slavery? Dei (2008) reminds us of the ways in which politics surrounding the safety/zero-tolerance rhetoric is not neutral. Rather, these zero-tolerance policies are symptoms of deep-seeded racist ideologies, which maintain a racial hierarchy. As African students, we are aware of the ways in which we are perceived. We are aware that we are criminalized and over-policed, and at times we may internalize these perceptions, which is damaging to our well-being. In another report by James and Turner (2015), "Fighting an Uphill Battle," which focused on the presence of systemic anti-Blackness within Peel District School Board (PDSB); African student participants expressed the frustrations of being subjugated to racial stereotypes by teachers and school officials.

Streaming

Through their findings, James and Turner (2017) report that African students were underrepresented in academic leveled programs and overrepresented in applied and essential leveled programs. From the years of 2006–2011, 53% of African students were enrolled in academic-level courses in comparison to 81% of White students and 80% non-African racialized students. It is imperative that we understand that these numbers are not simply percentages and are rather a manifestation of anti-Black racism, a reflection of commonly held stereotypes. James and Turner argue that African students were seen by their teachers and guidance counselors as academically incapable of achieving success. In the report, African student participants, community members, educators, and parents had all agreed that African students were systemically streamed into applied and essential programs. African students and African community members expressed that educators within TDSB were streaming African students into applied and essential-level programs based on anti-Black racist perceptions of African students being intellectually inferior to non-African students. The study provides in-depth narratives directly from African students and parents. For example, in the report one African student explains that:

> Black students are as capable, as competent, as creative, and as determined as all other students. The ways that Black students are constantly misjudged and mistreated by teachers and guidance counsellors is an injustice to our community. As educators who seek to enrich an increasingly diverse nation, it is your duty and responsibility to encourage, motivate, challenge and strengthen Black students like all others. When you begin to see Black students as part of your community, only then will you effectively fulfill your job as an educator. (p. 52)

There is a shared common experience of being African in public schooling where school educators and guidance counselors operate to further marginalize and undermine the academic potential of African students. For many African students, school becomes a space of violence and oppression, where they are subjugated to the racist assumptions of teachers and school officials and streamed into programs deemed fit for them. In the same sense, we must question the entire system: Why are specific students placed into a specific academic level? What is the purpose of such a system? This brings us back to Moreau's (1997) telling of the history of Halifax's public schooling during the early 1900s, whereby African women were educated solely for the purpose of servitude positions and to fulfil the under-class labor force.

Nonetheless, the African community in Canada has always been critical of the public school system and the dominance of Eurocentric pedagogies. The African community has had a long history of calling for culturally relevant schooling. For example, in 1997,

Dei, along with his graduate students at the Ontario Institute for Studies in Education, conducted and published a research report on the anti-Black politics of public schooling. The report, "Reconstructing 'Drop-Out': A Critical Ethnography of the Dynamics of Black Students' Disengagement from School, argued that the experiences of racism impacted the learning experiences of African students and influenced their engagement with education (as cited in Hampton, 2010). Three central concerns were detailed; the treatment based on race, the exclusion of Black/African Canadian curriculum, and the lack of African educators. Two years prior to Dei's report, the Nighana Afrocentric Transitional Program, an Afrocentric public school program, became the first official and publicly known movement calling for Afrocentric schooling (Dei & Kempf, 2013). The program began as a response to the marginalization of African students in Toronto schools. The African community had been demanding that schooling be culturally relevant to African students.

Curriculum

The Ontario curriculum is an important Canadian site of analysis for anti-racism educators. As mentioned previously, Ontario has the highest concentration level of African people, of all other Canadian provinces and territories; therefore, the Ontario curriculum plays an important role in the education of African people living in Canada.

For example, the Equity Studies program is offered through TDSB to students in grade 11 and 12 and is the only discipline in the curriculum invested in social justice-oriented theories. The Equity Studies program's overview is as follows:

> Equity studies examines various aspects of diversity, including those related to gender, race, ethnicity, religion, socio-economic background, and ability. The four equity studies course[s] differ in their focus. Yet, regardless of whether the topic is social justice, gender studies or world cultures, all of these courses at their core, address similar fundamental issues: the social construction of identity; the nature and impact of power relations; the importance of respecting diversity; and the role of personal engagement and social action. (Government of Ontario, 2015).

The four courses offered are as follows: (a) Gender Studies (Grade 11 university/college preparation), (b) Equity, Diversity, and Social Justice (Grade 11 workplace preparation), (c) Equity and Social Justice: From Theory to Practice (Grade 12 university/college preparation), and (d) World Cultures (Grade 12 university/college preparation).

Not surprisingly, the only discipline in the curriculum invested in social justice-oriented theories does not offer any type of independent critical race study. In a province with the highest population of African people, addressing race and offering

Black Studies courses would be relevant. However, the absence of race and Black studies from the curriculum speaks to the erasing of African presence in this country. Above all, there is no aspect of the curriculum that specifically speaks on the experience of African people in Canada and the unique historical specificities of anti-Black racism. Rather, in 2018, anti-racism studies and Black studies are further marginalized in the curriculum, given a limited position to other forms of social inquires. However, in all, this is not surprising, as Canada continues to conceal the realities of anti-Black racism. It is the repetition of colonial historical knowledge that has allowed the school system to avoid an honest intellectual examination of anti-Black racism in this country. African students are not offered any courses in the curriculum that would specifically speak on the experiences and histories of African people.

The analysis of power relations and knowledge production is key in understanding the ways in which knowledges are strategically produced. White supremacy in Canada is very much a historical continuity phenomena that continues to work in very insidious ways. It may be subtler than in the United States; however, this does not mean it does not exist or is less harmful, but rather it has chosen to use a different methodology. Nonetheless, anti-Black racism in Canada works to erase the presence and history of African people. The presence of African people in Canada can be traced back to the 17th century, mostly populated in Nova Scotia and later on New France (modern Quebec) (Cooper, 2007). We must ask ourselves, "Why has Canadian history erased the historical presences of African people in Canada?" George Elliott Clarke (2007) argues,

> The avoidance of Canada's sorry history of slavery and racism is natural. It is how Canada prefer[s] to understand themselves: we are a nation of good, Nordic, "pure," mainly White folks, as opposed to the lawless, hot-tempered, impure, mongrel Americans, with their messy history of slavery, civil war, segregation, assassinations, lynching, riots, and constant social turmoil. (p. xii)

The desire to erase historical realities has to do with Canada maintaining its reputation as a peaceful humanitarian nation. But not only is the erasure of slavery and racism from the narrative a tool to reproduce a false Canadian reputation, it is also done to maintain White dominance and anti-Black racism.

The need for Afrocentric spaces of learning is crucial; African students need spaces where they are not pathologized and policed. We as anti-racism educators must be invested in creating these spaces, with an understanding of the history of anti-Blackness and policing and the psychological oppression that comes from being criminalized in a space of learning. Education must be openly political, with a determination to shape students' racial and cultural consciousness. Education must be rooted in community and rely on ancestral knowledge. There is a necessity for Afrocentric education to help develop the political consciousness of African students.

The Afrocentric Paradigm

As defined by Molefi Kete Asante (1991), a pioneer in developing the Afrocentric paradigm, "Afrocentricity is a frame of reference wherein phenomena are viewed from the perspective of the African person. The Afrocentric approach seeks in every situation the appropriate centrality of the African person" (p. 171).

Afrocentricity does not simply demand us to study African history; it calls for us to decolonize our epistemological assumption and to study our history from an African perspective. Afrocentricity calls for Africans to be the subject rather than objects, in all fields of study (Mazama, 2001). In a world where the dominant global narrative asserts that Africans do not have a history of their own, where the dominant consent is Africans do not or have never contributed to human development, Afrocentricity merges as a counter-discourse. As such, Afrocentricity works to expose the intellectual dishonesty that exists within mainstream intellectual circles that place Africans at the margins of world history. Afrocentricity calls on the dismantling of Eurocentric academic hegemony. It calls out the universalization of Eurocentric epistemologies as part of the colonial project. Afrocentricity is not a reactionary comeback to Eurocentrism; rather, it is about the reclaiming of African cultural self-determination and decolonizing the consciousness of oppressed peoples (Dei, 1994).

Afrocentricity works to expose the disillusion of European supremacy and to recenter the African experience (for African people). Within this process of decolonizing our mind, the epistemological centeredness of the African cultural experience is key to our liberation (Mazama, 2003).

The Afrocentric paradigm provides a solid foundation for Afrocentric scholarship. As outlined by Mazama, the Afrocentric paradigm encompasses three dimensions: the cognitive, structural, and functional. The cognitive dimensions consist of the theoretical framework, with a set of principles dedicated to the centrality of an African ontology. The structural dimension is the community of Afrocentric scholars. The Afrocentric paradigm functions within a space of dedicated scholars committed to Afrocentricity, invested in advancing and recentralizing an African-centered epistemology.

The third dimension that distinctly separates Afrocentricity from any other paradigm is its functionality. The Afrocentric paradigm must function to liberate African people from the chains of White supremacy, with a systemic investment in developing the self-determination of African-descended people (Mazama, 2003).

An Afrocentric approach uses key concepts in understanding the ways in which people view their own reality. They are as follows: center/location, dislocation, and relocation (Mazama 2001). *Center* (which can also be place or location) argues that a person's cultural, biological, and historical identity determines identity and that identity should inform perspective on reality. *Dislocation* is the opposite of center, where individuals use "borrowed cultural terms and/or when one apprehends reality through another group's center" (pp. 397–398). For example, Africans (continental and Diasporic) dismissing the validity of African spiritual traditions in favor of European religions shows cultural dislocation. These concepts, overall, are the basis of Afrocentric location theory.

Theoretical Framework (Afrocentric Education)

Earlier, the chapter discussed the marginalization of the African experience in education and the role education plays in continuing to reinforce a White supremacist global order. It is so important for anti-racism educators to understand that education is not an objective entity. Rather, it reinforces clear Western philosophical positions. As explained by Dei & Kempf (2013), it is

> [a] mode of thought and action in which the centrality of African interests, values, and perspectives predominate. Concerning theory, it is the placing of African people in the center of any analysis of African phenomena. Thus, it is possible for anyone to master the discipline of seeking the location of Africans in a given phenomenon. In terms of action and behavior, it is a devotion to the idea that what is in the best interest of African consciousness is at the heart of ethical behavior. (p. 95)

The Afrocentric approach conceptualizes centricity in education in a very specific way. Education becomes productive when it uses culturally relevant pedagogies, and within that context, students' cultural realities are centralized. In the Afrocentric tradition, centricity within education locates students within the context of their cultural reality (Asante, 1991). In Canada and much of the Western world, Eurocentric education differs as it does not allow for a pluralistic approach; rather, it is interested in dominating.

In order to work toward African self-determination, African students need Afrocentric education. Dei (1994) argues, "To be successful the Afrocentric pedagogue must move away from a manipulation of 'victim status and exploiting white guilt' to work toward finding solutions to pressing problems of educating students of African descent" (p. 17). The objective of Afrocentric education must be the liberation of African people and challenging the dehumanization of the African reality.

We as anti-racism educators must acknowledge that education is a state apparatus that works to reinforce a system of White supremacy and dominance.

Afrocentric Pedagogies

Afrocentricity calls out the miseducation of African students and the indoctrination of Western values that contradict with the realities of African people. It allows for an interrogation of Eurocentric curriculums and pedagogies that work to dehumanize or erase African people and their cultures. The Afrocentric approach to education centralizes the cultural and ancestral knowledges of African-descended peoples and incorporates it within learning spaces.

Afrocentric pedagogies work to decolonize the ways we view learning. As argued by Dei and Kempf (2013), Afrocentric approaches to education must allow for both the teacher and student to affirm their identities in order for students to relate and actualize the material. Dei and Kempf highlight seven important themes that must be practiced within Afrocentric education. The first theme is representation:

> Representation: [T]he visual culture/landscape of the school, knowledge representation of different bodies, and physical representation of exceptional Black and other minority educators and administrative staff who are well grounded in their communities. (p. 170)

The lack of African teachers and administrative staff in public schools plays a significant role in the marginalization of African students. For example, as mentioned previously, African students make up 12% of the student population in the TDSB, but only 5% of the teachers are Black, while 77% of all teachers are White (James & Turner, 2017). Even in schools where the student population is predominately African, there is significantly less African teachers. This limits the development of the student's political Black consciousness. According to C.E. James, educators must understand the significance of the racial identity of the teacher. He argues that teachers have the power to make some students "feel invisible and insignificant and that their differences are irrelevant" through their pedagogical approaches (as quoted in Carr & Klassen, 1997, p. 69). Similarly, Schick (2010) argues that in the face of liberalism, teachers are portrayed as objective, unbiased, caring individuals; however, the historical evidence proves that teachers have always played a political role in maintaining state control and are dedicated to maintaining the status quo.

Teachers must be deeply connected to the communities from which their students come from. Teachers must be, as Dei and Kempf (2013) describe, both activists and scholars who remain connected and engaged with their communities. With that said, the names of schools whose student are predominately Black, do no reflect the communities in which they reside or the student population itself. For example, C.W. Jeffery's Collegiate Institute, a high school in the Jane and Finch area with a large Black presence, is named after a White Canadian artist who has zero relevance to the cultural make-up of the student population. Representation is important; this includes culturally relevant spaces of learning with educators from the communities.

The second theme is language. As Dei and Kempf (2013) write, language is "the teaching of African and other Indigenous languages apart from the dominant local, regional, or national language" (p. 131). We must also focus on the power of language. Through the continuous process of colonialism and the history of enslavement, many Africans in the Diaspora have been disengaged from their indigenous languages. African languages are also discouraged, and African people globally are encouraged to adopt European language, mainly English and French. Ngũgĩ wa Thiong'o (1986) explains the connection between cultural affirmations and the language in which we use, as he writes,

> Language as communication and as culture are then products of each other. Communication creates culture: culture is a means of communication. Language carries culture, and culture carries, particularly through orature and literature, the entire body of values by which we come to perceive ourselves and our place in the world. How people perceive themselves affects how they look at their culture, at their places politics and at the social production of wealth, at their entire relationship to nature and to other beings. Language is thus inseparable from ourselves as a community of human beings with a specific form and character, a specific history, a specific relationship to the world. (pp. 15-16)

Language is thus interconnected with identity. Language reflects our cultural values, and the importance of decolonizing the ways in which we communicate cannot be undermined. Students of African descent deserve to have spaces to learn and engage with African languages that reflect African values.

The third theme is family/community and school partnerships "with the focus on shared responsibility: meaningful engagement with the local communities as significant invaluable partners in delivery of education" (Dei & Kempf, 2013, p. 170).

Family and community have always played a central role in African values. In an Afrocentric educational approach, community must place a central role in a politicized understanding of community. Community collectiveness must work to challenge dominant Western capitalist discourses that promote individualism. Western discourse individualizes social realities and devalues collective responsibility (Dei, 2008).

In contrast, collective responsibility is paramount to Indigenous African cultures (Dei, 1994). For this reason, Afrocentric pedagogies emphasize the importance of individuals' responsibility to their communities. Communalism plays a central role in Indigenous African philosophical traditions.

The fourth theme is co-operative education: "education that stresses cooperative learning, multiple forms a student excellence, and in doing away with many hierarchical structures of schooling" (Dei & Kempf, 2013, p. 131).

The fourth theme challenges the hierarchical and authoritative nature of Eurocentric schooling. Education in Ontario specifically and generally in North America takes on a positivism approach. Positivism is a philosophical ideology that claims that all truth must come from scientific verification and that only one truth exists by claiming neutrality, objectivity, and rationality. The positivism approach takes an authoritative approach to knowledge, which many educators today continue to practice. Students are often told what is valid knowledge and what is illegitimate knowledge. They are expected to internalize these dominant knowledges. However, historically we know for African people this meant the "scientific" justification for their enslavement and colonialization. This is why we as Afrocentric educators must facilitate learning spaces where both the teachers and students are able to critically engage with each other in knowledge searching. Our public school systems are hierarchically designed, whereby students are not engaged in the development of education. Students in school are expected to reach excellence through individualism, and collective student learning is considered "cheating" and discouraged. An Afrocentric approach to education expects students to work together to obtain knowledge.

The fifth theme discussed is equity and values education: "the linkage of issues of power and social differences with schooling processes and knowledge production" (Dei & Kempf, 2013, p. 131). As mentioned previously, education is not a neutral social apparatus; rather, it is philosophy embedded with specific cultural values. However, the public discourse pretends these values are universal and transcultural (Asante, 1991). This is not the case. Western European culture is the dominant culture, and therefore education reflects this culture. It is within this process that Eurocentric hegemony knowledge takes up a civilizer complex.

The functionality aspect of Afrocentricity places a significant emphasis on social justice activism. Mazama (2001) reminds us that from the Afrocentric perspective, knowledge must be produced for a purpose and that purpose must centralize our liberation; it must work to "activate our consciousness" (p. 8). Our spaces of learning must be political spaces, which expand our understanding of colonial power and prioritize social justice values. Knowledge production within these spaces must call for a critical interrogation of White-washed multiculturalism and work to expose the deeply embedded colonial power relations existing within the liberalized version of multiculturalism.

The sixth theme is indigenous/community knowledge: "cultivating multicentric knowledge systems in schools by affirming off-school and local cultural resources knowledge bases, as well as lifelong learning" (Dei & Kempf, 2013, p. 131). At the current state, our educational spaces work to either exclude Indigenous knowledge or reduce it to "primitive myth." It is within these oppressive spaces that African-descended students are told that the knowledge they bring from their communities is uncivilized and will not benefit their educational journey. Public education teaches us that colonial knowledges are civilized and humane; however, this is historically inaccurate. Colonial knowledge has been used to justified the dehumanization of Indigenous people on a global scale. The enslavement and genocide of African peoples was the result of colonial knowledge. As a matter of fact, it has been African indigenous knowledge that has called for equity and social justice for all people. Dei and Simmons (2012) speak on

> the limitation of the school curricula and the way in which schooling and education problematically speak to the experiences of different peoples are

> the utmost concern to anti-colonial education. Indigenous, local cultural knowledges can help disrupt Eurocentric narratives embedded within conventional spaces of learning. (p. 77)

The successfulness of our resistances throughout the centuries in the face of colonialism and enslavement has been due to our commitment in employing our Indigenous ancestral knowledge.

Most importantly it must be mentioned that Afrocentric pedagogies encourage multicentric knowledge systems. What Afrocentricity does condemn is the hegemonic nature of Eurocentricity (Asante, 1991). Centricity is a process in which the students enable their perspectives to locate knowledge within the context of their own cultural values. Within this process multi-centrics can occur, without a hierarchy of knowledge.

The last theme discussed is spirituality: "evoking learners' understandings of the self, inner strength/environments and connections to the group and outer environments, as well as stressing the body-mind soul interface and the society-nature-culture nexus" (Dei & Kempf, 2013, p. 132).

Afrocentricity challenges the prioritization of Eurocentric individualism, which is very much embedded in Western liberal democracies. It challenges the notion that individualism is the more advanced stage of societal development. The disconnect from the larger community (outside of the traditional Western nuclear family), and the objectification of the environment and all nonhuman living things, has been deemed in the public discourse as the most optimum human reality. Eurocentric individualism undermines collective responsibility, and in return does not value social justice (Dei, 1994).

The functional aspect of Afrocentricity works toward the liberation of African people, and for that reason it cannot be lessened to just an intellectual paradigm (Mazama, 2001). Afrocentric education must facilitate a space and perspective that centralizes the African worldview, the spiritual relation between human, spiritual beings, community, and the environment (Dei, 1994). The spiritual ontology of African people is the profound connection between the individual, community, and nature. Afrocentricity acknowledges the spiritual being of nature and its connections to the community. Afrocentricity calls out the objectification and exploitation of the natural world.

There is also the deep commitment to the knowledge of the ancestors. People cannot disconnect from their ancestral roots. A commonality among African culture is the devotion to the ancestors and the valuing of ancestral knowledge. The ethical standards of the living are based on the teachings of the ancestors. African spirituality recognizes the presence of ancestors among the living (Dei, 1994). In the African philosophical tradition, life is conceptualized as infinite, and the living and spiritual world exist in a unified manner. Mazama (2002) writes, "Indeed, when we think if the African selves, we cannot be satisfied with an individualistic approach but must understand that we are an organic part of a whole that included diverse spiritual and physical entities" (p. 222). The need to centralize spirituality and the spiritual world in the classroom is crucial for the well-being of students. The Afrocentric student must be able to connect to the natural world in a divine way and understand the deep connection between the living and the ancestral spirits.

The Revolution Must Continue to Self-Reflect and Grow

As mentioned earlier, the first Afrocentric school opened its doors in the fall of 2009. The school is currently located within the Sheppard public school, serving Junior Kindergarten (JK) to eighth-grade students; it was the first Black-focused school in Toronto (Toronto District School Board, 2018). The opening of the school became a source of controversy, with two polarizing sides, one in favor of the school and the other in opposition. In January 2008, the TDSB trustees cast their votes; however, months prior the voting process discussions surrounding education, race, anti-Black racism, and multiculturalism circulated national media and were brought to public consciousness.

Despite racist oppositions and anti-Black racism that was obviously engrained in the debate, TDSB was successful in launching the school. However, as anti-racism educators we must be critical of the reality that the Africentric Alternative School operates as a TDSB school. This critique is not meant to undermine the exhausting work done by the African community in establishing the first Black-focused school, but we must also be aware of the limitations of working within a colonial system. For Afrocentric education to fully work toward decolonizing learning spaces, it must operate outside of colonial educational institution. The third dimension of the Afrocentric paradigm speaks to the functionality of Afrocentricity, as a force to liberate African people from the chains of White supremacy. Afrocentric education cannot fully achieve liberation and self-determination if it works in partnership with White settler colonial systems. There is no denying that in order for the current Africentric Alternative school to continue to exist and receive funding it must fall in line with the Eurocentric standards of TDSB.

For example, in order for the Africentric Alternative School to be deemed "successful," educators are expected to continue to employ Eurocentric pedagogies such as standardized testing and the grading system. A 2015 news article entitled "Africentric School Outcomes Hindered by Unclear Vision, Limited Resources" was published by a Canadian major news outlet, *CBC*, to report on whether the Africentric Alternative School was working toward successful results. Throughout the report, the standards of assessing success are measured within a neoliberal capitalist context. The news article reads:

> When looking at report card results from 2011-2012, the report found: The proportions of students in Grades 1 to 4 who achieved levels 3 (the provincial standard) and 4 in reading, writing and mathematics were higher than the

> TDSB average. The proportions of students in Grades 5 to 8 achieving levels 3 and 4 were higher than the TDSB average in mathematics, but lower than the TDSB averages in reading and writing. Between 2011-12 and 2012-13, the three-year rolling average of EQAO (standard provincial test) scores from the school was 4.3 per cent, which showed a higher rate of improvement than the TDSB (1.54 per cent) and the province (0.88 per cent), although results for the school were below those from the board and the province (CBC, 2015).

The reproduction of standardized forms of testing within the Africentric Alternative School exposes the continuous dominance of Eurocentric education within this space. African students within the Africentric Alternative School are expected to perform for the White gaze and achieve success using the standards of colonial systems. In order to truly have an Afrocentric learning space, we cannot continue to use colonial standards in measuring success. With that said, this chapter firmly argues that for Afrocentric educational spaces to truly work toward African liberation they must operate completely independently from colonial systems. Afrocentric educational spaces must be operated by the African community as an independent entity in order to truly practice self-determination. As we self-reflect and work toward decolonization we must also be critical of our spaces and reimagine new spaces.

Conclusion

As a student of Afrocentricity, I am in a process of intellectual decolonization. Those of us, Africans who have been dislocated from our cultural realities, forced to assimilate to a culture that was forced on us, have a responsibility. Our responsibility lies in our commitment to resist and to decolonize our spaces. However, we must work collectively as a community to create these anti-colonial spaces. Steve Biko (1979), one of the most revolutionary African thinkers to ever walk the earth reminds us:

> The myth of integration as propounded under the banner of the liberal ideology must be cracked and killed because it makes people believe that something is being done when in reality the artificially integrated circles are a soporific to the blacks while salving the con-sciences of the guilt-stricken white. (p. 22)

References

Apple, M. W. (1999). The absent presence of race in educational reform. *Race Ethnicity and Education, 2*(1), 9–16.

Asante, M. K. (1991). The Afrocentric idea in education. *Journal of Negro Education, 60*(2), 170–180.

Biko, S. (1979). *I write what I like*. New York, NY: Harper & Row.

Carr, P., & Klassen, T. (1997). Different perceptions of race in education: Racial minority and White teachers. *Canadian Journal of Education*, 22(1), 67–81.

CBC News. (2015, November 19). Unclear vision, resource shortage hinder outcomes for city's Africentric school: Report. Retrieved from https://www.cbc.ca/news/canada/toronto/africentric-school-report-1.3326447

Clarke, G.E.(2006). "Foreword." In *The Hanging of Angélique: The Untold y and the Burning of Old Montreal*. A. Cooper (Ed.). Toronto: Harper Collins, pp. xi-xviii.

Cooper, A. (2007). *The hanging of Angélique*. Athens, GA: University of Georgia Press.

Cooper, Afua (2016). Black Canada and the Law: Black Parents and Children in the Legal Battle for Education in Canada West: 1851-1864. In A. & Abdi, A. (Eds.) *The Education of African Canadian Children: Critical Perspectives*. (pp. 19 – 39). Montreal: McGill-Queen's University Press.

Dei, G. (1994). Afrocentricity: A cornerstone of pedagogy. *Anthropology & Education Quarterly*, 25(1), 3–28.

Dei, G. (2008). Schooling as community. *Journal of Black Studies, 38*(3), 346–366.

Dei, G. (2018) "Black like me": Reframing Blackness for decolonial politics. *Educational Studies*, 54(2), 117–142.

Dei, G., & Kempf, A. (2013). *New Perspectives on African-centred Education in Canada*. Toronto, Canada: Canadian Scholars Press.

Dei, G. J. S., & Simmons, M. (2012). Reframing anti-colonial theory for the Diasporic context. *Postcolonial Directions in Education, 1*(1), 67–99.

Government of Ontario. (2015). *Ministry of Education*. Retrieved from http://www.edu.gov.on.ca

Hampton, R. (2010). Black learners in Canada. *Race & Class*, 52(1), 103–110.

Howard, P. (2013). The smack of self-determination: A Fanonian analysis of the Africentric Schooling Debate in Toronto. In G. Dei & M. Lordan (Eds.), *Contemporary Issues in the Sociology of Race and Ethnicity* (pp. 43–68). New York, NY: Peter Lang.

James, C., & Turner, T. (2015). Fighting an uphill battle: Report on the consultations into the well-being of Black youth in Peel region. *Region of Peel*. Retrieved https://exchange.youthrex.com/report/fighting-uphill-battle-report-consultations-well-being-black-youth-peel-region-0

James, C. E., & Turner, T. (2017). *Towards Race Equity in Education: The Schooling of Black Students in the Greater Toronto Area*. Toronto, Ontario, Canada: York University.

Mazama, A. (2001). The Afrocentric Paradigm. *Journal of Black Studies*, 31(4), 387–405.

Mazama, M. (2002). Afrocentricity and African spirituality. *Journal of Black studies, 33*(2), 218–234.

Mazama, A. (2003). *The Afrocentric Paradigm*. Trenton, NJ: AWP.

Moreau, B. (1997). Black Nova Scotian women's experience of educational violence in the early 1900s: A case of colour contusion. *The Dalhousie Review*, 77(1), 179.

Ontario Human Rights Commission. (2003). *The Ontario Safe Schools Act: School discipline and discrimination*. Retrieved from http://www.ohrc.on.ca/en/ontario-safe-schools-act-school-discipline-and-discrimination

Schick, C. (2010). Whatever happened to anti-racist education? *Our Schools, Our Selves*, 19(3), 47-58.

Thiong'o, N. W. (1986). *Decolonising the Mind*. London, UK: James Currey.

Toronto District School Board. (2018). *Africentric Alternative School*. [online] Retrieved from http://schoolweb.tdsb.on.ca/africentricschool/About-Our-School

CHAPTER 15

The Intersection of Afrofuturism and African Indigenous Knowledge Systems: The Implications for Black Studies

Dr. Gloria Emeagwali

What is Afrofuturism? What are its origins as a concept, its conceptual and philosophical underpinnings, its multidisciplinary manifestations, its exponents, and, most relevant for our discourse, how does it intersect with African Indigenous Knowledge Systems—an interdisciplinary intellectual enterprise with its own unique epistemological frame of reference? What are their points of interconnection and also difference? These are some of the issues that we reflect on in this chapter.

The Origins and Significance of Afrofuturism

Should we locate the origins of Afrofuturism to about 5,000 years ago in Egypt, given the ancient Egyptian preoccupations with another world and another lifeform, and "their incredibly detailed meditations on life and death," as suggested by Greg Tate (Dery, 1994, p. 210)? What about W. E. B. Du Bois (1920), and his short tale, "The Comet," in *Dark Water, Voices from within the Veil*, where an extraterrestrial force lands on Earth and spares but two survivors in the region in a rather dystopic world? By 1990, Samuel Delany would have written *Jewels of Aptos, Towers of Toron, Cities of a Thousand Suns, Nova, Tides of Lust, Captains of the Flame,* and about 30 other science fiction novels and short stories. Octavia Butler, by that same year, 1990, had produced *Patternmaster, Mind of my Mind, Survivor, Kindred, Wild Seed, Clay's Ark, Adulthood Rites, and Imago* (Francis, 2010). Sun Ra, the flamboyant Egypt-centric keyboard maestro, along with his *Arquestra,* by 1993 would have created 200 records and numerous poems, interviews, and performances (Youngquist, 2016). In 1993, Sun Ra passed away and "returned" to Saturn. Three years before that, the alternative hip-hop rapper Def Jef (Jeffrey Fortson) launched his explosive 10th single, "Black to the Future." "Afrofuturism," the cryptic concept coined by Mark Dery in 1994, in his often-cited interview with Samuel Delany, Greg Tate, and Tricia Rose, emerged in the context of these preexisting artistic and intellectual activities of a host of Afro luminaries. In fact, Def Jef's lyrics for "Black to the Future" introduce Dery's (1994) interview with Delany, Tate, and Rose, in *Flame Wars.*

Afrofuturism may be also defined as combining "the colonial past, global capitalist present and apocalyptic future" (Olutola, 2018, p. 67). It sheds a perspective on political and cultural aspects of science, science fiction, and technology in a nonlinear time frame and with what Thrasher (2015) describes as an artistic combination of mysticism, politics, and metaphysics. Afrofuturism combines science fiction with fantasy to reexamine "how the future is currently imagined" (Brooks, 2018, p. 101). It involves the exploration of histories, new experiences, as well as the past, from the innovative lens of new methodologies and innovative epistemologies. The future is re-envisioned and conceptualized.

"Everyone I read about in Sci-Fi was white, and most were male, so I really did have to write myself in," explained Butler about her motivation to write science fiction in an interview with Juan Williams (Francis, 2010, p. 174). Imaginative writing, Butler said, should be "grounded in the world we live, where we come from, and in the bodies and minds we inhabit not only physically but mortally and spiritually," clarifying further her views about inspiration (Francis, 2010, p. 134).

In his review of mainstream science fiction, Russell (2018) documents the portrayal of Blacks in terms of # "comic subservience and menacing sub-humanity" in the 1940s and 1950s, and in the 1960s, as "post-apocalyptic atavistic black barbarian" (p. 83). To date, White anxieties are projected on to the "digitally generated alien cybernetic creations," which are hunted down as fugitive slaves in some cases" (p. 91). Afrofuturists have shattered that tradition in a move that "destabilizes previous analyses of blackness" (p. 16)

Octavia Butler felt compelled to explore the heroic nature of women like her mom, who underwent humiliating experiences just to keep a roof over her family's head. Her ancestors did not accept "disgusting behavior" without a cause (Francis, 2010, p. 79). Butler also wanted to reach people emotionally, in a way history may not. A science - fictional lens enabled the reconceptualization of race and the re-imagining of possible futures (Womack, 2013). Even so, Butler warned that her work offered a "cleaned up" version of history (Francis, 2010, p. 29) without the "ugly, awful, intimate details" (p. 135) as "there are limits to what people will put up with when reading a novel," she added (p. 44).

Afrofuturism has enabled temporary escapism as well. Sun Ra, born Herman Poole Blount in Alabama in 1914, was adamant in his indignation. "I wouldn't be caught dead in a planet like this," he insisted (BBC, 2018). Egyptology was a major motivation for Le Sony'r Ra, abbreviated to Sun Ra, a symbol of light, life, and divinity (Youngquist, 2016). Sun-Ra, the father of Astro-Black mythology, argued that "if you are not mad at the world you don't have what it takes" (p. 66). One of his mantras was "Space is the Place" (p. 212). Imagination was "a magic carpet" on which we may soar, stated one of his poems (p. 6). For Sun Ra, a conscientious objector to enlistment in World War II, planet Earth was an inveterate prison (p. 31). Planet Earth produced "the dead bodies of humanity" (BBC, 2018). Space was emancipatory, liberating, and free from domestic terror. "The precarity of certain kinds of black bodies" that Olutola (2018) made reference to in her discussion of Hopkinson's "Brown Girl in a Ring" (p. 67) would be absent.

Black people "live the estrangement that science fiction writers imagine, states Tate, in his interview with Dery (Dery, 1994, p. 212). The imaginary Black planet that Sun Ra seemed to hope for would stimulate spiritual awakening and provide a safe haven from oppression. Kodwo Eshnu considers that it was "a hyperbolic trope" to explore forcibly inspired dislocations. The idea was "to infiltrate the past and the present" with new Black "futurities" (Maynard, 2018, p. 29). This would provide "virtual, augmented and real spaces" (Brooks, 2018, p. 106) and encourage Africans to reconstruct, redefine, and decolonize their identity without apology. Afrofuturism is therefore a sociohistorical and intellectual genre, as well as a means of exploring alternative possibilities in a world of "racialized economic [power] structures" and "Black erasure" (Olutola, 2018, p. 64). It is a cultural force, an episteme, and a reflection on what histories matter (Dery, 1994).

Epistemological Underpinnings of Afrofuturism

The integration and synthesis of multiple spheres of knowledge production is the hallmark of Afrofuturism, a system that facilitates the fusion and convergence of film, dance, fashion, wearable art, music, and paintings with Africana cosmology, mysticism, occultism, teleportation and numerology, musicology, herbalism, plant-based medicine, and Africana science and technology. Broyld (2018) conceptualizes the famed Underground Railroad in Afrofuturistic terms, pointing also to the significance of astronomy—in particular the North Star—in the liberating undertakings of Harriet Tubman. The Underground Railroad and its freedom seekers, the so-called "runaways," symbolized "the convergence of science, metaphysics, and liberation". Afrofuturism reflects "the intersection of imagination, technology, the future, and liberation." Afrofuturistic encounters do not limit themselves to Western science or religion, and as pointed out by Jalondra Davis (2018), we have the consistent infusion of African-based spirituality and rituals. The redefinition of technology to embrace shape shifting techniques would thus bring into focus maligned and ignored technologies. Aisha Matthews (2018) also points to the integration of Afro Caribbean and other Afro Diasporic projects within the larger narrative of Afrofuturism. Afrofuturists point out that knowledge production is not exclusive to a particular race, region, or rationality, and excursions into the past, present, and future, and Africana forms of medicine, technology, cosmology, and science, transcend the dualism of mind and matter and "break with epistemological violence" (Davis, 2018, p. 24)

So how does Afrofuturism intersect with African Indigenous Knowledge Systems (AIKS) as an intellectual enterprise? We shall define, first, AIKS and its goals and reflect on the points of intersection between Afrofuturism and the latter. This will be followed by observations on the areas of difference between the two schools of thought and spheres of engagement. We conclude the address with a focus on the implications of Afrofuturism and African Indigenous knowledges for Black Studies.

Convergence and Difference between Afrofuturism and African Indigenous Knowledge Systems (AIKS)

AIKS is a conglomerate of intersecting epistemologies, disciplines, and value systems by scholar activists and researchers that work within African-centered paradigms. Indigenous knowledge emerges from specific geographical, ecological, and environmental contexts and are often derived from local experimentation and accumulated economic, sociocultural, and political experiences. Although methodological pluralism is at the center of the discourse, a holistic, African-centered framework aimed at the rediscovery, retrieval, documentation, and evaluation of knowledge accumulated over multiple generations is at the core. Scholars of AIKS reject Eurocentric dogma and view the methodologies and epistemological framework of AIKS as central in the decolonization process.

Scholars of AIKS reject the dehumanizing caricatures and pathological narratology of Eurocentric discourse that privileges one part of the globe above its other constituent parts in racialized discriminatory discourse, representations, and assessments. The objectives and aspirations of scholars of AIKS do not fundamentally diverge from Afrofuturistic practitioners in this regard.

AIKS discourse aims at decentering hegemonic epistemic systems and involves restorative research through collective consultation and the activation of credible ways of knowing about the world and environments as inherited, discussed, and articulated in ancestral and Diasporic communities. Accumulated knowledge has emerged from trial and error experimentation as well as tested empirical practices and paradigms related to ecological, botanical, environmental, geographic, economic, medical, social, and other traditions of existence. AIKS is essentially anti-colonial and anti-racist and may involve collaborative activism, coalition building, and even linkages with social movements, where applicable. The end goal is the development of respect, self-esteem, representation, skills enhancement and knowledge, and an understanding of African contributions to the intellectual world of Indigenous knowledge.

It has also been argued that AIKS should be at the center of development as well, in such a way that there is a shift away from toxic programs of maldevelopment and neocolonialism. The use of AIKS in development strategy implies consultation, dialogue, and rapport with the people for whom development programs are intended to assist. Dei (2014) suggests that development must be situated in Indigeneity and Indigenous knowledge and should involve the interrogation of ancient and existing practices in the solution of problems. Genuine development strategy must renegotiate the Eurocentric, neocolonial agenda and bring Indigenous knowledge into the center of intellectual activity. Such activities do not necessarily conflict with the fundamental aspirations of Afrofuturists.

The enormous economic success of Disney's *Black Panther* (2018), directed by Ryan Coogler, points to the economic viability of Afrofuturistic endeavors and their significance for costume design, fashion, music, and the entertainment industry. *Black Panther* took in more than $1 billion, granted the main beneficiary was Disney (Saunders, 2018). We may note also the highly successful Afrofuturistic ventures of Janelle Monae and to a lesser extent Beyonce and Nicki Minaj, all of whom would use androids and space paraphernalia in selected performances (Anderson & Jones, 2016).

But there are also differences between the two spheres of intellectual activity. When asked about her writing techniques with respect to *Wild Seed*, Butler informed the interviewer that she used maps and visited the area and that her fictional character Anyanwu was associated with and read books on Nigerian history and Igbo history in particular, citing some historical sources. Afrofuturists often rely on secondary sources, unlike their AIK counterparts, who often engage in primary research in areas neglected by mainstream researchers. Butler also made a distinction between her work and that of the historian. She wanted to connect "emotionally in a way that history tends not to" (Francis, 2010, p. 197). In her view, fiction writers "can't be too pedagogical or too polemical. If people wanted to be lectured to they would take a class" (p. 25). The entertainment factor is at the heart of a good story (Francis, 2010). It should be pointed out that a core segment of AIKS falls outside of these parameters.

There are other significant points of divergence. In Butler's *Kindred*, the protagonist travels back in time to antebellum America and relives past experiences. In *Wild Seed*, the protagonist changes gender and race and transforms into animals. Practitioners of AIKS do not have such absolute freedom of expression and imagination in their historical, anthropological, and sociological research activities. Afrofuturists can omit, add, and modify information, in the context of poetic license and artistic privilege, and face no professional penalties. Wakanda, the technologically superior kingdom of *Black Panther*, is a fictional location, although the screenwriter infused the film narrative with numerous factual references about culture and aesthetics. Costume designers were able to capture aspects of African culture and infuse this with futuristic fancy, but the narrative falls more securely within the Afrofuturistic genre than that of AIKS research, granted there are areas of overlap in the literary and cosmological terrain. In AIKS, magical realism and interplanetary futuristic discourse are often confined within the boundaries of literature, religion, and cosmology and, relatively speaking, may not crossover into primary historical and anthropological research, for example. Verification, justification, falsifiability, and provability variables are more firmly anticipated in AIKS. The general tendency is for AIKS scholars to be less concerned with "what if" than *when, how,* and *why,* Butler points out in her interview with Lisa See (Francis, 2010). This is not to undervalue the significance of Afrofuturist expositions since speculative fiction and futuristic narratives stimulate thought, open windows to new possibilities and inspiring imaginaries, and "stretch the imagination beyond the conventions of our time" (Womack, 2013, p. 16).

In the case of extraterrestrial travel, the difference between AIKS and Afrofuturism is also significant. Sun Ra donned a space hat "blinking red and green" and initiated, through the Arkestra and "space music," interplanetary journeys out of planet Earth, working "on the other side of time" (Youngquist, 2016, p. 212). Sun Ra and his followers traveled on waves of sound in the context of astro-Black mythology and fantasy—with lifelike images of Heru and Tehuti in the background. So too did George Clinton's parliament and funkadelic engage in fantasy, with Dr. Funkenstein strutting out of the mothership in flamboyant attire. Except for the literary components of AIKS where cosmology and imagination could take center stage, the major focus of AIKS practitioners, as far as space is concerned, is in astronomical research where mythology and narratives about the celestial bodies may provide avenues to tangible and practical understanding about the universe. Kreamer's (2012) *African Cosmos* is a prime example of an Africa-centered project that harmonizes with AIKS research. For Afrofuturists, Africa's science and technology fuse with fantasy and fictional narration to produce new perspectives and interpretations about the past, present, and future.

Implications for Black Studies

African, Africana, African American, and African Diasporic studies emerged out of four somewhat contradictory enterprises in the post-World II environment. We use the term *Black studies* to encompass African, Africana, African American, and African Diasporic studies as a whole. The first was a culmination of the passion, enthusiasm, and *Black consciousness* of Pan-Africanist luminaries such as Edward Blyden, George Padmore, W.E.B Du Bois, and others. The second was the systemic bipolarity of the Cold War involving the United States and the USSR, leading to the establishment of Area Studies in the United States for academic, espionage, and information-gathering purposes. Third, we have the anti-colonial nationalist movements, the product of liberation struggles and agitation to regain independence—from British, French, Spanish,

Portuguese, German, Dutch, Belgian, and Italian hegemony in Africa and the Americas. The U.S civil rights movement constituted the fourth factor with significant impact on the establishment of Black studies here in the United States in response to organized protests and pressure groups in the 20th century. In Afrofuturism and AIKS we see combined and collective responses to these four important sociocultural and political movements in the 21st century.

With the institutionalization of Black studies, a cornucopia of textbooks and monographs on sociopolitical, economic, and cultural aspects of Black Studies emerged. Afrofuturistic and AIKS approaches clearly and unapologetically reject some of the pathetic, pathological caricatures and representations associated with some of these works. Russell's insightful discourse of the portrayal of Blacks in mainstream science fiction is equally applicable with respect to the portrayal of Blacks in the writings of mainstream historians. In *Africa and the Academy: Challenging Hegemonic Discourse on Africa* (Emeagwali, 2006), I highlighted the questionable representations and toxic insinuations in World History textbooks and others. The rise of Afrofuturism and AIKS is not disconnected from this important movement and epistemological revolution—directly and indirectly inspired by the work of Molefi Asante and other Afrocentric and Africa-centered researchers. To date, the full integration of ancient Egypt, Nubia, and Ethiopia into continental and diasporic African studies is a work in progress and a goal that unifies both Afrofuturists and AIKS researchers and protagonists.

Sun Ra, the father of Afrofuturism, made Egypt a center of his intellectual world and recognized its significance for African spirituality and history. His library of about 15,000 books included numerous tomes on the mystical and spiritual aspects of Egyptian civilization (Youngquist, 2016). Wilkinson's five-volume work on the manners and customs of the ancient Egyptians of the 1840s apparently inspired Sun Ra's choice of Thmei, an Egyptian goddess of truth and justice, as an important spiritual guiding force. For scholars of AIKS, the knowledge of Indigenous Africa is crucial, and ancient Egyptians and Nubians fit within this portfolio.

The discipline and sphere of intellectual activity of AIKS is necessarily anti-colonial and anti-racist given its fundamental aim to decenter orthodox Eurocentric epistemology, interrupt the "infantilization" of Africa, and create intellectual space for Indigenous knowledge across space and time (Dei & Jaimungal 2018).

For practitioners and scholars, students, tutors, and professors associated with Black studies, the gauntlet has been thrown, so to speak, and the challenge is clear. Black studies in its African, African American, and African Diasporic contexts must pay close attention to these major intellectual systems of knowledge and gain valuable insights and inspirations from them not only in terms of representation, value systems, goals, and epistemologies, but also in terms of research trajectories and instructional and pedagogical techniques with a view to develop a more inclusive, equitable, decolonial, and decolonized academy.

References

Anderson, R., & Jones, C. (2016). *Afrofuturism 2.0. The Rise of Astro-Blackness*. Lanham, MD: Lexington B.

Asante, M. (1998). *The Afrocentric Idea*. Philadelphia, PA: Temple University Press.

BBC. (2018). Sun Ra: Brother from Another Planet [Video file]. Retrieved from https://www.youtube.com/watch?v=IeiN1WuobMo

Brooks, J. (2018). Cruelty and Afrofuturism. *Communication and Critical Cultural Studies, 15*(1), 101–107. http://doi:10.1080/14791420.2018.1435078

Broyld, D. (2018, November). The Underground Railroad and Afrofuturism: Enslaved Blacks That Imagined Freedom, Futures and Space. Paper presented at the Department of History Seminar, New Britain Connecticut: Central Connecticut State University.

Davis, J. (2018). Power and Vulnerability: Black Girl Magic in Women's Science Fiction. *Journal of Science Fiction, 2*(2), 13–30.

Dei, G. (2014). Reflections on African Development. Situating Indigenous Knowledges and Indigeneity. In E. Shizha & A. Abdi (Eds.), *Indigenous Discourses on Knowledge and Development in Africa* (pp. 15-30). New York, NY: Routledge.

Dei, G., & Jaimungal, C. (2018). *Indigeneity and Decolonial Resistance*. Gorham, ME: Myers Education.

Delany, S. (2015). *A, B, C: Three Short Novels*. New York: Vintage Books.

Dery, M. (Ed.). (1994). *Flame Wars: The Discourse of Cyberculture*. Durham, NC: Duke University Press.

W. E. B. Du Bois. (1920). *Dark Water, Voices from within the Veil*. New York, NY: Harcourt.

Emeagwali, G. (Ed.). (2006). *Africa and the Academy: Challenging Hegemonic Discourses on Africa*. Trenton, NJ: Africa World Press.

Francis, C. (Ed.). (2010). *Conversations with Octavia Butler*. Jackson, MI: University of Mississippi Press.

Kreamer, C. (2012). *African Cosmos*. New York, NY: Monacelli Press & Smithsonian National Museum of African Art.

Matthews, A. (2018). Foreword. *Journal of Science Fiction, 2*(2), 5-6.

Maynard, R. (2018). Reading Black Resistance through Afrofuturism: Notes on Post-Apocalyptic Blackness and Black Rebel Cyborgs in Canada. *Canadian Journal of Cultural Studies, 39*, 29–47.

Olutola, S. (2018). Blood, Soil and Zombies: Afrofuturist Collaboration and Re-appropriation in Nalo Hopkinson's Brown Girl in the Ring. *Journal of Science Fiction, 2*(2), 64-81.

Russell, J.G. (2018). Frozen Journey: Science Fiction, Blacks, Race, and the Limits of Speculative Practice. *Journal of Science Fiction 2*(2), 82-105.

Saunders, R. (2018). Profitable Imaginaries of Black Power. The Popular and Political Geographies of Black Panther. *Political Geography, 69*, 139–149.

Thrasher, S. (2015, December 7). Afrofuturism: Reimagining Science and the Future from a Black Perspective. *The Guardian*. Retrieved from https://www.theguardian.com/culture/2015/dec/07/afrofuturism-black-identity-future-science-technology

Womack, Y. (2013). *Afrofuturism: The World of Black Sci-Fi and Fantasy Culture*. Chicago, IL: Lawrence Hill.

Youngquist, P. (2016). *Sun Ra and the Birth of Afrofuturism*. Austin, TX: University of Texas Press.

Biographies

GHANAIAN-BORN GEORGE SEFA DEI is a professor of social justice education and director of the Center for Integrative Anti-Racism Studies at the Ontario Institute for Studies in Education of the University of Toronto (OISE/UT). He has written extensively on anti-racism education, minority youth, and schooling, Indigenous knowledge, Blackness, and Black Indigeneity. He received the 2016 Whitworth award for Educational Research from the Canadian Education Association (CEA) that is awarded to the Canadian scholar whose research and scholarship have helped shape Canadian national educational policy and practice. He is a fellow of the Royal Society of Canada. Most recently he was named the 2019 Paulo Freire Democratic Project, Chapman University, Social Justice award winner. In June of 2007, Professor Dei was installed as a traditional chief in Ghana, specifically as the Gyaasehene of the town of Asokore, Koforidua, in the New Juaben Traditional Area of Ghana. His stool name is Nana Adusei Sefa Tweneboah I.

EZINWANNE (EZI) ODOZOR is a Nigerian-born writer and scholar based in Toronto. Her work, whether fiction or nonfiction, focuses on themes of identity, culture, gender, race, health, and intimacy. Her work is featured in literary journals such as *Room Magazine* and in exhibits such as OLUSEYE's "A Room Full of Black Boys," which was also featured by the Canadian Broadcasting Company (CBC). Ezinwanne recently completed a master's in Education (MEd) with a collaborative specialization in global health at the University of Toronto. Ezi's work focuses on race, Black feminisms, anti-colonialism, and global health. Specifically, she has written about new ethics for Black feminist theorizing and anti-colonial interventions for global health. Ezi also holds an honors bachelor of science (HBSc) from the University of Toronto in the areas of human biology (global health) and English.

ANDREA VÁSQUEZ JIMÉNEZ is an Afro-Latina born to Colombian parents in what is dominantly known today as Toronto, Canada. She is a community organizer, community educator, previous 2018 Ontario NDP candidate, and a scholar-warrior. Andrea is codirector and cofounder of the Latinx, Afro-Latin-America, Abya Yala Education Network (LAEN), a Toronto-based grassroots organization where she creates, supports, and facilitates spaces that center the voices, experiences, and needs of historically and present-day marginalized populations such as Afro/Black Latinxs, Indigenous Peoples of Abya Yala, and Latinx LGBTQQIA+ peoples, including their multiple intersectionalities. Andrea is a lead organizer against the School Resource Officer program, which negatively impacts Black/African Diasporic, Indigenous, and/or undocumented students/youth. With others, she successfully pushed to end the program at the largest school board in Canada, the Toronto District School Board. Andrea is completing her master's in social justice education at the Ontario Institute for Studies in Education at the University of Toronto, where her activism feeds into and off of her academic work. Her scholarship and organizing is committed to all forms of liberation and premised on the development of transformative spaces that continuously and consciously challenge and dismantle white supremacy both in relation to, and within, Latinx communities.

Index